D1522186

METAPHOR AND COGNITION

STUDIES IN COGNITIVE SYSTEMS

VOLUME 13

EDITOR

James H. Fetzer, *University of Minnesota, Duluth*

ADVISORY EDITORIAL BOARD

Fred Dretske, *Stanford University*

Ellery Eells, *University of Wisconsin, Madison*

Alick Elithorn, *Royal Free Hospital, London*

Jerry Fodor, *Rutgers University*

Alvin Goldman, *University of Arizona*

Jaakko Hintikka, *Boston University*

Frank Keil, *Cornell University*

William Rapaport, *State University of New York at Buffalo*

Barry Richards, *Imperial College, London*

Stephen Stich, *Rutgers University*

Lucia Vaina, *Boston University*

Terry Winograd, *Stanford University*

The titles published in this series are listed at the end of this volume.

METAPHOR AND COGNITION

An Interactionist Approach

by

BIPIN INDURKHYA

Computer Science Department,
Boston University, Boston, MA, U.S.A.

KLUWER ACADEMIC PUBLISHERS

DORDRECHT / BOSTON / LONDON

Library of Congress Cataloging-in-Publication Data

Indurkhya, Bipin, 1959-
  Metaphor and cognition : an interactionist approach / Bipin
Indurkhya.
      p.   cm. -- (Studies in cognitive systems ; v. 13)
  Includes bibliographical references and indexes.
  ISBN 0-7923-1687-8 (hard : alk. paper)
  1. Symbolism (Psychology) 2. Metaphor--Psychological aspects.
3. Analogy--Psychological aspects. 4. Similarity (Psychology)
5. Cognition. I. Title. II. Series.
BF458.I53 1992
153--dc20   92-7189

ISBN 0-7923-1687-8

Published by Kluwer Academic Publishers,
P.O. Box 17, 3300 AA Dordrecht, The Netherlands.

Kluwer Academic Publishers incorporates
the publishing programmes of
D. Reidel, Martinus Nijhoff, Dr W. Junk and MTP Press.

Sold and distributed in the U.S.A. and Canada
by Kluwer Academic Publishers,
101 Philip Drive, Norwell, MA 02061, U.S.A.

In all other countries, sold and distributed
by Kluwer Academic Publishers Group,
P.O. Box 322, 3300 AH Dordrecht, The Netherlands.

Printed on acid-free paper

On the Cover: *Other World* by M.C. Escher.
© 1947 M.C. Escher / Cordon Art – Baarn – Holland
Collection Haags Gemeentemuseum, The Hague

All Rights Reserved
© 1992 Kluwer Academic Publishers
No part of the material protected by this copyright notice may be reproduced or
utilized in any form or by any means, electronic or mechanical,
including photocopying, recording or by any information storage and
retrieval system, without written permission from the copyright owner.

Printed in the Netherlands

In the memory of my grandmother
and
to Xela

SERIES PREFACE

This series will include monographs and collections of studies devoted to the investigation and exploration of knowledge, information, and data-processing systems of all kinds, no matter whether human, (other) animal, or machine. Its scope is intended to span the full range of interests from classical problems in the philosophy of mind and philosophical psychology through issues in cognitive psychology and sociobiology (concerning the mental powers of other species) to ideas related to artificial intelligence and computer science. While primary emphasis will be placed upon theoretical, conceptual, and epistemological aspects of these problems and domains, empirical, experimental, and methodological studies will also appear from time to time.

The nature of metaphor and the nature of cognition are both illuminated in this stimulating study by Bipin Indurkhya. Beginning with a distinction between conventional metaphors, similarity-based metaphors, and similarity-creating metaphors, he elaborates the idea that similarity-creating metaphors, which affect an interaction between the source of the metaphor and its target, fulfill a fundamental role in human cognition. In addition to the development of his own account, Indurkhya thoughtfully examines alternative theories and evaluates their strengths and weaknesses. By placing the problems of metaphor within the framework of cognition, this work makes an exceptionally valuable contribution to understanding the nature of the mind.

J. H. F.

Contents

Acknowledgments   xv

Prologue   1

I   The Problem   11

1   Characterizing Metaphor   13

   1.1   Introduction 13

   1.2   Some Examples of Metaphors 14

   1.3   Characteristics of Linguistic Metaphors 17

   1.4   Degrees of Metaphoric Content:
The Conventional vs. the Metaphorical 19

   1.5   Metaphors in Non-Linguistic Domains 21

   1.6   Metaphors, Similes, Analogies and Models 26

     1.6.1   Metaphors and Similes 26

     1.6.2   Metaphors and Analogies 28

     1.6.3   Metaphors and Models 34

   1.7   Conclusions 36

2   Enter Similarity-Creating Metaphors   39

   2.1   Introduction 39

   2.2   Some Examples of Similarity-Creating Metaphors 40

   2.3   Psychological Studies of the Creation of Similarity . . . 45

   2.4   Creation of Similarity in Metaphor-Related Phenomena 48

2.4.1   Simile   48

2.4.2   Analogy   49

2.4.3   Models   54

2.5   Similarities and Creative Problem Solving   56

2.5.1   Similarities Before and After the Metaphor   57

2.5.2   Similarities After but Not Before the Metaphor   59

2.5.3   Similarities Before but not After the Metaphor   63

2.6   Conclusions: The Problem of Similarity-Creating Metaphors .   63

3   Approaches to Similarity-Creating Metaphors   65

3.1   Introduction   65

3.2   Max Black   68

3.3   Paul Ricoeur   74

3.4   Carl Hausman   75

3.5   Wheelwright - Mac Cormac   76

3.6   The Lakoffian Approach   78

3.7   My Earlier Approach   84

3.8   Kittay's Perspectival Theory   86

3.9   Conclusions   90

4   Cognition as Interaction   93

4.1   Introduction   93

4.2   Empirical Support for the Interaction View of Cognition . . .   94

4.2.1   Concepts are More than Aggregates of Sense Data . . .   95

4.2.2   Concepts can Organize the World Differently 100

4.2.3   Concepts Cannot Organize the World Arbitrarily . . . 104

4.2.4   'Universals' and the Physiological Basis of Cognition . 105

4.2.5   Summary 111

4.3   From Kant to Goodman: Worldmaking 111

4.4   Piaget's Constructivism 116

4.5   Lakoff-Johnson: The Bodily Basis of Cognition 124

4.6   Conclusions 127

II   A Theory   129

5   An Interactionist Approach to Cognition:
Informal Overview   **131**

   5.1   Introduction 131

   5.2   An Example 135

   5.3   Concept Networks 151

   5.4   Environments and Sensorimotor Data Sets 158

   5.5   Cognitive Relations and Coherency 161

   5.6   Accommodation and Projection 164

   5.7   Cognitive Models 169

       5.7.1   Groupings on the Environment 170

       5.7.2   Accommodation and Projection: Another Perspective . 174

       5.7.3   Representation and Description 176

       5.7.4   Some Other Miscellaneous Notions 178

   5.8   Layered Cognitive System and Multiple "Worlds" 179

   5.9   Summary 187

6   An Interactionist Approach to Cognition:
Formal Concepts   **189**

   6.1   Introduction 189

   6.2   Classes and Groupings 191

   6.3   Relations and Induced Groupings 194

       6.3.1   Preliminary Definitions 194

       6.3.2   Difunctional Relations 196

       6.3.3   Relations Within a Class 201

   6.4   Functions and Operators 202

       6.4.1   Functions 203

       6.4.2   Operators 204

   6.5   Algebras and Structures 205

       6.5.1   Algebras 205

       6.5.2   Descriptions and Structures 209

       6.5.3   Closures and Generating Classes 214

	6.5.4	Closure Over Operators 216
	6.5.5	Computability of Operators 216
6.6	Subalgebras and Finite Generativity 217	
6.7	Groupings on Algebras: Algebras of Classes 220	
6.8	Relations Between Algebras: Correspondences 223	
	6.8.1	Products of Algebras and Correspondences 224
	6.8.2	Groupings Induced by Correspondences 227
	6.8.3	Difunctional Correspondences 229
6.9	Cognitive Models 232	
	6.9.1	Basic Definition 232
	6.9.2	Local Coherency and Coherency 234
	6.9.3	Some Characteristics of Cognitive Models 235
6.10	Cognitive Models Over an Environment 236	
6.11	Projective and Accommodating Models 239	
6.12	Finite Representability and Coherency 241	

7 An Interaction Theory of Metaphor   **245**

7.1	Introduction 245	
7.2	Metaphor as Projection 246	
7.3	Nomenclature Associated with Metaphor 253	
7.4	Modes of Metaphor 256	
	7.4.1	Similarity-Based (Comparative) Metaphors 256
	7.4.2	Similarity-Creating (Projective) Metaphors 271
7.5	Summary 279	

III   The Implications   **283**

8 Some Metaphor-Related Issues   **285**

8.1	Introduction 285	
8.2	The Thesis 'All Knowledge is Metaphorical' 286	
	8.2.1	Version 1: All Knowledge is Projective 287
	8.2.2	Version 2: All Thought is Comparative 289

8.2.3   Version 3: All Conventional Meanings Arise By Way of Metaphor 290

8.2.4   Lakoff-Mac Cormac Debate 292

8.3   Metaphor and Correctness 301

8.3.1   Correctness, Truth and Coherency 301

8.3.2   Understanding vs. Correctness 305

8.3.3   Conventional and Metaphorical Correctness 306

8.4   Aptness (Quality) of Metaphor 309

9   On Predictive Analogy and Induction   **315**

9.1   Introduction 315

9.2   Predictive Analogy and Metaphor 318

9.3   The Search for Logical Justification of Predictive Analogy . . 322

9.3.1   Predictive Analogy as an Inductive Process 323

9.3.2   Predictive Analogy as a First Order Generalization . . 325

9.3.3   Predictive Analogy as a Second Order Generalization . 327

9.4   The Search for Empirical Justification of Predictive Analogy . 329

9.4.1   Evidence from Classroom Experiments 329

9.4.2   Evidence from Real-World Problem-Solving Activities . 332

9.5   The 'Dark Side' of Predictive Analogy 334

9.6   Predictive Analogy and Cognition 339

9.7   The Problem of Induction 343

9.8   The Sampling Principle, Randomness, and the Generalized Grue Paradox 344

9.9   The 'Dark Side' of Induction 350

9.10 Induction in Cognition 352

10 On Computational Approaches to Metaphor and Analogy 357

10.1 Introduction 357

10.2 Computational Approaches to Linguistic Metaphors 360

10.3 Computational Approaches to Predictive Analogy 365

10.4 A Computational Model of Creative Analogies: Douglas Hofstadter 376

10.4.1 An Aside: Context-Sensitivity of Descriptions in Evans'
Approach 378

10.4.2 Resumption: Hofstadter and Mitchell's Copycat 384

10.5 Projective (Similarity-Creating) Metaphor in Artificial
Intelligence 392

10.5.1 Projection as 'Top-Down' Grouping 392

10.5.2 Novel vs. Conventional Projection 395

10.5.3 The Creation of Similarity 400

10.6 Modeling Metaphor as Change of Representation 401

10.7 Conclusions 408

Bibliography   **411**

Name Index   **433**

Subject Index   **439**

Acknowledgments

I would like to express my thanks and appreciation to the following people who have contributed to this manuscript in various ways:

- To Remko Scha for providing encouragement, ideas, and much constructive criticism through the entire project.

- To Mark Johnson for providing an encouraging feedback on a long essay that I wrote as an abridged version of the book in 1988.

- To Erica Melis for providing many useful comments on the abridged version of the book and on earlier drafts of some chapters.

- To Sylvia Candelaria de Ram for a thorough reading of early drafts of Chapters 1, 5, 6 and 7. Her numerous comments, especially on Chapter 6, were instrumental in adding to the clarity of the final draft.

- To George Lakoff for providing an encouraging feedback on an earlier draft of Chapter 7 and for providing valuable comments.

- To Melanie Mitchell for painstakingly going through a very rough version of the entire manuscript. Her detailed comments were an invaluable aid in revising the manuscript.

- To Margo Guertin and Scott O'Hara for reading through countless drafts and catching many syntactic and semantic errors.

- To Mary Atkins, Regina Blaney and Beryl Nelson for reading parts of the final draft and offering comments.

- To Doug Hofstadter and Melanie Mitchell for providing extensive comments on parts of the final manuscript.

- To Spyridon Braoudakis and Dan Solis for carefully going over the entire final draft and making numerous comments.

- To Marie-Dominique Gineste and an anonymous reviewer for Kluwer Academic Publishers for writing very positive and encouraging reviews of the manuscript, and for making comments on various parts of it that were quite helpful during revisions.

xvi

- To Simon Ross for doing a wonderful job as the editor in getting the manuscript reviewed promptly, and in offering much useful advice in getting the copyright permissions and in the preparation of the camera-ready copy.

- To the National Science Foundation for grant No. IRI-9105806, which supported in part the preparation of the manuscript.

I would also like to express my gratitude to various individuals and institutions for allowing me to include some copyrighted material in this book:

- *Other World* by M.C. Escher (on the cover): ©1947 M.C. Escher / Cordon Art – Baarn – Holland, Collection Haags Gemeentemuseum, The Hague. Reproduced with the kind permission of Cordon Art and Haags Gemeentemuseum.

- *Fog* by Carl Sandburg (page 2): From CHICAGO POEMS by Carl Sandburg, ©1916 by Holt, Rinehart and Winston, Inc. and renewed 1944 by Carl Sandburg, reprinted with the permission of Harcourt Brace Jovanovich, Inc.

- *Park bei Lu(zern) (Park near Lu(cerne))* (1938) by Paul Klee (plate 1): Paul Klee-Stiftung/Kunstmuseum Bern, ©1991 by VAGA, New York; reproduced with the kind permission of Kunstmuseum Bern.

- *The Marriage of Giovanni (?), Arnolfini and Giovanna Cenami (?),* (1434) by Jan Van Eyck (plate 2): The National Gallery, London, reproduced with the kind permission of the National Gallery.

- Quotations from Alfred Hitchcock (pages 24 and 44): ©1967 by Francois Truffaut, revised ©1984 by Francois Truffaut, reprinted in the U.S. and Canada with the permission of Simon & Schuster, and elsewhere with the kind permission of Secker and Warburg.

- *White Hawthorn in the West of Ireland* by Eavan Boland (page 41): ©1989 by Eavan Boland, originally published in The New Yorker, reprinted with the kind permission of Eavan Boland and The New Yorker.

- Excerpt from *Seascape* by Stephen Spender (page 42): from COLLECTED POEMS 1928–1985 by Stephen Spender, ©1946 by Stephen Spender, reprinted in the British Commonwealth (excluding Canada) with the kind permission of Faber and Faber Limited, and elsewhere with the permission of Random House, Inc.

- *Composition with Blue and Yellow,* (1935) by Piet Mondrian (plate 3): Hirshhorn Museum and Sculpture Garden, Smithsonian Institution, Gift of Joseph H. Hirshhorn Foundation, 1972, (photograph by Lee Stalsworth); reproduced with the kind permission of Hirshhorn Museum and Sculpture Garden.

- Quotation from Piet Mondrian (page 43): ©1986 by Harry Holtzman, reproduced with the kind permission of Mr. Holtzman and G.K. Hall & Co.

- *Le Gouter (Tea Time),* (1911) by Jean Metzinger (plate 4): Philadelphia Museum of Art: The Louise and Walter Arensberg Collection, reproduced with the kind permission of Philadelphia Museum of Art.

- Figures from P.A. Kolers' *Aspects of Motion Perception* (page 99): ©1972 by Pergamon Press, reprinted with the kind permission of Pergamon Press.

- Figure from A.R. Luria's *Cognitive Development* (page 103): ©1976 by the President and Fellows of Harvard College, reprinted with the kind permission of Harvard University Press.

- Quotations and figures from T.G. Evans' "A Program for the Solution of a Class of Geometric-Analogy Intelligence-Test Questions" (Section 10.4.1): ©1968 by MIT Press, reproduced here with the kind permission of MIT Press.

Prologue

This book is about metaphor and cognition, and about the relationship between the two. While there remains much dispute about what metaphor is, how it works, and what role it plays in cognition, there seems to be general agreement that metaphor involves two objects or situations and some kind of transference from one object or situation to the other. One object is referred to as the topic, the tenor, the primary subject, or the target domain, and the other object as the vehicle, the secondary subject, or the source domain. For instance, in "The chairperson of the meeting plowed through the agenda," the target is the meeting, the source is the act of plowing, and the transference exists in being able to describe the meeting meaningfully by using the semantically distant term of 'plowing'.

It is also generally accepted that metaphors are not limited to individual words, or even phrases, but a whole poem or a novel can be metaphorical as well. Anyone who has read Dylan Thomas' *The force that through the green fuse drives the flower*, Melville's *Moby Dick*, or Hemingway's *The Old Man and the Sea* would know that these works become much more interesting and insightful when given an interpretation other than the literal one. Here, while the source is explicitly given, the target is not specified at all; it is up to the individual reader to find her own target and carry out her own interpretation. The point is that one needs a target domain and a meaningful interpretation in order for the work to become metaphorical. For instance, I once read an interpretation of Frank Baum's *The Wizard of Oz*, a popular fantasy book that described it as a satire of the American political situation existing at the turn of the century, when the book was first published.[1] To get the satirical effect, however, the characters of the book need to be given an appropriate interpretation in that context—that the Wicked Witch of the East be identified with the financial institutions of the Northeastern U.S., the Tin Woodman be identified with the industrial workers, the Emerald City be identified with Washington D.C., the capital of the U.S., and so on.

Classification of metaphors themselves is somewhat controversial. But for our purpose, we need only make a distinction between conventional metaphors, similarity-based metaphors, and similarity-creating metaphors. Conventional metaphors are those metaphors that are so much a part of everyday speech that they seem hardly metaphorical. The 'plow' metaphor mentioned above is a case in point. Conventional metaphors are evidence to the fact

---

[1] I remember reading it in the Sunday edition of the *Buffalo News* sometime in December 1987.

that metaphoric transference is not something confined to poetry and literature, but is very much a part of our everyday speech. They have been studied extensively by George Lakoff and his colleagues [Lakoff & Johnson 1980; Lakoff & Turner 1989]. In this study, however, conventional metaphors play only a minimal role. My main concern is not so much with why our everyday concepts are structured in one way rather than another, but with how new concepts and meanings emerge.

Similarity-based metaphors invite the reader to make a comparison between the source and the target, as the transference of meaning is based on some existing similarity between them. For instance, in "The sky is crying" the reader is drawn into comparing the rain falling down from the sky with the tears falling down from the eyes of a person. These metaphors have been captured in what is commonly known as the comparison theory of metaphor [Henle 1958].

In a similarity-creating metaphor, however, there are no similarities between the source and the target when the metaphor is first encountered. Yet, after the metaphor is assimilated, (if it is assimilated at all,) there are similarities between the two. Thus, the metaphor *creates* the similarities between the source and the target. To appreciate the force of a similarity-creating metaphor, try the following experiment. For each of the following pairs of words, try to enumerate the similarities between the referents of the two words: *snake-eel, dog-computer, snowstorm-automobile, cat-fog, fog-clock.* For instance, for the *snake-eel* pair, you might say that they are both long, slithery, etc. If you cannot find any similarities, just say so. Give yourself, say about five minutes, for each pair.

Now consider Carl Sandburg's beautiful poem *Fog:*

> The fog comes
> on little cat feet.
>
> It sits looking
> over harbor and city
> on silent haunches
> and then moves on.

After reading the poem, the fog at once appears similar to the cat! They both creep up on you ever so silently. Moreover, I would be very surprised if this similarity was included in your initial comparison of fog and cat, unless you peeked ahead, or you were already familiar with the poem, and the words *fog-cat* reminded you of it. Thus, it would be appropriate to acknowledge that the metaphor created the similarities. If you need more convincing to accept the phenomenon of creation of similarity, I present many more examples in Chapter 2, since similarity-creating metaphors are my primary concern in this book.

The existence of similarity-creating metaphors has not been universally acknowledged. The reason is that in a similarity-creating metaphor, there are always similarities after the metaphor is presented and understood. So if a person is presented with a metaphor, and then asked to explain her understanding of it, she would invariably give a similarity-based account. But this fails to address the question of whether the similarities were there before the metaphor or not. (One notable exception is the interesting study of Camac and Glucksburg [1984], which is discussed in Chapter 2.) Consequently, it might not be surprising that almost all the research on metaphor in cognitive science has been in the pursuit of similarity-based metaphors. Empirical studies and theories have sought to articulate exactly what kinds of similarities underlie metaphors [Gentner, Falkenhainer, & Skorstad 1987; Gentner & Stuart 1983; Malgady & Johnson 1980; Ortony 1979]. Following these leads, the computational models have focused either on how the similarities might be computed, given a source and a target (Weiner 1984, 1985; Fass 1989); or on how the similarities might be used if they are explicitly given (Carbonell 1982; Martin 1988). Similarity-creating metaphors have been left out in the cold.

Interestingly, however, an approach to metaphor in the philosophical tradition—an approach that is widely known as the *interaction theory*—was created expressly to account for similarity-creating metaphors. Originating in I.A. Richards' *Philosophy of Rhetoric,* the interaction theory owes its present form largely to the works of such scholars as Max Black [1962; 1979], Carl Hausman [1983; 1984; 1989], and Paul Ricoeur [1977]. Harshly criticizing the comparison theory of metaphor for its inability to address the creation of similarity, interaction theory proposes that every metaphor involves an interaction between its source and its target, a process in which the target (and possibly the source) is reorganized, and new similarities between the source and the target emerge. This account, which is examined in Chapter 3, is, however, quite vague, and even paradoxical at times.

For instance, it neither pins down what exactly this mysterious 'interaction' is, nor specifies exactly how the new similarities emerge. There is a crucial problem here: the creation of similarity is obviously not an arbitrary process. If it were, then anything would be meaningful and there would be no way to maintain a distinction between what is genuinely metaphorical and what is certainly nonsensical. But then what constrains this creation process? It cannot be the similarities between the source and the target, for this would turn the interaction theory into nothing but a variant of the comparison theory, and all the criticism that the interactionists directed against the comparison theory can be directed at themselves. So the question is still unanswered: where do the created similarities come from?

A few scholars have tried to elaborate the interaction theory and tackle some of these issues head on, but again, by and large, either these elaborations are quite vague themselves, relying on metaphors and analogies to communicate the key concepts involved in their explanations, or they turn the interaction theory into a variant of comparison theory. Hausman [1983], for instance, postulated 'uniqueness' and 'extra-linguistic' conditions to explain how metaphors can create new meanings and similarities, but these conditions themselves are not spelled out with much clarity. Verbrugge [1980] proposed that a metaphor works by 'transforming' the target into the source, thereby making it similar to the source, but then it is not specified exactly what this transformation process is, and what constrains it so that arbitrary transformations are ruled out. Tourangeau and Sternberg [1982] proposed a 'domains-interaction' view, which is purported to be a 'more specific formulation of the interaction view,' but which, in essence, turns out to be the comparison view in disguise, because it assumes an underlying analogy to be the basis of every metaphor. A notable exception is provided by Kittay's [1987] perspectival theory, which comes quite close to providing a reasonable explanation of the creation of similarity. But, for the most part, we see that the interaction theories have still retained their fuzzy character, which may well be the single most important reason cognitive science researchers have shied away from them [Waggoner 1990].

There is also a minor inconsistency in the interaction view that is sometimes overlooked. At one place in his classic essay 'Metaphor,' Black remarked, "If to call a man a wolf is to put him in a special light, we must not forget that the metaphor makes the wolf seem more human than he otherwise would." This clearly implies a symmetry in the interaction between the source and the target. However, at other places in his discussion there is a clearly implied asymmetry. For example, in his later essay 'More about Metaphor,' in a deeply insightful section titled 'Thinking in Metaphors' Black considers how different concepts can organize the figure of the Star of David differently. In organizing the figure of Star of David as three parallelograms with their axes one hundred and twenty degrees apart, the process does not, at the same time, organize our concept of parallelograms as a part of the figure of the Star of David—that is, the parallelogram does not appear to be

Star-of-David-like after the interaction.

While a few interactionists, such as Verbrugge and Kittay, see the interaction view as essentially asymmetrical, others, Hausman for instance, have emphasized the symmetry aspect of the interaction. Hausman [1989, p. 67] went as far as to argue that one need not distinguish between the source and target of a metaphor. A result of this confusion has been that many scholars now accept the symmetry property to be a key aspect of the interaction theory [Waggoner 1990], and some, such as Lakoff and Turner [1989, pp. 131–133], use arguments against the symmetry property as a way to discredit the whole interaction theory. Black's insightful observations in 'Thinking in Metaphors' seem to have been grossly overlooked.

Then there is the problem of explaining the role of metaphor in cognition. It has been recognized for quite some time now that metaphor is not just a phenomenon of language, but pervades all aspects of cognition. It has been claimed that metaphors play a key role in learning and education [Holstein 1970; Petrie 1979; Sticht 1979], and they are an invaluable aid to problem solving [Schön 1963]. In the early stages of formulating a scientific theory, metaphors are often indispensable [Gruber 1978; Hesse 1980; Miller 1978; Rothbart 1984, pp. 611–612]. Religious scholars have emphasized time and again that religious symbols (scriptures, rituals, etc.) derive their significance due to their metaphorical nature, and should not be taken literally [Brown 1983; Soskice 1985; Tillich 1961; Wheelwright 1954]. For instance, the Christian ritual of taking communion is meaningful only if one understands it metaphorically. If one does not believe in the transsubstantiation doctrine, then neither is the bread literally the body of the Christ, nor is the wine literally His blood, and a metaphorical interpretation is required to render the ritual meaningful. Even if one adopts the transsubstantiation doctrine, a metaphorical interpretation is still required to attach significance to what would literally be a cannibalistic act. The well-known mythologist Joseph Campbell [1949; 1986; 1988] argued throughout his prolific career that myths are metaphorical ways of capturing the very essence of the experience of living, and, with an appropriate metaphorical interpretation, various ancient myths are still as relevant as they might have once been.

Besides literature, metaphors pervade various other art forms. The abstractionism prevalent in contemporary arts particularly requires a metaphorical interpretation for a work to be meaningful. Willem De Kooning's *Excavations,* Barnett Newman's *Achilles,* and Jackson Pollock's *Cathedral* are all examples of paintings that require metaphorical interpretations to be understood. John Cage's composition *4'33"* which is essentially 4 minutes and 33 seconds of silence, is another case in point. (See Cage's 'Lecture on Nothing,' in Cage [1961], pp. 108–127. See also Rowell [1983] for the role of metaphors in music, including an interpretation of *4′33″* [p. 220].) Fox [1982], in introducing the works of six modern sculptors, Vito Acconci, Siah Armajani, Alice Aycock, Lauren Ewing, Robert Morris, and Dennis Oppenheim, has further emphasized the reliance of contemporary art on metaphor to communicate its meaning. Whittock [1990] has analyzed several different types of metaphors in feature films, many of which were consciously introduced by the directors. For instance, the classic shower scene from Alfred Hitchcock's *Psycho* is seen as an act of spiritual cleansing: Marion Crane (Janet Leigh), having decided to go back and return the money she absconded with, is not just washing away her body, but is also ridding herself of the guilt [Wood 1989, p. 146]. This identification enhances the shock of her subsequent murder a great deal [Whittock 1990, p. 53].

Finally, anthropologists have pointed out that many of our own social, cultural and moral values result from the metaphors that are prevalent in our society and culture [Kempton 1987; Lakoff & Kövecses 1987; Quinn 1987; Reddy 1979; Schön 1979; Turner 1974]. For instance, Quinn's study found that there are different metaphors underlying the modern American concept of marriage: 'a manufactured product,' 'an ongoing journey,' 'an investment,' and so on. She also found that an individual's perception of whether his or her marriage is a success or a failure, whether there is some problem facing the marriage, and if so, how it might be corrected, etc. are all determined by the underlying metaphor.

Given this overwhelming evidence for the variety of roles metaphors play in cognition, one would expect a theory of metaphor to shed some light on what it is about metaphor that makes it pervade so many different facets of cognition. In fact, the evidence is so strong as to suggest that a theory of metaphor should perhaps be set within a framework of cognition. That is, there should be a general account of cognition, and metaphor should be presented as one of the mechanisms used in cognition.

In exploring this hypothesis, we find that there exists a problem in cognition that is remarkably parallel to the problem posed by similarity-creating metaphors. This problem has to do with a view of cognition according to which the world view of a cognitive agent does not reflect some pre-existing structures in the external world, but is *created* by the cognitive agent. Yet, this creation is not arbitrary, but is constrained by the external world. Perhaps not surprisingly, this view is referred to as *the interaction view of cognition,* since it sees cognition as a process of interaction between a cognitive agent and its environment.

While a version of the interaction view of cognition is implicit in Kant's celebrated *Critique of Pure Reason,* it is only in this century that it has been articulated as such, in the monumental works of Ernst Cassirer [1955], Nelson Goodman [1978], and Jean Piaget [1936; 1945; 1967; 1970]. In the past few decades, many scholars from various disciplines as diverse as philosophy, psychology, neurophysiology, linguistics, and anthropology, have provided persuasive evidence and arguments in support of the interaction view of cognition.

Yet, like the interaction theories of metaphor, most accounts of the interaction view of cognition remain somewhat vague. While they offer helpful analogies and metaphors, they do not explicitly address some of the key problems. For instance, what exactly is the nature of interaction? Exactly how does the external world constrain the world view of the cognitive agent? Notice that there seems to be a paradox here, for to talk explicitly of the interaction, the external world needs to be given an ontology; and to talk of the external world constraining the world view of the cognitive agent, there is the implicit assumption that the external world has a structure that is independent of the cognitive agent. However, both these features are inconsistent with the central thesis of the interaction view of cognition, which is to deny a mind-independent ontology and structure to the external world.

It is the vagueness on such issues that is primarily responsible for some misunderstandings of the interaction view of cognition, especially by its critics. For instance, the interactionists often talk of 'coherency' as a way to specify that the cognitive agent's world view must 'fit' the external world. However, for lack of a precise characterization of coherency, it is sometimes confused with the internal consistency of cognitive structures [Mac Cormac 1985, pp. 211–215].

Given that interactionism in cognition and interactionism in metaphor are both concerned with the issue of creativity, and that there are some obvious similarities between the key problems facing each of these views, one would expect that it should be possible to address them in a unified framework. Moreover, if it turns out that metaphors involve an interaction not unlike the interaction of cognition, then this might explain exactly what role metaphor plays in cognition, and why metaphor is an asset to so many cognitive activities.

Indeed, the study presented in this book is undertaken in this very spirit. My chief objective is to present a unified framework for the interaction view of metaphor and the interaction view of cognition. I lay out this framework in detail—even including a mathematical version in the tradition of formal semantics—so as to dispel much of the fuzziness that has surrounded the earlier versions of each of the interaction views. I also attempt to resolve the apparent paradoxes and inconsistencies of each view mentioned above.

As far as metaphors are concerned, my focus in this study, perhaps obviously, is on similarity-creating metaphors. However, the account of metaphor presented here also includes a treatment of similarity-based metaphors, since these too have a role to play in cognition—albeit a different role than the one played by similarity-creating metaphors—and a unified theory of metaphor ought to include both types of metaphor. Moreover, in this way, the reader will be better able to appreciate the different cognitive force of each type of metaphor.

This book is organized in three parts. Part One of the book introduces, in greater detail, the problems of metaphor and cognition. In Chapter One, I characterize my use of the term metaphor, and articulate the range of phenomena that I cover under it. It is important to do so, for there are significant variations in the literature as to what exactly is considered a metaphor, and how it is related to simile, analogy, models, etc. In Chapter Two, similarity-creating metaphors are introduced. It starts out with some examples of similarity-creating metaphors, and then reviews a few research efforts that have been made to empirically demonstrate the creation of similarity. It is also argued that in phenomena often considered to be closely related to metaphor—namely simile, models, and analogy—there exist counterparts of similarity-creating metaphors. It then highlights the role played by similarity-creating metaphors (as opposed to similarity-based metaphors) in cognition. The chapter concludes with a discussion of the problems posed by similarity-creating metaphors.

Chapter Three discusses various attempts that have been made to address the problems of similarity-creating metaphors. As one might expect, this chapter is essentially an overview of various interaction theories of metaphor, taking note of their insights as well as their shortcomings. Chapter Four introduces the interaction view of cognition, and points out some of its problems that parallel the problems of similarity-creating metaphors. It also examines three different versions of interactionisms, giving special attention to the views of Nelson Goodman and Jean Piaget, and analyzes how far the problems of the interaction view are resolved in each version.

In Part Two of the book, I lay out my framework for metaphor and cognition. In Chapter Five, I present my interaction view of cognition informally, including a detailed, though somewhat artificial, example to illustrate all the key concepts of the theory. Chapter Six contains a formalization, using some elementary concepts from Universal Algebra, of the framework introduced in Chapter Five. While this chapter can be safely skipped without affecting the readability of the rest of the book, it may be of interest to formal semanticists and anyone else interested in formal models of cognition. As far as the mathematical background required to read this chapter is concerned, only some very basic mathematical fluency—familiarity with sets, functions, relations, etc.—is required, as I have kept the discussion slow-paced and provided many examples. Following that, in Chapter Seven, I present a theory of metaphor within this framework of cognition. My account treats both similarity-based metaphors and similarity-creating metaphors, and I argue that different cognitive mechanisms are called into play for each class of metaphors.

In Part Three of the book, I present some implications of this framework of metaphor and cognition. Chapter Eight examines some issues related to metaphor including the literal-metaphorical dichotomy, the thesis that all knowledge is metaphorical, and metaphorical truth and aptness. In Chapter Nine, I examine the problems of predictive analogy—also known as analogical reasoning—and induction. I argue that both these processes are best seen as cognitive processes that are useful at times, and yet, much like our visual system, create their own illusions that can be detrimental to cognition at other times. It is erroneous to see them as processes that are somehow justified, even in a probabilistic sense, by the structure of reality. Chapter Ten takes a look at computational approaches to metaphor and analogy. Here, after pointing out the failure of most of the existing computational models of metaphors and analogy to address the creativity issue, I go on to argue that there exist artificial intelligence systems that are capable of generating creative metaphors and analogies.

Obviously, my views in this book present a convergence of many points that have been made in different contexts by various scholars of metaphor and cognition, and is a distillation of the resulting framework. While I have provided explicit references throughout the book, I would like to acknowledge here in a general way my intellectual debt to Max Black, Ernst Cassirer, Nelson Goodman, Paul Ricoeur, and most of all to Jean Piaget, whose numerous writings have been a source of constant impetus to me in carrying out this research. A reader acquainted with any of their works should not be surprised to find familiar themes reverberating beneath the views presented here.

Part I

The Problem

Chapter 1

Characterizing Metaphor

1.1 Introduction

Before we begin this study, it is necessary to characterize the term 'metaphor' itself, for in the literature it is used with a wide variety of meanings. In the narrowest sense, metaphor refers to a specific way of using the words and phrases of a language, and in a broad sense it is applied to the process of conceptualization itself, leading to the aphorism "All thought is metaphorical." Then there are the phenomena of simile, analogy, and models, that are considered to be closely related to metaphor, but there are wide variations in how these relations are perceived. Researchers do not always state explicitly the range of phenomena covered by their use of the term metaphor, leaving this task to the reader. This practice has sometimes generated needless controversy about the nature of metaphor due to misunderstood positions, as we will see in Chapter 8.

To avoid this unnecessary confusion, this chapter is devoted to articulating the exact sense in which I am using the term metaphor in this book. My objective here is not so much to come up with a precise definition of metaphor, but rather to give you some idea about the range of phenomena I am covering in my use of the term. I start by considering some examples of linguistic metaphors in Section 2 in order to isolate their identifying characteristics. These characteristics are summed up in Section 3. In Section 4, I point out that the metaphoric content of a statement (or a piece of text) is a matter of degree. There is a continuum from conventional metaphors, which are so much a part of the everyday speech that they hardly seem metaphorical, to novel metaphors that are vibrant and creative at once. It is the novel-metaphor end of the continuum that is most interesting for this study, because my main objective is to explore how new concepts and meanings emerge through metaphors, and how similarities are created.

In Section 5, I present examples of metaphors in the non-linguistic domains of paintings, films and religion, and extend my characterization of metaphor to include them also. I also show here that non-linguistic metaphors share many of the characteristics of linguistic metaphors. Then, in Section 6, I briefly examine the relationship of metaphors to similes, analogies, and models. Again, the objective here is not so much to establish one correct way to relate these things to metaphors, but rather, given the focus of this study, to show to what extent similes, analogies and models embody the cognitive mechanism that renders novel metaphors meaningful. It is important to clarify this because I use examples of what are considered similes, analogies and models to illustrate and analyze the creation of similarity and other characteristics of metaphors in Chapters 2 and 7. Finally, Section 7 summarizes the main points of this chapter.

1.2   Some Examples of Metaphors

Consider a simple metaphor, "The sky is crying." What makes it a metaphor, as opposed to, say, "John is crying," which is considered literal? First of all, notice that each of the statements is a description of some object or event (real or imagined). Let us call this real or imagined object (or event) *the target*. Now in "John is crying," the description can be applied to the target (John) using conventional meanings of the words. (By the term 'conventional meanings' I refer to the meanings that can be obtained by looking up the words in some standard dictionary.) However, in "The sky is crying," the word 'cry' cannot be applied to the target (sky) in a meaningful way while using its conventional meaning. Still, most people would understand it to mean that it is raining. This understanding is derived from interpreting the word 'cry' unconventionally in applying it to the target. The basis of this interpretation is an underlying similarity between teardrops falling down the cheeks of a crying person, and raindrops falling from the sky. Once this interpretation has been arrived at, it can be extended (more or less,) depending on one's imaginative potential and willingness to do so. For instance, in understanding "The sky is crying," one might associate a certain mood of universal sadness with this utterance, based on its similarity with the emotion usually associated with crying.

Thus, the interpretation does not just involve the concept 'cry' in its meaning, but also brings into play other concepts associated with 'cry,' such as 'teardrops,' 'sadness,' and so on. Let us call the part of the description that is given an unconventional interpretation, as well as all the related concepts it calls into play the *source.*

Consider now another example, "The defense counsel created a smoke screen of witnesses." Here the target is a certain action that the defense counsel took. As with the last example, the description cannot be applied to the target by using the conventional meanings of the words. In particular, the term 'smoke screen' cannot be conventionally applied to the target. According to Webster's dictionary, 'smoke screen' means 'a screen of smoke to hinder enemy observation of a military force, area, or activity.' To make the description meaningful, 'smoke screen' and its related concepts (the source) have to be given an unconventional interpretation. The basis of the unconventional interpretation is the similarity between the effect the witnesses called by the defense counsel are having, and the effect the smoke screen has during a military maneuver.

In both the above examples of metaphor, the target was explicitly mentioned in the description. However, this might not always be the case. For instance, consider "The old rock is becoming brittle with age." The description might have been of a rock, in which case it would be interpreted conventionally. However, one could have also said it of an old professor. In this case, it is the context alone that specifies the target, and all the concepts used in the description (and their related concepts) become the source of the metaphor, and have to be given unconventional interpretations.

In fact, even when the target seems to be explicitly mentioned in the description, the context can change it. For example, in discussing "The sky is crying," we tacitly assumed that it is about the sky, which became the target. But the same statement could also have been intended to describe a person with big pale blue eyes who is crying. The face of the crying person now becomes the target, and the sky and its related concepts become the source. Thus, context plays a dominant role in identifying the target, which, in turn, affects (given a description) what is considered to be the source of a metaphor.

Let us now consider "The chairperson of the meeting plowed through the agenda." The target here is how the chairperson conducted a certain meeting. If we take the conventional meaning of 'plow' to be, 'to move in a way resembling that of a plow cutting into or going through the soil,' then it cannot be applied to the target as it is; an unconventional interpretation is called for. Such an interpretation can be arrived at based on the underlying similarities between the actions of a farmer in plowing and the actions of the chairperson. The farmer keeps a straight course with her plow, uprooting dead roots, weeds, small stones, and whatever happens to come in her way. The chairperson sticks to the agenda and summarily brushes aside pointless objections and discussions.

However, the dictionary meaning of 'plow' also includes 'to proceed steadily and laboriously,' and with this meaning the description can be conventionally applied to the target, and would no longer be considered metaphorical. (In fact, one reviewer of this manuscript objected to my using the above statement as an example of metaphor. She noted in her review that she, having grown up in a city, learned this meaning of 'plow' first. To her, the above description of a meeting was not metaphorical at all.) Thus, we see that which interpretations are considered conventional and which ones are considered unconventional, whether something is considered metaphor or not, is quite subjective.

In all of the examples seen so far, there was basically one way of interpreting the source in the target unconventionally, though this basic interpretation could be extended in different ways subjectively (as in attributing sadness to the sky). However, this is not always the case. Once I heard a call-in show on the radio where the host asked the listeners to call in with a description of their love life in terms of food. Here the target was fixed. The source was also fixed in the sense that the love life had to be described using food concepts only. But people calling in with their descriptions reflected different ways of applying food to their love lives. For instance, one caller described her love life as an onion (it smells and makes you cry). Another caller described his love life as a fresh fruit (it is seasonal). In fact, even if we take one particular description, say 'love life as a fresh fruit,' different people would interpret it differently. (It is good and healthy, it is sweet and juicy, and so on.) Thus, we see that the unconventional interpretations that make metaphors meaningful are not unique, but are subjective.

The subjectivity of metaphors is even more pronounced in the cases where no target is supplied, either explicitly by the statement or implicitly by the context. This is often the case with metaphors of poetry and, as we will see later, of arts. For instance, consider Melville's *Moby Dick*. There is no target mentioned or hinted there. Of course, the story is quite meaningful as it is—as a conventional description of an imagined event. But it is certainly possible to interpret it metaphorically in many different ways in many different domains.

Now consider "Sincerity plowed through depravity," and assume that the context does not help you at all in identifying a target. What could the description be about? What could it possibly mean? You might consider it to be a statement about emotions, but then 'plow' with its conventional meaning cannot be applied to this target. If you cannot come up with any interpretation of this statement, then it would have to be discarded as anomalous or meaningless.

However, with a little bit of imagination, even the above statement can be made meaningful. Imagine some government department where corruption permeated everything until an honest and sincere administrator took over. Her high standards of moral integrity and her concern for the employees of the department touched the hearts of many of them, and soon the corruption was weeded out. The above description would be quite meaningful and appropriate in this context.

Well, my scenario might not be so convincing. You can try to make one of your own; I am sure it would not be very hard. Or you can look up the interesting studies of Pollio & Burns [1977] and Pollio & Smith [1979]. The point here is simply that the distinction between meaningfulness and anomaly is not so easily drawn. Yet, in any given context, there are statements that are clearly anomalous, for to any one individual, even one who is quite imaginative, not all statements are meaningful. Therefore, not every unconventional juxtaposition of words and phrases constitutes a metaphor.

Consider now "These highways are snakes" and "Snakes are highways." These two examples illustrate the asymmetry of metaphors. The first description is about highways. The unconventional interpretation of 'snakes' one makes here is that these highways are long and windy. The second description, which is about snakes, appears anomalous at first. With some effort, we can perhaps imagine a long snake, with ants running up and down along the length of its body, and render the sentence meaningful. Comparing the two interpretations, however, we see that they are quite different. Thus, we see that a metaphor is not a symmetric comparison between the source and the target, and reversing the source and the target might change the meaning of the metaphor drastically; it might even turn the metaphor into an anomaly. (See Connor & Kogan [1980]; Malgady & Johnson [1980]; and Verbrugge [1980] for empirical studies of asymmetry in metaphors.)

1.3 Characteristics of Linguistic Metaphors

We can now summarize the main characteristics of metaphors, at least in the linguistic setting, that were gleaned from the discussion of the examples in the last section.

1. A metaphor is a description of an object or event, real or imagined, using concepts that cannot be applied to the object or event in a conventional way. The object or the event being described is called the target, and the concepts that cannot be applied conventionally are called the source. The source does not just include the concepts mentioned in the description that cannot be applied conventionally to the target, but other related concepts as well.

2. The source of a metaphor is always supplied by the description (the text). The target may be explicitly hinted at by the description, may be determined by the context, or may not be provided at all. Whenever the target is provided, context plays a more dominant role in determining it than the description.

3. The metaphor is made meaningful by interpreting the source unconventionally in the target. The unconventional interpretation can be arrived at on the basis of some underlying similarity between the source concepts and the target. If no interpretation can be found, then the description is considered anomalous.

   This suggests that the similarities between the source and the target might be one of the identifying characteristics of metaphor. However, as I demonstrate in the next chapter, certain metaphors *create* the similarities between the source and the target. Taking the phenomenon of creation of similarity for granted at the moment, let us say that there are always similarities between the source and the target *after* the metaphor is understood, if it is understood at all.

4. Whether a statement is considered metaphorical or not is quite subjective. There are two reasons for it. One is that what one takes as the conventional meaning of a word or a phrase is subjective. So, what is a conventional description for one might be a metaphor for another. Secondly, varying degrees of imagination are required to make sense of what seems like an anomaly, and since different persons have different imaginative potentials, what is an anomaly for some might be a deeply insightful metaphor for another.

5. What a metaphor means is itself quite subjective, though different metaphors leave more or less room for subjectivity of meaning. Whenever the target of a metaphor is not specified, the reader can choose

her own target (as in interpreting Melville's *Moby Dick* metaphorically). When the target is specified by the context, or mentioned explicitly in the description (the text), different readers can give unconventional interpretation to the source in different ways (as in 'love life as a fresh fruit' metaphor). Even when there is a rather unambiguous interpretation of the source in applying it to the target unconventionally (as in "The sky is crying,") there are other connotations (such as the aura of sadness in the above example) that might be present, which heighten the emotive force of the metaphor differently for different readers.

6. Metaphors are asymmetric. That is, when the source and the target of a metaphor are reversed, the meaning can change dramatically, and the description may even cease to be a metaphor.

1.4   Degrees of Metaphoric Content: The Conventional vs. the Metaphorical

The examples discussed above clearly suggest that the metaphoric content of a description in a given context is not something that is all there or is completely absent, but is a matter of degree. For instance, "John is crying" is clearly non-metaphorical or literal; "The sky is crying" and 'love life as a fresh fruit' are clearly metaphorical; but "The chairperson of the meeting plowed through the agenda" is not so clear cut. Some scholars, such as Mac Cormac, would rather call it literal but use the term 'dead metaphor'—recognizing that it was metaphorical once, before the meaning of 'plow' that is transferred by the metaphor became so frequently used that it became a part of the conventional meaning, and was incorporated in the dictionary—to distinguish it from examples like "John is crying." Others, such as Lakoff, concede that the term 'plow' is used with its conventional meaning, but argue, nonetheless, that this example still evokes the image of metaphorical transference in the minds of at least some readers, and, consequently, prefer to call it a 'conventional metaphor.' As the issues of what is a metaphor, what is a conventional metaphor, what is a dead metaphor, and what is literal are quite controversial [Lakoff 1986; Lakoff 1987a; Mac Cormac 1985, Chap. 3]—a controversy that is analyzed in Chapter 8—I would like to clarify my own position here, especially since I have characterized metaphors in contrast with the conventional.

Clearly, there is a continuum with respect to the degree of metaphoric content. On one end are the novel metaphors such as 'love life as a fresh fruit.' Then come the metaphors that are widely used in a language and culture but still retain their interpretive nature, such as "Their marriage is on a rocky road." At the other end of the continuum are those metaphors that have become so much a part of the conventional language (as reflected in the dictionary meaning) that to many people there is no element of interpretation or transference. "The chairperson plowed through the meeting agenda" is a case in point. The only reason to call such examples 'metaphors' is to draw attention to the fact that they were novel metaphors once. I refer to this continuum as the *metaphoric-content* continuum, and identify its two ends as *novel-metaphorical* and *conventional* respectively. Contrasting with this continuum, there is, of course, the literal that includes examples such as "John is crying."

Obviously, one would like to exclude literal statements from being called metaphorical; and one would like to include the novel-metaphorical end ('love life as a fresh fruit') and the middle of the metaphoric-content continuum ('marriage as a rocky road') under the term 'metaphor.' So the only bone of contention is the conventional end of the metaphoric-content continuum ('conducting the meeting as plowing.') In emphasizing that a metaphorical interpretation has to be unconventional, I seem to be excluding this end of the continuum from being included in the metaphorical.

While many people would have no problem with this usage, Lakoffian scholars might object, since they have been using examples from the conventional end of the metaphoric-content continuum to argue that metaphors pervade our everyday speech, actions, and behavior. I do not dispute this remarkable feat accomplished by Lakoff and his colleagues. In fact, it only provides additional motivation for this study that undertakes to address how new concepts and meanings emerge through metaphors, and how similarities are created. If many of what we now regard as conventional meanings, conceptual organizations, and perceptions of similarities between two situations started out as novel metaphors, then this is all the more reason to find out how novel metaphors work, and how they create new meanings and new similarities. But then for this objective, it seems reasonable to take conventional metaphors, which already form a part of day-to-day, accepted conceptual organization as given, and focus on unconventional and novel metaphors that break the conventional barriers, and yet communicate meaningfully, and often insightfully.

Of course, one could also focus on conventional metaphors by rolling time back, and analyzing how "The chairperson of the meeting plowed through the agenda" would be rendered meaningful if 'to proceed steadily and laboriously' were not a part of the conventional meaning of 'plow.' Such an approach would be unavoidable if there were a dearth of novel and unconventional metaphors. But given the abundant supply of fresh and vibrant metaphors that stretch language in new and unconventional ways, this approach is unnecessary.

A consequence of my characterizing the metaphorical in contrast with the conventional is that a conventional-metaphorical dichotomy is automatically created. Since some scholars have argued, quite vehemently at times, that all knowledge is metaphorical, the position I am taking might be seen as opposing this view. I take up this issue in Chapter 8, where I argue that my views are, in fact, quite consistent with this "All knowledge is metaphorical" thesis, and the apparent conflict comes from the different ways in which the term 'metaphor' is used.

1.5   Metaphors in Non-Linguistic Domains

Let us now move beyond the metaphors of language, and see if a similar phenomenon can be found in non-linguistic domains such as paintings, films, and religion. Before doing so, we need to generalize the concept of 'text.' What are the kinds of things we might possibly consider as metaphorical? A religious ritual, a painting, and a certain juxtaposition of images in a film are all examples of things that have the potential of being metaphorical. A general term that subsumes them all is perhaps a *complex symbol* or a *structured set of symbols*.

The next thing is to extend the dichotomy between the conventional and the metaphorical so that it applies to symbols. Here again, there seems to be little problem, since most symbols have conventional interpretations associated with them. In order for something to act as a symbol, it has to represent something else, and that something else becomes the interpretation of the symbol. Moreover, most symbols work within a larger social or cultural setting, so that their interpretations are fixed by convention. Thus, we can look for metaphors among non-conventional interpretations of symbols.

Consider paintings, for instance. Clearly, a painting of a park that shows trees, rolling greens, a pond, lovers strolling arm-in-arm, little children feeding the ducks, and so on, shows all these things through conventional meanings. A picture of a tree conventionally refers to a tree, just like the word 'tree' in English refers to a tree. However, in Paul Klee's *Park near L(ucerne)* [Plate 1] we see a more abstract symbolism. Here, it seems more appropriate

PLATE 1: Paul Klee, *Park bei Lu(zern) (Park near Lu(cerne))*, 1938, Paul Klee-Stiftung/Kunstmuseum Bern, ©1991, by VAGA, New York.

PLATE 2: Jan Van Eyck, *The Marriage of Giovanni (?), Arnolfini and Giovanna Cenami (?),* 1434, The National Gallery, London.

to say that the figures refer to trees and people metaphorically. Another example of metaphorical interpretation in a painting is Jan Van Eyck's *The Marriage of Giovanni (?), Arnolfini and Giovanna Cenami (?),* [Plate 2]. Here, the image of a single candle in the chandelier (which conventionally refers to a candle, of course) is supposed to allude to the presence of the Holy Spirit, the shoes on the floor and the brush in the background are meant to symbolize the sanctity of the moment, the dog represents loyalty, the apple in the window sill is supposed to convey the relationship between sexuality and the Fall of Man, and the bed is symbolic of the consummation of the marriage vows [Whitford 1987, pp. 64–65]. (Some of these interpretations might have been conventional during a certain period.)

Consider the symbolism of religion. In the Christian ritual of taking communion, the reference to the bread and the wine, respectively, as the body and the blood of the Christ is very much a part of the accepted Catholic convention. However, when you drink wine and eat bread with your supper, these acts are not considered symbolic in any way, for they do not refer to anything outside of themselves in that context; they do not function as symbols. What makes the same actions taken at the communion symbolic is their reference to the blood and the body of the Christ. So to regard it as metaphorical would be like saying that when the word 'tree' refers to trees, since the reference is not literally to the word 'tree,' the interpretation is metaphorical. Thus, from my point of view, the communion ritual, if it is considered metaphorical at all, lies at the conventional end of the metaphoric-content continuum.

On the other hand, Joseph Campbell's interpretation of communion as a way of becoming one with Him ("The Christ is in me!")—an interpretation which is consistent with the message of the Thomas gospel—is certainly quite unconventional [Campbell 1988, p. 57]. Another excellent example of interpreting religious symbols metaphorically is Campbell's interpretation of Christ's death and resurrection, wherein death is seen as consciousness leaving the body and resurrection is seen as consciousness joining with the universal consciousness of which all life is a manifestation [Campbell 1988, pp. 56–57]. In fact, both these interpretations by Campbell, with which many Christians might feel quite uncomfortable, echo the theme of Buddhism. Nevertheless, if one is willing to suspend the conventional ways of interpreting the Bible in the Christian tradition, Campbell's meaning comes across with absolute clarity; the meaning is indisputably metaphorical.

Consider symbolism in films now. Alfred Hitchcock's *Rear Window* opens up with the perspiring face of James Stewart. The camera then moves on to reveal his leg in a cast, then to a nearby table that has a broken camera and a stack of magazines on it, then to the wall, where there are pictures of racing cars toppled on the track. The juxtaposition of images clearly suggests that it is a hot summer day, and that Jimmy Stewart is a professional photographer, who broke his leg taking pictures of a car race. Now getting all this information from the montage undoubtably requires an element of interpretation, but all the necessary interpretations are quite conventional. On the other hand, Charlie Chaplin's cut from a flock of sheep to a crowd descending into an underground station in *Modern Times* evokes a metaphorical comparison. [Whittock 1990, p. 51.]

The use of the shower scene in Hitchcock's *Psycho* to indicate spiritual cleansing that was mentioned in the prologue is another example of metaphorical interpretation. It lies at the middle of the metaphoric-content continuum—like the 'marriage is a journey' metaphor. It is reminiscent of ritual bathing (as in Hinduism), dipping in Holy Water (as in the Christian tradition of baptism), and washing the hands, feet and mouth before visiting a holy shrine (as in Buddhism). In each of these cases, the act of washing the body symbolizes a cleansing of the spirit and washing away of sins. In fact, this symbolism has also been used in other films. In Richard Benjamin's *Mermaids*, Charlotte Flax (Winona Ryder), a teenager who has strong religious feelings, kisses her boyfriend in a fit of passion. Immediately afterwards, she is overwhelmed by feelings of guilt, and we see her taking a shower while having thoughts (heard aloud in the background) of guilt and repentance.

Another example of metaphorical use of symbols with a similar degree of metaphoric content is in David Lean's *Doctor Zhivago*, when Yuri (Omar Sharif) and Lara (Julie Christie) "first touch, accidentally, on a trolley, Lean signals their mystic union with a spark from the trolley's overhead wires." [Anderegg 1984, p 129.]

There are also many examples of symbolism in film that lie at the novel-metaphorical end of the metaphoric-content continuum. Whittock discusses a particular striking example from Michelangelo Antonioni's *Il Deserto Rosso (The Red Desert):*

"Giuliana (Monica Vitti) is seen against a wall that has large blotches of paint spattered upon it. [The Shot to which I am referring is illustrated on p. 273 of Stanley J. Solomon, *The Classic Cinema: Essays in Criticism* (New York: Harcourt Brace Jovanovich, 1973).] Because of her position, she is both linked and juxtaposed to these blotches. Although their presence has

a literal explanation—colors are being tried out before the room
is repainted—the striking nature of their irrational shapes, set
against the trim figure of the woman, suggests the presence of
an emotional disturbance in Giuliana that belies her outer calm-
ness." [Whittock 1990, p. 59]

In fact, in all of the few color films Antonioni made, the colors have been used
economically, but quite deliberately and often metaphorically to enhance the
cinematic impact [Rifkin 1982, Chap. 5].

Another interesting metaphorical use of the screen image is provided in
Alfred Hitchcock's *The Birds*. In Hitchcock's own words:

"At the beginning of the film we show Rod Taylor in the bird shop.
He catches the canary that has escaped from its cage, and after
putting it back, he says to Tippi Hedren, 'I'm putting you back in
your gilded cage, Melanie Daniels.' I added that sentence during
the shooting because I felt it added to her characterization as a
wealthy, shallow playgirl. And later on, when the gulls attack the
village, Melanie Daniels takes refuge in a glass telephone booth
and I show her as a bird in a cage. This time it isn't a gilded cage,
but a cage of misery, and it's also the beginning of her ordeal by
fire, so to speak. It's a reversal of the age-old conflict between
men and birds. Here the human beings are in the cages and the
birds are on the outside." [Truffaut 1984, p. 288.]

David Lean's classic cut from an extinguished match to a desert sunrise in
Lawrence of Arabia is another case in point. The cut serves as an anchor
for several metaphorical interpretations. The boldness with which Lawrence
(Peter O'Toole) extinguishes a lit match by squeezing the flame between his
fingers becomes a powerful metaphor for his later defiance of the unforgiving
sun in the desert. Also, the desert sunrise becomes a vibrant metaphor for
the beginning of a career for Lawrence that would soon reach the sizzling
intensity of the midday desert sun. (See also Anderegg [1984], p. 111.)

Thus, we see that metaphors are not limited to language, but pervade
many forms of symbolism. It is interesting to note here that non-linguistic
metaphors share many of the characteristics of linguistic metaphors that were
pointed out in Section 4. Non-linguistic metaphors also work by describing
or representing some object or event in a way that requires the symbols used
in the description (or representation) to be interpreted in an unconventional
way. So, the source-target dichotomy can be applied to non-linguistic metaphors as well. The target is the object or event being described, and the

source is the set of symbols used in the description that cannot be conventionally interpreted (as well as related symbols that are called into play). For instance, in Antonioni's metaphor mentioned above, the emotional state of Giuliana is the target, and the blotches of paint on the wall are the source.

Then, while the source is always explicitly provided by the symbols used in the representation, the target might or might not be explicitly given. For instance, in the Van Eyck painting, the target is explicitly indicated by the title and the way the woman and the man are dressed. In Antonioni's metaphor, the target is hinted at very subtly. In Lean's cut from the extinguished match to the desert sunrise, the target is not provided at all.

In almost all the examples presented here, the unconventional interpretation of the source symbols is based on an underlying similarity between the meanings of the source symbols and the target object or event. For instance, in the Klee painting, various shapes resemble (abstractly) trees and profiles of the human body; it is this similarity that makes the painting meaningful. In Chaplin's metaphor in *Modern Times,* it is the similarity between the flock of sheep and the crowd that renders the juxtaposition of the images meaningful. (Of course, there are also many instances of non-linguistic metaphors that *create* the similarities between the source and the target, but they are discussed in the next chapter.)

Then, of course, non-linguistic metaphors can also be understood differently by different people, or not understood at all. For instance, three times in Luis Buñuel's *The Discreet Charm of the Bourgeoisie,* we see a sequence where the six main characters of the film are walking along a road which runs through a barren landscape. This sequence is interpreted by film critic Gwynne Edwards: "[T]he shot creates a sense of the characters' suspension in space and time, of their universality, and also of their bewilderment and isolation." [Edwards 1982, p. 263.] Virginia Higginbotham writes about the same sequence: "The leitmotif of the characters heading down the highway seems to stress the importance of motion in the lives of the elite. For Buñuel, their perpetual activity is often mindless and without direction." [Higginbotham 1979, p. 172.] Critic John Simon, on the other hand, considers the sequence quite trite, if not meaningless: "[T]he three or four recurrences of the shot with incremental variations tell us no more than that our bourgeoise sextet is trudging down the road of life with a different expression on each face." [Simon 1978, p. 366.]

Finally, there are two characteristics of linguistic metaphors that are much more pronounced in non-linguistic metaphors. One is that non-linguistic metaphors are more obviously asymmetric than the linguistic ones. This is because the relation between a symbol and its referent is, in general, a unidirectional one. (How could the emotional state of Giuliana be a symbol for the blotches of paints on the screen?) The other is that many more non-linguistic metaphors seem optional, like the metaphorical interpretations of *Moby Dick* and *The Wizard of Oz,* than linguistic metaphors. In all the examples presented here, with the exception of the Klee painting, the complex symbol (whether it be a screen image, a painting, or a piece of religious text) is meaningful conventionally. One can certainly look at the Van Eyck, read the New Testament, and watch *The Birds,* and understand and enjoy each activity without interpreting anything metaphorically.

1.6   Metaphors, Similes, Analogies and Models

Metaphors are often considered close cousins of, if not identical with, sim-iles, analogies, and models. However, there is no consensus among various researchers as to what these relationships are, and a review of the literature reveals only a maze of conflicting views and opinions. For the purpose of this study, I would like to articulate my own position on these relationships, since I use examples that might be considered similes, analogies, or models by some of you. As some of these examples are crucial to my arguments, it is important that I clarify at the outset how and why I see these phenomena as relevant to the study of metaphors.

1.6.1   Metaphors and Similes

Consider similes first. Similes are characterized as statements of the form "X is like Y," as in "These highways are like snakes." However, as Ortony [1979] has pointed out, the presence of the word 'like' is not sufficient by itself to form a simile, since there also exist statements of literal similarity such as "Encyclopedias are like dictionaries."

To see how a simile (or a statement of literal similarity) relates to meta-phors, we must figure out the target of the description expressed by the simile. There are two possibilities here. Most often, the simile "X is like Y" is intended to be a statement about X. That is, "These highways are like snakes" is supposed to be about these highways. In this case, we can see what happens when the simile is applied to the target. The only part of the description that might be problematic is 'like snakes.' However, the word 'like' conventionally means 'similar to' (and not 'identical with.') So, the statement is conventionally saying that these highways are similar to snakes in certain respects, and, therefore, no unconventional interpretation is called for. The same can be said of the statements of literal similarity.

The second possible target for "X is like Y" is the likeness between X and Y. That is, the statement "These highways are like snakes" might be intended to describe the likeness between these highways and snakes. In this case, the description is interpreted conventionally even more so than in the previous case. Thus, as long as X and Y are similar in certain respects, "X is like Y" does not call for an unconventional interpretation, and disqualifies as metaphor (given my characterization of metaphor.)

This conclusion, however, rests on the conventional meaning of the word 'like' and a purely linguistic analysis. It would be useful to dig a bit deeper to see what cognitive mechanism might be involved in interpreting a simile. In applying the description "These highways are like snakes" to the highways, you have to figure out in what respects the highways are like snakes. In interpreting the metaphoric paraphrase "These highways are snakes," you have to do the exact same thing. You have to figure out how to interpret 'snakes' so that they might apply to highways. Given that many such interpretations are based on the similarities between the source and the target, you have to determine how these highways might be like snakes. Thus, both the simile and its metaphoric paraphrase seem to require the same cognitive process, except that the process of comparison is explicitly signaled by the presence of the word 'like' in a simile.

From this vantage point, we can also better appreciate the difference between the statements of literal similarity and similes. In applying 'dictionary' (and its related concepts) to encyclopedias, the degree of unconventionality is much less than in applying 'gold mines' to encyclopedias (in interpreting the simile "Encyclopedias are gold mines.") Thus, statements of literal similarity are much less metaphoric than similes, if indeed they are metaphoric at all. (The conclusion that the same cognitive process underlies similes and metaphors is bolstered in the next chapter, where it is shown that similes can also create similarities just like metaphors.)

Given that similes explicitly signal comparisons, it might be worth noting whether or not that makes them special in any way (cognitively speaking). There seem to be two possibilities here. One is that the presence of the word 'like' can affect one's ability to comprehend the intended meaning (perhaps make it easier). There is some empirical research that has investigated this issue, though the results are quite inconclusive, and at times contradictory,

as to exactly what the effect is. For instance, Verbrugge [1980] noted that
similes are often treated as symmetric comparisons between X and Y (the
target is the likeness between X and Y), whereas when paraphrased without
'like' ("X is Y"), they are treated as asymmetric statements where the source
Y is being used to describe the target X. Reynolds and Ortony [1980] noted
that children, 7–12 years of age, when asked to choose an appropriate ending
(from a given set of endings) for a given short story, prefer similes to the "X is
Y" form. Contradicting this result, Winner *et al.* [1980], experimenting with
children aged 6, 7, and 9 years, found that both similes ("Raindrops were
like tears falling from the sky") and predicative metaphors ("Raindrops were
tears falling from the sky") have about the same degree of comprehensibility,
which was less than the comprehensibility for topic-less metaphors ("Tears
fell from the sky"). Later experiments by Vosniadou, Ortony, Reynolds and
Wilson [1984] confirmed Reynolds and Ortony's findings, and contradicted
those of Winner *et al.*

The other possible way in which the presence of the word 'like' might
make similes special is by taking away some of the emotional intensity that
accompanies the "X is Y" form by reducing the impact of the shock that
we feel initially due the semantic distance between X and Y. As this emotional intensity might be an important factor in poetry and literature, it is
understandable that literary theory would want to distinguish similes from
metaphors, as is done in Nowottny [1962].

1.6.2   Metaphors and Analogies

The term 'analogy' is used in the literature in many different senses [In-
durkhya 1989]. I would like to distinguish two different senses of analogy.
One has to do with similarities between the two situations—whether noticing the existing similarities or creating new ones—and the other has to do
with predicting further similarities between the two situations based on the
existing ones. These two usages of analogy are usually not distinguished, but
it is very crucial to do so for this study, since there is a great epistemological
chasm separating them. Consequently, I would like to say a few words here
elaborating each sense of analogy and relating it to my characterization of
metaphors.

Simple Analogy

The first sense of analogy concerns similarities between two objects or situations. As I would like to defer my discussion of the creation of similarity to the next chapter, let us just focus on analogy as noticing some existing similarities between two situations. I refer to this sense of analogy as *simple analogy*. A simple analogy can take the form of a linguistic expression, as in "White blood cells fight germs as soldiers fight an invading army." In this way, they seem identical to similes, and, consequently, the remarks I made above concerning similes apply here also. In particular, simple analogies couched in linguistic terms do not require unconventional interpretations, technically speaking, but use the same cognitive mechanism as the one used in understanding metaphors. Of course, one should note that simple analogies are even more explicit than similes. (The simile corresponding to the above simple analogy would be "While blood cells are like soldiers.") Though the more explicit form might make it easier for one to arrive at the intended interpretation of the analogy, it still requires that the source (soldiers in the army and related concepts) be given an unconventional interpretation in order to apply it meaningfully to the target (the immune system).

Simple analogies are more often encountered in cognitive settings than in purely linguistic settings. For instance, one could explain the structure of the atom to a physics student by analogy to the solar system: "An atom is like a miniature solar system." Or there is the parable of the sower that Jesus tells his disciples to make the point that His teachings would be useful only if taken to heart [*Matthew 13; Mark 4; Luke 8*]. (According to the parable, as a sower was sowing seeds, some (seeds) fell along the path, some fell on rocky grounds, some fell upon thorns, and some fell on good soil. Those that fell along the path were eaten up by the birds. Those that fell on rocky grounds sprouted immediately but, because they could not develop roots, were scorched when the sun came out. Those that fell upon thorns were chokes up by the thorns. Only those that fell on good soil brought forth grain.) I am limiting myself here to the use of these analogies to illustrate certain features of an object or situation (the target) by pointing the features of an analogous situation (the source) that is easier to understand. The use of analogies to make further inferences about the target is discussed later.

All such simple analogies make use of a cognitive process that is like the one used in interpreting metaphors. The more familiar source concepts are applied to the less familiar target phenomenon, requiring an unconventional interpretation of the concepts in the process.

One thing you might notice from these examples of simple analogy is that there is less of an asymmetry (than metaphor) between the source and the target. The atom-solar system analogy can equally well be used to communicate the structure of the solar system to someone who has studied some atomic physics but not astronomy. "Soldiers fight an invading army like white blood cells fight germs" can be used to tell a microbiologist about warfare. The meanings transferred when the simple analogy is used in one direction and when it used in the other direction are more or less the same, unlike the situation with linguistic metaphors. Perhaps, extrapolating the findings of Verbrugge [1980], there is a gradual eclipse of asymmetry from non-simile metaphors, through similes, and to simple analogies. This eclipse becomes total for certain variants of simple analogies commonly known as *proportional analogies,* which are completely symmetrical.

Proportional Analogy

Proportional analogies are characterized as relations of the form "A is to B as C is to D." Like simple analogies, they might also come from verbal domain, as in "Gills are to fish as lungs are to humans." In fact, all simple analogies can be paraphrased as proportional analogies: "Defending soldiers are to an invading army as white blood cells are to germs" and "Electrons are to the nucleus as planets are to the sun." The symmetry of proportional analogies is evident in the fact that the terms B, D can be interchanged with the terms A, C, respectively, without affecting the meaning of the analogy. For instance, "Lungs are to humans as gills are to fish" captures the same meaning as the version presented above. (Proportional analogies are symmetric in another way. The terms B and C of an analogy can be interchanged without disturbing the analogy. For instance, "Gills are to lungs as fish are to humans" also forms an acceptable analogy, though one could argue that this analogy does not quite mean the same things as the version presented above.) Proportional analogies can also be formed in perceptual domains. For instance, Figure 1.1 shows a proportional analogy relation involving geometric figures. In fact, such analogies often form the staple of standardized intelligence tests, such as the Miller's Analogy Test.

We encounter some immediate problems in assimilating proportional analogies with our characterization of metaphor, for we ask: What is the target of the proportional analogy? What is the analogy about? What is the description? What are the symbols? What are the conventional interpretations of the symbols? And so on. It is important to clarify these issues, since, as I show in the next chapter, proportional analogies provide a key insight into solving the riddle of creative metaphors.

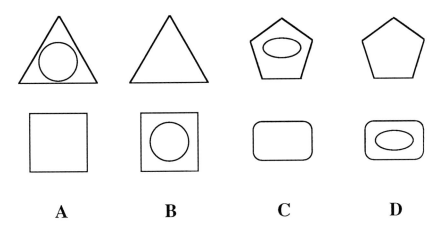

FIGURE 1.1: A proportional analogy relation ('A is to B as C is to D')
involving geometric figures.

At least for proportional analogies involving words, all these problems
are easily addressed. For instance, in the gills-lungs analogy, fish and gills
form one situation, and humans and lungs form the other situation. While
the symmetry of the proportional analogy precludes us from distinguishing
the source from the target, one could regard either one as a complex symbol
(the source) that is being applied to the other situation (the target). For
instance, we could view the process of comprehending the analogy as that
of interpreting the lungs-humans relationship in the fish situation, or vice
versa. This interpretation may well be regarded as lying at the middle, or
even at the conventional end, of the metaphoric-content continuum, because
the relevant relationship is 'organ of breathing,' which subsumes the gills-
fish relation under its conventional meaning. However, like the situation
with 'plow' we encountered earlier, there is some subjectivity involved in
rendering this judgement, for, after all, the physiologies of humans and fish
are quite different.

Consider, however, an interesting example provided by Hofstadter [1981-
85]: "Who is to Great Britain as Nancy Reagan is to the U.S.?" (Nancy
Reagan was the wife of the then U.S. president.) Here, the relationship
in question, 'the wife of the president,' cannot be directly applied given the

political structure in Great Britain, for there is no president there. Moreover, like many metaphors, it is possible to come up with different, and yet quite acceptable interpretations, leading to different answers. For instance, one could interpret 'president' as 'prime minister' and answer 'Dennis Thatcher,' who was the husband of the then prime minister of Great Britain. Or one could interpret it as 'queen,' leading to the answer 'Prince Philip.' Thus, we see that the notion of metaphorical interpretation is quite applicable here.

We can now turn to proportional analogies in perceptual domains, such as the one shown in Figure 1.1. Here the two situations can be identified based on the figures that form the four terms A, B, C, and D of the analogy. For the example in Figure 1.1, we might consider A and B to form one situation and C and D to form the other. Next, we figure out what is the relation between the two terms of one situation, and then interpret it in the context of the other situation. Should we choose to regard A and B as the source, the relation becomes 'move the circle from the inside of the upper triangle to the inside of the lower square.' Note that this description is essentially a structured set of symbols, for the terms 'inside,' 'upper,' 'triangle,' and 'square,' are symbols that are interconnected in a certain way in the description. In interpreting this description in the context of the target object consisting of figures C and D, we need to interpret 'triangle' as 'pentagon,' 'circle' as 'ellipse,' and 'square' as 'rectangle with rounded corners.' This interpretation is clearly non-conventional, and can be likened to the interpretation of the concept 'president' in the context of the British system of government. Thus, proportional analogies involving geometric figures also reveal an underlying cognitive mechanism that is like the one responsible for metaphors. It is important to appreciate this link between the process of interpretation that is taking place in perceptual domains, as seen in Figure 1.1, and verbal and cognitive metaphors. As I show in the next chapter, this domain of geometric proportional analogies provides the most convincing evidence of the creation of similarity. It also leads us to some key insights into how the creation of similarity takes place.

Predictive Analogy

Finally, we come to the other sense of analogy that I mentioned earlier, namely the process of predicting further similarities between two objects or events on the basis of some existing similarities between them. Here it is assumed that the fact that there are existing similarities is sufficient by itself to 'justify' the conclusion that there might be other similarities as well. For instance, suppose a person has never steered a boat before.

However, he has driven automobiles, and from what he knows about boats and automobiles, he sees many similarities between the two. From these similarities, he might 'justifiably' conclude that pushing the rudder to the left in the boat—being analogous to turning the steering wheel to the left in the automobile—would cause the boat to turn left. I refer to this sense of analogy as *predictive analogy,* which is also variously known as 'analogical reasoning' and 'analogical inference.'

This sense of analogy is in widespread use [Carnap 1962, p. 586; Gentner 1983; Gick and Holyoak 1980, 1983; Hesse 1966, pp. 101–129; Von Wright 1965, pp. 134–136]. Cognitive scientists have found in it a valuable source of heuristics for problem solving, have conducted many experimental studies about it, and have proposed a number of theories of predictive analogy. Logicians have done their part by taking seriously the challenge of providing some sort of logical foundation for predictive analogy so that an inference from predictive analogy comes across as more probable than, say, a random inference, and have developed mathematical frameworks to justify it.

For my part, I would like to distance my use of the term 'metaphor' from 'predictive analogy.' The reason is that, to me, metaphor is the process of meaningfully interpreting something as something else, and in this process, the fact that some parts of the interpretation have been carried out successfully, does not justify in any way that other parts of the interpretation can be carried out as well. For example, when you understand "The sky is crying," the fact that you can identify tears with raindrops does not 'justify' that other aspects of crying, such as 'saltiness of tears,' 'sobbing noise,' 'wet eyelashes,' and 'wet cheeks,' can all be interpreted as well. Of course, they might all be candidates for interpretation, and one might be able to extend the interpretation to a varying degree depending on one's imagination. But there is no 'justification' here. In Chapter 7, I discuss a certain mode of metaphor that captures this open-endedness, which is very much like predictive analogy minus the 'justification.' Lest this might seem a small technicality on which to base the claim that my characterization of metaphor has nothing to do with predictive analogy, let me emphasize that this 'justification' is very much the lifeblood of predictive analogy. Without it predictive analogy loses *all* its force as a problem solving heuristic—the role which is the sole reason that predictive analogy has been so much in the mainstream of cognitive science research.

Given that analogy is widely used in the sense of 'predictive analogy,' and its cognitive potential is highly rated, it is only appropriate to place it in the context of the framework of metaphor and cognition that I am developing in this book. I undertake this task in Chapter 9, where I review the various attempts that have been made to justify predictive analogy, and argue that it is best seen as a cognitive process that, while useful at times, can also be a serious obstacle to cognition at others. Until then, however, let me emphasize once more that my term metaphor does not cover predictive analogy in any way, and the two should not be confused.

1.6.3   Metaphors and Models

By 'models' I mean things like a small scale replica of a ship, the Stone Age village in a natural history museum, a picture of a dress accompanied by a sample of the fabric in a catalog, wind tunnels used by aircraft designers, an arrangement of colored marbles put together by a chemistry professor to explain the molecular structure of benzene to her students, the hydraulic model of electricity, a computer simulation of the traffic flow at a city planner's office, the Keynesian model of the economy, and so on. In each case there is an object (or situation, or phenomenon) being modeled (the target), and there is another object (the source), which can be regarded as a structured set of symbols, that represents (or describes) the target. There is also an element of interpretation involved, since the parts of a model (the symbols) must be interpreted appropriately in the context of the target for the model to be meaningful. This interpretation, at least for the examples presented above, is based on an underlying structural similarity between the source and the target.

However, most models are deliberately constructed to represent the phenomenon being modeled in certain respects, and so there is an intended interpretation that goes with them. These interpretations are not unlike interpreting the wine at the communion as the blood of Christ. For instance, a scale model of a ship has a conventional interpretation that is a necessary condition of its being the model; without the interpretation, it is not a model at all. Of course, this is not to say that different models of the ship might not have different interpretations. Obviously, a model of the ship that is used at a travel agency for showing its customers the types of available accommodations needs a different interpretation than the model used by a marine engineer to determine how much the ship is likely to roll during squalls. But for any given model, there is a conventional interpretation that goes with it, and using the model with that interpretation does not seem like metaphor at all. Thus, if such models were to be considered metaphorical at all, they would lie at the conventional extreme of the metaphoric-content continuum.

Of course, a model might be interpreted in rather unconventional ways, as noted by Goodman in an amusing little anecdote that I cannot resist recounting here:

> "Let me tell you two stories—or one story with two parts. Mrs. Mary Tricias studied [an upholsterer's] sample book, made her selection, and ordered from her favorite textile shop enough material for her overstuffed chair and sofa—insisting that it be exactly like the sample. When the bundle came she opened it eagerly and was dismayed when several hundred $2'' \times 3''$ pieces with zigzag edges exactly like the sample fluttered to the floor. When she called the shop, protesting loudly, the proprietor replied, injured and weary, 'But Mrs. Tricias, you said the material must be exactly like the sample. When it arrived from the factory yesterday, I kept my assistants here half the night cutting it up to match the sample.'
>
> This incident was nearly forgotten some months later, when Mrs. Tricias, having sewed the pieces together and covered her furniture, decided to have a party. She went to the local bakery, selected a chocolate cupcake from those on display and ordered enough for fifty guests, to be delivered two weeks later. Just as the guests were beginning to arrive, a truck drove up with a single huge cake. The lady running the bake-shop was utterly discouraged by the complaint. 'But Mrs Tricias, you have no idea how much trouble we went to. My husband runs the textile shop and he warned me that your order would have to be in one piece.'" [Goodman 1978, pp. 63–64].

The interpretations of the proprietor are certainly unconventional, and they can be considered metaphorical. In spite of their seemingly arbitrary nature, they do preserve certain similarities between the model and the object being modeled. In fact, what this story reveals is that many of our conventional interpretations that we take for granted are not the only ones possible.

Interesting as this example is, such unconventional interpretations are quite rare. So I must conclude by noting that while models do have the potential for sustaining unconventional interpretations, they are interpreted conventionally almost all the time. Noticing their potential for forming metaphors is important, hence the anecdote from Goodman, for similarity-creating metaphors can and do arise from models. But this is an issue I discuss in the next chapter.

1.7 Conclusions

The purpose of this chapter has been to characterize metaphor and to explicate its relationship with simile, analogy and models. The issue at stake is not that there is one correct meaning of metaphor, and we ought to find out what it is, but rather that we must clearly demarcate the range of phenomena covered by my use of the term. To do so is important because whenever I present an example of metaphor in a later chapter, it would be helpful to you not to have to wonder whether the example really is a metaphor. Also, clarifying my usage of the term metaphor reduces the possibility of confusion and misunderstanding of the arguments in this book.

With this goal in mind, the characterization of metaphor I use is that a metaphor is an unconventional way of describing (or representing) an object, event, or situation (real or imagined) as another object, event or situation. The object being described is called the target, and the object that is being used to unconventionally describe the target is called the source. The source participates in the process essentially as a structured set of symbols that have to be applied to the target in unconventional ways so as to render the description meaningful. The unconventionality of interpretation is emphasized because the objective of this book is to study the process by which metaphors create new meanings and concepts, and create similarities.

In examining the relationship of similes, analogies, and models to my characterization of metaphor, I noted that similes make use of the same cognitive mechanism as metaphors, though technically they can be regarded as conventional. I distinguished between two senses of analogy. One, which I call simple analogy, refers to comparing two objects or events and noticing their similarities. Simple verbal analogies behave in the same way as similes; they have the same underlying cognitive mechanism as metaphors. Simple non-verbal analogies and proportional analogies (a variant of simple analogies), especially those involving perceptual domains such as geometric figures, are more overtly metaphorical. The other, more popular sense of analogy, which I call predictive analogy, refers to the process of inferring further similarities between two objects or events based on the existing similarities, and is quite different from metaphor. Considering models, we saw that while they have the potential to sustain an unconventional interpretation, their interpretations are usually conventional.

As a last note, I would like to emphasize that most of the metaphors discussed in this chapter, including similes, analogies, and the unconventional interpretations of Mrs. Tricias' proprietor, are based on some underlying similarities between the source and the target. For the rest of the book, I refer to such metaphors as *similarity-based metaphors,* in contrast to *similarity-creating metaphors,* which are introduced in the next chapter.

Chapter 2

Enter Similarity-Creating Metaphors

2.1 Introduction

As I mentioned in the prologue, the interaction theory of metaphor has been proposed primarily to account for the creation of similarity that, it is claimed, accompanies certain metaphors. The proponents of this theory however—almost all of them philosophers—take the phenomenon of creation of similarity more or less for granted. That is, while they use this phenomenon to discredit the comparison theories of metaphor, and articulate their version of the interaction theory to account for it, the fact that certain metaphors can, indeed, create similarities is itself not established in any reasonable fashion, beyond occasionally mentioning a fleeting example.

As a result of this, what I consider to be essentially a methodological slip, we have on one hand philosophers trying to formulate theories of a phenomenon that has not been empirically demonstrated—a factor that may have been the primary cause of the fuzziness surrounding most versions of the interaction theories. And we have, on the other hand, psychologists and cognitive scientists all focusing their attention on comparative, similarity-based metaphors, notwithstanding the criticisms of the interactionist philosophers, since here they have a phenomenon they can put their hands on. Indeed, there have been quite a few empirical studies of how existing similarities between the source and the target form the basis of a metaphor, what kind of similarities can form the basis of a metaphor, how these similarities can be computed from the given representations of the source and the target, and so on. (See, for example, Gentner, Falkenhainer & Skorstad 1987; Gen-

39

tner & Clement 1988; Gick & Holyoak 1980; 1983; Malgady & Johnson 1980; Ortony 1979.) So great has been the impact of these studies, that the cognitive science research on metaphor has been completely dominated by similarity-based accounts.

In order to not make the same mistake and have a book focusing on a phenomenon of the existence of which you may not be convinced, I devote this chapter to demonstrating that similarity-creating metaphors are quite real, and that they play an important role in cognition. I do so by introducing similarity-creating metaphors with several examples in Section 2, and arguing that these metaphors do, indeed, create similarities between their source and their target. Then, in Section 3, I review the few psychological studies that have sought to demonstrate the creation of similarity. In Section 4, I show that the creation of similarity can also result from the phenomena of simile, analogy, and models that were related to metaphor in the last chapter. In Section 5, I contrast the roles of similarity-creating metaphors and similarity-based metaphors in cognition, and argue that similarity-creating metaphors are evident in many of the creative acts of cognition. Finally, I summarize the main points of this chapter in Section 6, and highlight the key problems posed by similarity-creating metaphors.

2.2   Some Examples of Similarity-Creating Metaphors

As mentioned in the prologue, it is somewhat tricky to demonstrate the creation of similarity convincingly, since even in a similarity-creating metaphor, there are always similarities after the metaphor. So, if a metaphor is simply presented, it is hard to be convinced that there were no similarities before the metaphor. After I presented Carl Sandburg's *Fog* in the prologue the way I did, it would not surprise me if some of you thought: "Of course, fog and cat are similar—they both creep on you silently. I just did not see this similarity before." But this is precisely my point. Objectively speaking, any two objects are similar in some respect. By creation of similarity, I mean the creation of similarity in the conscious mind of a cognitive agent.

I present several more examples here to convince you of the fact that certain metaphors can create similarities between their source and the target. In doing so, I follow the same approach as in the prologue. I provide you with pairs of objects, and you are invited to try to articulate all possible ways in which you consider the two objects in each pair to be similar. (Take your time in doing this experiment.) Here are the pairs: ocean and chicken, piano and farm, wild flowers and water, river and computer, computer and harp, ocean and harp, harp and spaceship, spaceship and bone, bone and ocean.

Now consider the beautiful poem *White Hawthorn in the West of Ireland* by Eavan Boland.

> I drove West
> in the season between seasons.
> I left behind suburban gardens.
> Lawnmowers. small talk.
>
> Under low skies, past splashes of coltsfoot,
> I assumed
> the hard shyness of Atlantic light
> and the superstitious aura of hawthorn.
>
> All I wanted then was to fill my arms with
> sharp flowers,
> to seem, from a distance, to be a part of
> that ivory, downhill rush. But I knew,
>
> I had always known,
> the custom was
> not to touch hawthorn.
> Not to bring it indoors for the sake of
>
> the luck
> such constraints would forfeit—
> a child might die, perhaps, or an unexplained
> fever speckle heifers. So I left it
>
> stirring on those hills
> with a fluency only water has. And, like water, able
> to redefine land. And free to seem to be—
>
> for anglers,
> and for travellers astray in
> the unmarked lights of a May dusk—
> the only language spoken in those parts.

The poem is filled with vibrant and creative metaphors. In fact, the poem as a whole can be interpreted metaphorically in more than one way. While I leave the pursuit of such interpretations and their analyses to your individual leisure and fancy, I would like to draw your attention to one particular metaphor that is dominant throughout the poem: namely wild flowers as water. The metaphor is evident in phrases such as "splashes of coltsfoot" and "ivory, downhill rush," but it climaxes, to my feeling at least, in the sixth verse: "stirring on those hills... redefine land." The similarities between the wild flowers (hawthorns here) and water that the metaphor makes us see are very much created similarities, for I would be very surprised if they were a part of your earlier comparison of water and wild flowers.

As another example, consider the following lines from Stephen Spender's well-known poem *Seascape:*

> There are some days the happy ocean lies
> Like an unfingered harp, below the land.
> Afternoon gilds all the silent wires
> Into a burning music for the eyes.
> On mirrors flashing between fine-strung fires
> The shore, heaped up with roses, horses, spires
> Wanders on water tall above ribbed sand
>
> The motionlessness of the hot sky tires
> And a sigh, like a woman's from inland,
> Brushes the instrument with shadowy hand
> Drawing across those wires some gull's sharp cry
> Or bell, or shout, from distant, hedged-in, shires;
> These, deep as anchors, the hustling wave buries.

Here again, after reading the poem, we are at once struck by the similarities between the harp and the ocean. Yet, these similarities could not have been a part of your earlier comparison of the harp and the ocean.

Let us now turn to arts. Consider Piet Mondrian's *Composition with Blue and Yellow* [Plate 3]. The painting literally contains eighteen rectangles, two of which are colored, one blue and one yellow, and nine thick black lines, five of which are horizontal and the other four vertical. What can this painting be about? What can it 'mean,' if anything at all? There seems to be no way to interpret the painting conventionally.

A second look at the painting, however, reveals a tension between various components. We see that the arrangements of lines and rectangles, and of colors, exhibits a certain dynamics and equilibrium. (See Whitford [1987],

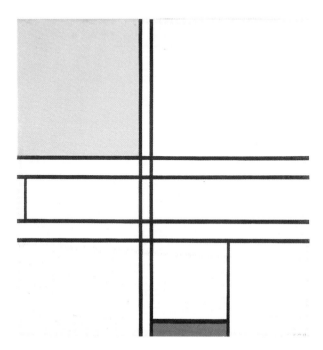

PLATE 3: Piet Mondrian, *Composition with Blue* and *Yellow*, 1935, Hirshhorn Museum and Sculpture Garden, Smithsonian Institution.

pp. 12–20; and Champa [1985], Chap. 12, pp. 113–126.) In fact, this dynamic equilibrium is a characteristic of many of Mondrian's compositions. What can this dynamic equilibrium be about? What could it be saying about life, or anything else for that matter? We need not go very far, for Mondrian himself has written a lot about his art, and how his art relates to life. For instance, in one article he wrote:

> "Good and evil—the two principal oppositions of life—all the world knows them, all the world suffers or is happy because of the one or the other. But not everyone realizes the true value of this opposition, and in general we do not even see their necessity: we demand good, and avoid evil as much as possible. Intuitively, man wants the good: unity, equilibrium—especially for himself. Thus he falls back into the search for false ease and static equilibrium, which is inevitably opposed to the dynamic equilibrium of true life. He satisfies himself with the false unity and in seeking it rejects the duality of oppositions, which, while difficult to perceive, is nevertheless very real to us. It is evident that until the present man generally has felt the profound unity of true life, but living in this disequilibrated world he does not accept the two oppositions simultaneously: he does not live life as a whole so that the duality can be resolved. ... However, life shows us that its beauty resides in the fact that precisely these disequilibrated oppositions compel us to seek equivalent oppositions: these alone can create real unity, which until now has been realized only in thought and in art." [Mondrian 1934, pp. 283–284.]

The same theme is echoed in many other places in Mondrian's writings. This interpretation, however, which is reminiscent of Buddhist metaphysics, makes the Mondrian painting deeply meaningful at once. Moreover, the similarities between the unity of life and the painting that the interpretation suggests are created ones.

Finally, let us take a quick look at the symbolism in films for the evidence of similarity-creating metaphors. In Stanley Kubrick's classic film *2001: A Space Odyssey,* the movement of a bone thrown in the air by Moon-Watcher (an ape-man) is transformed into the movement of a space-ship in the twenty-first century by means of a cut that may well be one of the most dramatic cuts in the history of films. Though the cut seems to have the character of an unobtrusive join, for the movement of the spaceship is closely matched with the movement of the bone, its effect, on the contrary, is quite shocking. (See also Whittock [1990], pp. 51–52.) We realize that they are both expressions of human technological prowess—a prowess that, in the light of the subsequent events of the film, seems quite hollow. In fact, that single cut serves as the anchor for linking the Moon-Watcher sequence to the rest of the film. For instance, critic Thomas Allen Nelson notes:

> "At Hilton Space Station 5, in the Howard Johnson Earthlight Room, Floyd's empty ritual of sounds in the company of Soviet scientists hardly has any more value as communication than Moon-Watcher's grunts of bewilderment or screams of triumphs. At this second waterhole, Kubrick shows that battles for territory and tribal dominance persist even in the rarefied air of space;..." [Nelson 1982, p. 108.]

Thus, the similarities that the juxtaposition of the bone and the spaceship evoke go far beyond whatever you may have come up with earlier.

In fact, the use of juxtaposition to create similarities is considered an accepted technique in cinema. Alfred Hitchcock comments on it in his conversations with Francois Truffaut, while discussing his film *Rear Window:*

> "In one of [Pudovkin's] books on the art of montage, he describes an experiment by his teacher, Kuleshov. You see a close-up of the Russian actor Ivan Mosjoukine. This is immediately followed by a shot of a dead baby. Back to Mosjoukine again and you read compassion on his face. Then you take away the dead baby and you show a plate of soup, and now, when you go back to Mosjouskine, he looks hungry. Yet, in both cases, they used the same shot of the actor; his face was exactly the same.
>
> In the same way, let's take a close-up of Stewart looking out of the window at a little dog that's being lowered in a basket. Back to Stewart, who has a kindly smile. But if in the place of the little dog you show a half-naked girl exercising in front of her open window, and you go back to a smiling Stewart again, this time he's seen as a dirty old man!" [Truffaut 1984, pp. 215–216]

This example unambiguously demonstrates that similarities can be created, for one cannot say, in the case of Mosjoukine, that the same face contained both compassion and hunger, or in the case of James Stewart's smile in *Rear Window,* that it contained both kindliness and lust at the same time, and that the other image was merely highlighting the appropriate emotion. The similarities between the two images that are seen after the second image is presented are *created*—in every sense of the word—by juxtaposition.

2.3 Psychological Studies of the Creation of Similarity

The examples presented in the last section suggest the existence of similarity-creating metaphors. Given that, it seems reasonable to wonder if any systematic study has been done to provide empirical evidence for their existence. I should emphasize here that while there have been many empirical studies to show that metaphors are based on some underlying similarity between the source and the target, these studies do not refute the creation of similarity in any way, for their approach is to present a metaphor to the subjects, and then ask them to explain the metaphor. If the subjects then explain it on the basis of the similarities between the source and target, this is evidence of the fact that there are similarities after the metaphor. Nothing whatsoever can be concluded about whether these similarities were created or not, unless it is known what the similarities were before the metaphor.

The problem in demonstrating the creation of similarity is to find out what the similarities between the source and the target are prior to the metaphor, but without giving away the metaphor. In the study by McCabe [1983], the problem was partially solved by having one group of subjects rate similarities between given pairs of nouns, and another group rate the aptness of metaphors formed by using the two nouns in each pair. I am saying 'partially' because one might quite reasonably wonder if the subjects in the group that is assigned the task of rating the similarities may not be trying to interpret the noun pairs metaphorically. Still, McCabe's results were surprising. She found that when the metaphors were presented in isolated, formulatic sentences ("Dew is veil") then there was a significant correlation between similarities and aptness of metaphors. However, when the metaphors were presented in extended, natural contexts, then the aptness of metaphors was not correlated at all with the similarities between the source and the target. This suggests that, at least in their extended contexts, existing similarities between the source and the target have no bearing on whether their juxtaposition will form an appropriate metaphor or not.

In a later study, Camac and Glucksberg [1984] sought to show the creation of similarity directly. They used the lexical decision paradigm to solve the problem of determining similarities between source-target pairs without giving away the metaphor. In this paradigm the subject is presented with pairs of random strings of letters, and for each pair she has to respond 'yes' when both strings form English words, and 'no' when either or both of the strings do not form English words. The response time is measured for each pair, which is taken to be an indication of the associations between the two words in the pair (when both strings in the pair do form words). The response time is shorter when both strings in the pair form words than when either of them does not; and it is even shorter when the two words are associated. Thus, the response time for *doctor-nurse* would be shorter than the response time for *doctor-lion,* which in turn would be shorter than the response time for *koot-akel.* In this paradigm, using a number of word pairs that are known to be associated, one can determine whether a new word pair is associated or not by comparing its response time to the average response time of the associated word pairs.

Camac and Glucksberg used this paradigm to test the hypothesis that metaphors can be used to create associations between words, words which were not associated prior to the metaphor. They presented ten subjects with four sets of word-word pairs. One set contained metaphor pairs, where both the words in every pair could form a metaphor. This set included pairs like *job-jails, surgeon-butchers,* etc. The second set contained scrambled metaphor pairs, which were words taken from the first set and randomly paired, with the restriction that they did not form a metaphor. This contained pairs such as *surgeon-jails.* The third set had standard associated pairs like *doctor-nurse.* Finally, the fourth set had scrambled standard associates, which were words from set three that were randomly paired, with the restriction that the words in a pair were not associated.

When the response times for all these four sets were measured and averaged over the pairs and across the subjects, a surprising result emerged. Whereas the mean response time for the the standard associated pairs was 782 milliseconds, it was 910 milliseconds for the scrambled [standard associated] pairs. There is a 128 milliseconds difference in processing time between word-pairs that are associated and word-pairs that are not. For the metaphor pairs however, the metaphor pairs set had an average response time of 954 milliseconds, and the scrambled [metaphor] pairs had the average response time of 971 milliseconds, showing only a 17 milliseconds difference. This suggests that the metaphor word pairs were not associated. However, since each pair in this set forms a reasonable metaphor, as in "Surgeons are butchers," the experiment suggests that metaphors can create associations between words that were not associated before.

In a different study, Kelly and Keil [1987] asked the subjects to compare two semantic domains before and after some metaphors connecting the two domains were presented. In order to measure the subjects' perception of similarity between the two domains before the metaphors, and without giving them any hint of the metaphorical connection between the two domains, they came up with the following methodology. The subjects were given a number of concepts from one domain, and they were asked to rate each concept on a given set of semantic differential scales. Then they were given a number of concepts from the other domain, and asked to do the same, with the same set of scales. The similarity between any two concepts, one drawn from each domain, was then taken to be simply their degree of correspondence on the semantic differential scales.

For instance, one pair of domains was periodicals and food. The subjects were given items, such as *New Yorker, Reader's Digest* and *Wall Street Journal,* from the periodical domain, and were asked to rate each item on a given set of dimensions, including *tasteful-tasteless, healthful-unhealthy,* and *spicy-bland.* Then, they were given a number of concepts from the food domain, which included *quiche, spinach,* and *hamburger,* and asked to do the same thing. From this information, the difference between, say *New Yorker* and *quiche,* along the *tasteful-tasteless* dimension would be the absolute value of the difference between the ratings of these two items along that dimension. Adding the differences along all the dimensions would provide a measure of how dissimilar these two concepts are perceived to be.

This procedure was repeated twice for the same pair of domains, and with two groups of subjects. For one of the groups, however, four instances of metaphor involving the two domains were presented before the procedure was repeated the second time. For instance, a metaphor for the periodicals-food domains that was used in this experiment was "The New Yorker is the quiche of newspapers and magazines." It was found that, for the subjects who were in the group that was presented with the metaphors, their perception of similarity between the two domains changed considerably after the metaphors, thereby demonstrating that metaphors can change one's perception of similarity between the two domains.

Technically, Kelly and Keil's experiment demonstrates that the similarities between the domains change, and not that new similarities are created. Indeed, the authors themselves interpret their results in the context of Ortony's model [Ortony 1979], where a metaphor is seen as using the highly salient attributes of the source to highlight the less salient attributes of the target. In this model, the attributes of the source and the target are all there to begin with, only their relative salience is changed by the metaphor.

However, this is easily explained by the fact that Kelly and Keil's subjects were provided with a fixed list of semantic dimensions, from which their perception of similarity was determined. There was no mechanism in the design of the experiment to test if new attributes were created. But one thing the experiment did demonstrate is that similarities are not objective, mind-independent, properties of two given objects, situations, or domains. For otherwise, how could the similarities between them change? And if similarities along a certain fixed set of semantic dimensions can change, it is quite conceivable that new dimensions of similarity can be created as well.

2.4   Creation of Similarity in Metaphor-Related Phenomena

In the last chapter we saw that the phenomena of simile, simple analogy (and its variant proportional analogy) and models are closely related to metaphor, for each has the potential to sustain an unconventional interpretation in describing the target as the source. Given that, it is natural to wonder if the creation of similarity can also arise from these phenomena. Indeed, as I show in this section, each of these phenomena can create similarities between two disparate objects or situations.

2.4.1   Simile

The case of simile is easily settled. In the verses of Boland and Spender, there were two instances of metaphor that could technically be considered similes, for they explicitly indicate that a comparison is being made by including the word 'like.' However, this does not diminish the emotive and cognitive force of the metaphor in any way, and the similarities that we see remain very much the created ones. For instance, in *Seascape,* even though the word 'like' is mentioned in the second line, if, on your first reading of the poem, you were to pause there, and ponder on how could the ocean be like an unfingered harp, you would probably not be able to come up with the similarities between the two that the later lines of the verse evoke. In fact, the presence of the word 'like' seems to have no impact on the emotional impact of the metaphor. (Kittay [1987, pp. 17–19] makes essentially the same point by considering T.S. Eliot's simile "The evening is spread out against the sky like a patient etherized upon a table" in *Love Song of J. Alfred Prufrock,* which creates similarities between the evening and a patient.)

2.4.2 Analogy

Let us consider simple analogies now. Clearly, as far as verbal simple analogies are concerned, all the examples of similarity-creating metaphors provided so far constitute evidence that simple analogies can also create similarities. This is because each example can be paraphrased as a simple analogy, as in "The afternoon sun was reflecting on the waves in the ocean like someone was strumming the strings of a harp." As noted in the last chapter, this paraphrasing might make it easier for someone to arrive at the interpretation of the metaphor. While this may rob the metaphor of some (or even most) of its emotive force, it does not alter the fact that the similarities in the metaphor were the created ones, for they were not present in the earlier comparison of ocean and harp.

Simple analogies in non-verbal cognitive settings can also create similarities. Consider computer software and myth. What are the possible similarities between the two? They seem quite disparate things at first. However, Joseph Campbell recalls that while he was learning to use computer software, he had a sudden revelation about mythology [Campbell 1988, p 20]. Just as computer software requires the user to follow certain steps in order to get the desired effects, a myth also requires its symbolism to be interpreted in a certain way in order to become alive and meaningful. And just as the sequence of signals that produces some desired effect with one piece of software may not work with another piece of software, the way a particular myth is interpreted may not work with another myth. This analogy, which had a significant cognitive value for Campbell, created similarities between software and mythology in his mind. For otherwise, it would not have appeared as a revelation to him.

As an even more bizarre analogy, consider Jean Metzinger's *Le Goûter* [Plate 4] and compare it with quantum mechanics. Let your imagination soar, and see if you can come up with any similarities. Well, Metzinger's painting presents perspectives from different angles at once. For instance, the head shows a full-face view and a profile simultaneously, and the teacup combines the view from the top with the eye-level view, whereas quantum mechanics lets us see the same thing simultaneously as a particle and as a wave.

You might have had a hard time seeing the similarities in this example, or maybe they were obvious at once. But if you try to transport yourself back in history to just before quantum mechanics was developed, it would certainly be impossible to come up with any similarities between the Metzinger and a particle. Yet, a Metzinger (not *Le Goûter* but another—the exact Metzinger does not matter for this argument) might well have been the driving force behind Niels Bohr's search for a theory that allowed the concepts of wave and particle to be interchangeable, so that a particle can be a wave at once, and vice-versa. (See Andersen [1967], p. 322; and also Miller [1978].) If we accept this claim, then the quantum theory itself becomes a product of analogy, in which there were no similarities between the source and the target to begin with, but after a new theory was created, then there were similarities between the two. (See also the fascinating study by Shlain [1991], where it is shown how many of the revolutionary ideas in physics, especially modern physics, were preceded by movements in arts that seem to have anticipated them.)

In order to contrast all these instances of analogy where the similarities are created, I use the term *creative analogy,* and restrict the term 'simple analogy' so that it only applies to similarity-based analogies.

Let us now turn to proportional analogies. While verbal proportional analogies can create similarities in the same way as simple analogies ("What are to the ocean as the strings being strummed are to the harp?"), it seems that perceptual proportional analogies are not capable of exhibiting this phenomenon. Looking at the figures A and C in Figure 1.1 (Chapter 1), one wonders how is it possible for anyone not to see the similarities between the two figures initially, but then see them immediately after the figures B and D are added.

The apparent problem here, in admitting the hypothesis that perceptual proportional analogies might also create similarities, must be appreciated for two major reasons. First, the resolution of this problem can provide the most convincing evidence yet of the creation of similarity. Second, it can give us some refreshing insights into how the creation of similarity takes place. So let me elaborate on why it seems that perceptual proportional analogies may not be capable of creation of similarity.

It seems quite reasonable to concede that verbal concepts usually have so many associations that a person might not be able to bring all the associations to mind at once. Given this, a cognitive scientist who wishes to claim that all metaphors are similarity-based might offer the following explanation of what I have been calling the creation of similarity. When a person is asked to compare, say a cat and the fog, she cannot bring to mind all the different things associated with the concepts of cat and fog. Consequently, not all the similarities between the two would be included in her initial account. However, when an appropriate context is presented, as by Sandburg's poem, these hidden associations are highlighted at once, and the person is able to see the similarities. But the similarities were there all the time, a comparison

PLATE 4: Jean Metzinger, *Le Gouter (Tea Time)*, 1911, Philadelphia Museum of Art: The Louise and Walter Arensberg Collection.

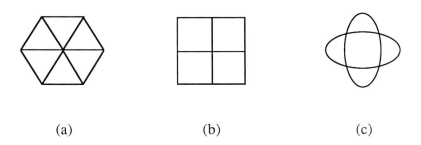

FIGURE 2.1: Three geometric figures. You are to compare each pair of figures: (a) with (b), (b) with (c), and (a) with (c). Write down all possible ways in which each pair seems similar.

theorist would argue.

When we look at the perceptual proportional analogies in the light of this argument, it seems that the objects in question (such as the figures A and C in Figure 1.1) are simple geometric figures, and they are right in front of the person in all their entirety. There are no hidden meanings or associations. The figures are reasonably simple. There is no symbolism involved, as it would be if the figures were of animals or houses. So, all the person has to do is to compare the two figures, and come up with the similarities. And whatever is included there must be the possible similarities between the two figures. Context can pick out different similarities from this list, but it cannot add new things to it.

Well, I hope you get the point. Now, consider Figure 2.1. It shows three geometric figures. Take figures (a) and (b), and compare them. Write down if they appear similar to you, and if so, then in what ways. Then do the same with figures (b) and (c), and then with figures (a) and (c).

Now look at Figure 2.2. Do the four figures there form a proportional analogy relation "A is to B as C is to D?" If you answer "No!" take another look. Do you see the relations involved? Do you see how figures A and C are similar? But they are the same as figures (a) and (b), respectively, in Figure 2.1. Are the similarities you see in Figure 2.2 included in what you wrote down after seeing Figure 2.1? Repeat the same experiment with Figure 2.3, which uses figures (a) and (c) of Figure 2.1 to form a proportional analogy relation.

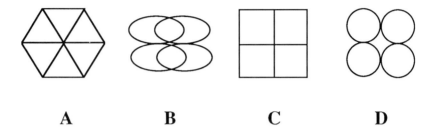

A   **B**   **C**   **D**

FIGURE 2.2: A proportional analogy relation ('A is to B as C is to D')
involving geometric figures. Note that the figures A and C are the same as
Figure 2.1 (a) and (b), respectively. Compare the similarities between the
figures you see now with what you wrote down after seeing Figure 2.1.

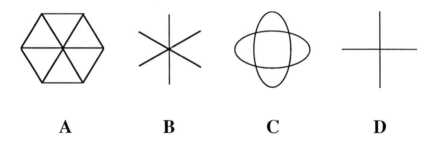

A   **B**   **C**   **D**

FIGURE 2.3: A proportional analogy relation ('A is to B as C is to D')
involving geometric figures. Note that the figures A and C are the same as
Figure 2.1 (a) and (c), respectively. Compare the similarities between the
figures you see now with what you wrote down after seeing Figure 2.1.

I hope this experiment is the last nail in the coffin of any doubts that might still linger in your mind about the phenomenon of creation of similarity. Let me now address, in the light of this example, the not-so-hypothetical account of the creation of similarity in a comparison theoretic framework mentioned above. To explain the creation of similarity as merely highlighting and downplaying of certain attributes of the source and the target that were there to begin with, the description of every object and situation (a potential source or target of a metaphor) must include numerous—potential infinite— attributes. The description of a relatively simple figure, such as Figure 2.1(a), must include *all* possible ways of describing it: that it has four parallelograms in it arranged in such-and-such fashion, it has three trapezoids with their axes 120 degrees apart, it has six triangles with their vertices coinciding and their axes 60 degrees apart, and so on and on. And I did not even consider attributes like the thickness of the lines, the texture of the paper on which they are drawn, etc., though any of these can easily be made relevant for a proportional analogy by choosing the terms B and D appropriately. And please bear in mind that this is a simple figure!

The point here is that if the similarities are assumed to be there from the start, then every object must be given a description that is astronomical in size, if not infinite. Otherwise, there would always be attributes left out that may be needed in comprehending some metaphor. However, with the descriptions so huge, they become completely unworkable in any reasonable model of cognition. First, there is the obvious memory space problem. Second, there is the inefficiency of having to search through this huge description list to find the right description for any given context. With the description of Figure 2.1(a) that includes all possible ways of looking at it, it may be a very long time before one sees in it a hexagon with all its major diagonals connected.

However, if we admit the possibility of creation of similarity, then there is no such problem. One can have small workable descriptions of objects and situations, and there would be similarity-based metaphors that are based on the underlying similarities between these given descriptions. At times, however, new similarities are created, similarities not seen from the existing descriptions.

The examples of Figures 2.2 and 2.3 also provide a valuable clue to the source of the created similarities. Notice that to understand the analogy relation in each case, one must look at Figure 2.1(a) differently. It has to be described differently. For the analogy of Figure 2.2, it needs to be described as four parallelograms in a certain configuration. For Figure 2.3, it needs to be seen as three trapezoids with their axes 120 degrees apart. Thus, each time, the description of the figure is changing, and a new description is being created. The created similarities are with respect to this new description. Thus, the problem of creation of similarity collapses into the problem of redescription.

This foreshadows the account of similarity-creating metaphor to be proposed in Chapter 7. However, two things should be noted here about rooting the creation of similarity in redescription. One is that this observation is not something new, but can be found implicitly or explicitly in the writings of Max Black, Mary Hesse, and Paul Ricoeur, among others. The other is that this observation alone merely passes the buck, and does not address the problems raised by the phenomenon of creation of similarities; problems such as: Where do created similarities come from? What constrains created similarities from being arbitrary? And so on. For similar issues can be raised about the redescription process: How does the new description emerge? What prevents the new description from being arbitrary? And so on.

2.4.3   Models

In the last chapter, we saw that a model is usually a deliberate creation meant to represent certain aspects of the object, situation, or phenomenon being modeled. Consequently, there is a conventional interpretation that goes with each model, though it is possible that one might not be aware of it, and decide to interpret the model in an unusual way. Thus, with my emphasis on unconventionality in metaphors, models are generally non-metaphorical, though they have the potential to become metaphors.

The term model, however, is also applied to what might be termed as 'pre-theoretic models,' which are models before their interpretation is fixed and becomes conventional. These pre-theoretic models can be found by historically tracing the origin of what are now regarded as conventional models. There is usually a target phenomenon that is not well understood, and a source that is more concrete and well understood. But there is no good connection, or transference between the two, so that the source can be meaningfully interpreted in the target domain. There is only some vague idea in the mind of the scientist. Sometimes, there is not even a vague idea but an emotional drive that keeps the scientist seeking some connection. However, once the connection is found, the model starts to become entrenched. If we compare the states of the source and the target before and after the model became entrenched, the creation of similarities can be seen quite clearly.

The influence of Metzinger on Bohr's theory of quantum mechanics mentioned above serves as a good example of a pre-theoretic model. Here the creation of similarities can be seen rather starkly, since there was no quantum theory before the metaphor. Several other examples of pre-theoretic models have been noted by historians of science. Gruber [1978], on analyzing Darwin's notebooks in which he kept notes while working on his celebrated theory of evolution, noted that the image of an irregularly branching tree kept on recurring in his thoughts, and may have served as the primal metaphor for his natural selection principle. Rothbart [1984, pp. 611–612] has noted that Newton's investigation of optics was greatly influenced by the theory of acoustics—that is, the theory of acoustics was a pre-theoretic model for optics. More examples are presented in the next section along with a discussion of the role of similarity-creating metaphors in creative problem solving and cognition.

I should emphasize that all these examples of pre-theoretic models cannot be explained from a similarity-based account, though every pre-theoretic model, if it is successful, always gives rise to similarities between the phenomenon being modeled and the model. It is important to underscore this point because the proponents of what I call predictive analogy often cite the same examples as evidence that noticing existing similarities between two situations is a justification for positing that there might be other similarities as well. However, the so called existing similarities are always similarities after the fact, at least in all the examples presented here. It is not as if Bohr saw certain similarities between the cubist style of painting and the behavior of atomic particles. Rather, cubism presented him with an idea, namely that a particle can be a wave at the same time. Finding this idea aesthetically pleasing, he worked hard to see if such a theory might in fact be developed.

The same can be said about Darwin's image of the irregularly branching tree. Miller's account cites several excerpts from Darwin's notebooks to show that it was not some existing similarities between the tree image and whatever was known about the evolution at that time that kept Darwin searching for what other similarities might be found. On the contrary, it was an emotional drive that kept up his intellectual commitment to articulating an account of evolution that matched the tree image. It was not as if Darwin was searching for similarities, rather he was formulating them. This process was actually fraught with several problems that appeared to invalidate the model, but Darwin's intellectual commitment to the idea kept him from throwing away the image altogether. Instead, he improvised and sought different ways to render the image meaningful.

2.5 Similarities and Creative Problem Solving

Now that we have seen that similarity-creating metaphors are real, we need to assess what role, if any, they play in cognition; and to contrast this role with that of similarity-based metaphors. This is the task undertaken in this section. In highlighting the role of similarity-creating metaphors in cognition, I focus on creative problem solving as the domain of cognitive activity. By using the qualifier 'creative' I am restricting myself to those problem-solving activities that require some new innovation, new idea, or new way of thinking.

It is now considered an established fact that metaphors play a key role in creative problem solving [Broad 1985; Canguilhem 1963; Gentner 1982; Gentner & Jeziorski 1989; Gick & Holyoak 1980; 1983; Gitter *et al.* 1964; Gordon 1961; Gordon 1965; Gruber 1978; Hesse 1966; 1974; 1980; Holstein 1970; Koestler 1964; Libby 1922; Miller 1978; Polya 1945; Schön 1963]. Many of these studies, however, do not make a distinction between similarity-based metaphors and similarity-creating metaphors, and end up analyzing metaphors in an 'after the fact' fashion. Since there are always similarities after the metaphor, such analyses are taken to suggest that noticing the existing similarities between two objects or situations is a key to creative problem solving, as these similarities can be used to make further hypotheses about the unsolved problem that are likely to lead to a solution. This way of using metaphors turns them essentially into predictive analogy. While I defer a full discussion of predictive analogy to Chapter 9, it would be useful here to analyze various studies on the role of metaphor in creative problem solving with respect to similarities before and after the metaphor.

A careful analysis, in this respect reveals three different ways in which metaphors show up in creative acts: (1) There are similarities before the metaphor and after the metaphor, (2) there are no similarities before the metaphor but similarities are created by the metaphor, and (3) there are similarities before the metaphor, but not after the metaphor. Obviously, the first of these roles corresponds to similarity-based metaphors and the second corresponds to the similarity-creating metaphors. The third role of metaphors is somewhat unusual, but a few examples that fit this category are rather interesting, and I include them here for completeness sake. I now examine each of these three classes of metaphors in turn.

2.5.1 Similarities Before and After the Metaphor

In this case, one notices some existing similarities between the source and the target. These existing similarities provide a way to map parts of the source to parts of the target. Based on this initial mapping, hypotheses can be transferred from the source to the target. These hypotheses, if verified in the target, might provide useful additional knowledge of the target domain.

An example is provided by Gentner and Jeziorski [1989]. In creating the theory of thermodynamics, Carnot used an analogy from the flow of fluids. Gentner and Jeziorski provide a long quotation from Carnot that lays out the analogy. From the existing similarities between the fluid-flow and the heat-flow, namely that fluid flows from the higher level to lower level and the heat flows from the higher temperature body to the lower temperature body, Carnot suggested the hypothesis: Could it be that the rate of heat-flow is proportional to the temperature difference between the two bodies? (Just like the rate of fluid-flow is proportional to the difference in levels.)

This example is clearly an instance of similarity-based metaphor. Moreover, the suggestiveness of metaphor can be seen as a manifestation of the open-endedness of metaphor that we saw in Chapter 1. (In understanding "The sky is crying," one may attach a feeling of universal sadness to the meaning of the metaphor.)

This particular role of metaphor in cognition comes closest to predictive analogy, and therefore it is crucial to distinguish between the two. In predictive analogy, the existing similarities between the source and the target are seen as justifying that the hypotheses transferred from the source are likely to hold in the target as well. Whereas, in similarity-based metaphors, the similarities that have been found so far carry no such justification about whether additional similarities would be found or not. Lest this seem a trite technicality, let me point out that this technicality is the basis of a major point of divergence between how similarity-based metaphors and predictive analogy might be used in cognition. If the existing similarities are seen as justifying additional similarities, then this, at once, suggests that when we are faced with an unsolved problem with the target, our best bet may be to find the most similar source, based on whatever is known about the target so far, and then to import hypotheses from the source to the target. But similarity-based metaphor, since it carries no justification, suggests no such mechanism. Of course, the fallacy of seeing a hypothesis as justified just because there are some similarities between the two domains works as a cognitive blind spot, as is shown in Chapter 9. For now, this important difference must be kept in mind so that this open-ended use of similarity-based metaphor is not confused with predictive analogy.

The use of similarity-based metaphors in this way involves little creativity. If we admit the hypothesis that the similarities between fluid-flow and heat-flow were known, as in Gentner and Jeziorski's account, then it does not require a particular deep insight to generate the above mentioned hypothesis. It seems obvious at once!

A somewhat more creative use of similarity-based metaphors can be seen in what William J.J. Gordon calls 'direct analogy' [Gordon 1961, pp. 42–45]. Here, faced with some problematic situation, one searches one's experience and memory for an image that is like the problem at hand, and makes a conscious comparison of the parallel facts between the problem and the source image. This is perhaps best demonstrated by an example provided by Gordon where a group was faced with the task of designing a dispenser for various products such as glue, nail polish, etc. The dispenser was to be in one piece (without a reclosable top), and therefore its mouth must open for dispensing and then close tightly after each use. The direct analogy that led to solving this problem came from that of a horse excreting. As a member of the group reminisced:

> "When I was a kid I grew up on a farm. I used to drive a hayrack behind a pair of draft horses. When a horse would take a crap, first his outer ... I guess you'd call it a kind of mouth, would open. Then the anal sphincter would dilate and a horse ball would come out. Afterwards, everything would close up again. The whole picture would be as clean as a whistle." [Gordon 1961, p. 42].

Here it is easy to see that there were similarities between the source and the problem to be solved before the solution was achieved. Moreover, these similarities were preserved in the solution process. Here, once more, I must emphasize that Gordon's direct analogy should not be confused with predictive analogy. When one finds a source that is similar to the problem at hand, there is absolutely no guarantee—not even an increased likelihood—that this will lead to the solution. Also, if there are two sources, and one of them is more similar to the problem than the other, direct analogy does not by any means suggest that the more similar source is more likely to lead to the solution (which is one of the predictions that predictive analogy makes). The point of direct analogy is simply that sometimes recalling a similar image may suggest a new way to solve the problem.

2.5.2 Similarities After but Not Before the Metaphor

Even though most of the recent research has concentrated on what role, if any, similarity-based metaphors and predictive analogy play in problem solving, there exist a few studies of how many creative and original ideas originated from metaphors that created the similarities between their source and the target. What is even more interesting is that all these studies are from 'real-world' problem-solving situations—that is, situations where the solution of the problem was not known a priori. (This is in contrast with somewhat contrived experiments that have been done to support predictive analogy. In these experiments a group of subjects are presented with a problem, the solution of which is known, and a number of sources, one of which is analogous to the problem and also leads to the solution of the problem. I discuss such studies, and the fallacy of concluding from them that predictive analogy is the key to creative problem solving, in Chapter 9.)

Let us look at one such example in detail. The example is taken from Schön's excellent study of creativity in *Displacement of Concepts*. One of the main concerns of Schön in this study was to remove himself from the fallacy of 'after-the-fact' analysis of creative acts. After a creative idea has been successfully applied to solve a certain problem, it is always easy to analyze it, to see the underlying similarities between the source of the idea and the problem at hand, and attribute the success of the idea to those similarities. However, this analysis sheds little, if any, light on how to solve another problem. What is crucial for studying creative problem solving is a 'during-the-fact' analysis: What ideas came to mind in solving the problem? Which ideas were rejected and which ones were tried out? And so on.

The example from Schön's study that I have chosen to present here concerns a group of researchers who were engaged in improving the performance of a synthetic-bristle paintbrush. (See Schön [1963, pp. 74–76], and also Schön [1979].) Compared to the natural-bristle paintbrush, the synthetic-fiber brush delivered the paint to the surface in the form of discontinuous stripes, giving it a gloppy appearance. Their model of painting a surface— and the role of a paintbrush in it—accounted for the process as the brush smearing the paint on the surface. The model, obviously, was sufficient for painting various surfaces with natural paintbrushes. However, when a synthetic brush was used, the model could not explain why the painted surface would not be as smooth as when a natural brush was used. In vain, the researchers tried to extend their model by making some other features of natural brushes relevant to the process of smearing and then incorporating them in the synthetic brush. For instance, they noticed that the natural bris-

tles have split ends and, thinking that this feature might affect the smearing
process, they tried to split the ends of the synthetic bristles, but with no
improvement in the performance.

Finally, the breakthrough occurred when a theoretically oriented physical
chemist suggested an unorthodox model that a paintbrush might work like
a pump. In projecting the pumping model on the process of painting the
researchers noted that the paint is not smeared on the surface, but actually
forced, by a pumping action, through the space between the bristles. This
perspective gave a totally different ontology to the process of painting, and
the role of a paintbrush in the process was radically transformed. And the
similarities between the paintbrush and a pump were created in this process
of transforming the perspective on painting and the role of paintbrush in
it. Thus, there were no similarities before the metaphor, but the similarities
were created by the metaphor.

From this transformed view of painting, when the actions of natural and
synthetic paintbrushes were compared, it was found that whereas the natural
bristles formed a gradual curve when pressed on the surface, the synthetic
bristles formed a sharp bend. Note that this difference becomes relevant only
with the new ontology. When painting is seen as the process of smearing paint
on the surface, the angle of bend of the bristles is irrelevant since it plays no
role in the process. Speculations that the sharp angle of bend of the synthetic
bristles might be the reason for gloppy appearance of the painted surface led
to a number of innovations. Some of these innovations were implemented
to produce a gradually bending bristle, and the resulting brush did, indeed,
produce a smooth painted surface.

Schön presented several other examples like this. He used the term *projection* to refer to the process of juxtaposing two dissimilar situations as a
means of gaining fresh insight into one of them.

William J.J. Gordon, whose direct analogy was cited above as an example
of creative use of similarity-based metaphors, has provided many more examples of real-world problem-solving situations where similarities were created
[Gordon 1961]. He proposed two mechanisms that are often useful in creative
problem solving. One of them is *making the strange familiar,* which works by
imposing a familiar point of view on a problem with which one is unfamiliar.
The role of cubism in Bohr's development of quantum mechanics and the role
of the tree image in Darwin's articulation of evolutionary theory can both be
seen as examples of this mechanism. 'Making the strange familiar' can also
be evidenced when we are faced with a problem from a domain about which
we know very little, and we impose a familiar perspective on the domain

to solve the problem. Some examples of this phenomenon are provided in Gordon [1965], including one of a student who, when asked to prove a theorem about endomorphisms (a function with the same domain and range), constructed an analogy of looking at oneself in the mirror to arrive at the proof. In all these examples the similarities are created, since initially there is so little known about the domain that few similarities, if at all, can be seen between it and whatever familiar domain happens to be the source of the theory.

Gordon's other mechanism is even more interesting, and he refers to it as *making the familiar strange*. Here one is familiar with the problem domain, but the familiar perspective cannot help in reaching the solution. So the thing, Gordon suggests, is to view it strangely by juxtaposing it with strange domains. The juxtapositions initially seem quite crazy, but then one of them might lead to an illuminating insight that can prove to be the key to the solution. This mechanism is, in fact, quite the opposite of predictive analogy, which looks at the most similar source to import hypotheses into the problem domain. According to Gordon's view—a view that is supported by many case studies provided there—any such attempt would only lead to mundane and not particularly insightful hypotheses. This is because a similar domain is not going to change the perspective on the problem domain.

Schön's paintbrush example cited above serves as a good example of this mechanism. The pumping domain was not chosen for its existing similarities with painting, and had the researchers limited themselves to seeking sources that were similar to the painting domain they would have been stuck with the painting-as-smearing point of view.

In another example of 'making the familiar strange'—one presented by Gordon—a group of researchers was faced with solving the problem of having a shaft turn at the constant speed of 400 revolutions per minute (rpm), while the speed of the power-source shaft varies from 400 to 4000 rpm. A blackbox was drawn with a shaft labeled '400 to 4000' entering and a shaft labeled '400 constant' exiting. The members of the research group tried to make this familiar problem strange by metaphorically entering the box and attempting to maintain the required speed constancy of the outgoing shaft by using their bodies. Here is, for instance, an excerpt from one member of the group:

> "...I'm in the box and I am trying to be a governor ...to be a feedback system ...built in. ...Let's see. If I grab the out-shaft with my hands ...and let's say there's a plate on the in-shaft so that my feet can press against it. I put my feet way out on the periphery of the plate and ...what I really would like is for my

feet to get smaller as the speed of the in-shaft increases because
then the friction would be reduced and I would hold on to the out-
shaft for dear life and its speed might remain constant. ... The
faster the in-shaft went the smaller my feet would become so that
the driving force would stay the same." [Gordon 1961, p. 39].

Based on this idea, one member of the team designed a hydraulic clutch,
which turned out to work as expected but was quite inefficient and not suitable as a power transmitting device. But then, another member of the team
designed a mechanical clutch from the analogy with the hydraulic clutch that
proved to work quite satisfactorily.

Here the approach to the problem is quite unorthodox, to say the least.
Moreover, it is not inspired by any existing similarities. However, once the
mechanical clutch is built, one can see that the actions of the person inside
the box are quite analogous to it.

Some other studies of creative problem solving that fit this category can
now be noted in passing. Libby [1922] cites several examples, including that
of Kekule who came up with the idea that the carbon atoms in the benzene
molecule might be arranged in the form of a ring when he dreamt of a serpent
swallowing its own tail. Here there was an image that led to the solution of
a problem. After the solution, one could see the similarities between the
molecular structure of benzene and a snake swallowing its tail. But before
that, there were no similarities. The image of the snake suggested an idea
that turned out to be fruitful. One cannot say that Kekule was aware of
some existing similarities between the snake and benzene that led him to the
hypothesis that the snake swallowing its tail might be the molecular structure
of benzene.

Koestler [1964, pp. 199–207] has provided many examples of similarity-
creating metaphors in problem solving. In one particular example, he traced
Benjamin Franklin's invention of the lightning conductor, concluding with:

> "There are two successive Eureka processes involved in this story.
> In the first, the bisociative link was what Franklin called 'the
> power of points'; it gave rise to the analogy: pointed finger dis-
> charges Leyden jar, pointed rod discharges cloud. It may have
> been attained by ideation on a relatively conscious level, probably
> with that aid of visual imagination. The second stroke of genius
> was the use of the kite to reach the thunderbolt. It illustrates
> the argument I have put forward earlier in this chapter: one can
> hardly say that a hidden analogy was pre-existent in the universe

between a kite used as a sail by a boy floating on a lake, and a lightning conductor." [Koestler 1964, p. 204.]

All these examples provide plentiful evidence that similarity-creating metaphors do, indeed, play a central role in cognition. They even suggest that, in any act of cognition involving creativity, similarity-creating metaphors might play a much more prominent role than similarity-based ones.

2.5.3   Similarities Before but not After the Metaphor

A few examples of the role of metaphor in creative problem solving fit this category. Here, a similarity-based metaphor provides an initial solution of the problem, which is not very satisfactory. The initial solution is then modified until it becomes satisfactory. In the modification process, however, the source is no longer used, so that the final solution of the problem ends up bearing little or no resemblance to the source.

Broad [1985] provides some classic examples of this phenomenon in Edison's prolific inventions. For instance, Edison's invention of the kinetoscope, a motion picture machine, was made from analogy with his earlier invention of the phonograph. One of the earlier designs of the kinetoscope showed a cylinder on which a sequence of images were laid out spirally. The cylinder was meant to be viewed through an eyepiece, so that as the cylinder was rotated, the images would be viewed in sequence. The design was rather awkward, and so he made many further modifications. The final kinetoscope bore little resemblance with the phonograph. Thus, we see that the role of metaphor here is basically to provide a first foothold in an unfamiliar domain. After that the connection with the source is severed, and later developments destroy the similarities that were the basis of the foothold. The process is, perhaps, not unlike the series painted by Piet Mondrian as the study of objects like a tree or a lighthouse. In the tree series, for instance, the initial painting looks very much like a tree, but each subsequent painting becomes more and more abstract, until the final one, which hardly looks like a tree.

2.6   Conclusions: The Problem of Similarity-Creating Metaphors

We have seen in this chapter that the phenomenon of creation of similarity is quite real, and that it can be evidenced in many creative acts of cognition.

Given this, the problem for any theory of metaphor is to explain the creation of similarity. Where do the created similarities come from? What was left implicit in all the examples of similarity-creating metaphor presented in this chapter is that the creation of similarity is far from arbitrary. That is, juxtaposing any random domain may not result in any creation of similarity, and even when it does, the created similarities may not be particularly insightful ones, and even when they are, the insights may not be helpful in solving a certain problem with the target domain. For instance, Gordon [1961, pp. 45–48] noted that when a group of researchers were engaged in developing a jacking mechanism that would fit into a four by four inch box, and yet would extend up to three feet and support four tons, the researchers tried to use a biological metaphor ("[A] biological jack where the power source would be a kind of virus culture. You drop some 'food' into the culture and the animals breed and occupy more space thus offering a power source.") and a chemical metaphor ("[A] slow burning powder that would develop energy as you added oxygen to it.") but in vain. (The final solution was arrived at by the analogy from the Indian rope trick, which is another example of similarity-creating metaphor.) Schön noted that the group working on the paintbrush problem also considered 'painting as masking a surface' metaphor, but it led to no useful insights [Schön 1979, p. 259]. In the case of Hitchcock's *Rear Window,* while James Stewart's face can be made to express kindness or lust by juxtaposing it with an appropriate image, it cannot be made to express horror, anger, or frustration. All these examples demonstrate that the creation of similarity seems to work in mysterious ways. Sometimes it works, and sometimes it does not. It is as if every domain had a mind of its own, and it would do unpredictable things when juxtaposed with another domain.

The problem for any theory of metaphor, and certainly for the one developed in Part II of the book, is to shed some light on this mystery, and to answer questions such as: What constrains the creation of similarity? When two domains are juxtaposed, what is actually going on? This is not the first time, however, that these questions have been raised. As I mentioned in the prologue, the interaction theories of metaphor have been proposed primarily to account for the creation of similarity, and to answer these questions. Given that, it would be useful to examine how far such theories have come to providing an adequate explanation of the creation of similarity. This is the subject of the next chapter.

Chapter 3

Approaches to Similarity-Creating Metaphors

3.1   Introduction

We saw at the end of the last chapter that similarity-creating metaphors present us with a paradox. On the one hand, they show that similarities hitherto unseen can be made real. On the other hand, the creation of similarity seems to be quite constrained. The problem is to resolve this paradox somehow and to show how the similarities are created, where they come from, and to make explicit the invisible hand that constrains this creation.

Of course, an attempt is made to solve this problem in the comparison theory of metaphor [Kittay 1982]. You may recall that, according to this theory, all metaphors are based on some existing similarity between the source and the target. The existing similarity is also seen to constrain the creation of similarity. It is argued that the 'creation' is in merely highlighting similarities with respect to less salient attributes and relations of the target. This process is not arbitrary, since there must be some existing similarities, albeit not prominently visible due to their low salience, between the source and the target in order for their juxtaposition to be meaningful. But this account encounters the problem that the representation (or description) of any object has to be infinitely large, as it must include every possible attribute, every relation and every possible way this object can be seen as similar to any other object. I have emphasized this point in the last chapter in the context of proportional analogies involving geometric figures.

This failure of the comparison theory and its variants to explain the creation of similarity has been one of the key factors behind the development of what is generally known as the interaction theory. Though the roots of it can be traced back to I.A. Richards' *Philosophy of Rhetoric,* the interaction theory is most often identified with the views presented by Max Black in two thoughtful essays written about twenty years apart [Black 1962; 1979]. Black's articulation of the interaction theory, however, is quite vague at its very best. While he provides some analogies and metaphors to communicate the key concepts of the theory, these analogies and metaphors are not elaborated sufficiently to address the creation of similarity satisfactorily. To make matters worse, his account contains some paradoxes and the images provided by his metaphors and analogies are sometimes in conflict with one another.

Several other scholars have proposed variations of the interaction theory in order to remove the problems inherent in Black's version. However, most of these accounts are equally vague, often introducing more ill-defined concepts in their attempts to clarify and elaborate the interaction theory. In all this confusion, it is hard to know what exactly any particular version of the interaction theory entails. One of my objectives in this chapter is to reveal the vague, paradox-ridden nature of the interaction theories, thereby justifying the need for a concise framework such as the one I present in Part II of this book.

In spite of this muddled picture of interactionism, some of the imagery that has been used to articulate it is quite insightful, given some elaboration and a sympathetic interpretation. My second objective in this chapter is to clearly identify such insights (with my elaborations and 'sympathetic' interpretations), for they have been incorporated in my own framework. This also allows me to acknowledge an intellectual debt to those interactionists whose views have greatly influenced my own.

The few works I discuss here have been chosen on the basis of their notability and relevance to my framework. Given the prominence enjoyed by Black's interaction theory, I begin by discussing it at some length in Section 2. I follow this, in the subsequent two sections, with a brief presentation of the interactionisms of Paul Ricoeur and Carl Hausman, respectively, who have also wrestled with the problem of the creation of similarity. In Section 5, I take note of Wheelwright's epiphor-diaphor distinction, and Mac Cormac's attempt to formalize it by using fuzzy set-theory.

A non-interactionist approach to the creation of similarity comes from the work of George Lakoff and his colleagues [Johnson 1987; Lakoff 1987; Lakoff and Johnson 1980; Lakoff and Turner 1989], which I refer to as the Lakoffian approach. Although Lakoff and his colleagues have largely focused on what might be called conventional, frozen, or dead metaphors, showing how many of our everyday concepts are structured by these conventional metaphors, they have not only duly recognized the potential of metaphors to create similarities, but also shed some light on how the similarities are created. Consequently, I present the Lakoffian approach to the creation of similarity in Section 6. We see there that the Lakoffian approach can, in fact, be easily seen as a variant of the interaction theory, even though Lakoff and Turner [1989, pp. 131–133] explicitly reject the interaction theory; their rejection turns out to be based on a quite myopic view of interactionism. We also see that the Lakoffian approach is itself put forward quite vaguely, leaving fundamentally unresolved the paradox of the creation of similarity. In spite of this, a key insight of the Lakoffian approach is to explicitly recognize that in order to explain the creation of similarity, one needs to look at it in the broader framework of cognition, and reexamine some fundamental assumptions about the nature of cognition.

Noticing the ambiguities inherent in the interaction theory, several attempts have been made to articulate it precisely using some mathematical formalism or another. There is my earlier attempt [Indurkhya 1986; 1987] that, although it does not fully resolve the paradox of the creation of similarity, does have certain interesting features that have been preserved in the theory developed in this book. Therefore, I briefly review my previous approach to metaphor in Section 7. Then there is Kittay's perspectival theory [Kittay 1987]. Though her theory is embedded in a framework of compositional semantics that makes it limited to linguistic metaphors, Kittay's explanation of the creation of similarity comes quite close to resolving the paradox. I review Kittay's approach in Section 8, since it is directly relevant to the account of metaphor I am going to present in Part II of this book. Finally, in Section 9, I summarize the main points of this chapter.

Often various scholars use different terms to refer to what I have been calling the source and the target. The target is variously referred to as the primary or principal subject and as the topic. The source is sometimes called the secondary or the subsidiary subject and sometimes the vehicle. To avoid the unnecessary confusion that might result from using different terms to refer to the same thing, I continue to use the terms source and target in discussing other authors' approaches to metaphor.

3.2   Max Black

The first detailed account of the interaction theory was presented by Max Black in his classic essay 'Metaphor' [Black 1962], which, in a nutshell, can be explained as follows. The two subjects of a metaphor, namely the source (the subsidiary subject) and the target (the principal subject), are to be regarded as 'systems' rather than isolated words or predicates. For instance, in "Man is a wolf," it is not just the word 'wolf' that acts as the source, but a lot of our general knowledge and conventionally held beliefs about wolves that must be brought into play. Black refers to all this knowledge and these beliefs as 'associated commonplaces,' and it is the associated commonplaces of wolf that would serve as the source system in this example.

In understanding a metaphor, the source and the target systems 'interact' with each other, a process in which the associated commonplaces of the source system organize the target system, selecting, emphasizing, and suppressing features of the target system in the process. For instance, in the man-wolf metaphor, the associated commonplaces corresponding to wolf, which might include beliefs like wolves are ferocious, territorial, and possessive, organize our view of man. In this process, certain human characteristics, such as walking on two legs, are pushed in the background, while other characteristics, such as ferociousness, are rendered prominent.

The creation of similarity is explained here by arguing that, in organizing the target in terms of the associated commonplaces of the source, the target is made to look similar to the source. Moreover, since the target has its own associated commonplaces, they serve to constrain the creation of similarity. But this explanation is reminiscent of the comparison theoretic account to the creation of similarity that I mentioned at the beginning of this chapter, as it essentially explains the creation of similarity in terms of highlighting-downplaying features of the target. So one naturally wonders: What, then, is new about the interaction theory? What is it that makes the interaction different from mere comparison? Interestingly perhaps, the most illuminating answer to this question is provided by Black in terms of a metaphor:

> "Suppose I look at the night sky through a piece of heavily smoked glass on which certain lines have been left clear. Then I shall see only the stars that can be made to lie on the lines previously prepared upon the screen, and the stars I do see will be seen as organized by the screen's structure. We can think of a metaphor as such a screen and the system of 'associated commonplaces' of the focal world as the network of lines upon the screen. We can say

that the [target] is 'seen through' the metaphorical expression—
or if we prefer, that the [target] is 'projected upon' the field of
the [source]. (In the latter analogy, the implication-system of the
focal expression must be taken to determine the 'law of projection.')" [Black 1962, p. 41].

This analogy contains two key insights. First of all, it provides an account of
the creation of similarity that is quite different from the comparison theory.
When we see the stars through the smoked glass, and see them arranged
along certain lines, it is the smoked glass (the source) that is *imposing* an
organization on the stars (the target). The similarities (between the smoked
glass and the stars) are created because this new organization is not a part
of the target. For, if we remove the smoked glass, then there are no lines in
the sky. It cannot be said that the lines were already there, but less salient,
and the smoked glass is merely making them more prominent. In fact, there
might be an infinite number of geometric patterns that can be traced on the
smoked glass, and the stars in the sky might be seen in the corresponding
pattern. One cannot argue that all these patterns are already there in the
sky.

This creation of similarity is constrained, however, because just holding
a smoked glass with certain lines etched on it is not sufficient by itself to
see that pattern in the sky. There must be stars in the sky. Moreover, the
stars must be in certain positions in the sky with respect to the smoked glass
so as to be visible through the etched lines. Both of these are attributes of
the target that are independent of the source, and can block the creation of
similarity.

The other illuminating insight of this analogy is that it presents metaphor
as an inherently asymmetric process. For one cannot look at the smoked glass
through the starry sky. Even if we assume that one could reverse the source
and the target—suppose that the 'sky' is a huge black screen with tiny holes
and illuminated from behind—what you will see when you view the smoked
glass through the black screen is certainly not the points of light arranged
along the lines etched on the glass.

Unfortunately, however, Black did not elaborate on this analogy and cap-
italize on the valuable insights it contained. To worsen the matter, some
of his other remarks in the same essay serve only to hide these insights,
and sometimes even contradict them. For instance, immediately after the
smoked glass analogy, Black presented another example to clarify the nature
of interaction:

"Or take another example. Suppose I am set the task of describing a battle in words drawn as largely as possible from the vocabulary of chess. These latter terms determine a system of implications which will proceed to control my description of the battle. The enforced choice of the chess vocabulary will lead some aspects of the battle to be emphasized, others to be neglected, and all to be organized in a way that would cause much more strain in other modes of description. The chess vocabulary filters and transforms: it not only selects, it brings forward aspects of the battle that might not be seen at all through another medium. (Stars that cannot be seen at all, except through telescopes.)" [Black 1962, pp. 41–42.]

This example seems to fall back into explaining the role of metaphor as highlighting and downplaying the existing attributes of the target, and a key insight of the first analogy is obscured. Black, of course, mentions that new aspects of the battle might be made visible through the source, but in the absence of a concrete example, his arguments do not appear convincing. The analogy with a telescope is not very apt, for a telescope brings in new information in a different way.

The asymmetry of metaphor that was inherent in the smoked glass analogy is also explicitly contradicted by Black at another place in the same essay: "If to call a man a wolf is to put him in a special light, we must not forget that the metaphor makes the wolf seem more human than he otherwise would." [Black 1962, p. 44.] The remark suggests that metaphor is symmetric, and that the result of interaction also affects the source.

This pattern of insightful observations interlaced with contradictory statements is repeated in Black's elaboration of the interaction theory in his later essay 'More about Metaphor' [Black 1979]. The most insightful part of this essay is the section titled 'Thinking in Metaphors' [pp. 32–34]. Consider the figure of the Star of David shown in Figure 3.1(a). The figure can be described, or thought of, in various ways: as two equilateral triangles, one of which is inverted and set upon the other [Figure 3.1(b)]; as a regular hexagon with an equilateral triangle on each of its edges [Figure 3.1(c)]; as three parallelograms superimposed on each other with their axes 120 degrees apart [Figure 3.1(d)]; etc. In each case, the resulting description of the figure of the Star of David is a result of an interaction between the figure itself (the target) and the concepts chosen for the description: triangles, hexagon and triangles, parallelograms, etc. (the source).

In this example, the deep insights of the starry-sky-through-the-smoked-

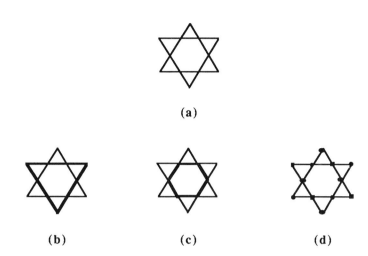

FIGURE 3.1: Black's Illustration of 'Thinking in Metaphors.' The familiar figure of the Star of David (a) can be thought of (or described) in terms of two equilateral triangles (b), a hexagon and six triangles (c), and three parellelograms (d).

glass analogy resurface. We get a glimpse of exactly how the interaction takes place, and that it is not a comparison. In seeing the figure of the Star of David as three parallelograms, we are not comparing the parallelogram with the figure. Instead, we are reorganizing, or redescribing the figure of the Star of David in terms of the parallelogram. The example also clearly shows that both the source and the target participate in the interaction process. First of all, one can see how different sources affect the description of the same target, highlighting the role played by the source in the interaction process. And, of course, the same source would give different descriptions to different targets. Figure 2.1(a) [Chapter 2] can also be described in terms of equilateral triangles, in terms of hexagons and equilateral triangles, and in terms of parallelograms. But each of these descriptions is different from the corresponding description of Figure 3.1. Moreover, certain targets may be such that they could not be described at all in terms of a given source. For instance, Figure 2.1(c) [Chapter 2] cannot be described in terms of hexagons, equilateral triangles, or parallelograms. Thus, we see that the target also affects the result of interaction. All these examples provide valuable clues to resolving the paradox of the creation of similarity.

Notice that the Star of David example is also inherently asymmetric. For in organizing the figure of the Star of David as three parallelograms, the parallelograms (the source) do not start to appear Star-of-David-like. Yet, at another place in the same essay, Black again insists on the symmetry of interaction: "[The interaction] reciprocally induces parallel changes in the [source]." [Black 1979, p. 29.]

There are other contradictions as well, and some of Black's other examples and analyses in this essay make the interaction theory look like a variant of the comparison theory. I mention two such instances here.

First, Black vehemently maintained that the basis of a metaphor is an isomorphism between the source and the target [Black 1979, pp. 29–31]. That is, the implicative complex of the source, when projected on the target, mirrors an identical implicative complex in the target. For example, in "Marriage is a zero-sum game," the part of the implicative complex of the source, namely "A game is a contest," is projected onto the implicative complex of the target, namely "A marriage is a sustained struggle," and so on. This account however, makes the interaction theory a variant of the comparison theory. It also completely fails to address the creation of similarity, and the illuminating insights of the starry-sky-through-the-smoked-glass imagery and the Star of David examples are hopelessly lost.

Secondly, while in the initial formulation of the interaction theory both the source and the target were regarded as 'systems,' Black retracted this requirement for the target in his later account. He claimed that this requirement is "needlessly paradoxical, though not plainly mistaken" [Black 1979, p. 28]. The only justification he provided for changing his position was an example, Wallace Stevens' "Society is a sea," with Black arguing that Stevens was not viewing society as a system of social relationships.

There is a ring of truth here. We do not regard the figure of the Star of David as a system of triangles or parallelograms. For if we did, then there would be little or no possibility of reorganizing it in terms of different sources. For instance, if the figure of the Star of David is regarded as a system of parallelograms, and the source contains the concepts of hexagons and equilateral triangles, then there is no way that the figure can be reorganized as in Figure 3.1(c).

This problem, however, can be addressed by regarding the source and the target as systems at *different levels*. In the Star of David example, the target can be considered a system of line segments, which, while it can be organized in terms of hexagons, triangles, and parallelograms, resists arbitrary organizations. For instance, it cannot be organized or described in terms of circles and ellipses. Indeed, this is the way that the problem is approached in my own account, as we see in Chapter 7.

The problem with Black's solution of not regarding the target as a system at all is that then it is hard to explain how the creation of similarities is constrained. Recall that in my interpretation of the starry-sky-through-the-smoked-glass analogy I argued that it is the arrangements of the stars in the sky, an independent attribute of the target, that acts as a constraining factor in the creation of the similarity. In this interpretation, the target is seen as a system of stars which is being organized by the system of lines on the smoked glass. However, if the target is not regarded as a system, then the constraint on the creation of similarity must be explained in some other way. But Black does not provide any alternative explanation.

To sum up, we see that Black's interaction theory, while it contains a number of illuminating insights, is fraught with paradoxes and loose ends. A few other scholars, drawn to the interaction theory for various reasons, have also noticed this and made various attempts to clarify and elaborate the interaction theory. I now turn to an examination of some of these attempts.

3.3   Paul Ricoeur

Ricoeur's development of interactionism has been markedly influenced by
Black's views. However, in spite of the fact that Ricoeur has written much
more on metaphor than Black [Ricoeur 1976, Chap. 3; Ricoeur 1977, esp.
Chap. 7; Ricoeur 1978; Ricoeur 1982], his version of the interaction theory is
even more vague than Black's. Here, I present two key features of Ricoeur's
account that are particularly germane to my own framework.

One major feature of Ricoeurian interactionism is its notion of *split reference.* The allusion here is to the fact that a metaphor involves a non-
conventional interpretation. Since this means that the metaphor must have
a conventional interpretation as well (which is ruled out by the context), the
two interpretations together constitute what Ricoeur calls the split reference.
For example, in Spender's *Seascape,* there is the conventional referent, the
harp, and the metaphorical referent, the ocean.

Now it may seem that Ricoeur is merely coining a new phrase for something that is already well established, for most scholars of metaphors would
readily agree that every metaphor involves a dual reference. However, Ricoeur uses his notion of split reference in a novel way to explain how metaphors, particularly creative metaphors, are made meaningful. Unlike Black,
in whose account the tension in a metaphor arises from the interaction between the source and the target (regarded as systems), in Ricoeur's view the
tension in a metaphor comes from the two interpretations of the metaphor.
Moreover, it is these two apparently conflicting interpretations that sustain
a metaphor and make it meaningful by bringing the referents of the two interpretations into semantic proximity. Thus, in reading Spender's *Seascape,*
the harp and the ocean themselves are brought together. That is, the harp
and the ocean are seen as if they belonged to the same category.

This observation involves a bold step in involving the referents of the
source and the target. (In almost all of the earlier approaches, including
that of Black, the referents were not explicitly involved.) However, it fails
to address the main problem of creation of similarity: How is it that some
referents can be brought into semantic proximity but not others?

The second major feature of Ricoeur's theory provides a partial answer
to this question. Here, Ricoeur makes an implicit distinction between the
objects in the world and the linguistic means through which we can access
and describe these objects. The idea is that the linguistic expressions work
like models in giving us a cognitive access to the things in the world. In this
process, they present us with certain aspects of the world. And metaphor

permits us to change the models, thereby allowing us to change the way of seeing things and perceiving the world [Ricoeur 1982, p. 1886].[1] In other words, metaphor works by changing our representations of the world, and in doing so, offers us new information about the world [Ricoeur 1976, pp. 52–53]. It is of interest to note that Black also adopted a similar stance in his later essay on metaphor: "[T]he world is necessarily a world *under a certain description*—or a world seen from a certain perspective. Some metaphors can create such a perspective." [Black 1979, pp. 39–40. Emphasis Black's.] The framework for metaphor I present in Chapter 7 sharply reflects this theme.

3.4   Carl Hausman

The paradox raised by the creation of similarity occupies the centerstage in Carl Hausman's approach to metaphor [Hausman 1983; 1984; 1989, esp. Chap. 3]. However, in his solution to the paradox, which is more elaborate and less ambiguous than Black's, Hausman introduces several new concepts that are themselves somewhat vague. Moreover, Hausman, in breaking away from Black, also lets go of some of the key insights that are implicit in Black's account. I now briefly discuss the major features of Hausman's theory.

Hausman introduces three new concepts to explain the creation of similarity. The first is the *uniqueness* of referent. It is argued that a metaphor creates a new and unique referent that is different from the referents of the source and the target. It would be helpful to read Hausman's term 'unique' as 'autonomous,' for his point is that though the new referent might have acquired some of its attributes through the referents of the source and the target, the new referent is quite distinct and has its own autonomy. For instance, in Shakespeare's "Juliet is the sun" the referent is not the sun and not Juliet, but something that can at best be described as 'Juliet-the-sun.' Here, Hausman considers his account as paralleling that of Ricoeur, though his interpretation of Ricoeur is somewhat different from the one I presented above. Still, to me at least, it is not quite clear what the unique referent is. The best possible light in which I can present it is by saying that the juxtaposition of the two referents brings to view certain aspects of the two referents that are not there when each referent is viewed individually. Since these aspects have been created solely through the juxtaposition, one can view this process as if a new referent has been created with precisely those aspects.

---

[1] I am grateful to Prof. Marie-Dominique Gineste for translating parts of this paper for me.

The second key concept of Hausman's account is the *extralinguistic* condition. He argues that the unique referent that is created has attributes that are not all linguistic. In other words, the new referent brings in new information that cannot be explained in linguistic terms. A major consequence of this position is that a metaphor is seen as not amenable to a purely linguistic analysis. Also, it is these extralinguistic attributes of the metaphorical referent that are seen to constrain the creation of similarity by the metaphor.

The third concept that Hausman introduces is that of *individuality*. The referent created by the metaphor is seen as an individual in the sense of being ontologically real. Here, Hausman evokes Pierce's concept of *dynamical objects,* which are objects that can be apprehended by senses, and yet are grounded in objective reality so that they resist being described arbitrarily [Hausman 1989, Appendix]. The individuality condition is proposed so that the creation of similarity does not become a purely subjective process, since the extralinguistic attributes of the created referent are determined in part by its objective nature.

While some of Hausman's ideas are clearly echoed in my account of metaphor in Chapter 7, these ideas are presented only vaguely by Hausman. The general themes of his approach can be understood easily, but when one tries to get more specific, his theory leaves much to be desired. For instance, what exactly is the unique referent? How does it acquire extralinguistic attributes? Which ones come from the source referent and which ones from the target referent? And where do the others come from? These are only a few of the many questions not fully answered in Hausman's account.

Finally, Hausman's version of interactionism is quite symmetric. In positing that a new referent is created as a result of the interaction, there is an implied symmetry. Lest there be any doubt, Hausman explicitly endorses a radical version of the symmetry view, arguing that the source-target distinction is meaningless, and it is best to just say that a metaphor involves two domains [Hausman 1989, p. 67].

3.5   Wheelwright - Mac Cormac

Wheelwright [1962] suggested a theory of metaphor that recognized the comparative aspect present in some metaphors, while at the same time fully realizing the creative aspect of other metaphors that sprout new meanings and new bases for similarities. He divided metaphors into two kinds: epiphors and diaphors. Epiphors involve "outreach and extension of meaning through comparison" [p. 72] but the "similarity need not be obvious and comparison explicit" [p. 74]. Thus, epiphors correspond to what I have been calling similarity-based metaphors.

Diaphors, on the other hand, create new meanings through juxtaposition, corresponding to my similarity-creating metaphors. Wheelwright, however, does not offer much in the way of explanation as to how diaphors create new meanings. A vague analogy is offered with chemistry:

> "The essential possibility of diaphor lies in the broad ontological fact that new qualities and new meanings can emerge, simply come into being, out of some hitherto ungrouped combination of elements... Just as different atoms, molecules, etc. exist independently but give rise to interesting compounds when put together under proper conditions (temperature, pressure, etc.) (like H_2O from H_2 and O_2), similarly various meanings can exist alone but new meanings can be created by juxtaposition of previously unjoined words and phrases. This is a diaphoric synthesis." [Wheelwright 1962, p. 85–86].

This analogy does little to illuminate the creation of similarity, save pointing to the facts that the creation of similarity works sometimes, when some mysterious conditions are right, and not at other times; and, which similarities are created depends on which particular words or phrases are juxtaposed. But this merely amounts to acknowledging that the creation of similarity takes place sometimes, and does not provide any mechanisms that explain how and why.

About twenty years later, Mac Cormac [1982; 1985] undertook to formalize Wheelwright's ideas using the fuzzy set-theory of Zadeh [1965]. In fuzzy set-theory, the membership function of a set is not a two-valued boolean function, but a continuous valued function that maps every member of the universe to some real number in the range 0 to 1. The value of this function for an object is the degree of membership of that object in the set. Zadeh developed this theory to formalize many predicates we use in our everyday language, such as 'tall,' that admit degrees of membership instead of partitioning the universe of all objects into members and non-members.

Using the fuzzy set-membership function, it is still possible to define a notion of *belongs to* that can be used to determine the extent of the set. It works by specifying two bounds a and b, with $0 \leq b \leq a \leq 1$. Now given a fuzzy set-membership function f_A, and some object in the universe, say x, x *belongs to* the set A if, and only if, $f_A(x) \geq a$; x *does not belong to* the set A

if, and only if, $f_A(x) \leq b$; and x is *indeterminate* with respect to the set A if, and only if, $b < f_A(x) < a$. This system gives rise to a three-valued logic in which every expression evaluates to 'true,' 'false,' or 'indeterminate.'

Mac Cormac extended this three-valued logic system to a four-valued one by using three bounds a, b, and c, with $0 \leq b \leq c \leq a \leq 1$. The intervals $(0, b)$ and $(a, 1)$ are identified with membership and non-membership as before, resulting in true and false expressions respectively, but the middle 'indeterminate' interval is broken into two parts. The interval $[b, c]$ gives rise to diaphors and the interval $(c, a]$ gives rise to epiphors. Thus, according to this theory, if a predicate is attributed to an object, and the membership function of that predicate returns a value between b and c then the predicate is said to be metaphorically attributed to the object. In particular, it would be a diaphor. Similarly, if a predicate is applied to an object with its degree of membership lying between c and a then an epiphor would result. Perhaps needless to say, Mac Cormac's theory also includes elaborate mechanisms for locating various terms in a multi-dimensional semantic space, and for determining the semantic distance between two given terms so that the metaphoricity of their juxtaposition may be determined.

One can already see that this account is so far removed from Black's interaction theory that it is hard to see it as a variant of it, though Mac Cormac insists on it quite the same [Mac Cormac 1985, p. 5]. More importantly, it does not explain the creation of similarity at all, a fact that Mac Cormac himself acknowledges [Mac Cormac 1985, p. 140]. The reason for this is that Mac Cormac's approach takes a static view of language, since the semantic distances between various words are all predetermined, and these distances form the bases for determining the degrees of metaphoricity. Of course, one could raise other grounds for criticizing this approach, such as its judging diaphors as less true than epiphors, which in turn are deemed less true than literal statements, but that does not seem to be relevant here.

3.6   The Lakoffian Approach

An approach to metaphor that has become increasingly influential was developed by George Lakoff and his colleagues. The focus of their study has been what are generally regarded as conventional metaphors. Lakoff and his colleagues have put up the most impressive empirical demonstration of how many of our everyday concepts are structured by conventional metaphors [Lakoff & Johnson 1980], and how many of the novel metaphors in poetry can be analyzed as new extensions or new combinations of conventional metaphors [Lakoff & Turner 1989]. Nevertheless, these scholars have also emphasized that metaphors can create similarities where none existed before, and have tried to explain how this creation takes place [Lakoff and Johnson 1980, Chap. 22]. These views have been further elaborated in Johnson [1987], Lakoff [1987], and Lakoff & Turner [1989, Chap. 2]. Though their explanations do not fully resolve the paradox of the creation of similarity, they are successful in pointing out that the roots of the paradox run much deeper than it might first appear, and that its resolution requires certain views about cognition to be reexamined.

At the core of the Lakoffian explanation of the creation of similarity is a distinction between *objective similarities* and *experiential similarities*. Their contention is that objective similarities do not exist, and only experiential similarities are real. That is, we cannot ask whether two objects are similar or not independently of how these two objects are experienced and conceptualized. And since "The essence of metaphor is understanding and experiencing one kind of thing in terms of another" [Lakoff & Johnson 1980, p. 5], it follows that in conceptualizing the target as the source, the two are made to look similar. Thus, a metaphor creates experiential similarities between the source and the target.

This point can be illustrated with the examples of geometric figures that were introduced in Chapter 2 [Figure 2.1]. Comparing Figures 2.1(a) and 2.1(b), the objective similarities, if they were to exist, would include all possible ways in which these two figures are similar *independent of any observer or any conceptual organization*. Clearly, no such thing can exist, for it is the concepts that make two different objects appear similar. We see that they are both 'triangles,' or they are both 'trees,' or the river and the snake are both 'wavy.' Looking at Figures 2.1(a) and 2.1(b) one might say that they are both 'closed figures.' But 'closed figure' itself is a concept. If concepts are not admitted, then even two congruent triangles cannot be seen as similar.

So we conclude that in order to see whether two objects are similar or not, and if so then in what respects, requires that the objects be conceptualized in some way. The figures in Figures 2.1(a) and 2.1(b) can be thought of in terms of triangles, squares, hexagons, ellipses, etc. However, as soon the objects are conceptualized, any similarities that are gleaned between them now become very much dependent on the conceptualization chosen. In other words, they become *experienced similarities*.

And conceptualizations are subject to change. We can conceptualize Figure 2.1(a) in terms of triangles, trapezoids, or parallelograms, among others. As the conceptualization of one or both of the objects being compared

FIGURE 3.2: The figure used in the quotation
from Whorf. (From Whorf [1941].)

changes, the experienced similarities also change, as they are dependent on the conceptualizations. This is precisely how similarities are created. Every instance of creation of similarity is accompanied by a change of conceptualization of one or both objects.

There are three things about this explanation that I must emphasize. First of all, it essentially rearticulates a point made about forty years earlier by Benjamin Lee Whorf. Whorf [1941] presented empirical evidence to argue that different cultures can conceptualize the world differently so that their similarity metrics are different. That is, two situations that are considered similar in one culture can be regarded as very different in another culture. For instance, to English speakers, the sentences 'I pull the branch aside' and 'I have an extra toe on my foot' seem quite dissimilar. Setting aside the linguistic descriptions, even the two phenomena that the sentences describe would not be considered similar. Yet, in Shawnee, Whorf writes:

> "[T]hese two statements are, respectively, *ni-l'θawa-'ko-n-a* and *ni-l'θawa-'koθite* (the *θ* here denotes *th* as in 'thin' and the apostrophe denotes a breath catch). The sentences are closely similar; in fact, they differ only at the tail end. In Shawnee, moreover, the beginning of a construction is generally the important and emphatic part. Both sentences start with *ni-* ('I'), which is a mere prefix. Then comes the really important key word, *l'θawa*, a common Shawnee term, denoting a forked outline, like [Figure 3.2]. The next element, *-'ko*, we cannot be sure of, but it agrees in form with a variant of the suffix *-a'kw* or *-a'ko*, denoting tree, bush, tree part, branch, or anything of that general shape. In the first sentence, *-n-* means 'by hand action' and may be either a causation of the basic condition (forked outline) manually, an increase of it, or both. The final *-a* means that the subject ('I') does this action to an appropriate object. Hence the first sentence means 'I pull it (something like branch of tree) more open or apart where it forks.' In the other sentence, the suffix *-θite* means 'pertaining to the toes,' and the absence of further suffixes means that the subject manifests the condition in his own person. Therefore, the

> sentence can mean only 'I have an extra toe forking out like a branch from a normal toe.'" [Whorf 1941, p. 234.]

From many other examples like this, Whorf argued that one's language imposes an organization on the world according to which certain things are seen as similar and certain others as dissimilar. However, different languages can impose different organizations on the world, thereby creating different similarity metrics. Thus, we see that the idea that the creation of similarity is brought about by a change in conceptualization is not so new after all. Even though Whorf was not focusing on metaphors, his account contains a clear and unambiguous explanation of the creation of similarity that is essentially the same as the Lakoffian explanation.

The second thing about the Lakoffian account is that it echoes the themes that were at least implicit, if not quite explicit, in Black's and Ricoeur's accounts. Though the Lakoffian approach rejects the interaction theory [Lakoff and Turner 1989, pp. 131–133], faulting it for its stand on the symmetry of metaphor, this rejection is based on taking the symmetry to be the one and the only characterizing feature of interactionism, a view which is very shortsighted in light of what I have already discussed in this chapter. Black's starry-sky-through-the-smoked glass analogy and the Star of David example are both instances of the target being experienced through the source. Moreover, Black's account of how the similarities are created in each of these cases is very much like the Lakoffian explanation. Finally, both Ricoeur and Black made a distinction akin to what the Lakoffian approach refers to as experiential and objective realities by arguing that metaphors are models through which we have cognitive access to reality. All these facts strongly suggest that the approach of Lakoff and his colleagues is much closer to interactionism then they are willing to admit.

Finally, while the Lakoffian approach is better articulated. aided with numerous examples, than the other versions of interactionism, a careful analysis reveals that it does not really resolve the paradox of creation of similarity. To appreciate this point, let me elaborate the Lakoffian approach with a few examples. Consider first a case where the creation of similarities is not involved, just to understand how a metaphor works in the Lakoffian account. In the 'more is up and less is down' metaphor, exemplified by "House prices plummeted following the stock market crash," Lakoff argues, the source 'verticality' is already understood independently of any metaphor. In the Lakoffian approach, such concepts are referred to as 'directly emergent,' which means they come about due to our having bodies of a certain sort, and are directly understood as such. While the concept 'directly emergent' itself raises several questions and contributes to the vagueness of the Lakoffian approach [Mac Cormac 1985, pp. 66–70], let us grant them that notion here. Now, the target 'quantity' is seen as having the following structure: Whenever we add more of a substance, the level rises, and whenever we remove some quantity of the substance, its level falls. In fact, this structure is already described in terms of the metaphor, and shows structural correlations of 'more' with 'up' and 'less' with 'down.' Lakoff takes this structural correlation to be the key factor that makes the metaphor work. He even goes on to state that there is an isomorphism between the metaphorical mapping and the structural correlation [Lakoff 1987, pp. 276–278].

There is a small but crucial assumption here that must be brought out, namely that the target domain must also be independently structured before the metaphor. If it were not, then the correlation condition does not make sense. That is, if the metaphor caused the correlation (and there was no structure to 'quantity' before the metaphor), then Lakoff's account does not explain why 'verticality' is an appropriate source domain. Why can another source domain not introduce a different structural correlation? Why can the 'container' domain, another one of the so called directly emergent concepts in the Lakoffian account, not structure the 'quantity' domain by inducing the structural correlation? The 'verticality' domain just did. What makes the 'verticality' domain so privileged? All these questions undermine the Lakoffian explanation unless one admits that the target domain has a struc-ture before being conceptualized by the source domain and the structure is independent of any metaphor. Because then the correlation business can be explained by pointing out that it is the autonomous structure of the target domain that resists arbitrary source domains being applied to it.

But if the target already has a structure, then establishing a structural correlation between it and the existing structure of the source is nothing but finding some existing similarities between the two domains. And the Lakoffian approach becomes essentially a variant of the comparison theoretic account, in spite of their severe criticism of it.

To be fair, I should stress that Lakoff did not cite this example as a similarity-creating metaphor, and I am not sure if he would view it as one. But this analysis was merely to expose the hidden assumption in the Lakoffian account. Now let us look at an example that is considered a similarity-creating metaphor in the Lakoffian approach.

Lakoff and Johnson [1980, pp.147–148] present the example of the 'ideas are food' metaphor to argue that this metaphor creates the similarities be-tween 'ideas' and 'food.' In particular, they argue that the concept of 'swallowing' ideas comes only by virtue of the metaphor, and does not exist independently of it. But then why do ideas not generate some waste product after being digested? Why do ideas not start rotting if you leave them outside for a long time? Why can only some aspects of the 'food' source domain be imported but others not? And why would any other source domain, like 'verticality' not do as well? It must be that the target has an independent structure that resists arbitrary correlations. Or, if the target does not have an independent structure, then what is it that resists arbitrary correlations?

These problems creep up everywhere Lakoff and his colleagues try to get more specific about their account of the creation of similarity. For instance, Lakoff and Turner [1989, pp. 63–64] state that a metaphorical schema maps slots, relations, properties and knowledge of the source domain to the slots, relations, properties and knowledge of the target domain. They also state that while some of the slots, relations, properties and knowledge of the target domain may have existed before the mapping, some are *created* expressly by the metaphorical process for the purpose of the mapping. For instance, in the 'life is a journey' metaphor, the 'course of life' slot is created in the target domain of 'life' so that the slot 'path' in the source domain 'journey' can be mapped onto it. But then why are not slots created for 'conductor,' or 'steward,' 'luggage,' and so on. Of course, it is understood that the mapping is partial, and not everything in the source domain is mapped. But the point is that when it comes to inducing slots and relations, it seems quite arbitrary why certain slots and relations of the source domain can induce their counterparts in the target domain, but other slots and relations simply cannot.

Thus, either the Lakoffian approach has to admit that the target has a structure that is independent of any metaphorical structuring, so that it can be used as a constraint to determine which metaphors work and which ones do not, which seems to contradict the very foundation of the Lakoffian approach that vehemently maintains that many of our everyday concepts are inherently metaphorical, and cannot be characterized non-metaphorically. Or the Lakoffian approach must remain mystical for not being able to explain why only certain source domains can structure a given target—a target that can only be experienced through a metaphor, and not directly—and why, even when they do, they can only structure the target in certain non-arbitrary ways.

In spite of this failure of the Lakoffian approach to fully address the creation of similarity, it contains a crucial insight that is only cursorily presented in Black's later paper [1979]. This is the realization that the creation of similarity is rooted in a more fundamental cognitive phenomenon, and that the creation, in its essence, is really the creation of attributes (and relations etc.) of objects. Indeed, Lakoff and Johnson's experiential account is actually a framework of cognition. But I defer a further discussion of their cognitive framework until the next chapter, where I examine various interactionist views of cognition.

3.7   My Earlier Approach

Ever since I started being interested in metaphors, over ten years ago, I have been intrigued with the interactionist approach to metaphor—especially that of Black—and concerned with its ambiguity. My first attempt at formalizing the interaction theory, outlined in Indurkhya [1986; 1987], only partially addressed the phenomenon of creation of similarity. Nevertheless, it has some interesting aspects worth noting here, especially since my approach to the creation of similarity presented in this book can be seen as an evolution of my earlier theory. Moreover, I used a mathematical formalism to articulate my ideas precisely then, something that I do here in Chapter 6 as well, and it is important to emphasize that the use of formal tools is not as limiting as some researchers, such as Lakoff [1987, Chap. 14], take them to be. Even in my earlier approach, which made use of First-Order Logic, some key characteristics of metaphors, such as how different metaphors can organize the same target domain differently, could be neatly captured.

The source and the target domains, in my earlier approach, were characterized as systems of axioms that were closed under entailment. Thus, each domain had a 'vocabulary,' which was a set of constant and predicate symbols, and a 'structure,' which were the axioms that showed how the symbols were interrelated. Certain axioms of a domain were called 'derivations,' where every derivation defined some symbol in terms of other symbols. For instance, in the domain of family relationships, a derivation for 'child' might be "X is a child of Y if, and only if, Y is a parent of X."

A key feature of the theory was that the derivations were allowed to be *circular*. That is, it was permissible to have a derivation for X in terms of Y, while at the same time having another derivation for Y in terms of X. In the above example, that the symbol 'parent' can also be defined in terms of 'child.' An important consequence of incorporating this feature was that a domain could admit of *several possible choices of primitives*. For instance, the domain of family relationships could be described from the set of primitives {'male,' 'female,' 'child'} and also from the set of primitives {'male;' 'female,' 'parent'}.

A metaphor was defined as a partial structure-preserving mapping from the vocabulary of the source domain to the vocabulary of the target domain. That is, a metaphor was seen as relating some of the symbols in the source domain with some of the symbols in the target domain in such a way that when the structure of the symbols (how they are interrelated) in the source domain was transported to the target domain, it did not contradict the existing structure there.

This account might seem quite simplistic, but it could explain some important characteristics of metaphor. For instance, the role of a metaphor in reorganizing a domain was explained as follows. A metaphorical mapping only chooses certain symbols in the target domain, and the view of the target domain, as seen through the metaphor, is essentially as if those symbols were the primitives and the rest of the target domain were being described in terms of them. And since different metaphorical mapping could choose different symbols from the same target domain, they would suggest different ways of organizing it.

It also explained how a metaphor can induce new structure in the target domain. A metaphorical mapping allows additional structure to be imported into the target domain as long as it does not contradict whatever structure is there already. Two operators were explicitly proposed that extended the metaphorical mapping by inducing structure in the target domain. One operator, called 'augmentation,' made use of derivations in inducing structure. For instance, Lakoff and Turner's example of a 'course of life' slot being induced in the 'life' domain by the source domain 'journey' can be seen as in instance of augmentation. Here, the induced slot is quite constrained by what has already been mapped, and it is merely a new name for a quantity (attribute, relation, etc.) that is already there in the target domain. The second operator, called 'positing structure,' was much less constrained and could induce any arbitrary structure as long as it was consistent with the existing structure of the target domain.

In spite of being able to formally capture some intuitions about metaphor, this approach has a major limitation as far as the phenomenon of creation of similarity is concerned. The structure of the target domain was always increased monotonically. That is, new structure was added as long as it was consistent with the existing structure of the target domain. But this process would never invalidate the existing structure. Thus, this approach would not be able to explain Schön's 'paintbrush as a pump' metaphor, where it was necessary to discard the existing structure of the target domain 'painting,' since the metaphorical restructuring was inconsistent with the initial structure. Being aware of this limitation, I offered the following explanation at the time:

> "In general, in comprehending a metaphor, there is three-way tension going on rather than two-way tension as we assumed in our theory. The interaction taking place in understanding a metaphor is not merely between the source domain and the target domain but among the source domain, the target domain and the object or the concept that is represented in the target domain. Thus in interpreting the metaphor 'the ship plowed through the sea' the domains *plowing* and *sailing* interact with each other and with the actual process of sailing to produce an interpretation of the metaphor. The reason for this distinction is that our representation of an object or a concept reflects a certain perspective and in that sense is an approximation to the real nature of that object or concept. A metaphor can, by mere juxtaposition or other techniques, force us to look beyond our representation of the object in order to make sense of the metaphor. This process can give rise to a new perspective on the object that was missing from our representation." [Indurkhya 1986, pp. 546–547].

I include this long quote here because the approach to metaphor developed in this book is really a fruition of this idea, and it might be helpful to see its origin. Moreover, this is really an echo of what has been implicit in the interactionisms of Black, Hausman, and Ricoeur.

3.8   Kittay's Perspectival Theory

Another notable attempt at formalizing the interaction theory has been made by Kittay [1987]. Kittay refers to the interaction theory as the perspectival theory, for, as she sees it, the essential ingredient of interactionism is in arguing that metaphors function by providing perspectives on the target. (Black has himself endorsed this view, as noted at the end of Section 3.) Taking this vantage point, Kittay went on to develop an elaborate and formal framework to explain the working of metaphor, including the creation of similarity.

Kittay's theory is articulated in the linguistic framework of compositional semantics, according to which the meaning of any phrase or sentence is a function of the meaning of its constituents. (For example, the meaning of "The sky is crying," in compositional semantics, would be a function of the meanings of 'the,' 'sky,' 'is,' and 'crying.') Presented in this way, Kittay's account becomes essentially a theory of the metaphors of language. Moreover, her theory regards conventional meanings as more fundamental than metaphorical meanings in at least two ways: Conventional meanings are arrived at *before* metaphorical meanings, and it is some incongruity with respect to the conventional meanings that, at least in part, triggers the process of constructing metaphorical meanings. This, in turn, has two major consequences: (1) Understanding conventional meanings becomes a prerequisite to understanding metaphorical meanings, and (2) conventional meanings are seen as cognitively easier to understand, since the extra stage of processing where the second-order interpretations are derived is not necessary. Though the empirical research on this matter has not yet reached a consensus, there seems to be some evidence that, given a proper context, metaphorical meanings are no harder to comprehend than conventional meanings [Gerrig 1989; Hoffman and Kemper 1987]. Further, the empirical research also suggests that an attempt to focus on the conventional meaning often turns out to be counterproductive in figuring out the metaphorical meaning. In both these respects, Kittay's theory contradicts empirical findings.

Embedded in the linguistic framework, however, is a cognitive dimension, and Kittay's explanation of the creation of similarity runs primarily along this cognitive dimension. As my main interest here is in the phenomenon of creation of similarity, I present here Kittay's approach to it, which can be understood without recourse to the compositional semantics framework in which it is embedded.

At the heart of Kittay's account of the creation of similarity is the concept of *semantic field.* A semantic field captures the intuition that the meaning of a word cannot be specified in isolation, but is invariably connected with the meanings of the other words. Further, the meanings of different words are structurally related to each other, and it is these structural relationships that are referred to as semantic fields by Kittay. For instance, the meaning of 'rock' has a semantic feature 'solid.' But the feature 'solid' is related to the features 'liquid' and 'gas' that might occur in the meanings of other words. Moreover, the features 'solid,' 'liquid,' and 'gas' form an ordered contrast set. Any material is in one, and only one, of these three forms, and there is an ordering from 'solid' to 'gas.' Thus, there is a structural relationship among the features 'solid,' 'liquid,' and 'gas,' that can be called into play whenever the meaning of 'rock' is being processed.

Formally, a semantic field is comprised of a *lexical field* and a *content domain.* The lexical field is a set of uninterpreted (not yet meaningful) labels that are structured. For instance, a lexical field might contain three labels 'solid,' 'liquid,' and 'gas' that are structured in the sense that they are pairwise mutually exclusive, and there is a gradation from 'solid,' through 'liquid,' and to 'gas.' The content domain is the realm in which the labels are to be interpreted. An example of content domain would be material objects. A semantic field is formed when a lexical field is interpreted in a content domain. Thus, when we decide to classify all material objects as 'solids,' 'liquids,' and 'gases,' a semantic field is created. This process of interpretation is called *articulating the content domain.*

With this background, the process of interpreting a metaphor is described as follows. The conventional interpretations of the expressions occurring in the metaphor identify two distant semantic fields, the source (the vehicle) and the target (the topic). In overcoming the distance between the two fields, the field of the source is used to articulate the content domain of the target field. The process is structure preserving in that it must not violate the existing structure of the target content domain. However, the articulation may induce additional structure from the source field to the target content domain.

The creation of similarity is explained in this account as follows. In re-structuring the target content domain, it is made similar to the semantic field of the source. Moreover, this restructuring is constrained by the existing structure of the target content domain, which resists being organized arbitrarily.

Thus, we see that Kittay's account quite explicitly assigns a role to the referent of the target domain in the interaction. The content domains can best be identified as the pieces of reality that have been presented to our perceptual and conceptual system to be 'articulated,' or given form. Kittay's own explanation of what exactly a content domain is clearly suggests this:

> "[Content domains] may be perceptual and as general as the do-
> main of colour or shape, or as specific as that of ice-cream flavours.
> An identifiable activity, such as woodworking or fishing, may con-
> stitute a content domain, as may something as generally experi-
> ential as the life cycle. A domain could have its source in cultural
> institutions—for example, marriage and the socially significant
> kinship relations. A domain may be conceived of as conceptual,
> having its unity derived not from an activity or a perceptual mode
> but from an interrelation of concepts. Scientific theories would

be paradigmatic conceptual content domains. As these examples
suggest, a content domain is an area of thought, of inquiry, of activity about which we require or desire *information*. . . . In short,
a content domain is whatever a set of labels that have contrastive
and affinitive relations may be *about*." [Kittay 1987, p. 225].

There is a crucial issue here, though: Is a content domain structured prior to,
and independently of, being articulated by a lexical field? This issue is crucial
because if one answers it affirmatively, then one is committed to realism
where reality has its own objective structure prior to conceptualization. But
then it is hard to argue that a source semantic field that is not similar to
this objective structure can actually make the content domain similar to the
field. And if one answers the question negatively, then one is committed to a
relativism where any arbitrary source can induce similarities by articulating
the target content domain. Kittay is quite aware of the dilemma, but evades
the issue altogether:

"Put simply, whether we consider a content domain to have an
objective structure, which we need to capture with a set of contrasts and affinities, or whether we conceive of the content domain
as a continuum upon which we impose a scheme of contrasts and
affinities, it is the requirements of information that dictate the
articulation of the domain by contrasts and affinities." [Kittay
1987, p. 226].

Here, 'the requirements of information' are that the articulation somehow
provide 'conditional and differential information' about the content domain.
And a discussion of what exactly this conditional and differential information
is [Kittay 1987, pp. 121–139] fails to shed any light on how the content
domains resist being articulated arbitrarily.

Thus, we see that Kittay's incorporation of the referent of the target into
the metaphorical process fails to resolve the paradox of creation of similarity.
Still, it does come quite close to it by pointing out that the key to the
resolution of the paradox lies in understanding the interaction between the
lexical fields and the content domains. The paradox of creation of similarity
can now be stated as: How is it that different lexical fields can articulate a
content domain differently, but not arbitrarily? This again suggests that the
problem of creation of similarity is really a problem of cognition.

3.9   Conclusions

We saw in this chapter that despite numerous attempts at explaining the creation of similarity, its paradox is still not fully resolved. In particular, no theory has satisfactorily demonstrated how it is that a metaphor can create similarities between the source and the target, similarities that were not there before the metaphor, and how the creation of similarities is not arbitrary, but is constrained somehow.

We also saw that, in spite of the wide variation among different scholars' approaches to the creation of similarity, there are two key concepts that are implicitly or explicitly contained in most of them. First, there is the idea that the interaction involves not just the conceptualizations of the source and the target, but also their referents—at least the referent of the target. Second, there is the argument that similarity-creating metaphor invariably works by changing the familiar perspective on the target referent and creating a new one. And the similarities are created with respect to the new perspective on the target. That is, the source and the target do not appear similar from the familiar perspectives, but when the metaphor changes the perspective on the target, they become similar.

Lurking underneath this explanation are two crucial assumptions that are partially analyzed by a few scholars. One assumption, explicitly recognized in the Lakoffian approach, is that similarities are characteristics of the perspectives and not of the objects. That is, we cannot ask if two objects are similar or not independently of how they have been conceptualized.

The second assumption is that in changing perspectives on an object (event, situation, etc.) new attributes and structures can emerge. Thus, the creation of similarity essentially becomes the creation of attributes. But this is a cognitive claim. The problem of creation of similarity becomes a problem of cognition.

The realization that the paradox of the creation of similarity must be resolved within a cognitive framework, while it involves a deep insight, does not, however, resolve the paradox. It merely translates it into a cognitive paradox: How is it that an object can be conceptualized differently, with new attributes and structures being created, but this creation is not arbitrary? What constrains the creation of attributes and structures? Until these questions are satisfactorily answered, the paradox of the creation of similarity remains untamed.

It is exactly this paradox of cognition that has been a central theme in the works of those scholars who have tried to find a compromise between the extreme views of subjectivism and objectivism. Perhaps not surprisingly, the view of cognition proposed by these scholars is sometimes known as the inter- action view of cognition. Various articulations of this view, however, suffer from a lack of precision not unlike the vagueness surrounding the interaction theories of metaphor. This is what I endeavor to show in the next chapter.

Chapter 4

Cognition as Interaction

4.1 Introduction

At the end of the last chapter we saw that the creation of similarity points to a more fundamental cognitive phenomenon, namely that of the creation of attributes of an object, event or situation. This phenomenon has sprouted a certain view of cognition that is becoming increasingly prominent. I refer to it as the interaction view of cognition. According to this view, our concepts do not reflect some pre-existing structure in the environment, they *create* the structure. Yet, this conceptual organization cannot be arbitrary, and is somehow constrained by reality.

The interaction view of cognition has been speculated upon widely, especially in this century, by philosophers, psychologists, anthropologists, and linguists alike. There have been many empirical studies contributing to this view. And many theoretical frameworks have been proposed to elaborate and articulate the exact nature of the interaction.

The interaction view of cognition involves a paradox that is very much like the paradox of creation of similarity: How can the attributes be created, but not arbitrarily? The paradox is in positing a reality that can constrain our conceptual organization, and yet denying this reality a mind-independent ontology and structure. And if one maintains that reality does have a mind-independent ontology and structure, then the question naturally arises: Why is this ontology and structure not knowable? And if it would be knowable, then this would immediately lead to the view that reality has a pre-existing ontology and structure and our concepts can reflect it. But such a view would contradict the fundamental premise of interactionism.

This paradox has not yet been resolved, though elaborations of the inter-action view have implicitly dealt with it to varying degrees. In this chapter, I consider three different versions of interactionism and discuss what light, if any, each of them sheds on the paradox. The three versions, which are cho-sen for their notability and relevance to my own approach, are: Goodman's worldmaking, Piaget's constructivism, and Lakoff and Johnson's experiential account. As each of these versions originated in a different field—one in phi-losophy, one in psychology, and one in linguistics—a discussion of them also provides a multidisciplinary perspective on the interaction view.

This chapter is organized as follows. In Section 2, I present some empir-ical evidence in support of the interaction view of cognition. In the subse-quent three sections I review the three versions of interactionism mentioned above. I start out, in Section 3, by considering the philosophical approach to interactionism that started in Kant, matured in Cassirer, and climaxed in Goodman. In Section 4, I discuss Piaget's constructivism at some length, because my own approach to interactionism, laid out in chapters 5 and 6 of this book, incorporates many ideas of Piaget. In Section 5 of the current chapter, I present Lakoff and Johnson's experiential account that emphasizes the bodily basis of cognition. Finally, in Section 6, I summarize the main points of the chapter.

4.2   Empirical Support for the Interaction View of Cognition

Many empirical studies support the view that our concepts do indeed con-struct our world view, and are not reflections of some pre-existing, mind-independent structures in the world, and yet that this construction is not arbitrary. My objective in this section is to give you some feeling for the empirical foundation of interactionism. I do so by breaking up the interac-tion view into three separate hypotheses, and reviewing empirical evidence for each hypothesis. Then I discuss the issue of 'universals,' which are structures that are a necessary part of any conceptual organization. As an illustration, I then review the search for the existence of color universals and that attempts to ground them in the physiological structure of the brain.

Needless to say, my review is not meant to be exhaustive. There are many empirical studies that corroborate the interaction view, or refute the alternative views of cognition, and even a somewhat superficial survey of all these studies would easily fill a whole volume. In fact, given the overwhelming evidence supporting the interaction view, I wonder how anyone can reasonably subscribe to any other view of cognition. Unfortunately, cognitive science research abounds with approaches that completely disregard this mass of evidence. The research on metaphors, which has been dominated by similarity-based approaches that assume that attributes of an object are all given, provides one source of flagrant examples. Given that, my modest goal here is to review some of the evidence so that you do not regard interactionism as a far-fetched idea; and, if you already find it intuitively appealing, to provide some empirical grounding for this intuition.

4.2.1 Concepts are More than Aggregates of Sense Data

It is through our sense organs, by a process called perception, that we receive information from the world. Given that, it may seem reasonable to assume that sense data accurately reflect the state of the world. Moreover, it might also suggest that concepts are really aggregates of sense data. That is, the concept 'tree' is merely a label for a class of visual stimuli. This view implies an atomistic approach to cognition, so that any concept can be analyzed in terms of its component sensory stimuli.

Arguments refuting this atomistic view of cognition can be found as far back as Plato. In *Theaetetus,* the doctrine 'cognition is perception' is elaborately refuted [184b–186e]. It is argued that concepts such as 'sameness,' 'existence,' and 'difference' are themselves not directly apprehended through our senses. That is, you might see an object A and another object B and declare that they have the same color. But the concept of 'same color as' is not something that you can sense. From our modern perspective, Plato's point is easily made by citing the phenomenon of color blindness. If the concept 'same color as' can be sensed, then we merely need to expose a color-blind person to this sensation as a cure.

Towards the end of the nineteenth century, Christian von Ehrenfels, an Austrian psychologist, pointed out that the wholeness of a concept cannot always be expressed as the sum of its parts. When we hear a tune, there is a wholeness to it, namely the melody, that cannot simply be expressed as the sum of its parts, namely the individual notes appearing in the tune. We can shift the whole tune upward or downward on the musical scale, and yet it appears the same. In the process of shifting, however, all the individual notes (the 'parts') are changed. So what we recognize to be the same melody in the shifted tune (its 'whole') cannot be the same as the sum of its 'parts.'

(See Köhler [1930], pp. 164–165.)

But it was the *gestalt* movement in psychology that dealt a death-blow to the atomistic view of cognition. (See Köhler [1969] for an overview of gestalt psychology.) The origin of this movement can be traced back to 1912, when Max Wertheimer, a German psychologist, did experiments on apparent motion. Wertheimer found that when two dots are flashed near each other in quick succession, the subject viewing it reports a movement of the dot from the first position to the second. Lest this may be dismissed merely as an error of judgement on the subject's part, Wertheimer did another set of experiments to demonstrate the 'real' nature of this perceptual experience. There is a phenomenon known as the negative aftereffect of motion. If a subject views a uniform motion in a part of her visual field continuously for some duration of time, immediately followed by viewing some stationary object in the same part of the visual field, then the stationary object seems to be moving in a direction opposite to that of the previously viewed uniform motion. Wertheimer was able to demonstrate that the apparent motion exhibits negative aftereffects just like the real motion. These experiments clearly demonstrate that what we perceive in a given situation can be more than the sensory stimuli.

This process of local sensations combining into a meaningful whole that is more than their sum is referred to as *grouping* by the gestalt psychologists. Köhler did more experiments to show that (1) the grouping process is not always learned, and (2) the same grouping process that creates a whole out of the parts, can also make a whole disappear under suitable conditions. His favorite examples demonstrating both these points are shown in Figure 4.1. The figure in 4.1(a) contains the geometric form corresponding to the numeral 4, but subjects fail to see it at all. Clearly, the subject is used to recognizing the numeral 4 in isolation, but this ability does not help in recognizing it in Figure 4.1(a). In fact, Köhler explicitly tested this hypothesis in another experiment, where the subject is first repeatedly presented with the figure of a hexagon [Figure 4.1(b)]. After that, when the subject is presented with Figure 4.1(c), he completely fails to see that it includes the hexagon [4.1(b)] unless he intentionally searches for it. One might still object in these examples that the familiar figure is presented in an unusual and unfamiliar setting in each case, which affects its recognizability. Köhler countered it with the example of Figure 4.1(d) where the numeral 4 is also presented in an unusual and unfamiliar setting, and yet it is easily recognized. (See Köhler [1930], pp. 149–152.)

The original apparent motion experiments of Wertheimer were expanded

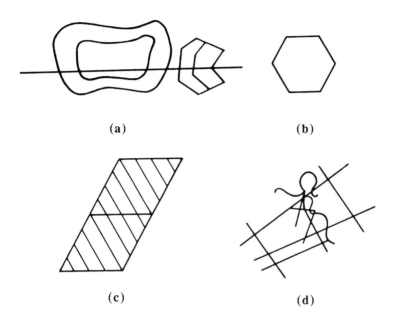

(a)   (b)

(c)   (d)

FIGURE 4.1: Examples used by Kohler to demonstrate some characteristics of 'grouping'. Figure (a) contains the familiar figure '4', but it is 'dissolved' in the background. Figures (b) and (c) explicitly show that past experiences do not affect this dissolution. Even after the subject is conditioned by showing figure (b) repeatedly, she fails to recognize its occurrence in (c), unless she is explicitly seeking it. Figure (d) shows that the dissolution is not always due to the unfamiliar background. The figure '4' is again presented in a 'strange' setting, yet it is easily recognized. (From Kohler [1930].)

more recently by Kolers [1972] to reveal the complex ways in which our visual apparatus adds to what is in front of the eye. He found, for instance, that when a circle and a square were flashed near each other in quick succession in a subject's visual field, the subject not only reported a movement from the first position to the second, but also a smooth transformation of the circle into the square during the movement. If the two figures were of different sizes, then the subject reported that the first figure grew or shrunk smoothly as it moved to the second position. If a barrier (in the form of a line) was imposed between the positions of the first and the second flashes, then the figure moved from the position of the first flash to the barrier, then moved forward (in the third dimension) to cross the barrier, back to the same plane, and then moved to the position of the second flash, with all perceived movement being smooth and continuous.

When the flashes consisted of groups of figures, instead of single figures, even more interesting phenomena were observed. Some examples of the pairs of figures used by Kolers in this study are shown in Figure 4.2. In each case, the group of figures in 4.2(a) was flashed first, followed by the group of figures in 4.2(b). In the first example, when the group of figures shown in 4.2[i](a) was flashed followed by the group of figures in 4.2[i](b), the three right figures in (a) moved as one unit, while the leftmost circle in (a) moved around to become the rightmost circle in (b). If a dot was flashed followed by four dots in four different directions (4.2[ii]), the subject saw the center dot 'explode' and move in four outward directions simultaneously. A remarkable thing was that under no circumstances did Kolers find that the apparent motion paths of different figures cross. For instance, when the group of figures in 4.2[iii](a) was flashed followed by the group of figures in 4.2[iii](b), then the top circle in (a) moved to the right to become the top square in (b), and the bottom square in (a) moved to become the bottom circle in (b).

Kolers' experiments with colored figures yielded the most surprising results. When a red dot was flashed followed by a green one, the subject saw a continuous motion all right. But as far as the color of the dot was concerned, the subject reported that the dot stayed red till about halfway, and then it abruptly changed to green. Kolers and Green's [1984] later experiments with color pairs, in which a pair of red-green dots was flashed followed by a pair of green-red dots (Figure 4.2[iv]), noted that the subject saw a linear movement of the initial pair of dots to the position of the second pair, with the colors of the dots abruptly changing from red-green to green-red about halfway.

All this evidence clearly points to the fact that our perceptual and cognitive apparatus is not a passive receptor of sensory stimuli, but asserts a

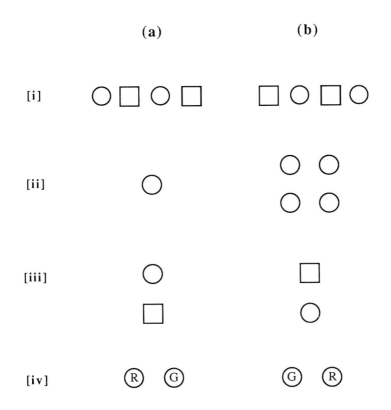

FIGURE 4.2: Kolers' examples that use apparent motion to demonstrate the complexity of the visual system. In each of the examples, the group of figures in (a) is flashed on the screen in front of the subject, followed by the group of figures in (b). The subject does not 'see' two succesive flashes, but a smooth and continuous motion. In (i) the three right figures in (a) move to the right as one unit, while the leftmost circle moves around to become the rightmost circle in (b). In (ii) the circle in (a) 'explodes' in four circles, which move outwards simultaneously to become figure (b). In (iii) the circle and the square in (a) move smoothly to the right (without crossing paths) while transforming into the square and the circle, respectively, to become figure (b). In (iv) the red-green pair of dots in (a) move smoothly to position (b), while the dots abruptly change colors to green-red about halfway. (From Kolers [1972] and Kolers & Green [1984].)

formative spirit in shaping the sense data through its concepts. Sometimes it makes us see some event even when the sensory stimuli corresponding to that event are not there. And, at other times, it makes an object disappear even though we are directly receiving sense data from that object. In either case, what we see in the mind's eye is not what is in front of the eye.

4.2.2   Concepts can Organize the World Differently

The second hypothesis concerning interactionism is that it is possible to organize the same environment, the same sense data, in different conceptual ways. (Note that both this hypothesis and its negation are consistent with the view that concepts are more than sense impressions.) I present two studies here, each of which corroborate the hypothesis in a different way.

One source of supporting evidence is provided by the seminal work of Benjamin Lee Whorf, whom I have already introduced in the last chapter. In fact, his study cited in the last chapter is relevant to this section as well, for it showed how different cultures can conceptualize the world differently so that their similarity metrics are different. In another study, Whorf [1950] showed that even what we consider as the most fundamental concepts can be different in different cultures and can lead to radically different world views. For instance, we organize the world in terms of space and time. We refer to spatial dimensions as 'here,' 'there,' 'ahead,' 'behind,' 'above,' 'below,' and so on. We also have the three tenses to refer to the temporal dimension. In the Hopi language, however, there is no concept of time. Instead, Hopi people divide their world into two grand concepts: 'manifested' and 'unmanifest.' The 'manifested' category corresponds to whatever is or was accessible to the senses. The mountain I am looking at now, and my recollection of the snowstorm I saw yesterday would both fit in this category. The 'unmanifest' category includes everything that is not manifest. Thus, anything that has not yet happened (my plans for what I will do tomorrow), plus everything that is imagined (what my daughter might be doing when I am at work) would fall into this category. In spite of this different conceptual organization, Whorf argued: "[T]he Hopi language is capable of accounting for and describing correctly, in a pragmatic or operational sense, all observable phenomena of the universe." [Whorf 1950, p. 58.]

Another study by a psychologist Alexander Romanovich Luria supports in a different way the hypothesis that there might be alternate ways of organizing sense data. Notice that the experiments of gestalt psychology, as well as many other phenomena of visual illusion that have been investigated since then, suggest that we do not always 'see' what is in front of the eye, but fabricate the objects of perception and cognition, at least partially. Given that, one wonders if people with different cultural backgrounds fabricate differently. For if so, then this would again suggest that one can conceptualize the same sense data, same world, in alternate ways. This is exactly what Luria demonstrated by studying the effects of cultural background on individual perception and cognition in Uzbekistan, the heart of what was Soviet Union then. (See Luria [1976]. Though this study was carried out in 1931–32, it was only published in 1976.)

Most of Luria's experimental subjects lived in remote villages of Uzbekistan. At the time the study was conducted, Luria notes, "[T]hese regions of the Soviet Union were undergoing especially profound socioeconomic and cultural changes. The period we observed included the beginnings of collectivization and other radical socioeconomic changes as well as the emancipation of women. Because the period studied was one of transition, we were able to make our study to some extent comparative. Thus we could observe both underdeveloped illiterate groups (living in villages) and groups already involved in modern life, experiencing the first influences of the social realignment." [Luria 1976, p. 14]. There were five groups of subjects: "(1) Ichkari women living in remote villages who were illiterate and not involved in any modern social activities. (2) Peasants in remote villages, who continued to maintain an individualistic economy, to remain illiterate, and to involve themselves in no way with socialized labor. (3) Women who attended short-term courses in the teaching of kindergartners. As a rule, they still had no formal education and almost no literacy training. (4) Active 'collective farm' workers and young people who have taken short courses. (5) Women students admitted to a teachers' school after two or three years of study. Their educational qualifications, however, were still fairly low." [Luria 1976, p. 15]. With these groups of subjects, Luria charted their performance for a whole range of perceptual and cognitive processes, such as color perception, visual illusion, abstraction, deduction, and so on. I review only two sets of experiments here.

The first set of experiments concerned the perception of color hues. The subjects were presented with 27 different hues in the form of skeins of wool, and were then asked to name the colors. The results were interesting because 59.5% of the Ichkari women came up with object-category names—that is, names that referred to the color by using a concrete object of that color (such as iris, liver, spoiled cotton, etc.) rather than some abstract color name (such as blue, green, etc.)—as opposed to only 16.3% of the women at teachers' school. Even more interesting was the case when the subjects were asked to group the colors according to whatever colors they thought were 'similar.' Whereas the last four groups gave what might be considered more or less 'normal' response, Ichkari women, who routinely engaged in embroidery, and who chose objects to name hues,

> "[P]resented us with an entirely different system. As a rule, the instruction to divide the colors into groups created complete confusion and called forth responses such as, 'It can't be done,' 'None of them are the same, you can't put them together,' 'They're not at all alike,' or 'This is like calf's-dung, and this is like peach.' The women usually began by putting different skeins together, then attempted to explain their color groups but shook their heads in perplexity and failed to complete the task." [Luria 1976, p. 27.]

In the forced classification part of the experiment, 70% of the Ichkari women refused. All this led Luria to conclude, "[T]he process by which [Ichkari women] group and classify colors differs markedly from that of assigning them to distinct categories as described in the standard literature on the psychology of color perception and encoding." [p. 30].

The second set of Luria's experiments concerned the perception of optical illusions. He tested the susceptibility of the subjects in each of the five groups to certain optical illusions. Two of the illusions used in Luria's study are shown in Figure 4.3, and Table 4.1 shows the percentage of subjects from each of the five groups who perceived these optical illusions. One can see from the table that there is a strong correlation between the social background of the subjects and their ability to perceive optical illusions: significantly fewer Ichkari women and peasants were able to see the illusions than collective-farm activists and women at teachers' school.

While acknowledging the somewhat tentative status of these findings, since such experiments cannot be easily replicated, Luria nevertheless argued that it "clearly shows that optical illusions are linked to complex psychological processes that vary in accordance with socio-historical development" and "perceptual processes hitherto regarded as purely physiological (and thus universal) are influenced by sociohistoric development." [Luria 1976, pp. 43–45]. It may be of interest to note here that Kolers, in his study of apparent motion, also found that some subjects were unable to see apparent motion at all. While he did not systematically investigate any correlation between the cultural background of the subjects and their inability to see apparent motion, he, nevertheless, noted that most of those who were unable to see apparent motion were engineers and physicians [Kolers 1972, p. 160]. (See

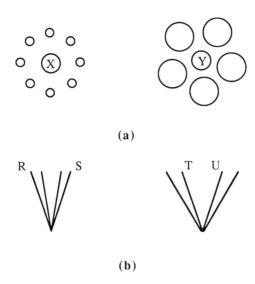

(a)

(b)

FIGURE 4.3: Optical illusions used in the study by Luria. In figure (a) the circles marked X and Y are of equal size, but X seems bigger than Y. In figure (b), the angles marked RS and TU are of equal size, but the angle RS appears bigger. (From Luria [1976].)

Group	No. of Subjects	Optical Illusion	
		Fig. 4.3(a)	Fig. 4.3(b)
Ichkari women	9	33.3%	11.1%
Peasants	25	20.8%	25.0%
Women in preschool courses	25	64.0%	36.0%
Collective-farm activists	40	85.0%	77.5%
Women at teachers' school	38	92.1%	71.0%

Table 4.1: Perception of Optical Illusions by Luria's Subjects. Percentage figures show the number of subjects in each group who perceived the corresponding optical illusion. (From Table 6, p. 44, in Luria [1976].)

also Segall, Campbell & Herskovits [1966]; and Deregowski [1980] for more studies of the effect of cultural background on visual perception.)

Thus, we see that while concepts can go beyond what is given to the senses in organizing the world, they do so in different ways, so that different people can see the world in different ways.

4.2.3   Concepts Cannot Organize the World Arbitrarily

Admitting that concepts can organize the world differently for different people, the next issue that naturally suggests itself is whether this organization is constrained in any way. Can concepts organize reality in any arbitrary way? The answer, a vehement "No!," might seem obvious to most people. Still, it would be useful to consider some empirical facts supporting this conclusion.

Anyone who has worked on a project involving assembly of physical components—building a model glider or a book-shelf; sewing a shirt; knitting a sweater; or even hanging a picture on the wall—knows that it is all too easy to make mistakes. What characterizes a 'mistake' is the fact that carrying out certain operations that one thought would lead to a certain state of affairs, results in a different state altogether. The glider does not fly. The picture falls down. And so on. Sometimes we can look back and realize what we did wrong. But at other times, we go over the instructions carefully again and again, but cannot find any place we might have made a mistake. And, yet, the glider does not fly. This feeling is quite common when trying one's first project involving a new skill. Reality does not care whether one followed the instructions carefully or not.

Or, consider the situation where you are lost in an unfamiliar town. If any conceptual organization is as good as any other, then you ought to be able to get to where you want to be by going in any direction, or even by not going anywhere at all. If your concepts can organize the world in any way, why can you not organize them so that far away places come closer at will, with only the effort of reconceptualization required. The point here is very simple: certain actions lead to the desired state of affairs and many others do not, in spite of our best efforts and intentions.

The prehistory of flight provides another rich source of examples where reality refused to accept many conceptual organizations imposed on it, with a few comic but mostly tragic consequences. In his thorough study, Hart [1985] provides a detailed look at the conceptual and theoretical background of the human attempts at manned flight, covering a period up to the end of the eighteenth century. He notes that the designs of the pre-flight flying machines were far from arbitrary. Rather they took into account metaphysical, theological, and cosmological arguments about the nature of air, empirical observations of the flight of birds, and various other logical and rational points of views. Yet, none of these attempts resulted in a successful flight. For instance, in 1772, Abbé Pierre Desforges of France designed an elaborate contraption and jumped from the top of Tour Guinette in Etampes. His design was quite sophisticated and took into account empirical observations of the flight of swallows. Desforges made provisions for his machine to be able to carry a 150 lb pilot and an additional luggage of 15 lb. He estimated, based on comparisons with the flight of swallows and with rowing a boat, that his machine would be able to cover 30 leagues an hour in favorable wind. In spite of the elaborate design and construction, attention to the details, numerous calculations and empirical facts that were taken into account, Desforges' contraption fell to the ground from the 100 ft tower. It was miraculous that Desforges escaped from the fall with only a bruised elbow. (See Hart [1985], pp. 159–163.)

Thus, we see that reality is not a passive receptor of our conceptual organizations, but ferociously asserts itself. It does not care whether we are following a certain set of instructions to the tee, or that we have spent years of intellectual, emotional and physical energy in formulating some elaborate theory or constructing a sophisticated machine. It does not even care how rational, logical, or coherent with empirical observations are our theories. The theory and the dreams of flying are easily shattered by the dispassionate and uncaring reality as the sophisticated flying machine plummets to the ground like a dead bird. Reality decides in its own mysterious way whether to accept or reject our conceptual organization.

4.2.4 'Universals' and the Physiological Basis of Cognition

The fact that reality imposes its own constraints on one's conceptual organization suggests an intriguing hypothesis: Could it be that all different conceptual organizations have a common denominator? Indeed, this hypothesis has been pursued vigorously by many scholars, who sought to find the common denominator underlying all conceptual organizations. As this hypothesis contradicts the interaction view of cognition—if the common denominator exists, one cannot say that it is *created*—it is important to review the empirical evidence supporting it.

Broadly speaking, there are two versions of the common denominator hypothesis that have been investigated. In one version, the objective is to demonstrate that reality has a mind-independent ontology and structure, and all conceptual organizations can be reduced to it. The origin of this 'reductionist' approach to the world can be traced back to Descartes' idea that the world is a machine that operates according to a certain fixed set of laws—an idea that received a strong impetus from Newtonian mechanics. However, with the advent of quantum mechanics, it has lost some of its appeal in this century. Though most physical scientists still work under the assumption that there are laws out there in the world, and it is the objective of science to *discover* what they are, several scholars have put forth strong and convincing arguments to show that the laws and the theories of physical sciences are not as mind-independent as it may seem, but are partly creations of the scientific community. (See Gerhart & Russell [1984], Jones [1982], and Turbayne [1962].)

The second version of the common denominator hypothesis argues that all conceptual organizations share some invariant structures, which are often referred to as 'universals.' It is precisely for this reason that anthropologists, linguists and psychologists have repeatedly sought to demonstrate the existence of universals across different languages and cultures. Then, in recent years, a new twist has been added to this version of the common denominator hypothesis. It is argued that universals, assuming that they exist, are rooted in the physiological structure of the cognitive agent's body and brain. This hypothesis is bolstered by the phenomenal leap that our knowledge of neurophysiology has taken in this century. It has been demonstrated that in animals with simple brain structures, such as horseshoe crabs and frogs, the processing of sensory information starts right at the receptors, and that this processing is goal-oriented. (See Hartline [1967]; and Lettvin *et al.* [1959].) For instance, certain cells in the frog's retina are specialized to detect bugs, while certain others are specialized to detect predators. Thus, at least for frogs, their universals of 'bugs' and 'predators,' if we may call them universals, can be seen to arise from their neurophysiology. The goal-oriented nature of perception has even been demonstrated for animals with more complex brains [Hubel 1988]. For instance, the visual system of cats, monkeys and humans has evolved so that it *looks for* straight edges.

In spite of all this, the attempts to demonstrate the existence of universals for animals with complex brains, such as us humans, and provide a neurophysiological basis for them, has not yet been fruitful. I demonstrate this point in this section by considering the universals for color terms, which have been intensively investigated.

In 1969, Berlin and Kay published a study demonstrating the existence of universals in naming color categories. They studied 20 languages experimentally, and considered the existing relevant literature on 78 other languages, to show,

> "First, there exist universally for humans eleven basic perceptual color categories, which serve as the psychophysical referents of the eleven or fewer basic color terms in any language. Second, in the history of a given language, encoding of perceptual categories into basic color terms follows a fixed partial order. The two possible temporal orders are:

$$\left. \begin{array}{c} \text{white} \\ \text{black} \end{array} \right] \rightarrow \text{red} \rightarrow \text{green} \rightarrow \text{yellow} \rightarrow \text{blue} \rightarrow \text{brown} \rightarrow \left[\begin{array}{c} \text{purple} \\ \text{pink} \\ \text{orange} \\ \text{grey} \end{array} \right.$$

$$\left. \begin{array}{c} \text{white} \\ \text{black} \end{array} \right] \rightarrow \text{red} \rightarrow \text{yellow} \rightarrow \text{green} \rightarrow \text{blue} \rightarrow \text{brown} \rightarrow \left[\begin{array}{c} \text{purple} \\ \text{pink} \\ \text{orange} \\ \text{grey} \end{array} \right.$$

> Third, the overall temporal order is properly considered an evolutionary one; color lexicons with few terms tend to occur in association with relatively simple cultures and simple technologies, while color lexicons with many terms tend to occur in association with complex cultures and complex technologies (to the extent that complexity of culture and technology can be assessed objectively)." [Berlin & Kay 1969, p. 104]

A comprehensive effort to provide a neurophysiological basis for Berlin and Kay's color universals has been made by Floyd Ratliff [1976]. Ratliff started by reviewing the existing research on the neurophysiology of color vision, which reconciles the opposition of the Young-Helmholtz theory of trichromatic additive color and the Hering theory of tetrachromatic opponent colors. According to the Young-Helmholtz theory, all color sensations are derived from suitable combinations of three 'primary' colors: red, green, and blue. This theory is supported by the fact that in our retina, there are three kinds of cones (the cells primarily responsible for color vision) that are most sensitive to the wavelengths corresponding to the colors red, green, and blue, respectively. The Hering theory, seemingly on the contrary, suggests that all color sensation results from combinations of two antagonistic pairs of colors: red-green and yellow-blue. This theory is supported by the fact that there are four psychologically basic colors—red, green, yellow, and blue—and, further, sensations of red and green suppress each other, and so do the sensations of yellow and blue. Thus, for instance, we can have a color sensation of reddish yellow (orange), or reddish blue (purple), or greenish yellow (chartreuse), or greenish blue (turquoise), but not of reddish green or yellowish blue.

In reconciling these two theories, Ratliff brought in the studies of De Valois and his colleagues on the visual system of the macaque monkey, which happens to be very similar to that of humans. (See De Valois, Abramov, & Jacobs [1966]; and De Valois & Jacobs [1968].) De Valois *et al.* monitored the response of single cells leading from the lateral geniculate nucleus to the visual cortex of the monkey. They found the presence of four types of spectrally opponent neurons. These spectrally opponent neurons are excited by light from one part of the spectrum and inhibited by light from another part of the spectrum. The four types of neurons are: red-excitatory and green-inhibitory, green-excitatory and red-inhibitory, yellow-excitatory and blue-inhibitory, and blue-excitatory and yellow-inhibitory. The presence of these four types of neurons clearly provides a neurophysiological foundation to the Hering tetrachromatic opponent color theory. Moreover, Ratliff brings in Abramov and Levine's model to explain how the three kinds of cones in the retina might be connected to the cells in the lateral geniculate nucleus so as to produce a response concurring with De Valois *et al.*'s observations. Thus, the two theories are "no longer regarded as contradictory, but as complementary. Each refers principally to a different level of the visual system." [Ratliff 1976, p. 317].

Taking all these findings into account, Ratliff then went on to provide grounds—in terms of neurophysiological, psychophysical, and psychological evidence—for the partial order of the color terms found in Berlin and Kay's studies. For instance, the grounds offered for the later position of blue (compared to red, green and yellow) in the order of development are: the weak and narrow sensitivity of the pigment in the 'blue' cones (compared to 'red' and 'green' cones); the fact that according to Abramov and Levine's model the response of 'blue' cones from the retina does not interact with that of the other cones until relatively late in the integrative process; the fact that the center of the fovea (the central part of retina) is blue-blind; and the fact that the lens and the macular pigment in the eye absorb blue light. Similarly, the reasons suggested for the early appearance of 'red' in Berlin & Kay's partial order are: the pigment in the 'red' cones is the most sensitive of the three; the response of 'red' cones from the retina is incorporated early on in the integrative process that produces opponent response and, moreover, these are the only type of cones that make a contribution to each and every one of the four types of opponent response cells; the center of the fovea is most sensitive to red; the chromatic aberration caused by absorption by lens and macular pigment in the eye favors the red; etc.

All the arguments advanced by Ratliff to explain the partial order of Berlin and Kay's color universals constitute what might be considered a very weak case of circumstantial evidence. I should emphasize here that the issue at stake is *not the color perception, but the names for colors.* You may recall Luria's study here which showed that Ichkari women on no account showed any deficiency of color perception. On the contrary, they refused to group different hues under one label, arguing that each of them is a different color altogether. Ratliff himself mentions the study by Heider and Olivier [1972] that demonstrated that Dani speakers, who have only two color terms in their language *mola* for 'white-warm' hues and *mili* for 'dark-cool' hues, are fully capable of distinguishing different hues, even though they are given the same name.

The issue at stake is the emergence of linguistic categories that group various hues together. And it is in this regard that Ratliff's arguments fall short. For instance, given all the facts suggesting dominance of red over blue, if one were to use them to show that our perception of the color red is better than that of blue, or that we are capable of making finer distinctions of hue in the red region of the spectrum than in the blue region, then there would be a reasonable argument subject to empirical confirmation. But to argue from those facts that a culture would develop the term for red before the term for blue constitutes a long leap from neurophysiological structures to linguistic structures without any satisfactory account of the processes or structures that mediate this transition.

An attempt to fill the gap between neurophysiological structures and linguistic structures for the color terms was made by Kay and McDaniel [1978]. Starting from De Valois *et al.*'s four types of opponent response cells, and positing that the two other types of non-opponent response cells—also studied by De Valois and his colleagues—encode the luminosity information, they went on to show how the responses of all these cells can be combined by using fuzzy set-theoretic operations of union and intersection to produce various other color terms. For instance, the term *mili* in Dani for dark-cool hues can be represented as 'black OR green OR blue,' where by OR we mean the fuzzy set-union operation. Similarly, the color orange is represented as 'red + yellow,' where + is a slightly modified version of fuzzy set-intersection operation. Thus, the fuzzy set-union and fuzzy set-intersection operations are seen to mediate the transition from neurophysiological structures to linguistic ones.

These operations themselves, however, are not grounded in the neurophysiological structure of the brain, at least in as far as we know. Thus, the question still remains: Why, when fifty-seven composite categories can be formed by applying the fuzzy set-union operation to two or more of the six fundamental neural response categories (black, white, red, green, yellow, and blue), do only three of them exist as universals? Even if we rule out those composites that include both categories of an opponent pair—that is, we do not want to consider those composites that include both black and white, or both red and green—there are still twenty possible composites. Why are only three of them universal? Why is 'red OR blue' not a color universal?

Unless these questions can be satisfactorily answered, the universals for color terms must remain essentially an empirical finding. Given that, it is perhaps not surprising that later research has cast doubts on Berlin and Kay's hypothesis. MacLaury [1987] cites the case of the 'yellow-with-green' category in Shuswap that is not included in Berlin and Kay's sequence of color universals. Moss [1989] uses the case of purple in Russian to argue against the Berlin-Kay hypothesis.

To sum up the discussion of this section, there are two key points. The first rather obvious point is that the structure of our brains and bodies does affect cognition, for the processes of perception and cognition take place in the brain. The second point is that though one could argue, in principle, that physiological structures might be a source of universals, the evidence for this can only be seen in animals with a relatively simple nervous system. The structure of the human brain is much too complex, and our knowledge of it is much too fragmentary, to try to look for a direct connection between universals, if their existence can be demonstrated convincingly, and the physiological organization of the brain.

Both these points are perhaps best demonstrated in a series of touching tales of his patients by Dr. Oliver Sacks in *The Man Who Mistook His Wife for a Hat*. Physical damage to the brain does indeed result in cognitive aberration, but what is more interesting is the variety of ways in which the rest of the brain compensates for these aberrations while preserving the identity of the person as a whole. This, if nothing else, definitely points away from a simple-minded identification of cognitive structures with physiological structures.

4.2.5 Summary

The research reviewed in this section clearly shows that the world we see in our mind's eye is a world that is not 'given' but is constructed by our cognitive apparatus. Yet, this construction is not arbitrary but is constrained by reality. One might say that the conceptual organization of the world is brought about by an interaction between the cognitive agent and the environment, a process in which each participant is actively involved.

The problem is in explaining the role of the environment in this interaction. If we assume that it has a preconceptual (mind-independent) ontology and structure, then we need to show how (and why) different conceptual organizations are created from it. If we assume that it does not have a preconceptual ontology and structure, then we need to show how it can reject arbitrary conceptual organizations.

So the problem remains. I now examine three different approaches to cognition that are interactionist in spirit, and analyze how far this problem is addressed in each of them.

4.3 From Kant to Goodman: Worldmaking

Nelson Goodman put forth a comprehensive framework of cognition in his two beautifully written books *Languages of Art* [1976] and *Ways of Worldmaking* [1978]. That he is a vehement supporter of the interaction view is rather obviously reflected in the titles of his works: 'Reality Remade,' 'The Fabrication of Facts,' and, of course, 'Ways of Worldmaking.' Since Goodman's framework is the culmination of a theme that was started by Kant and nurtured by Cassirer, it would be useful to take a brief look at Kant's and Cassirer's approaches to interactionism before delving into Goodman.

It is in Immanuel Kant's celebrated *Critique of Pure Reason* that we find the roots of a constructivist approach to cognition that is the hallmark of interactionism. Kant took his point of departure from the earlier traditions where knowledge was considered to be knowledge of the objects in the world. Instead, he focused on the process of cognition, which forces objects into the structure of concepts.

Kant acknowledged the metaphysical problem one faces in supposing that our conceptual organization, and our knowledge, conforms to some pre-existing structure in the world, namely that then one must be able to specify this structure at least in some respects, so that these specifications can distinguish between genuine knowledge and heresy. Noting the failure of various philosophers before him to address this problem, Kant argued that a better approach might be to reverse the supposition, so that the objects in the world are seen to conform to the structure of our concepts.

Kant's concepts, which he referred to as *categories,* are subjective in that they highlight the subject's role in cognition—they are a priori and exist independently of experience. Yet, categories are objective in that they do not vary from consciousness to consciousness. The relationships between categories are not unique for my consciousness, but are true in all consciousness. It was necessary to take this position to explain the objective nature of the natural sciences, which are essentially *categorical* in Kant's account.

As far as the external world is concerned, Kant made a distinction between the noumenal world, a world of *things in themselves,* and a phenomenal world, a world of *appearances.* The world of appearances is the world that is given to us by our senses, which we are in a position to know. The noumenal world, however, is not knowable, but one can think about it. It was necessary to posit a noumenal world that one can think about, since otherwise it would lead us to conclude that the world of appearances is made out of nothing.

Then Kant introduced *schemas* to mediate between categories and the world of appearances. The distinction between these three key concepts of Kant's account of cognition can be better appreciated with an example. When we say that the sum of the three angles of a triangle equals two right angles, we are referring to the category triangle, which is the abstract notion of a triangle. Being abstract, however, it cannot be imagined (you can imagine a particular triangle, but not the abstract concept triangle), and therefore, cannot be applied to figures that we see. It is the schema of triangle that allows us to imagine figures that are triangles, and it is through the schema of triangle that the concept of triangle becomes applicable to the world of appearances, which contains particular triangular objects. Thus, our categories organize our world of appearances through their respective schemas.

These are the key features of Kant's approach to cognition. While he enthusiastically endorsed the subject's role in cognition, he is quite silent about how the world of things in themselves constrains the possible ways in which the world of appearances can be organized by our categories. However, we should take note of Krausser's [1974] arguments that there are two postulates implied in Kant's philosophy. The first postulate is that in order to have an empirical structure in the sciences, we must be able to interact with and experience the world of things in themselves. Secondly, this world of things in themselves must have some order and structure, even though this order or structure is not knowable.

The metaphysical revolution that Kant started—regarding only the process of cognition as accessible and knowable but not the world of things in themselves—achieved its full intensity in the philosophy of Ernst Cassirer. He focused on Kant's schema, developed it into a theory of symbolic forms, and then proceeded to apply it to various human activities such as language, mathematics, natural sciences, myths and religion, etc. In this task Cassirer greatly benefited from certain developments in mathematics and the natural sciences since Kant, such as non-Euclidean geometries and the theory of relativity, as well as the availability of a great deal of research in anthropology, linguistics, mythology, religion, and animal cognition. (Cassirer's theory is outlined in his monumental *The Philosophy of Symbolic Forms* [1955], a summary of which can be found in his *An Essay on Man* [1944]. For some of the applications of his theory see *Language and Myth* [1946] and *The Problem of Knowledge* [1950]. See also Susanne Langer's *Philosophy in a New Key* [1942] and *Feeling and Form* [1953] for further elaboration of Cassirer's theory, and its application to the philosophy of art.)

The creation of symbols, for Cassirer, is the primary function of human consciousness. He saw cognition merely as one of the activities that manifests the symbolic function; notable among others being art and religion. The symbolic activity was properly called *creation* since it is only in the making of symbols that the kaleidoscopic flux of impressions is halted and given a form that can be comprehended. The multiplicity of symbolic forms, as well as their creative aspects is summed up nicely in the following passage:

"Every authentic function of the human spirit has this decisive characteristic in common with cognition: it does not merely copy but rather embodies an original, formative power. It does not express passively the mere fact that something is present but contains an independent energy of the human spirit through which the simple presence of the phenomenon assumes a definite 'meaning,' a particular ideational content. This is as true of art as it is of cognition; it is as true of myth as of religion. All live in particular image-worlds, which do not merely reflect the empirically given, but which rather produce it in accordance with an independent principle. Each of these functions creates its own symbolic forms which, if not similar to the intellectual symbols, enjoy equal rank as products of the human spirit. None of these forms can simply be reduced to, or derived from, the others; each of them designates a particular approach, in which and through which it constitutes its own aspect of 'reality.'" [Cassirer 1955, vol. 1, p. 78].

Here we see that the intersubjectivity of Kant's categories is turned into a multiplicity of symbolic worlds by Cassirer. Moreover, these multiple worlds are considered irreducible to one another. Thus, Cassirer's account explicitly endorses the view that reality can be conceptualized in alternate ways.

Cassirer elaborated at quite some length on what exactly is a symbol. He draws a distinction between signs and symbols. [Cassirer 1944, Chaps. II and III; Langer 1942, Chaps. II and III.] Signs are the basis of animal cognition. They are direct links between the sensory and effectory organs of an animal. For instance, we can train a dog to associate the sound of a bell to availability of food. The dog comes running to a preappointed place expecting food every time she hears the sound of the bell. It may even start some physiological reactions in the dog, such as salivation. In this case, the ringing of the bell acts as a sign for the dog. It is closely tied to the physical world. The dog cannot 'think' about it in the absence of the sign. Even when the sign is presented, it invariably results in some action.

Symbols, on the other hand, are taken to be the foundation of human intelligence: "Between the receptor system and the effector system, which are to be found in all animal species, we find in man a third link which we may describe as the *symbolic system*." [Cassirer 1944, p. 24.] Symbols can be looked upon as signs that have become independent and free-floating in that they are no longer directly connected to the sensory or the effectory organs. Thus, we may think of food in our idle moments, without being hungry, or the word 'food' being mentioned at all. Moreover, even when a symbol is explicitly mentioned, we can manipulate it, talk about it, without at once getting actively involved.

Symbols themselves are divided into three types: mimetic, analogical, and discursive, in the order of their development. [Cassirer 1955, vol. 1, pp. 186–197; Langer 1942, Chap. IV.] That is, mimetic symbols are supposed to be the first ones that a culture develops, followed by analogical ones, ultimately leading to discursive symbols. Mimetic symbols consist in replicating the sense impression caused by the object that is being designated. For instance, thunder might be designated by a thunder-like sound. In the second type, termed 'analogical' or 'presentational' symbols, the symbol is some kind of structural model of the object designated. All kinds of picture language falls in this category. Finally, discursive symbols are those in which there is no direct relationship between the symbol and the object designated. For instance, the English word 'cat' does not bear any resemblance with the animal species it designates.

Despite these elaborations of what a symbol is, it is not clear in Cassirer's account how the symbolic worlds are prevented from being arbitrary. If Kant's version of interactionism is seen as leaning too far in the direction of intersubjectivity by positing transcendental categories, then Cassirer's interactionism seems to bend too far in exactly the opposite direction by making the symbol all powerful creator of form, and reducing the role of the environment to a passive recipient.

It is in Nelson Goodman's approach that we find just the right balance between these two extremes. He embraces Cassirer in maintaining that there are different modes of cognition, and each creates its own 'world.' But he also argues that every 'world' has its own criteria of rightness that are objective, so that the judgment whether something is a fact or a fallacy within a given 'world' no longer depends on the whim of the subject. For instance, we can fix our frame of reference so that the earth is motionless. But then the rightness of the statement "the sun revolves around the earth" is a matter of objective verification, and cannot be decided arbitrarily. Thus, the role of the subject, in Goodman's worldmaking view, is seen in establishing the frame of reference, and the role of the environment is viewed in objectifying the facts relative to the frame of reference.

Goodman also emphasizes the need for having a frame of reference, using an analogy with the map [Goodman 1978, p. 114]. In order to use a map, we must first locate ourselves on it. And once we locate ourselves on it, the frame of reference gets fixed, and the 'world' acquires a fixed ontology and structure. Now in order to get to the train station, certain sets of directions are correct and others are wrong, and this correctness is a matter of objectivity.

This account, however, while it comes close to resolving the paradox of interactionism, does not quite do so. The problem is to explain how reality objectifies the 'world.' Notice that in the map analogy, it does so by virtue of a frameless structure. A map has certain fixed structure even before we locate ourselves on it. Moreover, this structure is knowable without locating ourselves on it.[1] And all frames of references can be derived from

---

[1] Film director Alfred Hitchcock reminisced that before coming to the Unites States, he was so fascinated by New York City that he had memorized its map. He knew the locations of the stores and theaters, the schedule of trains, and so on. When he would

this universal frameless structure, so its knowledge is useful.

In fact, the map analogy is not very apt here, because one of Goodman's points, a point that he argues rather well, is that it is not always possible to resolve conflicts between different worlds by reducing them to some frameless world. [Goodman 1978, VII, pp. 109–140.] But, if it is not some frameless world that is objectifying the relative 'worlds,' then what is? In answering this question lies the key to the paradox of interactionism.

4.4   Piaget's Constructivism

The pioneering work of Jean Piaget, the biologist, the philosopher and, most of all, the psychologist, provides another comprehensive framework of interactionism. Throughout his prolific career, Piaget was a staunch supporter of the view that reality does not have a pre-existing structure, but is actively constructed by the cognitive agent. This theme echoes in all of Piaget's writings. His numerous ingenious and meticulously executed experiments showed how various concepts—such as object permanence, time duration, temporal succession, speed; geometrical concepts like length, angle, curvature, area, and volume; logical concepts like class inclusion, 'all' and 'some;' multiplicative classification, seriation; numerical concepts; and so on—are gradually constructed by the child through increasingly complex interactions with the environment. (See Inhelder & Piaget [1959]; Piaget [1936, 1937, 1945, 1946, 1946a, 1981, 1983]; Piaget & Inhelder [1948]; Piaget, Inhelder & Szeminska [1948]; and Piaget & Szeminska [1941]. For an overview see Piaget & Inhelder [1966] and Piaget [1970].)

For instance, take the notion of object permanence itself. Piaget's experiments show that the world is not already cut up into numerous objects, but a child, as she grows and develops cognitively, arrives at the idea of an 'object' through successive constructions [Piaget 1937, Chap. 1]. Early on, the child's concept of object is inseparable from her actions. Something is an object as long as it can be grasped, or sucked. At this point, if the object is taken away from the child, she merely repeats her actions anticipating the reappearance of the object: the child would continue to make the sucking motions or the motions of opening and clenching her fists.

Later on, the child begins to associate different sensory stimuli resulting

---

meet Americans at parties, they would invariably ask him when he was last in New York. To which Hitchcock, to their utter amazement, would reply that he had never been there. [Truffaut 1984, p. 125.]

from the same object: she will shake a rattle in order to make the sound, or turn her head towards the sound in order to see the object making the sound, etc. But the child has no notion of object permanence yet. If something is not present to the senses directly, then it is simply not there. For instance, if one hides a toy with which the child has been playing under a handkerchief, the child will show no interest in recovering it, even if the act of hiding was carried out in full view of the child, and the child has the motor ability to remove the handkerchief.

Still later in her cognitive development, the child begins to actively search for objects. However, there is an interesting sequence of developments. At one point, the child will retrieve a toy that is hidden behind a screen by removing the screen, as long as the act of hiding is carried out in front of the child. But after the toy is hidden and retrieved from behind screen A several times, if the toy is hidden behind screen B, again in full view of the child, the child still looks behind screen A to retrieve it. Only later in the course of her development does the child make a more adequate association between the sequence of events witnessed and the location of the toy.

At this stage, invisible displacements still confuse the child. If a toy is put in a box, and the box is taken behind the screen, where the toy is taken out so that the child cannot see it, and the empty box is brought out again, then the child does not know where to look for the toy. Eventually, when the child does make the connection, she temporarily regresses to the earlier behavior so that she searches for the toy, hidden behind screen B, by lifting screen A, from where the toy was retrieved the last few times.

Thus, we see that the concept of object permanence is not a simple and primitive concept after all, but requires an elaborate intellectual construction. It is construction in the sense that the concept is embedded in the different ways in which the child can act upon an object. As the action repertoire of the child grows, the objecthood concept becomes increasingly complex, until the adult version of the concept emerges through abstraction.

This last point can be emphasized by considering the notion of identity. Adults can see an object preserving its identity through various transformations of orientation, position, form, shape, and size. For instance, a piece of string is the same string whether it is arranged in the shape of a circle or a square. However, a child, until a certain stage of her cognitive development, would insist that they are different things, for the child has not yet learned that in transforming an object in various ways, something is conserved, and it is this conservation that is at the heart of the concept of identity. This difference between the adult's and the child's concepts of identity reveals itself in an interesting way in the phenomenon of apparent motion. Recall that in Kolers' experiments, when a circle and a square were flashed in quick succession near each other in the visual field of an adult, the adult reported a uniform movement of the circle to the position of the square, during which the circle was smoothly transformed into a square. Children, on the other hand, report that the circle remains a circle until it is near the position of the square, where it abruptly changes into another object, a square. (See Piaget [1970], pp. 54–57.) (This is reminiscent of the adult's experience when the color, rather than the shape, of the flash was varied in Kolers' experiments. See also Goodman's [1978, V, 6, pp. 85–89] explanations.)

Based on many such studies, Piaget articulated his action-oriented approach, according to which, to know an object is to act upon it and to transform it, so that "Knowing reality means constructing systems of transformations that correspond, more or less adequately, to reality." [Piaget 1970, p. 15.] Moreover, the process of knowing itself works by transforming reality, "[K]nowledge results from continuous construction, since in each act of understanding, some degree of invention is involved; in development, the passage from one stage to the next is always characterized by the formation of new structures which did not exist before, either in the external world or in the subject's mind." [Piaget 1970, p. 77.]

Piaget, of course, elaborated in quite some detail his action-oriented approach. The key concept in his elaboration is that of an equilibrium between the complementary processes of assimilation and accommodation. This concept was borrowed from biological systems, which should not be surprising given that Piaget started his career as a biologist. The analogy is explicitly laid out in one of Piaget's earlier works:

> "The organism is a cycle of physiochemical and kinetic processes which, in constant relation to the environment, are engendered by each other. Let a, b, c, etc., be the elements of this organized totality and x, y, z, etc., the corresponding elements of the surrounding environment. The schema of organization is therefore the following:
>
> 1. $a + x \longrightarrow b$;
>
> 2. $b + y \longrightarrow c$;
>
> 3. $c + z \longrightarrow a$; etc.
>
> The processes (1), (2), etc., may consist either of chemical reactions (when the organism ingests substances x which it will

transform into a substance *b* comprising part of its structure), or of any physical transformations whatsoever, or finally, in particular, of sensory-motor behavior (when a cycle of bodily movements *a*, combined with external movements *x*, result in *b* which itself enters the cycle of organization). The relationship which unites the organized elements *x*, *y*, *z*, etc., is therefore a relationship of *assimilation,* that is to say, the functioning of the organism does not destroy it but conserves the cycle of organization and coordinates the given data of the environment in such a way as to incorporate them in that cycle. Let us therefore suppose that, in the environment, a variation is produced which transforms *x* into *x'*. Either the organism does not adapt and the cycle ruptures, or else adaptation takes place, which means that the organized cycle has been modified by closing up on itself:

1. $a + x' \longrightarrow b'$;

2. $b' + y \longrightarrow c$;

3. $c + z \longrightarrow a$; etc.

If we call this result of the pressures exerted by the environment *accommodation* (transformation of *b* into *b'*), we can accordingly say that *adaptation is an equilibrium between assimilation and accommodation.*

This definition applies to intelligence as well. Intelligence is *assimilation* to the extent that it incorporates all the given data of experience within its framework. ... [M]ental life is also *accommodation* to the environment. Assimilation can never be pure because by incorporating new elements into its earlier schemata the intelligence constantly modifies the latter in order to adjust them to new elements. Conversely, things are never known by themselves, since this work of accommodation is only possible as a function of the inverse process of assimilation. We shall thus see how the very concept of the object is far from being innate and necessitates a construction which is simultaneously assimilatory and accommodating." (Piaget [1936], pp. 17–19, emphasis Piaget's.)

I included this long quotation because to understand the cognitive mechanisms of assimilation and accommodation—and they are going to play a major role in my account of cognition laid out in the next chapter—it is helpful to see their biological roots. The analogy between biological systems and cognitive systems resurfaced in Piaget's later works [1967, 1974], though he used it in the reverse direction this time by applying his insights from psychological studies of cognition to biological systems. Some more recent studies have carried this analogy quite far by proposing elaborate theories that explain knowledge and cognition on a biological basis. [Maturana & Varela 1987; Barham 1990.]

In any case, my interest being in cognitive assimilation and accommodation, it would be useful to elucidate these mechanisms further with some examples. Assimilation is the process by which a cognitive agent sees every situation, every environment, through the structure of its pre-existing concepts, or *schemas*. For instance, an infant may attempt to suck at any object pressed to her lips, thereby assimilating the object to her 'sucking schema.' As far as this schema is concerned, every object is an object to be sucked. A rich source of examples of assimilation are children's playful activities, especially those involving 'pretend situations.' A child playing with a doll house is essentially assimilating the doll house and the dolls to her schema of domestic life.

Assimilation may lead to *differentiation,* as the object being assimilated may produce an unexpected, or otherwise interesting, response. For instance, a child who has developed the schema of 'grasp an object and bring it to the mouth to suck on it' may find the object visually interesting as well.

However, assimilation alone produces only a playful behavior and not an 'intelligent' one. The unexpectedness of response is lost unless it is *integrated* into the conceptual organization by suitably modifying it. Precisely this task is accomplished by the process of *accommodation*.

In accommodation the cognitive agent reorganizes its schemas by taking account of the environmental differences so as to preserve an overall unity. The overall unity comes from the fact that the cognitive agent, in assimilating the environment to its schemas, has 'expectations' that are fulfilled by the environment. When this overall unity is disturbed, either the cognitive agent does not survive (as the tragic failures of several heavier-than-air flight attempts before the Wright brothers testifies), or else it reorganizes its schemas so as to maintain the overall unity.

It is the accommodation that gives the cognitive agent a capacity to 'learn.' However, every act of accommodation presupposes a prior step of assimilation. Also, it is the interplay of assimilation and accommodation, in conjunction with *generalization,* that is responsible for generating new schemas via differentiation. In the example of the child who, in acting out the schema of 'grasp objects and bring them to lips to suck,' finds the object visually interesting also, integrating this observation into her network of schemas might result in a new schema of 'grasp *that* object and bring it to the visual field,' which can then be generalized into 'grasp *any* object and bring it to the visual field to look at it.' Various schemas that a cognitive agent may possess are not all isolated, but are interconnected as a network. For example, both the schemas just mentioned make use of, and are connected with, the schema of 'grasp objects.'

Many of the key concepts of Piaget's constructivism have been given precise characterizations using logical and algebraic tools. [Piaget 1953; Wermus 1971[2].] Two of these concepts play an important role in my framework. The first is the notion of an operation, which is an internalized action. Piaget requires an operation to have the following four characteristics:

1. "[A]n operation is an action that can be internalized; that is, it can be carried out in thought as well as executed materially." (Piaget [1970], p. 21.)

2. "[I]t is a reversible action; that is, it can take place in one direction or in the opposite direction. This is not true of all actions. If I smoke my pipe through to the end, I cannot reverse this action and have it back again filled up with the same tobacco... On the other hand, addition is an example of an operation. I can add one to one and get two, and I can subtract one from two and get one again." (Piaget [1970], pp. 21–22.)

3. "[An operation] always supposes some conservation, some invariant. It is of course a transformation, since it is an action, but it is a transformation that does not transform everything at once, or else there would be no possibility of reversibility. For instance, in the case of arithmetical addition we can transform the way we group the parts together. We can say $5 + 1$, or $4 + 2$, or $3 + 3$, but the invariant is the sum." (Piaget [1970], p. 22)

4. "[N]o operation exists alone. Every operation is related to a system of operations, or to a total structure as we call it." (Piaget [1970], p. 22. See also Piaget [1967], pp. 208–212.)

The *structure* that Piaget refers to above is an abstract *schema*. He attributes the following characteristics to structures:

---

[2]I am grateful to Ugo Buy for translating this paper from French.

1. "[A] structure is a totality; that is, it is a system governed by laws that apply to the system as such, and not only to one or another element of the system." (Piaget [1970], p. 22. See also Piaget 1967, p. 139.)

2. "[These laws] are laws of transformation; they are not static characteristics." (Piaget [1970], p. 23.)

3. "[A] structure is self-regulating ; that is, in order to carry out these laws of transformation, we need not go outside the system to find some external element. Similarly, once a law of transformation has been applied, the result does not end up outside the system." (Piaget [1970], p. 23.) This property is referred to as *closure*.

4. Structures may relate to each other, and elements of a structure can themselves be structures as a whole. (Piaget [1967], p. 140; Piaget [1970], p. 23.)

5. Structures, while maintaining closure, might still be *open to exchanges with the environment*. (Piaget [1967], pp. 154–158.)

It is this last characteristic that allows the structures to be applied to the environment, thereby making them *meaningful*.

Piaget's interactionism also explicitly took into account the role of the environment in ruling out arbitrary constructions. Piaget's views on this matter are best articulated in his last and most fascinating work that was only published posthumously [Piaget 1981; 1983]. It focuses on how children come to develop the concepts of possibility and necessity, and how it relates to their cognitive development in other respects, such as emergence of operational structures from simple sensory-motor action schemas. The term 'possibility' here refers to the cognitive agent's choices of actions or operations, and 'necessity' to the constraints imposed by the environment.

Piaget's studies, in collaboration with several other psychologists, led him to conclude that possibilities develop through successive differentiations. As the child's repertoire of schemas grows, and her organization becomes more complex, she sees newer ways of interacting with the environment, and therein lies the source of her possibilities. For instance, in one experiment [Piaget 1981, Chap. 7, pp. 70–77], children were given a number of objects, such as a piece of wood, a candle, three lead weights, a sponge, etc., and a cylindrical aquarium partially filled with water. They were then asked to use the objects to raise the water level in the aquarium as high as they can. Younger children were unable to differentiate between their own actions and the interactions between the objects. Some of them would start putting objects in the water in random order. One of them, when she needed more objects, merely took some objects out of the aquarium and put them back, as if that would make a difference. Some children noticed that some objects, like a sponge, float, and tried to use their hands to forcibly submerge them, expecting them to stay submerged. Older children, learn to use the heavier objects to keep the lighter objects submerged. Thus, we see that the action of putting objects in water to raise the level leads, by observing that it has different effects on different objects, to the discovery of the action to use heavier objects to keep floating objects submerged.

Necessity, while seen to be the constraint imposed by the environment, pertains, nonetheless, "to the compositions carried out by the subject and is not an observable datum inherent in objects." [Piaget 1983, p. 135]. In this respect, the source of necessity lies in the organization of the child's schemas, and it reflects the environmental constraint in as much as the organization of the child's schemas has integrated the results of the past interactions with the environment. The point here is simply that the environment responds in a certain way to the cognitive agent's actions, and this response is not always predictable. When the cognitive agent's predictions are not met, then it must reorganize its schemas to integrate this observation. Thus, it is through accommodation that the environment prevents a schema from having an arbitrary structure. But since it is the cognitive agent who decides which actions to carry out on which objects and which parts of the environment, the necessary constraints in the environment are still seen in terms of relationships between the cognitive agent's actions and schemas.

This observation implicitly resolves the paradox of interactionism. For one could argue now that a cognitive agent can act in an environment in a variety of ways. Which actions are actually carried out depends on the cognitive agent. But the results of these actions are determined by reality, and are not controlled by the cognitive agent (though it may have foreseen the results, and may even have initiated the actions expressly to achieve those results). And since these results affect the organization of the cognitive agent's schemas, we see that the cognitive agent's conceptual organization is determined in part by the cognitive agent and in part by the environment.

4.5   Lakoff-Johnson: The Bodily Basis of Cognition

In the last chapter, I discussed the Lakoffian approach to the creation of similarity, and pointed out that it explains the phenomenon by rooting it in a cognitive mechanism that is responsible for creating attributes of an object (or event, or situation). Though we saw there that the Lakoffian approach does not really resolve the paradox of the creation of similarity, this conclusion was arrived at without considering the Lakoffian approach to cognition. Now that we are examining the interactionist views of cognition, it would be interesting to see what additional light, if any, does the Lakoffian approach to cognition shed on either the paradox of the creation of similarity, or the paradox of interactionism in cognition. (The Lakoffian approach to cognition is briefly outlined in Lakoff & Johnson [1980], and elaborated in Johnson [1987] and Lakoff [1987].)

The intent of the Lakoffian approach is to strike a balance between the objectivist view, according to which there is some objective pre-existing ontology and structure of the world, and our concepts reflect this ontology and structure; and the subjectivist view, according to which there is no external constraint on meaning and experience, and concepts can arbitrarily organize one's experience. It would like to argue that reality can be conceptualized in alternate ways, and yet rule out arbitrariness. It wants to maintain that "there are real things, existing independently of us, which constrain both how we interact with them and how we comprehend them." [Lakoff & Johnson 1980, p. 226.] At the same time, it would also like to hold that "meaning is always meaning *to* a person... [and] will not depend on [her] rational knowledge alone but on [her] past experiences, values, feelings, and intuitive insights." [Lakoff & Johnson 1980, p. 227.]

There are two aspects of Lakoff and Johnson's work that must be distinguished here. One is their amassing of empirical linguistic data to show the need to find a balance between the two extremes of objectivism and subjectivism. This is their forte; since the evidence gathered by Lakoff and his colleagues is, indeed, quite impressive. The other aspect has to do with actually striking the balance between objectivism and subjectivism in some reasonable way. It is this second aspect of the Lakoffian approach that is of concern to us here, as we are interested in seeing what light it can shed on the paradox of interactionism.

To achieve all objectives, Lakoff and Johnson developed an *experiential* view of cognition. According to this view, "conceptual structure is meaningful because it is *embodied,* that is, it arises from, and is tied to our pre-conceptual bodily experiences." [Lakoff 1987, p. 267.] It is further suggested that certain experiences that we have are preconceptual in that they are di-rectly meaningful. For instance, our experience of up-down orientation is directly meaningful because of our having bodies of a certain sort. Moreover, these preconcepts have their own structure, or internal logic, that is directly accessible to us. For instance, the part-whole preconcept includes in its basic logic: "If A is a part of B, then B is not a part of A." [Lakoff 1987, p. 273.] And the link preconcept, the bodily basis of which is traced to the umbilical cord, includes as its basic logic: "If A is linked to B, then B is linked to A." [Lakoff 1987, p. 274.]

Other abstract concepts are made meaningful indirectly by the structures of directly meaningful preconcepts. Two mechanisms that can render indi-rect concepts meaningful are metaphor and metonymy. For instance, the abstract experience of marriage is made meaningful metaphorically by the part-whole preconcept: marriage is considered the creation of a whole with the spouses being the parts. A metaphor, in this process, works by mapping the preconcept structure into the abstract domain in such a way that the basic logic of the preconcept structure is preserved.

While in a general way the Lakoffian approach to cognition is quite appealing—its intentions are certainly quite appealing—it does not stand up to close scrutiny. I have already pointed out one major problem with this approach in the last chapter. We saw that the Lakoffian approach cannot explain how an abstract concept, the target of a metaphor, resists arbitrary structuring unless one posits that the target already has a preconceptual structure. For metaphors to map preconcepts into abstract domains, the ab-stract domain must have something that can be mapped into; it must have an ontology. And in order for the condition that the mapping preserve the basic logic of the preconcept to be significant, it must be possible for the abstract domain to sometimes not preserve this basic logic. But the abstract domain can do that, only if it already has its own logic, its own structure. Thus, the abstract domain must have its own preconceptual ontology and structure. But then a couple of other questions immediately arise: Why is it that this preconceptual structure cannot be understood directly and non-metaphorically? Is this preconceptual structure the same for everyone? If this second question is answered affirmatively, then it is only one step away from positing a universal, objective reality. But if it is answered negatively, then one wants to know what it is that structures the same domain dif-ferently for different people *before* the domain is conceptualized. (See also Mac Cormac [1985], p. 68.)

A similar problem, in fact, exists with the preconcepts as well. They are considered to have a gestalt structure that is directly understood. But if the preconcepts are already structured, then this structuring should be the same for everyone. Admitting that the structures are dependent on our bodies, preconcepts should be the same across human beings. But then that would make them 'universals' in the sense that the structure of these preconcepts should be constant across different cultures—a position that Lakoff *et al.* do not seem to want to take, for they oppose it vehemently at several places. Of course, Lakoff and Johnson explicitly mention that the body is not the only thing that structures our concepts, but "a vast background of cultural presuppositions" is involved as well. [Lakoff & Johnson 1980, p. 57.] But then, one needs some explanation of how cultural presuppositions enter the part-whole, up-down, or link preconcepts, which are so fundamental.

There is also the problem with respect to the genesis of preconcepts. Taking them as primitives completely overlooks their development. Piaget's numerous studies clearly show that all the basic level preconcepts of Lakoff and Johnson are a result of intellectual construction. For instance, children do not at once understand the notion of constraint or symmetry that is the basic logic of Lakoff's link preconcept. [Piaget 1936, pp. 323–331.] Of course, Lakoff might argue that he is making precisely the same point, for the genesis of these preconcepts is the evidence that they are rooted in experience. But then it seems quite arbitrary to distinguish them as preconcepts, since they can be analyzed in terms of other more primitive concepts (Piaget's schemas); and a case can be made for the abstract concepts that if their structuring in terms of the preconcepts is quite often used in a culture, and forms the basis of experiencing those concepts, as in 'more is up and less is down,' then why should we not regard them as preconcepts as well.

To sum up, the Lakoffian experiential account *articulates* the empirical phenomena, but *does not explain* them. That many of the conventional metaphors in language have physical domains as their source is an empirical fact. Calling them preconcepts merely captures this fact. That preconcepts are understood directly, is again an empirical fact (ignoring their genesis), as they are not understood as anything else. That abstract domains are understood metaphorically by preconcepts is another empirical fact. That an abstract domain can be structured in different ways by different preconcepts, but not arbitrarily, is yet another empirical fact. So far all these features of the experiential account are statements of empirical fact. The real problem is in explaining how this restructuring of abstract domains is possible, without being arbitrary. And why the abstract domains cannot be understood as such, like preconcepts. This is where the experiential approach is silent.

Anywhere Lakoff and Johnson come close to dealing with this problem, they vehemently assert that it is so—alternative conceptualizations are possible and they are not arbitrary—but say nothing whatsoever to illuminate how and why it is so. In particular, their experiential account is not much help in resolving the paradox of interactionism.

4.6   Conclusions

The main objective of this chapter has been to shed light on the problem of the creation of attributes and structures that occurs as a cognitive agent conceptualizes its environment. The problem is in explaining the apparent paradox that comes from maintaining, on one hand, that the attributes and structures can be created, and hence do not reflect some pre-existing ones, and, on the other hand, that this creation is not arbitrary, but is somehow constrained by the environment (which, nevertheless, does not have a pre-existing structure). In resolving this paradox lies the key to explaining the phenomenon of the creation of similarity, as we saw at the end of the last chapter.

I started with a brief review of some empirical evidence supporting both parts of the paradox. We saw that our minds do, indeed, create attributes and structures in the environment—attributes and structures that are 'seen' even when the corresponding stimuli are not present in the environment. Moreover, different people create different attributes and structures, and in different ways. As a result, the same environment can be conceptualized in radically different fashions—as in the European American view *vs.* the Native American views of the universe. But this creation cannot be arbitrary, as the prehistory of flight clearly attests. We also saw that though the physiology of our body and brain does affect cognition, it does not provide a sufficient set of conditions to rule out arbitrary creation of attributes and structures.

Then I presented, in some detail, three different elaborations of the inter-action view, and discussed what each of them has to say about its paradox. We saw that the development of interactionism in the philosophical vein, originating in Kant and culminating in Goodman, provides the illuminating insight that the cognitive agent asserts its role in establishing the frame of reference, and then the environment objectifies the truths and falsehoods with respect to that frame of reference. While this explanation comes close to resolving the paradox, it does not do so for the following reasons. When different frames of reference can be unified in a frameless 'world,' as in "The Earth moves relative to the Sun" that unifies "The Earth stands still and the Sun moves around it" and "The Sun stands still and the Earth moves around it," then Goodman's account does not provide a satisfactory answer to why one must have a frame of reference, and why one cannot know the environment in a frameless way. This issue is important because if one could know the environment without establishing a frame of reference, then that would become the universal objective knowledge of the environment, and all questions, with respect to any frame of reference, can be answered by consulting it, thereby leaving no room for creation of any kind. And when two frames of reference cannot be reduced to one another, and Goodman provides several examples of them, it is not clear what objectifies them, for one cannot say that it is the autonomous structure of the frameless 'world,' as in the previous case.

Following that, I discussed Piaget's constructivism at some length, since many of its ideas have played a central role in the development of my approach. Though Piaget did not explicitly address the paradox of interactionism, his account implies a clear resolution of it. A subject can act on an object in a variety of ways, but how the object responds to any of the actions depends on the object, and is thus determined by the environment. The equilibrium of interaction between the subject and the environment (that makes it so that the environment meets the expectations of the subject) can be ruptured by the environment, with possibly disastrous consequences for the subject unless an appropriate accommodation takes place. This is the key insight of Piaget that has been incorporated in my framework.

Finally, I presented the experiential view of cognition, being developed by Lakoff and Johnson, that emphasizes the bodily basis of cognition. Acknowledging the mass of empirical data from linguistics that Lakoff and his colleagues have gathered to strengthen the view that our concepts do not reflect some pre-existing mind-independent structure in the environment, which is a Herculean task in itself, we see, nevertheless, that the experiential account is quite vague, and sometimes even contradictory, on how the environment objectifies our conceptual structures (to prevent them from being arbitrary) without having a pre-existing and mind-independent structure itself. This is the problem I tackle, using the insights of Goodman and Piaget, in the next chapter.

Part II

A Theory

Chapter 5

An Interactionist Approach to Cognition: Informal Overview

5.1 Introduction

We saw in the last chapter that there is a paradox implicit in the interaction view of cognition. The paradox is in assigning reality the role of constraining our conceptual organizations, but denying it a mind-independent, preconceptual ontology and structure. (If reality is given a preconceptual ontology and structure, then this becomes the 'universal' knowledge structure, an idea that is expressly rejected by the interaction view.) We also saw that the theories of Goodman, Piaget and Lakoff & Johnson, each of whom approached interactionism by a different route, fail to resolve this paradox explicitly, though some of them come quite close to doing so. You might also recall, from Chapter 3, that resolving this paradox is necessary to give a satisfactory account of similarity-creating metaphors, and to address an analogous paradox raised by the phenomenon of creation of similarity.

In this chapter and the next, I lay out a formal framework for the interaction view of cognition that is specifically articulated to deal with its implicit paradox. This chapter is concerned with introducing all the key concepts of my approach informally and intuitively, and a precise mathematical treatment is taken up in the next chapter. It is hoped that the discussion of this chapter will motivate you to press on through the formal details of the next chapter, and will make them easier to digest.

To elaborate the exact nature of interaction, one must begin by pinning down its two components. On one side of interaction are the internal repre-

sentations of the cognitive agent, which I refer to as *concept networks.* Now
there is no problem in articulating precisely what the concept networks are.
They have been variously characterized as *schemas* by Piaget, as *network
models* by Hesse [1974, Chap. 2], as *cognitive domains* by Scott *et al.* [1979],
as *form* by Bateson [1979], as *mental spaces* by Fauconnier [1985], as *mental
models* by Holland *et al.* [1986], and as *idealized cognitive models* by Lakoff
[1987], to mention a few. For my purpose here, combining Piaget's schemas
and Cassirer's symbols, I choose a somewhat general characterization of them
as symbolic systems having an operational structure, which correspond to algebras.

On the other side of interaction is reality, which is a different cup of tea.
I have already emphasized the paradoxical position that the interaction view
creates with respect to the ontology and structure of reality. To resolve this
paradox, I first introduce the *sensorimotor data set,* which is reality that is
made available for conceptualization through the sensorimotor apparatus of
the cognitive agent. Then I argue that while the ontology of the sensorimotor data set is determined by the cognitive agent's perceptual and motor
apparatus, its structure (as seen from this ontology) is determined by reality.
The sensorimotor data set may not be cognitively visible to the cognitive
agent; we cannot 'see' the image on our retina, even though it forms the raw
data for our visual system. Following Piaget's action-oriented approach, the
sensorimotor data set is also formalized as an algebra.

Then I introduce the concept of *cognitive relations,* which are links that
connect concepts in the concept networks with parts of the sensorimotor
data set. Since the sensorimotor data set is rooted in reality, cognitive
relations become the links between the internal concepts of the cognitive
agent and reality. Moreover, following Cassirer, I maintain that it is only by
forming a cognitive relation—by instantiating concepts (symbols) of a concept network—that reality acquires an experiential ontology for the cognitive
agent. I refer to this experiential ontology as the *environment.* Thus, it is a
cognitive relation that makes a concept network *meaningful* and it is a cognitive relation that brings reality within the cognitive grasp of the cognitive
agent in the form of an environment.

A cognitive relation is formed by the cognitive agent. And since it is a
cognitive relation that gives an experiential ontology to the environment, it
follows that the ontology of the environment is determined by the cognitive
agent. However, the structure of the environment with respect to this ontology is determined by reality (which acts through the autonomous structure
of the sensorimotor data sets), and is external to the cognitive agent. In this

observation lies the key to resolving the paradox of interactionism.

A concept network instantiated by a cognitive relation is referred to as a *cognitive model.* In a cognitive model, two autonomous structures can be distinguished. One is the structure of the concept network (determined by the cognitive agent), and the other is the structure of the environment (determined by reality) as seen from the experiential ontology created by the cognitive relation. Ideally, one would like the two structures to be the same. At least this is the goal that the cognitive agent must strive for, if it wishes to use the cognitive model to make useful predictions about the environment. I refer to the structure preserving characteristic of some cognitive models (and cognitive relations) as *coherency.*

How can the cognitive agent maintain the coherency of its cognitive models? It cannot change the structure of the environment with respect to any given ontology. The only parameters under its control are the structure of the concept networks and the ontology of the environment (how the networks are instantiated via cognitive relations). Correspondingly, I introduce two mechanisms the cognitive agent might use, individually or in concert, to keep its cognitive models coherent. One mechanism, called *accommodation,* works by changing the structure of the concept network, while keeping the cognitive relation (and the experiential ontology of the environment) fixed. The other mechanism, called *projection,* works by keeping the structure of the concept network invariant, but modifying the cognitive relation, thereby changing the experiential ontology of the environment, so that its structure (which is determined by reality) can become coherent with the structure of the concept network.

For instance, mapping a terrain is an accommodating process. The meanings of concepts like 'land' and 'water' are kept fixed, but the relations between these concepts are altered to reflect the state of affairs in the environment. Notice, however, that it is the cognitive agent who determines what 'land' and 'water' mean. Lines of latitude and longitude, on the other hand, are examples of projection. The structure of the concept network is fixed and the environment is given an ontology accordingly. Reality, however, constrains the possible ontologies. That is, since it is reality that determines the structure of the environment with respect to any given ontology, if the cognitive agent wishes to see a certain structure in the environment, several possible ontologies are ruled out by reality, for they do not result in the requisite structure. The lines of latitude and longitude can be instantiated in more than one way, but the autonomous structure of reality rules out many possibilities. For instance, New York City, Copenhagen and Tokyo cannot be all assigned the same latitude. Moreover, once the system of reference is put in place, whether two given places have the same latitude or not is no longer a matter of arbitrary decision by the cognitive agent, but is a matter of objective verification.

Thus, accommodation is the process by which the environment affects (acting through the sensorimotor data set) the structures of the cognitive agent's concept network. And projection is the process by which the cognitive agent affects the structure seen in the environment. I am deliberately using the word 'affects' and not 'determines' here because in each of the two processes, both the cognitive agent and the environment play a role in determining the structure that results from the process. The difference lies only from the perspective of an outside observer, whereby projection can be viewed 'as if' the cognitive agent is the originator of the perturbations and the environment the recipient; and vice versa for accommodation.

Clearly, my projection corresponds to Piaget's assimilation. Why, then, am I coining a new term? The reason is that Piaget's assimilation has been given a very wide interpretation. As I pointed out in the last chapter, Piaget himself uses it in at least two different ways: biological assimilation, a mechanism by which an organism absorbs energy from its environment and transforms it to a form that it can use, a familiar example being ingestion; and behavioral, or cognitive assimilation, which is closer to my projection mechanism. Moreover, cognitive assimilation itself is given a broad scope: for instance, Piaget argues that it is primarily responsible for the formation of memory. (See Piaget [1976], p. 141.) Though I do not necessarily reject the idea that the very same mechanism can in fact underlie such seemingly diverse processes, I do not wish to see my projection—which is given a very precise meaning in my approach to interactionism—burdened by having to explain them all.

Of course, this is only a broad overview, and in the rest of this chapter I elaborate my interaction view of cognition by means of examples, definitions, and depictions. I first present a simple, yet surprisingly rich example to illustrate all the key concepts of my framework in Section 2. In the subsequent three sections I elaborate upon concept networks, environments and sensorimotor data sets, and cognitive relations. In Section 6, I examine the mechanisms of projection and accommodation in more depth. In Section 7, I present some features of cognitive models, such as 'groupings' induced on the environment, and introduce some useful terms. In Section 8, I introduce the concept of a 'layered cognitive system,' and point out how multiple 'worlds,' in the sense of Goodman, can be created. Finally, in Section 9, I summarize

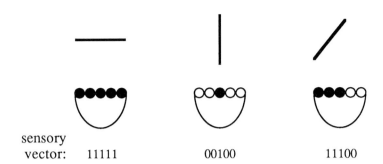

sensory
vector: 11111   00100   11100

FIGURE 5.1: Sensory organ of Spinner. The 'eye' consists of five cells that work in an on-off fashion. The off cells are shown as darkened. A line (or any other object) in front of the eye forms an image on it by casting a shadow and turning off certain cells. The 'states' of the eye are represented by sensory vectors. The three examples here show the image cast on the eye by lines in different orientations, and the corresponding sensory vectors.

the main theses embodied in my framework of interactionism.

5.2   An Example

To start with, I introduce a somewhat artificial, but nonetheless interesting and rich example to introduce all the various features of my framework of interactionism. Let us transport ourselves to the two dimensional world of Edwin Abbott's *Flatland*. We find ourselves in an area of *Flatland* that is inhabited by several straight-lines and a cognitive agent named Spinner. Spinner has very simple sensory and effectory organs that enable it to interact with its world. The sensory organ consists of five light sensitive cells, closely packed together and arranged in a row, as shown in Figure 5.1. Each cell works in an on-off fashion, meaning that when the light impinging on it exceeds a certain threshold then the cell turns 'on,' remaining 'off' otherwise. The cells respond instantly: that is, as soon as the light impinging upon a cell exceeds its threshold, the cell turns on, and when the light level falls below its threshold, the cell turns off immediately.

Uniform diffused light pervades all *Flatland*. When a straight-line is in front of Spinner's 'eye,' it casts a shadow on the eye and turns some cells off. Obviously, which cells get turned off depends on the length of the line as well as its position and orientation with respect to the eye. A few situations are shown in Figure 5.1. We can ignore the effect of the distance between the eye and the line. Also, it is assumed that all the lines have a small thickness, and the cells in the eye are closely packed together, so that when a line is perpendicular to the eye, exactly one cell in the eye is turned off.

I represent the image formed on the eye at any time by a five bit binary string. The bits, from left to right, correspond to the cells of the eye, also from left to right with the eye facing up. A 0 in any bit position means that there is no image formed on the corresponding cell (it is turned on) and a 1 in any bit position means that an image is formed on the corresponding cell (it has been turned off). I refer to any such binary string as a *sensory vector*. Thus, the sensory vector represents the output of the five cells in Spinner's eye in any given situation. In Figure 5.1, the sensory vectors are shown below the corresponding images.

The five cells in Spinner's eye also constitute its effectory organ. Spinner can emit a small jet-stream of air from any one (but not more than one) of these cells at any time. This stream can only be emitted in short bursts, but the intensity of a burst can be varied somewhat by Spinner. The jet-stream can cause the line facing the eye, if there is one, to be rotated or pushed back, as shown in Figure 5.2.

As for the sensory organ, activation of the effectory organ at any time is represented by means of an *effectory vector*. An effectory vector also has five positions corresponding to the five cells, and the value in each position indicates the input to the corresponding cell that determines the intensity of the burst emitted by that cell. However, instead of allowing only 0 or 1 in any position, I allow any number from 0 to 3. As one might expect, a 0 in any position means that the corresponding cell is inactive as an effectory organ. A non-zero number in a position means that the corresponding cell is active, where the magnitude of the number approximately represents the intensity of the burst. I say 'approximately' because whereas a 2-burst is stronger than a 1-burst and weaker than a 3-burst, it is not necessarily twice as strong as a 1-burst. I leave it at that because to make things any more precise would require a comprehensively worked out physics of motion for *Flatland*, which may be an interesting task in itself but an unnecessary and distracting one for this example. Valid effectory vectors are only those that have zeros in at least four positions. Effectory vectors for the activation patterns in Figure 5.2 are shown next to them.

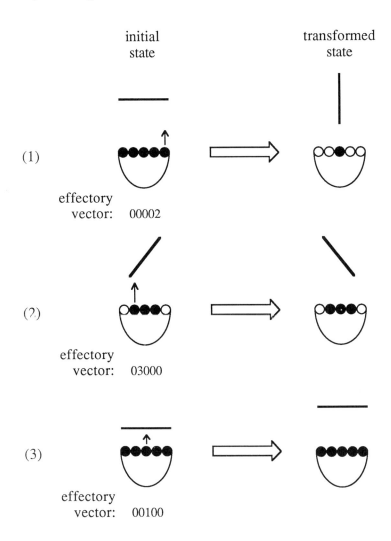

initial state   transformed state

(1)

effectory vector: 00002

(2)

effectory vector: 03000

(3)

effectory vector: 00100

FIGURE 5.2: Effectory Organ of Spinner. The cells in the eye double as effectory organs by emitting a jet-stream (shown by an arrow) of air. The jet-stream, emitted in bursts, may cause the line facing the eye to rotate. Spinner can emit a burst from only one of the cells at any one time, but the burst can be emitted in three possible strengths. Here, three examples are shown to demonstrate how Spinner may use its effectory organ to transform its world.

Notice that the sensory and the effectory organs of Spinner restrict its world view considerably. The sensory organ allows for only thirty two different states, and whatever world Spinner happens to be in, it is reduced to one of these states. Similarly, the effectory organ of Spinner allows fifteen possible actions that it can take in any situation at any time. Thus, the sensorimotor apparatus makes every world manifest to Spinner in a certain way. I refer to this manifestation as the *sensorimotor data set*. A sensorimotor data set has an *ontology*, which includes the sensory states and the actions of Spinner, and a *structure*, which shows how the sensory states are affected by the actions. Note here that though the ontology of any sensorimotor data set is completely determined by the sensory and effectory organs of Spinner, its structure is external to Spinner, and is completely determined by reality. For instance, given that the image on the eye of Spinner at some time is 11111 and it activates its effectory organ as 00002, the image that is subsequently formed on Spinner's eye is determined by the external reality. Three examples are shown in Figure 5.3. In each case it is the nature of the object facing Spinner that determines the outcome of this action.

Though the correspondence between the sensory states and the things in its world is rigidly fixed in the case of Spinner, a cognitive agent might be able to change it by altering the bias of its sensorimotor apparatus. But even then, the structure of the sensorimotor data set resulting from any given bias of the sensorimotor apparatus is determined by reality. I elaborate this point later in Section 8.

Now assume that the world of Spinner consists of various zones in the form of uniform parallel strips, as shown in Figure 5.4. The width of each zone exactly equals the length of Spinner's eye, and the boundaries between zones run perpendicular to the axis of the eye. Spinner can occupy any one zone at a time, and has the full view of the part of the zone facing the eye. It cannot change its orientation with respect to the inter-zone boundaries, but it can hop from one zone to another. This hop is, however, a discreet event so that Spinner can never have a view of more than one zone at any time.

Each zone is inhabited by exactly one straight-line, and the length of each line is equal to the width of its zone. Since all zones are of the same width, it means that all lines are of the same length also. Thus, when Spinner is in a zone, and the line occupying that zone is facing it and is parallel to its eye, the image of the line covers all five cells; that is, the sensory vector is 11111. The lines can move around in their respective zones. A line can turn around its middle point to any degree and in any direction, and can move horizontally and vertically, as long as none of the movements cause any part

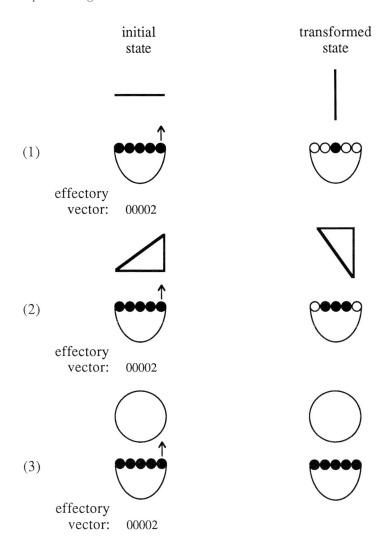

FIGURE 5.3: The three examples shown here demonstrate that the 'structure' of the sensorimotor data set is rooted in the external world. In all three cases, the initial state of the eye and the activation of the effectory organ are the same. Yet, the transformed state, which depends on the nature of the object facing the eye, is different in each case.

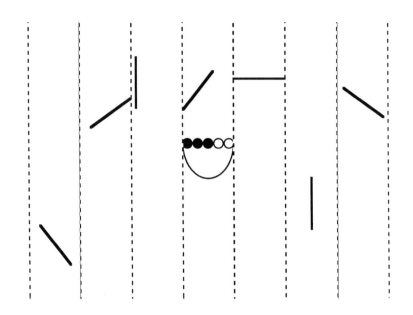

FIGURE 5.4: The Environment of Spinner. It consists of zones in the form of parallel strips. Each zone is inhabited by a line. The lines can turn around their middle point and move vertically and horizontally, as long as the movements keep them completely inside their respective zones. Spinner can hop from one zone to another, but that happens as a discreet event. Thus, Spinner can never view more than one zone simultaneously.

of the line to venture out of its zone.

The lines love to spin around, and can often be seen dancing wildly. Spinner can also cause the line in its zone, if there is one facing it, to spin. In fact, Spinner loves doing that, (and so do the lines,) so much so that over the generations 'mental structures' have evolved in Spinner that reflect its understanding of the behavior of the lines, as well as its ways of affecting this behavior. I show some of these mental structures, or *concept networks* as I refer to them from now on, in Figure 5.5. CN1 in 5.5(a) shows Spinner's concept network for making the lines spin; CN2 in 5.5(b) is a concept network for understanding the lines' behavior when they spin by themselves; and CN3 in 5.5(c) is a concept network Spinner uses for centering a line in its zone if it is off-center.

A concept network is essentially a structured set of concepts. I make a distinction between symbols (object-concepts) and operators (functional-concepts). In the concept network CN1, for example, 'vline' and 'hline' are symbols, whereas 'qturn' and 'e-lturn' are operators. An operator specifies how a symbol can be derived from other symbols. Thus, the operators of a concept network connect the symbols in specific ways, thereby imparting the concept network with a *structure.*

All concept networks are fully internal to the cognitive agent in that it can access and manipulate them as necessary.

Concept networks are best seen as *potential representations.* That is, as shown in Figure 5.5, the concept networks do not yet mean anything or refer to anything. (Though, since I mentioned the intended purpose of these concept networks above, you may have guessed what the 'conventional' referents of the concepts of Figure 5.5 might be. If not, it will become clear shortly.)

This much understood, I now come to the process of *interpreting* these concept networks. A concept network can be interpreted in a world by associating its concepts with parts of the world. Of course, since Spinner does not have direct epistemic access to the world, this process is necessarily mediated by the sensorimotor data set.

In Figure 5.6, I show how the concept network CN1 corresponds to the world of Spinner via its sensorimotor data set. Object-concepts of the concept network correspond to various lines in the world through the sensory organ. Operators correspond to the actions, via the effectory organ that can change the position of a line, thereby altering the sensory vector. The correspondence between the concept network and the world of Spinner is referred to as a *cognitive relation* and the interpreted concept network is referred to as a

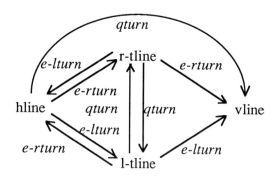

(a) Concept Network CN1: For making the lines spin.

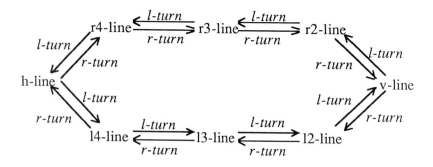

(b) Concept Network CN2: For understanding when lines spin by themselves.

$$2\text{line} \xrightarrow{h1\text{-}turn} 3\text{line} \xrightarrow{h2\text{-}turn} 4\text{line} \xrightarrow{h2\text{-}turn} \text{hline}$$

(c) Concept Network CN3: For centering the lines.

FIGURE 5.5: Concept Networks of Spinner. All operators are shown as arrows and take one argument. The result of applying an operator is to generate the symbol at the tip of the arrow from the symbol at its base.

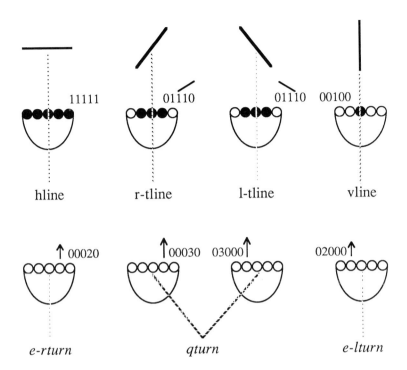

FIGURE 5.6: An interpretation of the concept network CN1. Symbols of the concept network correspond to the objects of the environment, and the operators correspond to the actions that might change these objects. In this case, actions are caused by the effectory organ of Spinner. Sensory and effectory vectors corresponding to the image on the eye and actions of Spinner are also shown.

cognitive model.

Two things should be noticed immediately about this interpretation. First of all, the symbols 'l-tline' and 'r-tline' correspond to two different lines in the world—or what is the same, a line in two different orientations—via the same sensory vector 01110. Thus, the cognitive model effectively allows Spinner to distinguish between two different situations in the world that both form the same image on its eye. Obviously, it is the effectory organ of Spinner that is making this distinction possible. Since the orientation of a line is thus detectable by the combined sensory and effectory organs of Spinner, I represent this information by putting an appropriately tilted line above the sensory vector when necessary. This notation is shown in Figure 5.6.

Secondly, notice that the operator 'qturn' corresponds to two different actions of Spinner—those given by effectory vectors 03000 and 00030. These two actions are said to be *grouped* by the cognitive model, since seen from CN1, their effects cannot be distinguished. This phenomenon of grouping can be evidenced in many facets of perception and cognition.

The interpretation of the concept network creates an experiential ontology of the world for Spinner. This experiential ontology is called an *environment*. The counterparts of the symbols and the operators, respectively, are referred to as the *objects* and the *transformations* of the environment. Thus, one can view the process of interpreting a concept network as that of establishing a correspondence between the symbols of the concept network and the objects of the environment, and between the operators of the concept network and the transformations of the environment. However, it must always be remembered that the objects and the transformations in the environment come to exist only through the interpretation of the concept network, and do not exist independently of the interpretation. This is not to say that reality does not exist prior to conceptualization, but only to say that *the ontology of reality does not exist prior to conceptualization.* This aspect of my framework essentially echoes the theme of Cassirer.

Another thing to be emphasized is that though the cognitive agent determines the ontology of the environment by interpreting a concept network, the structure of the environment with respect to this ontology is determined by reality. This point has its root in a similar observation made earlier with respect to the sensorimotor data set. The transformations of the environment are grounded in reality, and must be distinguished from the operators internal to the cognitive agent. Even though the transformations are actualized by interpreting the operators, once brought into existence, they affect objects in their own way, and need not follow the operational structure of

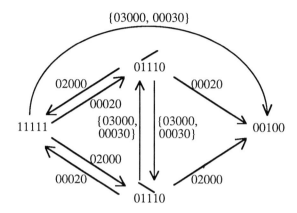

FIGURE 5.7: Spinner's 'world-view' as seen from the concept network CN1 under the interpretation of Figure 5.6. The symbols are replaced by the corresponding states of the environment, shown here as sensory vectors with tilted lines on the top to represent orientation of the lines, if relevant. The operators are replaced by corresponding transformations, which are activations of Spinner's effectory organ, shown here as effectory vectors. Notice that the transformations 03000 and 00030 are 'grouped' together, and are not distinguished in this 'world-view.'

the concept network. It is always up to reality to structure the environment.

Of course, a cognitive agent might be able to change the ontology of the environment by interpreting a different concept network, or interpreting the same concept network differently, thereby forcing reality to restructure the environment with respect to this new ontology. In fact, as I argue in Chapter 7, in this restructuring lies the key to metaphor.

The structure of Spinner's environment with respect to the ontology created by the interpretation of Figure 5.6 is shown in Figure 5.7. This structure happens to be isomorphic to the structure of the concept network CN1 [Figure 5.5(a)], but that might not necessarily be the case. When the two structures of a cognitive model (or cognitive relation) are isomorphic, I call the model (or the relation) *coherent*. Obviously, a cognitive model must be coherent if the cognitive agent is going to use it to plan its actions and successfully predict changes in the environment.

Thus, what the cognitive agent 'sees' in the world through a coherent cognitive model is an isomorphic copy of the concept network. This is a consequence of my assumption that the only way to give an ontology to the world is by interpreting a concept network in it. And once such an interpretation is made, the ontology of the environment is fixed. Its structure is then also fixed by reality, and this is the environment that the cognitive agent experiences in the world. And because the cognitive model is coherent, this experienced structure of the world is isomorphic to the structure of the concept network.

It must be emphasized here that coherency, as I have defined it, is a characteristic of cognitive models and cognitive relations and not of concept networks. Therefore, coherency should not be confused with the internal consistency of symbolic systems, as it directly relates to the autonomous structure of reality.

Coherency of cognitive models, however, is not something a cognitive agent can cognitively verify. For instance, the structure of Figure 5.7 is not directly accessible to Spinner, except via experimentation. And although experimentation can prove some cognitive models to be incoherent, it cannot prove them coherent. There is always the possibility that the environment, unbeknownst to Spinner, has changed so that it no longer has the same structure with respect to the ontology established by Spinner. In fact, I introduce such a possibility just a little bit later.

A word needs to be said about transformations. In Figure 5.6, the transformations that the operators of CN1 are made to correspond to are the actions of the cognitive agent itself. However, this might not always be the case. For instance, in an interpretation of CN2 (not shown here), the transformations corresponding to its operators are caused by the lines themselves. Moreover, in certain situations there might not even be any agent causing a transformation, and it might be merely the cognitive agent's way of understanding changes happening in the environment. Thus, operators of a concept network can represent actions of the cognitive agent as well as actions of other 'real' or 'hypothetical' agents. This is the reason I chose to call the counterparts of the operators 'transformations' rather than 'actions.'

Next I introduce the notion of conventional interpretation. If a concept network is habitually interpreted in a certain way, that interpretation (and the resulting cognitive model) is called *conventional*. The interpretation of Figure 5.6 can be dubbed conventional, if we assume that that the concept network CN1 is usually interpreted that way by Spinner. A concept network

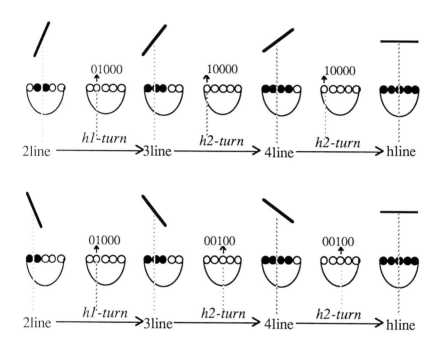

FIGURE 5.8: Two different interpretations of the concept network CN3.

might be genuinely ambiguous in having more than one conventional interpretation; just as a word can be ambiguous by having more than one literal meanings. For instance, concept network CN3 has several interpretations, two of which are shown in Figure 5.8. Moreover, all of these might well be preferred interpretations if Spinner is habituated to all of them.

So far we have kept Spinner in its natural world, and therefore it is not surprising that all the interpretations of its concept networks were conventional. Now let us transport it to an alien world that is very similar to its own, except that all the lines are slightly smaller. The lines in this new world are such that when they are parallel to the eye of Spinner, their shadows cover only four cells. In every other way, they behave just like the five cell long lines.

What does Spinner do in this new world? It still has its concept networks.

But they no longer have conventional interpretations. If we stick to the old interpretations, then they are no longer coherent, as the reader can easily verify. In order to keep them coherent, Spinner is forced either to *reinterpret* its concept networks, thereby changing the ontology of the environment (and its structure), or to *restructure* them. I refer to the process of reinterpreting existing concept networks as *projection* and the process of *restructuring* existing concept networks—of which creating new concept networks is a special case—as *accommodation*.

In projection, the structure of the concept network is kept invariant, and the correspondence between the parts of the network (its concepts) and parts of the environment (its objects and transformations) is varied until a coherent fit is reached. A projective interpretation of the concept network CN1 in the new environment is shown in Figure 5.9(a). The process might work by first interpreting a small set of symbols and operators and then extending this correspondence coherently. For instance, in this case, if 'hline' is interpreted as the sensory vector 01111 and 'e-lturn' as the effectory vector 00200, then the result of applying 'e-lturn' to 'hline,' namely the symbol 'l-tline,' must be interpreted as the result of applying transformation 00200 to the sensory vector 01111, which is the sensory vector 00110. Obviously, it might be necessary to go back and reinterpret the initial set of symbols and operators, or choose a different set to be the initial set, depending on one's objective. Notice that the interpretation shown in Figure 5.9 is very different from the conventional interpretation of Figure 5.6. The autonomous structure of the environment, with respect to the new ontology created by this reinterpretation of CN1 is shown in Figure 5.9(b).

You might notice that the interpretation of Figure 5.9 groups two different vertical positions of a line, that are otherwise distinguishable, in one category. Thus, as viewed from the concept network, these two different states in the sensorimotor data set are seen as one thing.

In accommodation, the concept network is restructured. Or if the old concept network is not discarded, we can say that a new concept network is created. However, the new concept network is created from the ontology provided by the cognitive agent's perceptual apparatus. The process works in a sort of 'bottom-up' fashion. Spinner plays with the sensory and effectory vectors until some pattern is detected. One such pattern that might result from this interaction is shown in Figure 5.10(a). Then this pattern is *generalized* to a concept network, as in Figure 5.10(b). Once generalized, the concept network can have the original pattern as a conventional interpretation, but is now capable of admitting other interpretations as well. Obviously,

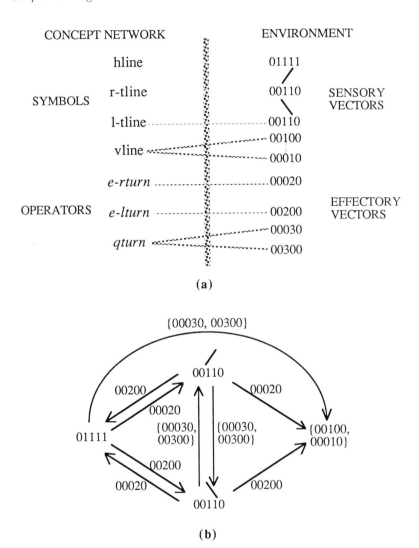

FIGURE 5.9: A projection of the concept network CN1 onto the new environment in which all lines are four cells long instead of five. The correspondence between the elements of the concept network and parts of the environment is shown in (a). The 'world-view' from the concept network CN1 with this interpretation is shown in (b).

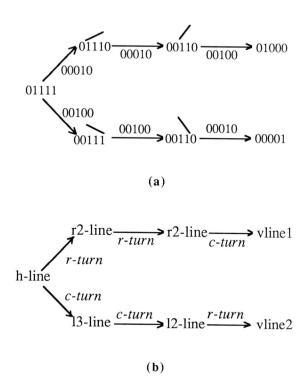

(a)

(b)

FIGURE 5.10: An example of accommodation. The pattern of interaction
shown in (a) reveals a structure of the environment based on the ontology
given to it by Spinner's sensorimotor apparatus. Generalizing this pattern
results in the concept network shown in (b).

accommodation involves learning and inductive generalization.

The example presented in this section was simple, but illustrated all the major features of the theory. I now examine these features in more depth one at a time.

5.3   Concept Networks

Concepts, while they have a referential function in being able to connect with our sense impressions, nonetheless enjoy an independent status that allows us to combine them in various ways to generate non-referential conceptual structures. The existence of mathematics, various forms of fiction, etc. clearly attests to this non-referential role of concepts. In this process, however, concepts show an inherent structure that precludes arbitrary combinations. For instance, each of the concepts 'child' and 'parent' is the converse of the other; and the concept of 'mother' is subsumed by the concept of 'parent.' Another example is provided by dictionary meanings. A dictionary essentially relates concepts to one another without connecting them to the things in the external world. Thus, we can talk about *concept networks,* which are structured sets of concepts. My concept networks correspond to the 'schemas' of Piaget, the 'schematas' of Goodman [1976, II, 6, pp. 71–74], and the 'idealized cognitive models' of Lakoff [1987].

A concept network, in my characterization, has two components: a set of symbols and a set of operators. Operators specify how certain symbols can be combined to generate other symbols. In the example above, all the operators were one-place operators, but this might not always be the case. I allow n-place operators for any finite n.

Consider some examples. The natural number system can be seen as a concept network. The symbols of this concept network would be all the positive integers including zero. We could have two binary operators: addition and multiplication. The addition operator '+' would take two numbers (symbols) as arguments and combine them to output another number (symbol). The multiplication operator '×' would be similar.

A street map provides an example of a different kind of concept network. One could take various places in the city to be the symbols of this network, and directions like 'go east one block,' and 'turn left at the second intersection,' to be the operators. Notice that the operators can be unary ('go east one block from X'), binary ('go one block from X in direction Y'), ternary ('go one block from X in direction Y and then turn and go two blocks in direction Z'), and so on, where X, Y, and Z are variables for the symbols. Here also, when an operator is applied to the given symbols, another symbol results.

In this second example, we see that while a concept network is necessarily internal to the cognitive agent, it might be manifested in some external object. Thus, the map is an external object that manifests the corresponding concept network. The symbols and the operators of this concept network are, nevertheless, fully internal to the cognitive agent. The idea that when going two blocks east from the train station, one ends up at the post office is an internal conceptual structure in the mind of the cognitive agent. The map, taken as an object by itself, is only a network of colored lines and regions, and there are no symbols or operators there.

Another thing to emphasize is that the action of the operators on the symbols should not be confused with the actual result of taking the corresponding actions in reality. The post office may not actually be two blocks east of the train station, but if this is what the map shows, then this is what the operator 'go two blocks east' gives when applied to the symbol 'train station.' Thus, concept networks are only *potential* representations of reality, and do not necessarily correspond to anything by themselves.

The operators play many useful roles in a concept network. First of all, they can be made to represent actions of the cognitive agent, as in CN1 above, thereby allowing it to 'foresee' the results of its actions without actually carrying them out. One can compare different routes to the airport to see which one might be shorter, without actually taking the routes. Secondly, by making the operators represent actions of other 'real' or 'hypothetical' agents causing changes in the environment operators make it possible for the cognitive agent to predict the changes in the environment. If your friend told you that she will be taking the subway from the airport going towards downtown, and getting off at the third stop, you could figure out from the map to which station you should go in order to meet her. Both these applications are extremely useful for any kind of planning involving a sequence of interchanges with the environment.

Thirdly, operators allow for a certain economy of representation, expression, and communication. For instance, in the concept network of the natural number system, one need not keep the infinite set of symbols in one's head. Since any number can be generated from '0' and '1' by applying an appropriate sequence of operators, only two symbols and two operators need be explicitly represented. Of course, if one has to deal with large numbers frequently, then this representation would be far from economical, but then some other finitary representation might be chosen. In the map concept network, it is not necessary to remember the location of every place on the map. If you know where the train station is, the location of any other place can be fixed giving directions for how to get there from the train station.

The operators of a concept network also endow its symbols with *structures*. An operator, we have seen, combines symbols to generate another symbol. The process, however, can also be viewed in reverse: that is, an operator can be seen as decomposing a symbol into other symbols. Some or all of these symbols can then be further decomposed into other symbols, and so on. Any such decomposition of a symbol into other symbols is called a *description* of it. For instance, the directions for going to the post office from the train station could be called a description of the symbol 'post office.' (The symbol 'post office' in the map is really 'the location of the post office,' and not 'the post office building.')

Obviously, a symbol can typically have many descriptions. There might be more than one way to get to the post office from the train station, though some of them might involve longer detours. In Figure 5.11, I show some descriptions of the symbols '3' and 'vline' in the concept networks natural number system and CN1 respectively. The descriptions are depicted as labeled ordered trees, where every leaf of a tree is labeled with a symbol of the concept network and every intermediate node having n children is labeled with an n-ary operator of the concept network.

For a given description of a symbol, the symbols that result from the corresponding decomposition process are called the *components* of the original symbol; and the sequence of operators is called the *structure* of the symbol (based on the given description). Thus, different descriptions of a symbol 'see' it as made up of different components and having different structures. One thing to notice here is that every symbol is a description of itself: the description that sees the symbol as an indivisible whole.

A concept closely related to decomposition is that of *generation*. Given a set of symbols of a concept network, it might be possible to generate other symbols from them by applying appropriate sequences of operators. The set of all symbols that can be so generated, along with the operators of the concept network, is called the *subnetwork* generated by the given set of symbols. If this subnetwork includes all the symbols of the concept network, then we say that the initial set of symbols is a *generating set* of the concept network. For instance, in the natural number system concept network, the set $\{0, 1\}$ is a generating set of the concept network, whereas the set $\{0, 2\}$ generates a subnetwork containing all the even numbers. In CN1, any of

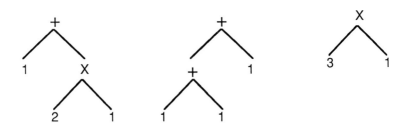

(a) Three different 'descriptions' of the symbol '3'.

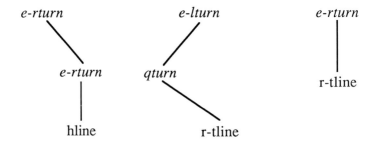

(b) Three different 'descriptions' of the symbol 'vline' in the concept network CN1.

FIGURE 5.11: Two examples to illustrate that a symbol in a concept network may typically have many 'descriptions'.

the symbols except 'vline' can generate the entire concept network. In the map concept network, all the places that can be reached from the train station (according to the map) form the subnetwork generated by the set {'train station'}. A small island that is in the middle of the lake would not be included in this subnetwork, unless the map concept network contains operators like 'swim' or 'take a boat.'

Another way of looking at this process of generation might be helpful. A given set of symbols can be viewed as a set of 'primitives.' The subnetwork generated by this set is that part of the concept network that can be described by using these primitives. Notice that every symbol in the subnetwork has a description with all its components included in the given set of primitives, implying that every symbol in the subnetwork can be described in terms of these primitives. A generating set of the concept network, from this view, is essentially a set of primitives, in terms of which the whole concept network can be described.

A generating set of a concept network is said to be *minimal* if no symbol in this set can be generated from the remaining ones. Thus, a minimal generating set contains the minimum number of primitives that are necessary to describe the concept network. For the natural number system concept network, a minimum generating set is $\{0, 1\}$; whereas for CN1 any of the sets {hline}, {r-tline}, and {l-tline} is a minimal generating set. Thus, since a concept network does not have to have a unique minimal generating set, it can be described in a variety of ways, and in terms of different primitives. This is a key factor in explaining various characteristics of cognition, including metaphor.

Speaking of requirements brings me to the constraints the concept networks must satisfy in my framework: so far, I have only said that a concept network consists of symbols and operators. The symbols and operators, in order to constitute a *concept network,* must meet the following three criteria:

1. The set of operators must be *finite.*

2. Every operator must be *physically realizable.* In other words, for every operator there must exist some physical system that implements it.

3. The concept network must be *finitely generated:* that is, it must have at least one finite generating set.

These three requirements on concept networks ensure their finite representability, thereby addressing the issues raised in Partee [1979].

It is easily verified that all the concept networks I introduced so far satisfy these three constraints. Notice that the set of symbols of a concept network can be finite or infinite. A concept network is said to be *finite* if its set of symbols is finite and *infinite* otherwise. Natural number system is an infinite concept network, whereas CN1 is a finite one.

At this point I would like to make some remarks relating my concept networks to some similar notions that have been proposed elsewhere. In doing so I must emphasize that mine is a precise and formal characterization, whereas the ones mentioned below, though based on empirical evidence, are nevertheless vaguely specified at best. For this reason I believe that much can be accomplished by bridging the gap between the two approaches: the empirical concept networks can be given a formal basis, and the usefulness and scope of this framework can be widened considerably.

- A concept network can have many operators that change a given set of symbols into another symbol. For instance, in the 'family' concept network, each of the operators 'gives birth to,' 'nurtures,' and 'contributes genetic material to' can change the symbol 'mother' into 'child.' Moreover, in instantiating the concept network, it is not necessary to instantiate every operator. Thus, the concepts 'mother' and 'child' can be applied solely on the basis of 'nurtures' operator. This allows my concept networks to show the *clustering* effect in the sense of Lakoff [1987, pp. 74–76].

  Given a concept network, one can ordain a certain subnetwork of it that includes a generating set of the concept network, to be the 'prototype.' Then, one can define a measure function that assigns a 'distance' to every symbol of the concept network depending on the length of the shortest description tree of that symbol rooted in the prototype subnetwork. This would give the concept network a *radial* structure in the sense of Lakoff [1987, Chap. 6]. For example, in the Dyirbal classification system that Lakoff uses to demonstrate the structure of radial categories, in the concept network corresponding to Balan, which includes women, fire, and dangerous things, the symbol 'women' can be considered a prototype (there might be other prototypes as well). Then 'dangerous things' would become a distant symbol of the concept network. This is because the derivation from 'women' to 'dangerous things' is a long one: going from 'women' to 'sun,' then to 'fire,' and finally arriving at 'dangerous things.' [Lakoff 1987, p. 100.]

  Both these features show that my concept networks can be conciliated with the *idealized cognitive models* of Lakoff.

- I believe that the concept networks as formalized here are able to characterize most folk and cultural models described by various linguists and anthropologists in Holland and Quinn [1987]. There is nothing in my characterization that requires concept networks to be complex. If necessary, additional constraints can be placed to guarantee that the complexity of any concept network does not exceed a certain level. For instance, one could limit the number of symbols, the number of operators, or the maximum arity of the operators. In fact, one such approach is used in the theory of cognitive development proposed by Halford and Wilson [1980], where the arity of operators is related to the stage of the cognitive development in the child. The first stage is characterized by unary operators, the second with binary operators, and so on.

- Finally, my concept networks fully capture Piaget's characterization of them as 'closed systems that are, at the same time, open to exchanges with the environment.' (See Piaget [1967], pp. 154–158.) The reason is that concept networks can be *circular*. A concept network is said to contain circularity if it has symbols, or sets of symbols, $X_1, \ldots, X_n$ such that X_1 generates X_2, X_2 generates $X_3, \ldots, X_{n-1}$ generates X_n, and X_n generates X_1. For instance, CN1 is circular in an obvious way. In fact, any concept network with invertible operations exhibits circularity. Circularity allows a concept network a choice of primitives and a variety of organizations depending on which symbols are directly interpreted in the world.

  This point is very important because it shows that the same concept network can organize reality in different way depending on how it is instantiated. In Lakoff's example of Balan in Dyirbal that was mentioned above, if the symbol 'fire' is considered a primitive and a prototype of the concept network, then 'women' becomes a distant symbol and 'dangerous things' becomes a more central one. Instantiated in this way, the concept network would structure the world differently than the way it does in Dyirbal.

Finally, a major issue that I have not yet touched upon is: How do concept networks come about in the first place? Though to fully address this question is beyond the scope of this work, I recognize three different ways in which a concept network may be formed.

1. A concept network might be *learned*. The learning might or might not have been guided by another cognitive agent such as a teacher.

2. A concept network might be *derived* from other existing concept networks. Just to mention a few possibilities: the cognitive agent might form a subnetwork of an existing concept network; extend a concept network by adding more symbols and operators to it; combine two or more concept networks to form a larger unified concept network, etc. (See also Goodman [1978], pp. 7–17.)

3. A concept network might be inherited genetically. That is, it might be implicitly manifested in the biological (or physical) structure of the cognitive agent. All this means is that I recognize that certain concept networks might be present without either being learned or being derived from other concept networks.

In closing, let me again underscore the fact that concept networks are purely syntactic systems that are meaningless unless interpreted appropriately in an environment.

5.4 Environments and Sensorimotor Data Sets

This brings us to the second component of the interaction process: reality. Here we are in deep water, for to characterize reality in any way gives it a preexisting structure. But not to characterize it leaves us no way to talk about how it might affect the process of interaction. To break out of this seemingly paradoxical situation, I distinguish between three levels of reality.

At one level is the reality that is not knowable by the cognitive agent, for it requires a God's eye view. This level of reality corresponds to the Kantian world of *things-in-themselves* and Jungian *Pleroma*. (See Jung's *VII Sermones ad Mortuos,* translated into English as *Seven Sermons to the Dead,* in Hoeller [1982], pp. 44–58.) For instance, the zonal structure of Spinner's environment, visible in our God's eye view, cannot be known by Spinner. As far as Spinner is concerned, the effect of a hop may well be to cause the old line to disappear and a new line to appear in a random orientation.

Here, however, I incorporate Krausser's [1974] two observations. One is that this level of reality is not an unstructured mass, but has a mind-independent autonomous structure that cannot be specified or known. The reason this structure cannot be specified is that no a priori ontology exists for this level of reality, and specifying a structure presupposes an ontology.

One might quite reasonably object here: How can I posit a mind-independent structure without positing a mind-independent ontology? My answer is that I can posit a mind-independent structure without needing a mind-independent ontology as long as I do not have to specify what the structure is, for it is only in specifying the structure that I need the ontology. Ascribing a mind-independent structure to this level of reality is like the existence proofs in mathematics, where the existence of some mathematical object is proved without specifying what the object is.

The second observation of Krausser that is incorporated is that the cognitive agent can interact with this level of reality. In fact, it is only by interacting with this reality that the cognitive agent can partially receive evidence of its autonomous structure.

The second level of reality corresponds to the world of sense impressions, and I refer to it as the *sensorimotor data set*. This level of reality is created by our sensory and motor apparatus interacting with the world of things-in-themselves. That is, it is our perceptual system that halts the continuous flux of things-in-themselves and brings the first level of reality to a manifestation. And our cognitive access to things-in-themselves is limited to this manifestation.

As our perceptual apparatus creates the sensorimotor data set, it necessarily follows that the ontology of the sensorimotor data set is determined by our perceptual system. However, as Eleanor Rosch [1978, p. 28] astutely noted in one of her landmark papers on the cognitive aspects of categorization, this world of sense impressions is not unstructured. Rather, reality, as it presents itself to us in the form of sensory stimuli that form the raw material for conceptualization and categorization, is already highly structured: certain sets of stimuli occur together, while certain others preclude one another. Moreover, this structure of the sensorimotor data set is determined by the mind-independent autonomous structure of the world of things-in-themselves. I elaborated this point in the context of Spinner's world, but let me now give another example. Suppose I am standing in front of a tree. It is the biological structure of my eyes that determines what image is formed on my retinas, what contrast I see, what colors I see, etc. (Of course, it also depends on the object in front of my eyes, the lighting conditions, etc. But different objects, or the same object under different lighting conditions, can all be considered different stimuli in the sensorimotor data set.) Similarly, as I walk towards the tree, it is the structure of my motor apparatus that determines what possible movements I can make. However, the effect of any such movement on changing one stimulus on my retina into another, possibly different, stimulus is determined by the structure of the external world. It is precisely in this sense that reality, while owing its form (as experienced by me) to my sensorimotor apparatus, nonetheless appears as an autonomous external entity to me.

Of course, this second level of reality is also not always directly accessible to us. Neither can we 'see' the image on our retina, nor can we activate every individual muscle in our body. Thus, the sensorimotor data set, while it forms the raw data that we receive from reality, does not reflect our conceptual world view. For this reason I posit a third, conceptual level of reality, corresponding to Kant's *phenomenal world* and Jung's *Created World*.[1] This is the level of reality that we experience every day. From here on, I reserve the term *environment* to refer to this level of reality.

An environment is essentially created by interpreting a concept network in the sensorimotor data set. Parts of the interpretation might be predetermined by the physical or biological structure of the cognitive agent, but there might be ample room for the cognitive agent to change the interpretations and create different environments in the same sensorimotor data set.

The same observations made about the sensorimotor data set can be made about the environments with respect to their ontologies and their structures. The ontology of an environment is determined by the cognitive agent (by interpreting a concept network), and therefore it must necessarily mirror the ontology of the concept network being used for interpretation. For this reason, an environment, in my formalization, consists of objects and transformations. Objects are counterparts of symbols, and transformations are counterparts of operators. There are no restrictions of any kind placed on the objects and transformations. The set of objects might be finite or infinite, the set of transformations might be finite or infinite, a transformation might or might not be algorithmic, and the objects might or might not be generated by a finite subset of them. It seems reasonable not to impose any kind of requirements on the environment since doing so would amount to imposing requirements on the autonomous structure of reality.

The structure of the environment, however, is determined by the world of things-in-themselves. Since this point is crucial to my framework of interactionism, I provide some more examples here at the risk of being redundant. First, consider a common object such as a table. Obviously, its status as an 'object' distinct from its surroundings, an 'object' that can be moved from one place to another, bought or sold, etc., is solely to the fact that we identify that chunk of reality with a symbol of our concept network. Thus, it owes its

---

[1]This term has also been translated as *Creatura* by Winstons [Jung 1963, Appendix V].

existence as an 'object' solely due to our perceptual and cognitive apparatus. However, the result of applying any transformation on it, such as setting it on fire, hitting it hard with the palm of our hand, selling it, etc., is determined by the external reality. Notice, in connection with 'selling,' that even those social and cultural institutions that are completely human creations—legal systems, monetary systems, marriage, come to mind as examples—do nevertheless acquire an 'objective reality' once their structures, that were once created by us, are shared by a group of people and used as a basis for their behaviors. (See Berger & Luckmann [1966].) As another example, consider the lines of latitude and longitude. There is no doubt here that they are created by our cognitive apparatus. Yet, once the ontology is created, the structure, which determines whether two given 'places' have the same latitude or not, is no longer an arbitrary matter, but is determined by the world of things-in-themselves. (The 'places' ontology also created by our cognitive apparatus.)

5.5   Cognitive Relations and Coherency

A cognitive relation is a link between a concept network and reality. It is a cognitive relation that makes a concept network meaningful, and it is a cognitive relation that brings reality within the cognitive grasp of the cognitive agent. Moreover, it is by forming a cognitive relation that environments are created out of the world of things-in-themselves (a process that is mediated by the sensorimotor data set).

Formally, then, a cognitive relation becomes a correspondence between the symbols of the concept network and the objects of the environment, and between the operators of the concept-network and the transformations of the environment. I allow a correspondence to be one-to-one, one-to-many, many-to-one, or many-to-many. The correspondence can be total as well as partial. However, each operator can only correspond to a transformation of the same *type,* meaning that n-ary operators correspond to n-ary transformations for all n. This may seem to be a stringent requirement, but it is a natural consequence of how environments are created. The objects and transformations in the environment do not exist independently of the cognitive agent, but are created by the cognitive agent by instantiating a concept network and forming a cognitive relation. So, if a symbol is instantiated, the resulting thing in the environment will necessarily behave like an object. If an n-ary operator is instantiated, then the corresponding thing in the environment will necessarily be an n-ary transformation. Of course, this does not mean that a part of reality can be given an ontology in only one way, since different concept networks can be instantiated in the same part of reality in different ways, resulting in many different ontologies (and creating many different environments).

Though the ontology of an environment mirrors the ontology of the concept network that created the environment, the structure of the environment is another matter. I have already belabored this point in the last section. So, it is natural to ask if a cognitive relation is such that the autonomous structure of the environment respects the structure of the concept network; or, in other words, if the actions of the transformations on the objects mirror the actions of the operators on the symbols.

We have already come across this problem when we transported Spinner to an alien environment. Let us consider some more examples here. Consider the concept network of natural numbers again. Let the environment consist of piles of stones. Each number—a symbol of the concept network—corresponds to all the piles, if any, containing that many stones. Obviously, this is a one-to-many correspondence. The operation of addition corresponds to the transformation by which two piles are combined to form a new pile. Now the correspondence will respect the actions of operators and transformations if, and only if, whenever we take any two piles of stones and their corresponding numbers, and apply the transformation of combining the piles to make a new pile, and the operation of addition on the two numbers, we find the resulting pile corresponds to the resulting number. To take another example, consider the concept network of a map. According to the map, if we go two blocks east from the train station, we should be at the post office. If that indeed happens when we take the corresponding action with respect to the object that is the train station, then the environment preserves the action of the operator 'go two blocks east' when applied to the symbol 'train station.'

To see an example of a correspondence that does not respect the actions of operators and transformations we only need to change the environment in the last example to groups of donkeys and/or carrots. Each number now corresponds to all the groups, if any, containing that many donkeys and/or carrots. Thus a group containing three donkeys and ten carrots corresponds to the number 13. The operation of addition still corresponds to the transformation by which two groups are combined to form a new group. It should be emphasized here that these groups of donkeys and/or carrots are real in the sense that all the members of a group have to be in close proximity. Also the transformation of putting two groups together is a physical transformation that is carried out by actually bringing the two groups together in close vicinity. Obviously now, the result of transforming two groups into a new group might not always yield a group that corresponds to the addition of the numbers corresponding to the original groups. For example, if a group containing ten carrots is combined with a group containing three donkeys it might not always result in a group corresponding to the number 13 since the donkeys might eat some carrots if they are hungry. A map of a city that has some errors in it provides another example of a cognitive relation where the structure of the environment does not respect the structure of the concept network.

The characteristic some cognitive relations have of preserving the actions of operators and transformations is called *coherency*. In practice, not all cognitive relations are coherent, as observed by Collins and Gentner [1987]. Moreover, a cognitive relation might be *locally coherent:* that is, the cognitive relation restricted to a part of the concept network and a part of the environment is coherent but taken as a whole it might not be coherent.

Local coherency is a much more useful concept than coherency for two reasons. Firstly, a cognitive relation that is to provide a useful basis for planning one's actions, and to go about day-to-day life, need only be locally coherent in the appropriate parts of the concept network and the environment. The second reason concerns finite representability. Assuming that a cognitive agent can examine only a finite part of the concept network at any time, it means that the cognitive agent can only establish local coherency within finite parts of the concept network. It would seem that a cognitive agent can never establish the coherency of a cognitive relation between an infinite concept network and an environment. However, the fact that even infinite concept networks are required to be finitely generated provides two different ways to tie local coherency within finite parts to the coherency of cognitive relations between infinite concept networks and environments.

One way to construct a fully coherent cognitive relation between an infinite concept network and an environment is as follows. A finite generating set of the concept network is given an interpretation in the environment by associating each symbol in this set with an object in the environment. Now the finite set of operations of the concept network is interpreted by identifying each operation with some transformation such that the resulting correspondence is locally coherent with respect to the generating set. This is no problem since the set is finite. Now the correspondence can be extended to all the symbols by associating each generated symbol with the appropriately transformed object. The correspondence does not have to be actually made—obviously it cannot be, since it would require that the infinite set of symbols be generated. But as long as this procedure is followed to extend the correspondence to any other subset of the symbols of the concept network, the result will always be coherent. This mechanism plays a key role in forming a cognitive relation by means of projection, an example of which I showed earlier when Spinner projected CN1 onto the alien environment, though the concept network there was a finite one. In our world, we use a similar method in using mathematical models to predict the real-world phenomena.

Secondly, it follows from the definition of coherency that any incoherency in a cognitive relation, even when the concept network is infinite, is always detectable locally within a finite part of it. This feature plays a key role detecting incoherency when a cognitive relation is being formed by accommodation. In the context of scientific theories, which are primarily formed by accommodation, this characteristic of cognitive relation is well known: a scientific theory can never be validated, it can only be refuted [Popper 1959; 1962].

5.6   Accommodation and Projection

Obviously, coherency of cognitive relations is an ideal that a cognitive agent must strive for. For it is the coherency of a cognitive relation that ensures that a prediction arrived at by reasoning from the concept network holds in the environment. Given that, we ask: how can a cognitive agent maintain coherency of its cognitive relations? Well, there are three components to a cognitive relation: the concept network, the environment, and a correspondence between the two. Moreover, the coherency condition requires the structure of the concept network and the structure of the environment to respect each other. So we need to ask: which of these parameters can be varied by the cognitive agent?

The structure of the environment is rooted in reality, so it cannot be varied by the cognitive agent (at least not without changing the ontology of the environment). But that leaves two parameters: the structure of the concept network and the correspondence between the concept network and the environment. Correspondingly, there are two mechanisms that can be used, individually or together, to maintain coherency of cognitive relations. These mechanisms, referred to as *accommodation* and *projection* respectively, have already been introduced in the context of Spinner example, and here I elaborate them further,

Accommodation works by keeping the correspondence between the concepts and the environment invariant, and then altering the structure of the concept network (recall that 'structure' here means how the symbols are interrelated) whenever an incoherency is detected. Projection works by keeping the structure of the concept network invariant, but changing the correspondence between the concepts and the parts of the environment. In fact, in changing the correspondence, the cognitive agent is in effect instantiating the concept network anew, thereby creating a new environment. Thus, projection works by indirectly altering the structure of the environment so that it better fits the structure of the concept network. I say 'indirectly' because what the cognitive agent is actually doing is giving a new ontology to the environment, and it is reality that is fitting this ontology with a structure.

The cognitive agent can use both these mechanisms in concert to maintain coherency of a cognitive relation: there might be some varying of the correspondence, and some restructuring of the concept network. However, it is possible to study each mechanism separately by holding the effect of the other mechanism fixed. In other words, we can study the effects of accommodation by keeping the correspondence between the concepts of the concept network and the parts of the environment fixed, and then noticing how the structure of the concept network changes so as to maintain coherency. A cognitive relation formed in this fashion is referred to as *accommodating* or *environment driven*. Similarly, we can keep the structure of the concept network invariant and then maintain coherency solely by varying correspondences between the concepts of the concept network and the parts of the environment. A cognitive relation arrived at by this process is referred to as *projective* or *concept driven*.

Let us first consider accommodation. As mentioned before, in forming accommodating relations, the correspondence between parts of the environment and the concepts of the concept network is kept fixed. The correspondence might have been fixed by a prior step of projection, or might have been hard-wired into the perceptual apparatus of the cognitive agent. The structure of the concept network is adapted to the structure of the environment so as to maintain coherency of the cognitive relation. In other words, it is the environment, acting through the fixed correspondence, that structures the concept network. This is the reason for naming the resulting relation 'environment driven.'

Some examples will perhaps be helpful here. Imitation comes to mind immediately as a typical activity that gives rise to accommodating relations. (See Piaget [1945], Part I, pp. 5–86, for a fascinating study of the role played by imitation in the early cognitive development of the child.) When one imitates an action, a sound, or a view, one is copying the environment in a sense. Notice here that any imitation is an imitation *only in certain respects.* If you were imitating my act of touching my nose with my left hand, you would have to decide whether your touching my nose or your nose would amount to an imitation. You would also have to decide if the nose should be touched with my hand or yours and if it should be the left or the right hand, not to mention deciding whether to imitate the place where I was standing or sitting, the direction I was facing, the clothes I was wearing at the time I touched my nose, etc. All this must be decided by a prior step of projection. (See also Goodman [1976], I, 2, pp. 6–10; and Hofstadter [1981-85], pp. 563–565.) However, once the relevant aspects are decided, the correspondence is established between the concept network and the environment; or, in other words, the ontology of the environment has been determined. The environment takes over from there and the cognitive agent adapts the structure of its concept network (the necessary sequence of actions that would result in the imitation) to conform to the structure of the environment (the act being imitated).

There are many other examples of accommodation. In drawing a geographical map, one is essentially carrying out a process of accommodation. The ontology of the terrain in terms of which its structure is to be mapped— rivers, lakes, land, ocean, etc.—is decided beforehand. The terrain takes over from there and the geographer must make the structure of the map correspond to the structure of the terrain. In determining the number of days in a year, one is again carrying out a process of accommodation, for the ontologies of day and year are already grounded in external phenomena, and it is the autonomous structure of the world that determines how these two phenomena are related.

It may be of some interest to note here that the Q-morphisms of Holland *et al.* [1987, Ch. 2] correspond to what I have been calling accommodating cognitive relations here. In their model of cognition, the environment is assumed to act on the cognitive agent via a set of feature detectors. These feature detectors establish the correspondence between the objects of the environment and the concepts of the concept network. However, since the nature of the feature detectors is fixed, the correspondence is predetermined. The cognitive agent can only modify its existing operators, or create new operators, to correspond to the transformations of the environment.

All these examples also help to show why the cognitive agent is not entirely passive in the formation of an accommodating relation. The process of establishing a correspondence between the concepts of the concept network and chunks of the environment is a prerequisite for the formation of an accommodating relation. This choice is made by the cognitive agent, consciously or not. In many cases the physical and biological structure of the agent might be such that the correspondence is predetermined and cannot be varied at all: the choices are already made by evolution or the system architect and the cognitive agent has no conscious control over it. However, if the cognitive agent does have some freedom in this respect, then it is capable of forming a projective cognitive relation, which I discuss now.

A projective relation is formed by keeping the structure of the concept network invariant but changing the correspondence between the concepts of the concept network and parts of the environment so as to maintain coherency. Since the structure of the concept network is kept fixed in the process, it is the structure of the environment that must conform. This is the reason for naming the resulting relation 'concept driven.' Of course, the structure of the environment does not actually conform, what this means is that the cognitive agent is asserting its formative power in changing the experiential ontology of the environment so as to be able to see the structure of the concept network reflected in it. And, of course, reality, which determines the structure of any experiential ontology created by the cognitive agent, asserts itself by limiting the possible ontologies that do end up reflecting this structure, if at all. Thus we see that 'concept driven' cognitive relations are not completely determined by the cognitive agent, just as 'environment driven' cognitive relations are not completely determined by the environment.

The most classic example of projection is the retinal inversion of image in our visual system. We all know that the image formed on the retina of our eye is actually inverted: everything is upside down. However, we do not 'see' things upside down. This, of course, is easily explained by the fact that our concept networks already take the inversion into account. In other words, the correspondence between our concepts and the images on our retina is such that the actions of all operators are preserved, and since 'upside down' itself is a concept embedded in our spatial concept network, it actually corresponds to those images that are rightside up on the retina. Suppose we now change the structure of our eyes so that the images on the retina are not inverted, a task easily accomplished by wearing the appropriate lenses in front of the eyes. Obviously, it immediately makes the earlier interpretations of our existing spatial concept networks incoherent. This experiment was, in fact, carried out by Stratton [1897] at the end of the last century. As one might expect, the incoherency resulted in vertigo and nausea. However, after about a week, everything started to appear normal. What might have happened? Surely it is too short a time to 'relearn' all the various skills in which the visual stimuli play a role, and restructure the spatial concept network.

This phenomenon is explained in my framework by the mechanism of projection. In order to 'see' everything normal, with the distorting glasses in front of the eyes, all that was necessary was to reinterpret the old concept networks by changing the correspondence between the concepts and the retinal images. As to be expected, Stratton encountered a similar experience when he took off the distorting glasses: it started out with a feeling of dizziness but after about a week everything was back to normal. I would say that the correspondences were back to what they were initially. This example also demonstrates that not all the correspondences between the concepts of our concept networks and parts of our sensorimotor data set are predetermined for us, thereby allowing us to use the mechanism of projection in forming cognitive relations. (See also Turbayne [1962], Chap. VIII, Sec. 4, for a very similar explanation of this phenomenon.) As I show in Chapter 7, it is this projection that makes metaphor possible, especially similarity-creating ones.

Other examples of projective relations can be found in the playful activities of children. When a child identifies a doll with herself, she is essentially projecting her image of herself onto the doll. In any such playful activity of children, the interesting thing is that the projection is far from arbitrary, and reveals a systematic structure that the child is attempting to preserve. (See Piaget [1945], Part II, pp. 87–212, for a detailed study of the role played by 'play' in the cognitive growth of children.)

As another example of a projective relation, consider the lines of latitude and longitude. Obviously, these lines do not exist in our environment and so they could not have been induced by it. It is a system of reference that we have developed for our convenience and then projected onto our environment. Similarly, our system for measuring time is an instance of a mostly projective relation. Notice here that though the concepts of *night* and *day* are induced by the environment, the concepts of *hour, minute,* and *second* are purely projective. It is also easy to see here that the environment, not a principal actor in projective relations, nonetheless plays a key role. It is true that we could have devised another system in place of lines of latitude and longitude, but once a system is devised and projected, it is the environment that determines whether two places are on the same 'latitude' or not. We could have chosen to divide the day into 43 'hours,' but even then whether two events took place within the same 'hour' or not is a matter that is determined by the environment.

Finally, I should emphasize again that most cognitive relations are not formed by either accommodation or projection acting alone, but instead by both mechanisms acting together. Perhaps the most interesting examples of these two mechanisms acting in concert are provided by Imre Lakatos [1976] in his beautiful essays on the role of counterexamples in mathematical proofs. When a counterexample to a certain theorem is found, there are two things one can do. One is to redefine the mathematical objects involved in the proof so as to exclude the counterexample. This amounts to projection, because the concepts are being instantiated anew. The other thing one can do is to declare the theorem invalid, and perhaps look for a weaker theorem. This amounts to accommodation, for the structure of the concept network (manifested in the statement of the theorem) is being altered to keep it true (coherent). Lakatos argues quite convincingly that in most situations we like to use a little bit of both the mechanisms to keep our concept networks significant, meaningful, and coherent (as far as we can ascertain it). (See also the account of learning given in Petrie [1979]. In his account, the teacher works by projecting a concept network so as to reveal an incoherency in the student's cognitive relations. The student 'learns' by changing the structure of her concept network—that is, by accommodation.)

5.7 Cognitive Models

I refer to a concept network that has been interpreted by a cognitive relation in an environment as a *cognitive model*. Cognitive models are experiential and conceptualized versions of reality, and thus they loosely correspond to the 'worlds' of Goodman [1978]. In this section I discuss how cognitive models 'group' parts of the environment together. Then I present a 'grouping' perspective on accommodation and projection. Then I discuss how parts of the environment are represented in the cognitive model, and how they acquire a description via the operational structure of the concept network. Finally, I introduce some terminology to refer to different characteristics of cognitive models.

I assume here that a cognitive model is coherent, unless explicitly stated otherwise. Since coherency is an ideal that a cognitive model must aim for, this assumption does not seem unreasonable. It is like assuming the absence of friction in order to discuss characteristics of motion.

5.7.1   Groupings on the Environment

A cognitive model 'groups' the objects and the transformations in the environment so that the structure in the environment seen with respect to these groups is isomorphic to the structure of the model. I now elaborate this grouping phenomenon with some examples.

Let us first consider groupings on the objects of the environment. We saw an example of this in Figure 5.9 when two different states of Spinner's eye, corresponding to the sensory vectors 00010 and 00100, were grouped together under one symbol 'vline.' Viewed from CN1, these two otherwise distinguishable objects of the environment cannot be distinguished at all. Another example, from the natural environment of Spinner, is shown in Figure 5.12(a) and (b). Here all the objects of the environment are grouped into nine categories. Thus, Spinner's 'world,' which was already simplified by its perceptual apparatus, is further simplified by the cognitive model.

These examples, of course, show grouping at a small scale, but it is due to Spinner's having a very simple perceptual apparatus to begin with. In our visual system, we know that the images on the retina are grouped into various classes according to the position and orientation of lines, edges etc. [Hubel & Wiesel 1979.] Of course, at the cognitive level the groupings are more obvious. All our 'words' correspond to several 'world-states.' This suggests that a cognitive relation, from the concept network to the environment, might typically be a one-to-many affair. One might even see the whole problem of cognition as that of grouping a vast number of 'world-states,' made possible by the perceptual apparatus, into a few categories. The empirical research of various linguists and anthropologists presented in Holland and Quinn [1987] certainly supports this view.

The transformations can be grouped in two interesting ways. The first way is to group the transformations in *sequences* and then relate the operators of the concept network with these sequences of transformations. An example of a cognitive model that groups transformations in this way is shown in Figure 5.13(a) and (b). The one operator of the concept network is identified with the sequence of transformations obtained by first applying the transformation 10000 followed by the transformation 01000: which may be written as 10000 o 01000.

Numerous examples of grouping transformations in sequences can also be found in our perceptual and cognitive apparatus. A simple action such as 'jump' or 'walk' actually translates into a sequence of muscle activations. Similarly, in planning a trip, we might use a concept network that has an

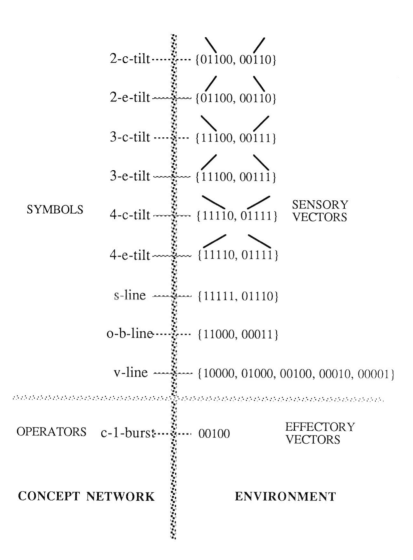

FIGURE 5.12 (a): An example of a cognitive model that shows grouping of objects in the environment. The structure of this cognitive model is shown in (b).

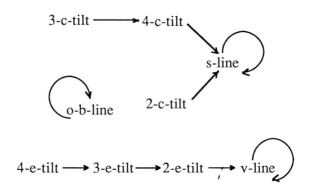

FIGURE 5.12 (b): Structure of the cognitive model shown in (a). Since there
is only one operator 'c-1-burst' all arrows refer to it.

operator 'get to the airport,' which actually corresponds to a sequence of
actions such as 'walk to the subway,' 'take the subway to the airport,' 'take
the airport shuttle to the terminal,' etc. (Forming sequences of transformations that take only one object as an argument seems straightforward. To
form sequences of n-ary transformations in general, one composes n m-ary
transformations with an n-ary transformation to yield an m-ary transformation. This is technically called *composition* and is formally defined in the
next chapter.)

The second way transformations can be grouped is as objects. We saw an
example of this in Figure 5.6 when the operator 'qturn' grouped the actions
of Spinner corresponding to effectory vectors 03000 and 00030. The idea here
is that if two or more transformations cause the same change, as seen from
the concept network, then they appear as one. For instance, there might be
several ways of getting to the airport, but at the level of abstraction where
we have the operator 'get to the airport,' all these 'details' are irrelevant and
indistinguishable.

Notice that these two ways of grouping the transformations can work
together to produce a grouping. All the different ways of getting to the
airport that correspond to the operator 'get to the airport' might themselves
be sequences of actions. Moreover, each part of any such sequence might
actually be realizable by two or more actions.

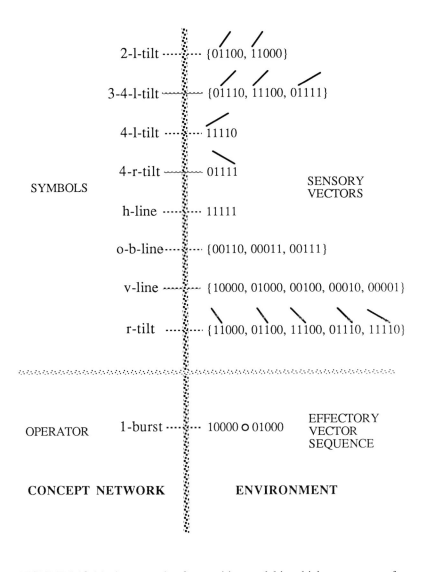

FIGURE 5.13 (a): An example of a cognitive model in which an operator of the concept network corresponds to a 'sequence' of actions. The structure of this cognitive model is shown in (b).

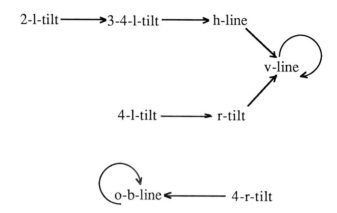

FIGURE 5.13 (b): Structure of the cognitive model shown in (a). All arrows represent the operator 'l-burst', which is effectory vector 10000 followed by 01000.

5.7.2 Accommodation and Projection: Another Perspective

With the phenomenon of grouping in the background, we can view the mechanisms of accommodation and projection from another perspective. Let us look at accommodation first. The perceptual apparatus of the cognitive agent provides it with an ontology for the sensorimotor data set. This ontology is structured by reality, as I have emphasized several times. Now since the sensorimotor data set is available for conceptualization, the cognitive agent can group its ontology in various ways, simplifying its world view in the process. Effectively, this is what goes on when a concept network is interpreted in the sensorimotor data set. The structure of the environment as seen from this grouped ontology depends partly on the autonomous structure of the sensorimotor data set, and partly on the way the grouping was carried out. The process of accommodation works by keeping the groupings of the sensorimotor data set fixed, and changing the structure of the concept network so that it reflects the structure of the environment in terms of these groupings. This process is graphically demonstrated in Figure 5.14. One might see it as the cognitive agent determining what goes into the groups, and the environment determining the structure.

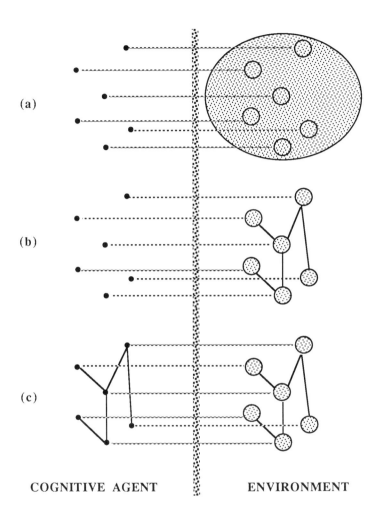

(a)

(b)

(c)

COGNITIVE AGENT   **ENVIRONMENT**

FIGURE 5.14: A perspective on accommodation. In (a) the cognitive agent gives an ontology to the environment. In (b) the environment determines the structure of this ontology. In (c) the cognitive agent adapts the structure of the concept network to reflect the structure of the environment.

For projection, the process works in the other direction. One already has a structure that comes from the concept network being projected. The problem now is in coming up with a grouping of the sensorimotor data set that respects this structure. Since the sensorimotor data set has an autonomous structure, it limits the possible ways in which it can be grouped so as to reflect the structure of the concept network. The cognitive agent selects one such grouping, though this selection process might also be constrained by the physical or biological structure of the cognitive agent. This process is shown in Figure 5.15. One might see this as the cognitive agent determining the structure and the environment determining what goes into the groups.

This view of accommodation and projection better explains how both the cognitive agent and the environment have a role to play in each of the processes. However, if we take the structure-determining role to be the primary one, then accommodation can be viewed as an environment driven process and projection as a concept driven process. The result in either case is that the cognitive agent sees in the world an isomorphic copy of the concept network.

5.7.3   Representation and Description

Looking at cognitive models from another angle, we might notice that they bring objects and transformations in the environment within the cognitive grasp of the agent. In a cognitive model, any object (or transformation) of the environment is said to be *represented* by a symbol (or operator) of the concept network if the two are related by the cognitive relation. Conversely, the concept is said to be a *representation* of the object. Obviously, since I allow many-to-many relations, an object can have many representations and a concept can represent many objects.

Recall that earlier I defined the term *description* in connection with symbols of a concept network. A description of a symbol is any way of specifying how that symbol can be decomposed into various other symbols; or, looking at it constructively, how various symbols can be combined to generate the symbol being described. This terminology is easily extended to the objects in the environment via the cognitive relation of a cognitive model. That is, a *description* of an object in a cognitive model is a description of any of its representations. Since it will always be clear whether we are talking about the environment or the concept network, using the same term for objects and symbols should not cause any confusion. On the contrary, it brings out a key feature of cognition: *objects in the environment acquire a description only by*

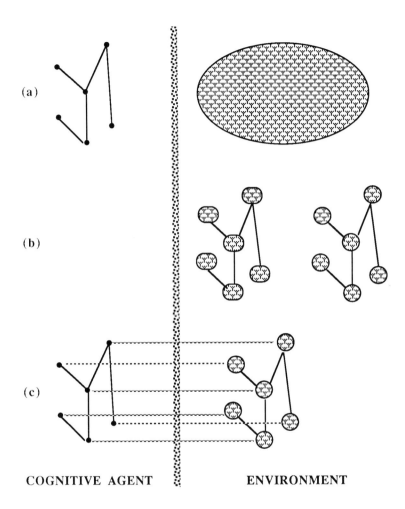

FIGURE 5.15: A perspective on projection. In (a) the cognitive agent selects a concept network with an autonomous structure. In (b) the environment, based on its autonomous structure, determines the possible groupings that respect the structure of the concept network. In (c) the cognitive agent in instantiating a cognitive relation, chooses one such grouping.

being represented in a concept network and via the operational structure of the concept network.

5.7.4   Some Other Miscellaneous Notions

With groupings, one can define some useful notions related to cognitive models. First of all, notice that a grouping can put an object (or transformation) of the environment into more than one group. Any cognitive model that groups its environment in this way is said to be *ambiguous*. For instance, suppose that in mapping a terrain it was decided to use the concepts 'wooded land,' 'hilly land,' 'flat grassy land,' 'flat dry land,' 'body of water,' and 'built-up land.' The map of the terrain using these concepts would be a cognitive model. However, the model is ambiguous because an area that is hilly and also wooded corresponds to two different concepts (assuming that such an area exists in the terrain being mapped). For a cognitive model that is being formed by accommodation, it is necessary that it be unambiguous, because otherwise the environment does not present the cognitive agent with an unambiguous structure that can be used to adapt the concept network. In the above example, it is not clear how a wooded hill is to be represented in the model, and how the map is to be structured.

Secondly, when two cognitive models A and B share the same environment, one of them, say A, is said to be a *refinement* of the other if the grouping induced on the environment by A is exactly like the one induced by B except that it splits at least one group into two or more groups. For instance, the map of a terrain using the concepts above (after removing the ambiguity) would be a refinement of another map that uses only the concepts 'land' and 'water' (assuming that the terrain includes some land with different features.) Thus, a refinement magnifies the world-view of the cognitive agent by making further distinctions possible.

A cognitive model is said to contain *synonyms* if at least two concepts in its concept network are related to exactly the same group in the environment. This should be obvious.

Since I allow a cognitive relation to be partial, there is the possibility that not all the concepts of the concept network correspond to some object in the environment. If they all do, we say that the cognitive system is *full*. All the cognitive models of Spinner that we have seen so far are full. A cognitive model that is conventional is likely to be full, but when a concept network is interpreted in an unconventional environment, then it is usually not full. Metaphorical interpretations provide many examples of cognitive models that are not full, as we will see in Chapter 7.

Similarly, not every object or transformation in the environment can be represented in the concept network. If every object is represented, then we say that the cognitive model is *complete*. Some clarification is needed here, since I emphasized earlier that the objects and transformations in the environment can only be created by instantiating the concepts of the concept network. So, if some object or transformation is not represented in the concept network of a cognitive model, how does it become an object or a transformation in the first place?

The answer lies in realizing that we rarely work with a single cognitive model in isolation. Though a certain cognitive model can be significant at some point in time, the cognitive agent might be aware of other cognitive models as well. And the environment is not just the environment created by the concept network that is in use, but might include dormant instantiations of other concept networks as well. Thus, we can talk about a cognitive model being incomplete without creating a paradox.

In the world of Spinner, the cognitive models formed by the concept networks CN1 and CN3 of Figure 5.5, along with their interpretations of Figures 5.6 and Figure 5.8 respectively, are incomplete. However, the cognitive model of Figure 5.12 is complete. Numerous examples of complete and incomplete cognitive models can be found in our world. A map of Paris is complete if the environment is restricted to the street layout of Paris, but incomplete with respect to France (or even with respect to Paris if houses are included as part of the environment.)

Some formal characteristics of cognitive models with respect to these defined properties are presented in the next chapter.

For those who are familiar with Goodman's 'notational systems' [Goodman 1976, Chap. IV], it may be instructive to note that I place much less stringent requirements on my cognitive models than Goodman. But then of course, Goodman's system was designed for a different purpose than the one that concerns me here.

5.8   Layered Cognitive System and Multiple "Worlds"

The process of establishing a correspondence between the parts of the sensorimotor data set and the concepts of the concept network seems very much

like the process by which the perceptual apparatus creates the sensorimotor data set out of the world of things-in-themselves. For instance, both
processes involve grouping: the perceptual apparatus makes many different
external states of reality correspond to the same sensory state, and the cognitive apparatus makes many different sensory states correspond to the same
symbol. This similarity suggests that it might be possible to view the process of establishing a correspondence between the parts of the sensorimotor
data set and the concepts of the concept network as if a 'cognitive eye' were
placed between the sensorimotor data set and the concept network. This
cognitive eye would create another ontology from the ontology that has been
provided by the perceptual apparatus. This, in turn, suggests that it might
be possible to view the actions of the perceptual apparatus and that of the
cognitive apparatus of the cognitive agent in terms of the same mechanisms
operating at two different levels. Let us explore this avenue in the context of
Spinner's world.

In the example presented in Section 2, the sensory organ of Spinner was
inflexible and fully predetermined. This made it so that there was a fixed
mapping from the states of the external world to the states of the eye (as
represented by the sensory vector.) In the case of the effectory organ, Spinner
had some degree of flexibility in controlling the intensity of its bursts. However, we could tacitly assume as the simplest case that the same activation
patterns of the effectory organ—that is, the activations corresponding to the
same effectory vectors—always resulted in the jet-stream bursts of the same
intensity, it also established a mapping—from the transformations possible
in the external world to the states of Spinner's effectory organ—that was
fixed once and for all. In fact, because of these fixed mappings, it is possible
to specify all cognitive relations shown in Section 2 by merely associating
the concepts of the concept networks with the sensory and effectory vectors.
The correspondence then automatically extends to the lines and jet-streams
of air in the external world via the fixed mappings created by the sensory
and effectory organs.

The situation would be different if Spinner could change the threshold of
the cells in its eye, or if different air particle densities in the external world
caused jet-streams of different intensities to be emitted for the same setting
of the effectory organ. To understand this phenomenon, let us just consider
the case when Spinner can change the bias of its sensory organ.

Imagine that, as in Abbott's original *Flatland,* there is a dense fog per-
vading the world of Spinner. The effect of the fog is to make the image on
the eye of Spinner dependent on the distance between the eye and the object,

as shown in Figure 5.16(a). However, by changing the threshold of the cells in its eye, Spinner can now cause different states of the eye—or different sensory vectors—to correspond to the same object in the world. This is shown in Figure 5.16(b). But does this process not seem very much like projection?

To make this point clear, suppose we construct concept networks at the perceptual level by considering the states of the eye as symbols and the states of the effectory organ as operators. The mechanisms of projection and accommodation can then be used to interpret these concept networks coherently in the external world. In projection, the structure of the concept network would be kept invariant and the correspondence between the states of the perceptual organs and the objects in the world would be varied by changing the threshold of the eye. In accommodation, the bias of the perceptual apparatus—that is, the threshold of the eye—would be kept fixed and the structure of the concept network would be adapted. In fact, this is exactly how the 'concept network' of Figure 5.10(b) came about. In Section 2, by keeping the perceptual apparatus fixed, we effectively limited Spinner to accommodating cognitive models between the world of things-in-themselves and the perceptual level.

Thus, we have a three layered cognitive system here: there is the cognitive layer, the perceptual layer, and the external world layer (Figure 5.17). If we focus on structural determination, then projection can be seen as working from the cognitive layer to the perceptual layer, and from the perceptual layer to the external world layer. Accommodation works in the opposite direction: from the external world layer to the perceptual layer, and from the perceptual layer to the cognitive layer. Notice that the structure of the external world layer is independent of the perceptual layer. The perceptual layer creates an ontology for the external world layer, by grouping the objects in various ways, but not its structure. Similarly, the structure of the information present at the perceptual layer is independent of the cognitive layer (it is derived from the autonomous structure of the external world layer). Of course, a cognitive model at the cognitive layer can restructure the 'lower-level' information present at the perceptual layer (by grouping it via a cognitive relation), but this restructuring is far from arbitrary. The autonomous structure of the information present at the perceptual layer resists and can be restructured only in certain ways, as I have emphasized time and again. The same holds for the interaction between the perceptual layer and the external world layer.

From here, it is only a small step further to realize that a cognitive system might well have several layers, with each successive layer representing a higher level of abstraction. The layers will be numbered from 0 to N, with the layer

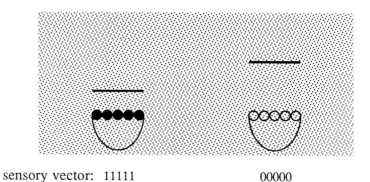

sensory vector: 11111   00000

(a) The fog's effect on the image on Spinner's eye.

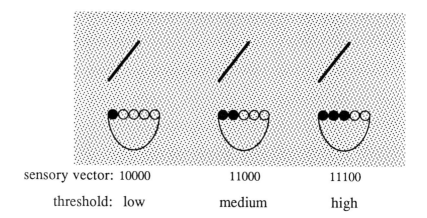

sensory vector: 10000   11000   11100

threshold: low   medium   high

(b) Spinner, by changing the threshold of the eye, can make the same object correspond to the different states of the eye.

FIGURE 5.16: An example to illustrate the effect of Spinner being able to change the bias of its sensory organ.

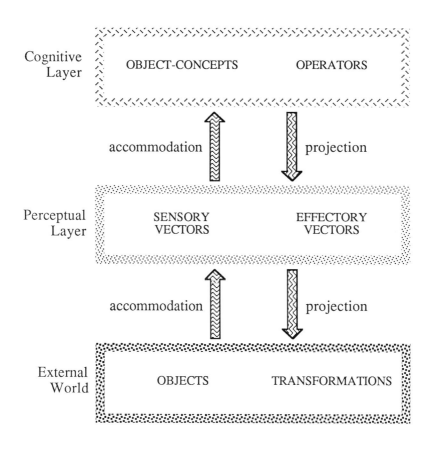

FIGURE 5.17: Three layered cognitive system of Spinner.

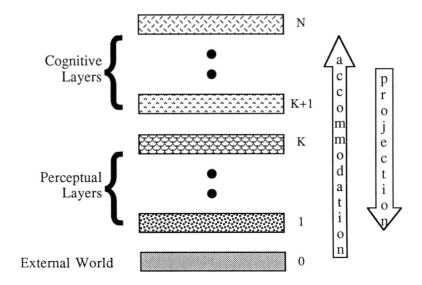

FIGURE 5.18: Multi-layered cognitive system.

0 corresponding to the external world, layer 1 corresponding to the immediate perceptual level (processing by a complex perceptual system might require more than one layers), and layer N corresponding to the highest level of abstraction (Figure 5.18).

Each layer can contain a variety of inherited, learned, or derived concept networks. The mechanisms of projection and accommodation work between adjacent layers to organize the 'lower-level' representations or 'raw-data' of the lower layer into the 'higher-order' categories or concepts of the upper layer. Since the 'lower-level' representations at the lower layer have their own autonomous structure, the process is essentially interactive. Projection works in a 'top-down' fashion by forcing the 'lower-level' representations, as far as they can be forced, to fit the concepts and categories of the upper layer. In other words, the organization of the concepts and categories in the upper layer is kept fixed and it is the mapping between the two layers that is altered to maintain coherency. Accommodation works in a 'bottom-up' fashion by first grouping the 'lower-level' representations in some way, and then reorganizing the concepts and categories—creating new ones, if necessary—of the next layer above to reflect the structure of the groupings. Here the correspondence between the two layers is kept fixed but the organization of concepts in the upper layer is changed. A cognitive relation between any two adjacent layers is formed by an interplay of these two mechanisms.

Given any pair of adjacent layers, the flexibility to project a concept network in the higher layer onto the structures in the lower layer can vary quite a bit depending on where the pair is located. In certain cases, the correspondences might be hard-wired so that the cognitive agent might have no recourse but to accommodate and adapt. In some other cases, there might be some flexibility, but certain correspondences might still be 'preferred' for biological or habitual reasons. Thus, we might still be able to refer to certain correspondences as 'conventional.'

Notice that as long as the ontology of the external world (created by the cognitive agent) at a certain layer in a cognitive system is kept the same, the structure with respect to that ontology in that layer can never be changed as a result of anything happening in the layers above it. Of course, it can be grouped differently, and thus 'seen' differently from a cognitive model in a higher layer. But its autonomous structure can be changed only via accommodation emanating from any of the lower layers. For instance, the nature of the stimulus on the retina of the cognitive agent experiencing apparent motion has its autonomous structure that does not depend on how that stimulus is 'seen' at the conceptual layer. Of course, the cognitive layer might change the bias of the retinal cell, but that would amount to a projection from the perceptual layer to the external world, a process in which the world is given a new ontology at the retinal level.

Viewing our visual system as a layered cognitive system might perhaps be helpful here. The actual scene that the cognitive agent is seeing would be in Layer 0. The images on the retina would be in Layer 1. Layer 2 might contain the description of the scene in terms of lines, edges, boundaries, etc. The description of the scene in terms of concepts like 'table,' 'books,' etc. would be contained in Layer 3. And so on. This view of the visual system is, in fact, fully consistent with what is known about our visual system in neurophysiology and the brain theory [Hubel 1988; Pinker 1985]. For instance, in a model of visual cognition by Ullman [1985], it has been suggested that the process proceeds in a 'bottom-up' fashion in the first few levels starting from the retinal image, and then 'top-down' routines are applied to the resulting representations to extract various other characteristics. This would suggest that in any layered cognitive system, the bottom few layers, referred to as 'perceptual layers' in Figure 5.18, might be mostly accommodating: meaning that the mapping between successive layers is predetermined and cannot be easily changed. The higher 'cognitive layers,' on the other hand, might be mostly projective: meaning that the structures of the concept networks there are not changed very often, but the 'lower-order representations' of the lower layers are grouped in various ways so as make them fit the structures of the concept networks.

I must hasten to add here that I am by no means implying that the layers of a cognitive system must correspond to the physiological structure in the cognitive agent's brain, as some layers of the visual system might; or even that it is always possible to cleanly separate any cognitive system (such as our visual system) into different layers. My point is simply that the process of integrating the autonomous structure of the sensorimotor data set into the structure of a concept network is best seen as happening in several stages; and at each stage, we can view the process as an interaction between two autonomous structures—the structured 'raw data' of the 'lower' layer and the abstract conceptual structure of the 'upper' layer. In this interaction process, the mechanisms of projection and accommodation are used together to integrate the raw-data into abstract concepts in a way that does not violate the autonomous structure of either layer.

Many characteristics of cognition cannot be explained without layered cognitive systems. For instance, as I discuss in Chapters 7 [§7.2] and 8 [§8.3], the distinction between understanding and truth can only be explained with cognitive systems that have three or more layers and, moreover, in which derived structures are allowed to exist in one of the middle layers.

Layered cognitive systems also explain why it is not necessary to carry out active experimentation in order to get a new insight or detect some misconception in one's beliefs. In a two layer view of cognition, any accommodation (that is, a change in the structure of a concept network so as to maintain coherency) is necessarily and directly caused by the environment. This cannot account for the fact that many of the adjustments in our concept networks—including new insights—happen in an arm-chair. With a layered cognitive system, this is no problem since it is only accommodation between layers 0 and 1 that require active interaction with the external world.

Finally, the concept of layered cognitive systems can explain how we can create a multitude of 'worlds'—in the sense of Cassirer and Goodman—that are not always reducible to one another. A slightly different grouping at a lower layer can result in an entirely different structure a few layers above. Though, my formalization suggests that it is theoretically possible to correlate two entirely different 'worlds' by bringing them to their lowest possible denominator, that is the layer at which the groupings leading to the two 'worlds' begin to diverge, practical limitations might prevent one from always realizing this possibility. The physical structure of the brain might be the source of one such limitation. Over time, certain projections can become 'hardened' so that they cannot be undone for regrouping. Or certain structures might become so rigid that they cannot be adapted any more. In spite of all that, we frequently do bring two disparate 'worlds' together, creating a metaphor in the process, which is the topic I discuss in Chapter 7.

In closing this section, let me emphasize that the idea of a layered architecture for modeling perception and cognition is not something radically new, but has been suggested several times in the past in different contexts. (See Arbib [1972], Chap. 6; Erman *et al.* [1980]; Holland *et al.* [1986]; Rumelhart *et al.* [1986]; and Lippman [1987].) What is new in my account, however, is the structural independence of the layers and the mechanisms of projection and accommodation that can be used in concert to maintain the coherency of these independent structures with respect to each other.

5.9 Summary

To conclude, I present below the definitions of the key concepts and the main theses underlying the interaction view of cognition that I outlined in this chapter.

- A concept network is a set of concepts having an operational structure. It is a potential representation of reality.

- A concept network can permit many different and non-overlapping sets of concepts to act as primitves. Which concepts actually do become primitives depends on how the concept network is instantiated in the external world. Moreover, depending on the concepts chosen as primitives, the same concept network can structure reality in different ways.

- Reality is given an ontology by instantiating a concept network in it, turning it into what I referred to as an environment. This process is mediated by the sensorimotor data set, which is reality as apprehended by the perceptual apparatus of the cognitive agent. Therefore, it follows that the ontology of the environment necessarily follows the ontology of the concept network.

- The structure of the environment, however, is autonomous. Reality asserts its autonomy by imposing a structure on the ontology (created by the cognitive agent) of the environment.

- A cognitive relation connects the elements of a concept network to the parts of the environment. It is through a cognitive relation that a concept network becomes 'meaningful,' and it is through a cognitive relation that reality becomes accessible to the cognitive agent.

- Coherency refers to the property of certain cognitive relations in which the structure of the concept network reflects the autonomous structure of the environment. Thus, coherency is a property of cognitive relations, and not of concept networks.

- The coherency of cognitive relations cannot be determined cognitively (without having the God's eye view), though incoherency can be so determined.

- A cognitive agent must try to keep its cognitive relations coherent as far as it can do so. The cognitive agent uses the mechanisms of projection and accommodation to maintain the coherency of its cognitive relation, whenever an incoherency is detected.

- In projection, the structure of the concept network is kept invariant, while the cognitive relation is altered to maintain coherency.

- In accommodation, the cognitive relation is kept invariant, while the structure of the concept network is altered to maintain coherency.

- A cognitive model is a concept network that is instantiated through a cognitive relation.

- In a cognitive model, the cognitive agent 'sees' an isomorphic copy of its concept network in the environment. The isomorphism is created by grouping the objects and transformations in the environment by the cognitive relation.

- Objects in the environment of a cognitive model acquire a description only by being represented in the concept network (through the cognitive relation) and via the operational structure of the concept network.

Chapter 6

An Interactionist Approach to Cognition: Formal Concepts

6.1 Introduction

In this chapter my goal is to carry out a formal exposition of the framework that was laid out informally in the last chapter. The key notions in my framework of interactionism are those of 'concept networks,' which are finitely generated algebras; 'structure,' which refers to how the operators of a concept network connect its object-concepts together; 'descriptions,' which refer to the ways in which an object-concept can be decomposed into other object-concepts and sequences of operators; 'generating set,' which refers to how certain object-concepts can be used as primitives in terms of which the whole concept network can be described; 'cognitive models,' which are relations from the algebras of the concept networks to the algebras of the environments; 'groupings,' an effect of the one-to-many cognitive relations on the sensorimotor data sets to group a number of different sensory states into one conceptual unit; and 'coherency,' which is the characteristic of those cognitive relations in which the structure of the concept network reflects the autonomous structure of the environment. Besides these notions, there are a few other important features such as the isomorphism in cognitive models, whereby the environment of a cognitive model is experienced by the cognitive agent as isomorphic to its concept network; and the finite representability of coherency, whereby a cognitive agent with a finite brain and without access to the God's eye view of the world can maintain coherency of its cognitive relations. All these notions are given a formal characterization in this chapter, and their properties are explored.

189

However, in this process I have tried not to lose sight of the audience for whom this book is primarily intended: cognitive scientists not necessarily fluent in mathematics. For this reason, I have, at times, sacrificed mathematical elegance in favor of easier readability. I have also included many examples to help understand the formal definitions better. Yet, I am sure that the subject matter of this chapter would put the greatest demands on my not-so-mathematically-inclined readers. I can only hope that the discussion of the previous chapters has provided enough of a motivation to such readers for undertaking this arduous journey.

As one might expect, I make use of several concepts from classical set theory and Universal Algebra in this chapter. However, no prior background is assumed and all the relevant concepts are introduced first with examples. A reader already familiar with these concepts may wish to merely skim the earlier sections, but I must caution that I do make use of some non-standard constructions, and for this reason it may be prudent not to skip anything altogether.

I start in Section 2 with a discussion of classes and groupings. Then, in Section 3, I introduce relations between classes and show how relations can induce groupings. A particular kind of relations called *difunctional relations,* which turn out to be significant later, are introduced here also. Section 4 presents functions and operators, as a prelude to introducing algebras. Algebras are introduced in Section 5, and I show how the operators of an algebra endow its objects with structures. The term 'generating class of an algebra' is defined here also.

Then, in Section 6, I present the concept of subalgebra. This concept is important because one may be interested in using only a part of the concept network, and not the whole concept network. Therefore, it would be useful to see how the algebraic structure, particularly generativity, is affected when the operators and/or the objects of an algebra are dropped.

Section 7 extends the concept of groupings (previously defined with respect to classes) to algebras. The term 'algebra of classes' is introduced here to refer to groupings with an algebraic structure. Then, in Section 8, the notion of relations and functions are extended to algebras, where they are referred to as correspondences and homomorphisms, respectively.

Section 9 uses all the previously defined concepts to formalize cognitive model. The terms 'coherency' and 'local coherency' are defined here, as well as some other terms like 'fullness' and 'completeness' [§5.7.4]. Section 10 discusses cognitive models over the same environment, and introduces the terms 'refinement' and 'extension.' Section 11 characterizes projective and accommodating cognitive models. Finally, in Section 12, I discuss the issue of finite representability of coherency.

6.2 Classes and Groupings

A *class* is any collection of objects. It can be defined by enumerating all the objects in the class, or by specifying a rule by which it can be decided whether any given object belongs to the class or not. An object belonging to a class is usually called a *member* of the class. Thus, the collections $\{2, 4, 5\}$, {Boston, Bombay, Sydney, Paris}, {Massachusetts, 5, Margaret Thatcher} are all examples of classes that are specified by listing all its members; whereas $\{x$ such that x is a state of New England}, $\{x$ such that x is an odd positive integer}, $\{x$ such that x is a rational number less than 3 but greater than 3 or x is a citizen of Australia} are instances of classes that are defined by giving a rule to determine class membership.

It must be emphasized that it is not necessary that the objects of a class have some feature in common. In other words, classes are not necessarily defined on the basis of some preexisting property that all the objects in a class are supposed to share. Instead, being the member of a class is itself a property, and in that sense, classes can *create* commonality.

If an object x is a member of a class A, it is written as $x \in A$. The unique class that has no members is called the *empty class* and is denoted by $\emptyset$.

Given two classes A and B, A is said to be a *subclass* of B, written as $A \subseteq B$, if and only if every member of A is also a member of B. A is *equal* to B, written as $A = B$, if and only if A is a subclass of B and also B is a subclass of A. In other words, two classes are equal to each other if, and only if, they have exactly the same objects as their members. A is a *proper subclass* of B, written as, $A \subset B$, if and only if A is a subclass of B but B is not a subclass of A. Thus, the class {Boston, New York} is a subclass of the class $\{x$ such that x is a city of the US}; in fact it is a proper subclass. The class $\{x$ such that x is a positive integer and x is less than 5 and x is greater than 3} is equal to, given standard arithmetic, the class $\{4\}$. The empty class is a subclass of every class but is equal only to itself.

A class is *finite* if the number of distinct objects in it is less than some number N, and is *infinite* otherwise.

Given two classes A and B, the *union* of A and B, written as $A \cup B$, is the class obtained by putting all the objects in A and all the objects in B together. The *intersection* of A and B, written as $A \cap B$, is the class of all those objects, and only those objects, that are members of A and also of B. Thus, if A is {French, Italian}, and B is {English, Spanish, French} then $A \cup B$ is the class {French, Italian, English, Spanish}; and $A \cap B$ is the class {French}. Two classes are said to be *disjoint* if their intersection is the empty class.

A key concept of my framework is *grouping*. Given a class A, a *grouping* of A is a class of subclasses of A. Intuitively, a grouping of a class represents a classification scheme for the objects in the class. Figure 6.1 shows some examples of groupings of a class. (Groupings may be induced by relations as explained below.)

Given a grouping of a class A, it is said to be *pairwise disjoint* if the intersection of any two members of the grouping is always the empty class; and *full* if the union of all the members of the grouping equals the class A itself. In Figure 6.1, the grouping shown in (b) is full but not pairwise disjoint, whereas the one in (c) is pairwise disjoint but not full. When a grouping is both full and pairwise disjoint it is said to be a *partition*. The grouping shown in 6.1 (d) is a partition.

I must remark here that axiomatic set theory makes a clear distinction between sets and classes. All sets are classes but only those classes that are members of other classes are sets. The reason for making this distinction is to avoid Russell's paradox that comes from considering 'the class of all such classes which are not a member of themselves.' The axioms of set theory delineate precisely all those classes that are sets by defining the empty class to be a set and then giving a bunch of other rules that allow new sets to be created from existing sets. In formalizing my framework, it might have been prudent to start out with sets instead of classes. However, I chose classes so as to spare me from having to explain, and you from having to understand, the axioms of set theory—especially since those axioms are not crucial to understanding my formalization. As far as Russell's paradox is concerned, we can simply rule out those classes that are members of themselves: they do not play any interesting role in my framework any way. A reader interested in the axioms of set theory and knowing further about the hows and whys of sets *vs.* classes should consult Mac Lane [1986], Chapter XI, or Levy [1979], Chapter 1.

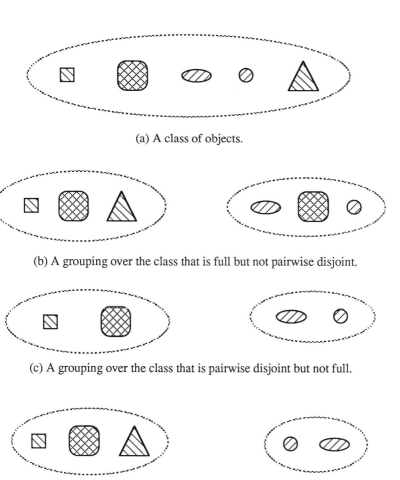

(a) A class of objects.

(b) A grouping over the class that is full but not pairwise disjoint.

(c) A grouping over the class that is pairwise disjoint but not full.

(d) A grouping over the class that is a partition.

FIGURE 6.1: Examples of grouping over a class.

6.3   Relations and Induced Groupings

In instantiating a concept network, the concepts of the network are related
to the parts of the environment. In this section I introduce the concept
of a relation formally. I limit myself to relations between classes here—
relations between algebras (which is how cognitive relations are formalized)
are saved for Section 8—until after I have introduced the concept of algebra.
I also show in this section how relations can induce groupings over classes.
I start with some elementary definitions, and then present a few interesting
characteristics of a special kind of relations called 'difunctional relations' that
induce partitions over their classes. Finally, I discuss relations within a class.

6.3.1   Preliminary Definitions

Given two classes A and B, the *product* of A and B, written as $A \times B$, is the
class of all ordered pairs such that the first element of each pair is a member
of A and the second element a member of B. If A is {Australia} and B is
{Sydney, Boston} then $A \times B$ is the class {⟨Australia, Sydney⟩, ⟨Australia,
Boston⟩}. The nth *power* of A, written as A^n, is the product of A with itself
n times. That is, A^2 is $A \times A$, A^3 is $A \times A \times A$, etc.

Given two classes A and B, a *relation* from A to B is a subclass of $A \times B$.
In other words, a relation assigns to each object of A zero or more objects of
B. The class A is said to be the *domain* of R and class B is said to be the
codomain. Examples of some relations are shown in Figure 6.2.

If R is a relation from A to B, then the *inverse* of R, written as R^{-1},
is the class of all pairs $\langle b, a \rangle$, with $b \in B$ and $a \in A$, such that $\langle a, b \rangle \in R$.
Obviously then, R^{-1} is a relation from B to A.

Given a relation R from A to B, and another relation S from B to C,
the *composition* of R and S, written as $R \circ S$, is defined to be the class of
all pairs $\langle a, c \rangle$, with $a \in A$ and $c \in C$, such that there is some $b \in B$ with
$\langle a, b \rangle \in R$ and $\langle b, c \rangle \in S$. In other words, for every object $a \in A$, consider all
the objects of B that are assigned to a by R, and then for every such object
take all those objects in C that are assigned to it by S, and assign them all
to a. Thus, $R \circ S$ is a relation from A to C.

Every relation between two classes induces groupings on each class. If R
is a relation from A to B, then for every object $a \in A$ consider the class of all
those objects in B that are assigned to a by R. This is obviously a subclass
of B. I refer to it as the *image* of a under R, and write it as $R(a)$. Now

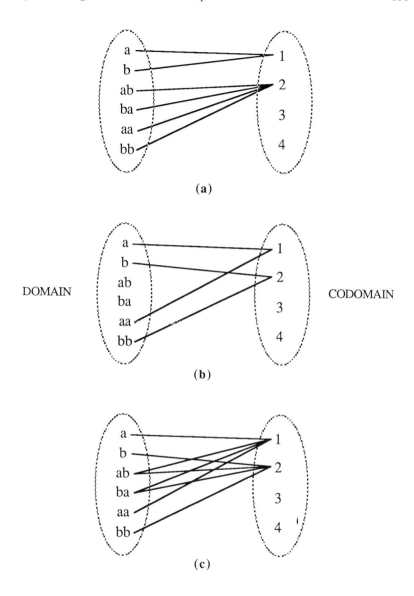

FIGURE 6.2: Three relations from the class {a,b,ab,ba,aa,bb} to the class {1,2,3,4}.

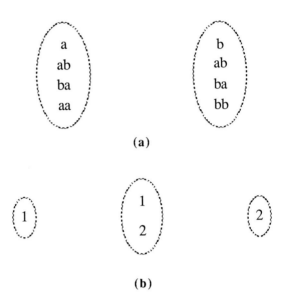

(a)

(b)

FIGURE 6.3: Groupings induced by the relation of Figure 6.2(c) on (a) its domain, and (b) its codomain.

the class of all those subclasses of B that are images of some object in A is a grouping on B. This is called *the grouping induced by R on its codomain.* Similarly, for every object $b \in B$ the class of all objects of A that are assigned to b by R is called the *pre-image* of b, and is written as $R^{-1}(b)$ since it is, in fact, the same as the image of b under the inverse of R. By considering the pre-images of all objects in B under R, we get *the grouping induced by R on its domain.* The groupings induced by the relation of Figure 6.2(c) on its domain and codomain are shown in Figure 6.3.

Notice that in this notational scheme we have $R \circ S(x) = S(R(x))$ and $(R \circ S)^{-1} = S^{-1} \circ R^{-1}$.

6.3.2   Difunctional Relations

A relation R from A to B is said to be *functional* if the grouping induced by it on A is a partition of A; *cofunctional* if the grouping induced by the relation on B is a partition; and *difunctional* if both the groupings are partitions of their respective classes.

Difunctional relations were studied by a French mathematician Riguet in the late 1940s.[1] (See also Mal'cev [1973], p. 23.) Here I note a few interesting characteristics of them. Before doing that, I introduce one more term. A relation R from A to B is said to be *full in A*, or simply *full*, if the grouping induced by it on its domain (A) is full. (Recall that a grouping is full if the union of all its members equals the class—A in this case—itself.) Thus, a relation is full if every member of its domain is related to some object in the codomain.

Now if we start with a subclass, say X, of A, then *the image of X under R* is the class $\{y$ such that $\langle x, y \rangle \in R$ for some x in $X\}$. We will denote it by $R(X)$. Similarly, starting with a subclass Y of B, we can define $R^{-1}(Y)$ to be the class $\{x$ such that $\langle x, y \rangle \in R$ for some y in $Y\}$. The following facts are now easily derived:

Fact: 6.1 *For any relation R from A to B, the following properties hold:*

1. *Given $X_1, X_2 \subseteq A$, whenever $X_1 \subseteq X_2$ then $R(X_1) \subseteq R(X_2)$.*

2. *For all $X \subseteq A$, $R(X) \subseteq R(R^{-1}(R(X)))$.*

3. *R is full if, and only if, $X \subseteq R^{-1}(R(X))$ for all $X \subseteq A$.*

Proof: The first two remarks are immediately obvious, and here I present the proof of the third remark only. First assume that R is full. Then for every x in A—and in particular for every x in X—there is a y in B such that the pair $\langle x, y \rangle$ is in R. In other words, for every x in X there is some y in $R(X)$ such that $\langle x, y \rangle$ is in R.

Let $R(X)$ be called Y. Now by definition, $R^{-1}(Y)$ is the class $\{x$ such that $\langle x, y \rangle \in R$ for some y in $Y\}$. But since for every x in X, there is some y in Y such that $\langle x, y \rangle$ is in R, we conclude that every x in X is also in $R^{-1}(Y)$; thereby proving half of the third remark.

To prove the other half, assume that for every $X \subseteq A$ we know that $X \subseteq R^{-1}(R(X))$. I must now show that R is full.

I prove this by contradiction. Assume that R is not full. It means that there is at least one object in A that is not related to anything in B by R. Call such an object a. Now let $X = \{a\}$. Clearly, $R(X) = \emptyset$, and therefore $R^{-1}(R(X)) = R^{-1}(\emptyset) = \emptyset$ also. Therefore, it is not the case for $X = \{a\}$

---

[1] I am grateful to Beryl Nelson for translating some theorems of Riguet from French into English for me.

that $X \subseteq R^{-1}(R(X))$, contradicting our assumption, and proving the second part of the third remark also. □

Since R^{-1} is a relation from B to A, we can also infer the dual of each remark in Fact 6.1. For instance, the dual of remark (3) is: R is full in B if, and only if, $Y \subseteq R(R^{-1}(Y))$ for all $Y \subseteq B$.

Given any class A, a *chain* in A is a sequence of non-decreasing subclasses of A: that is, a sequence $A_0, A_1, \ldots$ such that $A_i \subseteq A$ and $A_i \subseteq A_{i+1}$ for all i. For instance, if A is the class of all positive integers, then the sequence A_i defined as: $A_0 = \emptyset$, $A_1 = \{0\}$, $A_2 = \{0, 1\}, \ldots, A_i = \{x \text{ such that } x < i\}, \ldots$, is a chain in A. Now given a relation R from A to B, every subclass Y of B induces a chain in A under R, where the initial element of this chain is $R^{-1}(Y)$, and the element following A_i, for $i \geq 0$, is $R^{-1}(R(A_i))$. R is said to be *disconnected in A* if all such chains, for any $Y \subseteq B$, are constant: meaning that $A_0 = A_1 = \cdots$.

Similarly, every subclass X of A induces a chain in B, with the initial element being $R(X)$. We say that R is *disconnected in B* if all such chains, for any subclass X of A, are constant. We can now prove the following interesting fact:

Fact: 6.2 *Given that R is a relation from A to B, each of the following four conditions implies the other three:*

    1. The grouping induced by R on A is pairwise disjoint.

    2. The grouping induced by R on B is pairwise disjoint.

    3. R is disconnected in A. That is, $R^{-1}(Y) = R^{-1}(R(R^{-1}(Y)))$ for all $Y \subseteq B$.

    4. R is disconnected in B. In other words, $R(X) = R(R^{-1}(R(X)))$ for all $X \subseteq A$.

Proof: I first show that (1) implies (2) by contradiction. Assume that the grouping induced by R on A is pairwise disjoint but the one induced on B is not. This means that for all y_1, y_2 in B we either have $R^{-1}(y_1) \cap R^{-1}(y_2) = \emptyset$ or have $R^{-1}(y_1) = R^{-1}(y_2)$. On the other hand, there exists at least one pair of objects in A, say a_1 and a_2, such that $R(a_1) \neq R(a_2)$ and $R(a_1) \cap R(a_2) \neq \emptyset$. This means that there is at least one object, say b_{12}, that $R(a_1)$ and $R(a_2)$ have in common; and one of them, let us say $R(a_1)$ without loss of generality, has an object, say b_1, that is not in $R(a_2)$. This situation is depicted in Figure 6.4.

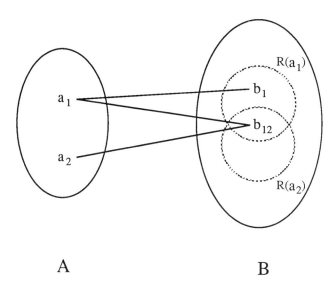

A   B

FIGURE 6.4: Property of relation R in the proof of Fact 6.2.

Now consider $R^{-1}(b_{12})$ and $R^{-1}(b_1)$. Clearly, a_1 and a_2 are both in $R^{-1}(b_{12})$. However, a_2 is in $R^{-1}(b_{12})$ but not in $R^{-1}(b_1)$. Thus, $R^{-1}(b_{12}) \neq R^{-1}(b_1)$, but $R^{-1}(b_{12}) \cap R^{-1}(b_1) \neq \emptyset$. This contradicts the assumption that the grouping induced on A by R is pairwise disjoint, and proves that (1) implies (2).

The proof that (2) implies (1) can be derived by duality—that is, by taking R^{-1} to be the relation in question, and applying the result I just proved—thereby proving that (1) and (2) are equivalent.

I leave it to you to complete the rest of the proof. It needs to be shown that (3) implies (4)—then (4) implies (3) follows from duality; (1) implies (3); and (3) implies (1). (Of course, one could follow some other path also.) The proof in each case is very similar to the one I presented here. Note that each proof is of the form 'M implies N.' To prove it assume first that M is true and N is false. From this show that the situation in Figure 6.4 (or its dual) exists. Finally, derive the negation of M from Figure 6.4, thereby completing the proof by contradiction. □

Facts 6.1 (3) and 6.2 together give the necessary and sufficient conditions for a relation to be difunctional. I now show one other important property of difunctional relations:

Theorem: 6.1 *Let R be a difunctional relation from A to B, and F and G be groupings induced by R on A and B respectively. Then for every X in F there exists a unique non-empty class Y in G, and for every Y in G there exists a unique non-empty class X in F, such that $R(X) = Y$ and $R^{-1}(Y) = X$.*

Proof: Since R is difunctional, it is full in both A and B. In other words, the empty class $\emptyset$ is neither in F nor in G.

Let us take any X in F. It cannot be empty, so it must have at least one object in it, say a. Also, by definition of grouping, there must be some object in B, say b, such that $R^{-1}(b) = X$. Now for every pair of objects x_1, x_2 in X, we have b in $R(x_1)$ and b in $R(x_2)$. From the definition of difunctional relation, $R(x_1)$ and $R(x_2)$ must be disjoint, or equal to each other. Since they are not disjoint—b is in both of them—they must be equal to each other. Thus, $R(X) = R(a)$, which is in G.

The second part, that $R^{-1}(R(X)) = X$, follows directly from Fact 6.2, if we realize that X is nothing but $R^{-1}(\{b\})$.

The proof that for every Y in G there is a unique non-empty X in F with the same properties is similarly derived. □

I may as well remark here that the above theorem essentially shows that the groupings induced by a difunctional relation on its domain and codomain are *bijective,* though the term *bijection* is formally introduced a little later.

6.3.3 Relations Within a Class

I now examine the case when the domain and codomain of a relation are the same class. R is then said to be a relation *over A*, meaning that R is a subclass of $A \times A$. An ambiguity immediately surfaces, since in general there are two different groupings that R induces on A, one by way of images of objects in A and the other from the pre-images of objects of A. I refer to them as *the forward grouping* induced by R on A and *the backward grouping* induced by R on A, respectively.

If a relation over a class is such that both the forward and the backward groupings induced by it are the same, we say that the relation is *symmetric*. Other ways of specifying the symmetry property are to say (1) that a relation R over a class A is symmetric if, and only if, it is such that whenever $\langle x, y \rangle \in R$, for some $x, y \in A$, then $\langle y, x \rangle \in R$; or (2) to say that R is symmetric if, and only if, $R = R^{-1}$. When a relation R over a class A is known to be symmetric, we can talk of *the grouping* induced by R on A, as the mention of forward or backward does not make any difference.

If a relation R over A is such that every object in A is related to itself—in other words, for every x in A, $\langle x, x \rangle$ is in R—then we say that R is *reflexive*. If a relation R over a class A is such that whenever for any $x, y, z \in A$ it is the case that $\langle x, y \rangle \in R$ and $\langle y, z \rangle \in R$ then $\langle x, z \rangle \in R$, we say that R is *transitive*. Another way of specifying the transitive property of a relation R is to say $R \circ R \subseteq R$.

A relation over a class that is reflexive, symmetric, and transitive, at the same time, is called an *equivalence relation*.

Fact: 6.3 *If a relation R over a class A is an equivalence relation, then the grouping on A induced by R is a partition of A. In other words, every equivalence relation is difunctional.*

Proof: Assume that R is an equivalence relation over a class A. Now in order to prove this fact, one must show (1) that the union of all subclasses in the grouping on A induced by R is equal to the class A, and (2) that the intersection of any two subclasses in this grouping is the empty class. I prove both parts by contradiction.

To prove (1), assume that it is not true. Since every member of the grouping is a subclass of A, the union of all the members can at most equal to A: that is, it is always a subclass of A also. Since we assumed that it is not equal to A, it must be a proper subclass of A. In other words, there must be at least one object, say a, in A that is not in any of the subclasses in the grouping. This means that for every x in A, a is not in $R(x)$. In particular, a is not in $R(a)$, implying that R is not reflexive and contradicting our initial assumption. Hence, (1) must be true.

To prove the second part, again assume its negation. That is, there are at least two distinct subclasses of A in the grouping induced by R such that their intersection is not the empty class. Let these be X and Y. Now since X and Y are not disjoint, they must have at least one object in common. Call such an object a. Also, X and Y are not equal, meaning that one of them have an object that is not in the other. Without loss of generality, let us say that there is an object b that is in X but not in Y. Now X and Y must be the image under R of two different objects in A. Let these objects be x and y respectively. So now we have $R(x) = X$, $R(y) = Y$, $a \in X$, $a \in Y$, $b \in X$, and it is not the case that $b \in Y$. However, this means that $\langle x, a \rangle \in R$ and $\langle y, a \rangle \in R$. From symmetry of R we know that $\langle a, x \rangle$ is also in R, and from transitivity of R we can further conclude that $\langle y, x \rangle$ is in R. We also have that $b \in X$ implying that $\langle x, b \rangle \in R$ and again from transitivity of R we infer $\langle y, b \rangle \in R$. However, this last fact means that $b \in Y$, thereby contradicting our assumption that X and Y are not equal. □

The inverse of this fact, however, is not true. In other words, there are difunctional relations that are not equivalence relations. As a very simple example, consider the class of two objects $\{a, b\}$ and the symmetric relation $\{\langle a, b \rangle, \langle b, a \rangle\}$ over it. The grouping induced by this relation is a partition of the class, but the relation is not reflexive or transitive, and is therefore not an equivalence relation.

6.4   Functions and Operators

In my framework, concept networks and environments are formalized as algebras, and an algebra is a class of objects and operators defined over the class. Consequently, as a prelude to introducing algebras, I introduce the concept of an operator in this section. I do so by first discussing functions, which are special kinds of relations, and then presenting operators, which are special kinds of functions.

6.4.1 Functions

Given two classes A and B, a *function* from A to B, is an assignment of a *unique* member of B to *each* member of A. If A were the class of all countries in the world, and B were the class of all capital cities of the world, then the assignment *capital-of* that assigns a unique capital city to each country is a function from A to B. A function is a special kind of relation, where, for every $x \in A$ there is one, and only one, pair $\langle x, y \rangle$, for some $y \in B$, such that the pair is in the relation. Of the relations shown in Figure 6.2, only the one in (a) is a function. The relation in 6.2 (b) is not a function because the objects 'ab' and 'ba' are not assigned anything, and the relation in 6.2 (c) is not a function because 'ab' and 'ba' are each assigned two objects of the class B.

It simply follows from the definition of a function that:

Fact: 6.4 *Every function is a functional relation. In other words, the grouping induced by a function on its domain is always a partition.*

However, the converse of this is not true: that is, there are functional relations that are not functions. The relation *is-a-city-of* from the class of all countries to the class of all cities that relates every country to all the cities in that country is a functional relation but is not a function.

The grouping induced by a function on its codomain need not always be a partition. However, when it is—that is, when a function is a cofunctional relation—we say that it is a *surjective* or *onto* function.

Since every function is a relation, we can also define composition of two functions and inverse of a function. If F is a function from A to B, and G is a function from B to C, then the composition of F and G, written as $F \circ G$, is a relation that assigns to every object a in A, the objects $G(b)$, where $b \in F(a)$. Notice that since F is a function, $F(a)$ contains exactly one object, say b, and since G is a function, $G(b)$ also contains exactly one object. In other words, $F \circ G$ assigns exactly one object of C to every object of A. This leads to the following fact:

Fact: 6.5 *The composition of two functions is a function.*

However the inverse of a function, in general, may not be a function. Consider the class of all positive and negative integers including 0, call it Z, and a function *square* from Z to Z that assigns to every number its square. The inverse of *square* is not a function because some numbers, such as 2 and 3, are not assigned any number by the inverse of *square* and also numbers such as 4 are assigned two numbers: $+2$ and -2. A function such that its inverse is also a function is said to be *bijective*.

Here again it should be noted that whereas every bijective function is difunctional, not every function that is also a difunctional relation is bijective.

6.4.2   Operators

An *operator* over a non-empty class is a function from some integer power of the class to the class itself. Thus, an *n-ary operator* on a non-empty class A is a function from A^n to A: a unary operator on A would be a function from A to A, a binary operator would be a function from A^2 to A, etc. If we consider the class of all positive and negative integers including zero, then addition, subtraction, and multiplication are all binary operators on it, whereas negation is a unary operator. Notice that an operator can be 0-ary, in which case it does not take any argument but returns a member of the class A.

Given any non-empty class A, there are some special operators on it that are given standard names. For each $n > 0$, there are n *identity* operators. The ith *n-ary identity operator,* written as $I_n^{(i)}$ (where $n \geq i > 0$), is the n-ary operator such that for any $a_1, \ldots, a_i, \ldots, a_n \in A$, $I_n^{(i)}(a_1, \ldots, a_i, \ldots, a_n) = a_i$. Similarly, for any member $a \in A$, the *n-ary constant operator with value a,* written as $C_n^{(a)}$ (where $n \geq 0$), is the n-ary operator such that for any $a_1, \ldots, a_n \in A$, $C_n^{(a)}(a_1, \ldots, a_n) = a$.

Given some operators over a class A, new operators can be derived from them by specialization and composition. If α is an n-ary operator, then a *specialization* of α is any operator that is derived from α by fixing one or more of its arguments. For instance, the binary operator *add* over the class of integers can be specialized as a unary operator *add3* by fixing the second argument to be 3, or as the 0-ary operator *2add5* by fixing the first argument to be 2 and the second argument to be 5. As one would expect, *add3* adds 3 to the argument number, and *2add5* accepts no arguments and always returns the number 7.

Though the composition of unary operators can be simply arrived at by composing them as functions, it may not be immediately obvious how to compose operators of arity other than 1. Given that α is an n-ary operator over a non-empty class A, and $\beta_1, \ldots, \beta_n$ are all m-ary operators over A, the *composition* of $\langle \beta_1, \ldots, \beta_n \rangle$ with α, written as $\langle \beta_1, \ldots, \beta_n \rangle \circ \alpha$, is the m-ary operator over A such that for all $a_1, \ldots, a_m \in A$, $\langle \beta_1, \ldots, \beta_n \rangle \circ \alpha(a_1, \ldots, a_m) = \alpha(\beta_1(a_1, \ldots, a_m), \ldots, \beta_n(a_1, \ldots, a_m))$.

An example may make this clearer. Consider the binary operator *sub* over integers that subtracts the second argument from the first argument.

Consider also two unary operators *add3* and *mult2* that are derived by specializing the operators of addition and multiplication respectively. Now the composition of $\langle add3,\ mult2\rangle$ with *sub* is the unary operator $(x + 3) - 2x$ where x is the argument number. Notice that the order in which the operators are composed is very important. If we compose *sub* with *mult2*, then we get *sub* $\circ$ *mult2* $= 2(x - y)$, which is a binary operator with x being the first argument and y being the second argument.

6.5 Algebras and Structures

In my framework, concept networks are formalized as finitely generated algebras. In this section I present a general characterization of algebras, and discuss how operators of an algebra endow its objects with an operational structure and make generativity possible. I start by defining what an algebra is and then characterize the notions of descriptions and structures within algebras. Following that, I introduce the concepts of closure and generating class of an algebra. Finally, I introduce the closure over operators (polynomial operations) and the computability of operators.

6.5.1 Algebras

An algebra is a pair $\langle A, \Omega \rangle$ where A is a non-empty class of objects and Ω is a class of operators over A. For convenience we assume that the class of operators of any algebra is always disjoint from its class of objects: that is, $A \cap \Omega = \emptyset$ for any algebra $\langle A, \Omega \rangle$. With each operator in Ω we associate its arity: a positive integer specifying the number of arguments that must be supplied to the operator. If $\omega \in \Omega$ has arity n then ω is a function from A^n to A. For any n we denote the class of all n-ary operators in Ω by $\Omega(n)$.

Examples of algebra abound. You are surely familiar with the algebra of integers, with its binary operators of addition, subtraction, and multiplication. Boolean algebra is the algebra of truth values ('true' and 'false') and has the binary operators 'and' and 'or,' and the unary operator 'not.' One need not limit oneself to the realm of mathematics to look for examples of algebra; they can be easily found in our day-to-day lives. Consider a construction kit for building a model of an ocean liner. The kit comes with a set of construction pieces that can be put together only in certain ways. Now all these construction pieces, as well as all possible configurations that can be assembled by using some or all of the pieces, can be viewed as objects of an algebra. The operators of this algebra are all possible ways in which two or more construction pieces, or partial assemblies, can be joined together to yield a larger assembly. Notice that from this viewpoint, the final assembled model of the ocean liner is merely an object of the algebra, and the class of objects includes all possible partial assemblies.

At this point, you may as well familiarize yourself with a couple of example algebras, shown in Figure 6.5 (a) and (b), that are very explicitly and fully specified, since I use these examples to illustrate many other concepts and constructions related to algebras in the rest of the chapter. Figure 6.5 (a) shows an algebra of strings of letters. The objects of this algebra are all possible non-null strings of letters 'a'...'z' such as: 'a,' 'mmxxn,' 'zzzzz,' etc. The algebra has six one-place operators: *succ, pred, copy, reverse, first,* and *last;* and one two-place operator: *conc.* The operator *succ* assigns to every character its successor, with the successor of 'a' being 'b,' that of 'b' being 'c,'..., and that of 'z' being 'a'; and to every string the string obtained by replacing every character in the original string by its successor. The other operators are similarly described. The operator *pred* is the inverse of *succ* and assigns to every string the string obtained by replacing every character by its predecessor, where the predecessor of 'y' is 'x,' of 'a' is 'z,' etc. The operator *copy* replicates the argument string and and then puts the two in sequence, and *reverse* reverses the order of characters in a string. The operators *first* and *last* return the first and the last character of the argument string respectively. The two-place operator *conc* accepts two strings as argument, and generates a string that is obtained by concatenating the two strings. A few instances of the strings generated by all these operators are shown in the figure, and should help one understand them better. I refer to this algebra as STRING.

The second algebra shown in Figure 6.5 (b), referred to as INTEGER, is the algebra of signed integers. As everyone must be familiar with it, I think that the figure is self-explanatory and no further explanation of its operators is needed here.

In these two algebras you may notice that some operators are derived from others by composition or specialization. For instance, in STRING the operator *copy* is the composition of a pair of unary identity operators with *conc:* that is, $copy = \langle I_1^{(1)}, I_1^{(1)} \rangle \circ conc$. Similarly, the operator *next* in INTEGER is a specialization of *add* in which the first argument (or the second argument) is fixed to be 1. The operator *sub* is also a composite operator, though its expression is somewhat complicated. I invite you to express *sub* in terms of other operators of INTEGER. A clue is that it uses the operators

Objects: All finite strings of letters 'a' to 'z'.

> Ex: a, aabb, mmnnxxppww, etc. (Note: Null string is not included.)

Unary Operators:

> SUCC Replaces every character in the string with its successor.
>
> Ex: SUCC(a) = b; SUCC(z) = a; SUCC(abz) = bca; SUCC(mnxx) = noyy; etc.

> PRED Replaces every character in the string with its predecessor.
>
> Ex: PRED(a) = z; PRED(z) = y; PRED(abz) = zay; PRED(mnxx) = lmww; etc.

> COPY Appends a copy of the string to itself.
>
> Ex: COPY(a) = aa; COPY(z) = zz; COPY(abz) = abzabz; etc.

> REVERSE Reverses the order of characters in the string.
>
> Ex: REVERSE(a) = a; REVERSE(abz) = zba; REVERSE(mnxx) = xxnm; etc.

> FIRST Returns the first character of the string.
>
> Ex: FIRST(q) = q; FIRST(zz) = z; FIRST(abz) = a; FIRST(mnxx) = m; etc.

> LAST Returns the last character of the string.
>
> Ex: LAST(b) = b; LAST(kw) = w; LAST(abz) = z; LAST(mnxx) = x; etc.

Binary Operators:

> CONC Appends the second string at the back of the first string.
>
> Ex: CONC(a,b) = ab; CONC(amn,wxz) = amnwxz; CONC(p,p) = pp; etc.

FIGURE 6.5 (a): Algebra STRING of strings of characters.

Objects: All positive and negative integers including zero.

Ex: 5, -245, 0, 3189, 1, -1, etc.

Unary Operators:

NEG Changes the sign of the number.

Ex: NEG(-5) = 5; NEG(8) = -8; etc.

NEXT Adds 1 to the number.

Ex: NEXT(-5) = -4; NEXT(7) = 8; etc.

Binary Operators:

ADD Adds the first number to the second number.

Ex: ADD(3,5) = 8; ADD(8,-2) = 6; etc.

SUB Substracts the second number from the first number.

Ex: SUB(-3,-5) = 2; SUB(6,2) = 4; etc.

MULT Multiplies the first number with the second number.

Ex: MULT(5,2) = 10; MULT(4,-3) = -12; etc.

FIGURE 6.5 (b): Algebra INTEGER of signed integers.

$$Objects = \{a_1, a_2\}$$
$$Operators = \{f_1, f_2, f_3\}$$

arguments		operators f_1	f_2	f_3
a_1	a_1	a_1	a_2	a_1
a_1	a_2	a_2	a_1	a_2
a_2	a_1	a_1	a_1	a_2
a_2	a_2	a_2	a_2	a_2

Table 6.1: Algebra ALG1

of *add, neg,* and two binary identity operators $I_2^{(1)}$ and $I_2^{(2)}$.

The two other algebras shown in Tables 6.1 and 6.2 are somewhat artificial. ALG1 has two objects and three binary operators, and ALG2 has three objects and two binary operators. The action of these operators on the objects of their respective algebras is shown by listing the results of applying each operator for all possible pairs of input objects. This can be done because they are finite.

An algebra $\langle A, \Omega \rangle$ is said to be *finite* if its class of objects A is finite, and *infinite* otherwise. Of the four algebras we just saw, INTEGER and STRING are infinite, whereas ALG1 and ALG2 are finite.

6.5.2   Descriptions and Structures

Intuitively, an algebra is a class of objects having structure. The operators of the algebra endow the class with a structure. An operator essentially specifies how a certain object can be *generated* from other objects. Therefore, it is possible to associate one generation history—or possibly more—with each object showing how that object was generated from other objects by applying a sequence of operators. For instance, in the construction kit algebra, the instructions that might accompany the kit are in fact specifying the generation history of the object that is the final assembled model. Similarly, in the algebra STRING, four different generation histories of its object 'aabbcc' are shown in Figure 6.6. Now a generation history of an object can be viewed as specifying how the various sub-units comprising the object are put together to form the object. But this is what is usually meant by the term 'structural description.'

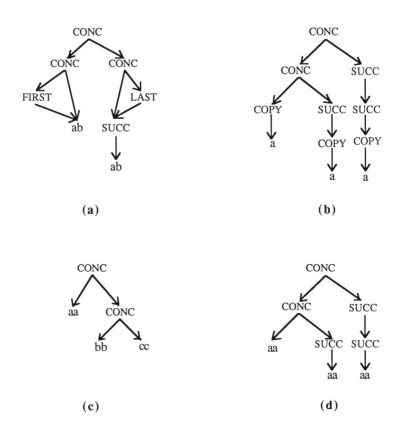

FIGURE 6.6: Four different generation histories of the string 'aabbcc'.

$$Objects = \{b_1, b_2, b_3\}$$
$$Operators = \{g_1, g_2\}$$

		operators	
arguments		g_1	g_2
b_1	b_1	b_1	b_3
b_1	b_2	b_2	b_3
b_1	b_3	b_3	b_3
b_2	b_1	b_3	b_3
b_2	b_2	b_2	b_2
b_2	b_3	b_3	b_3
b_3	b_1	b_3	b_3
b_3	b_2	b_3	b_3
b_3	b_3	b_3	b_3

Table 6.2: Algebra ALG2

I now formalize the notion of structural description. First I define the class of all possible structural descriptions over an algebra, and then associate structural descriptions with individual objects of the algebra. Given an algebra $\langle A, \Omega \rangle$, its *class of structural descriptions*, denoted by $S_\Omega(A)$, is defined recursively as follows:

1. For all $a \in A$, $a \in S_\Omega(A)$, and

2. Whenever $\omega \in \Omega(n)$ and $s_1, \ldots, s_n \in S_\Omega(A)$, then $\omega[s_1, \ldots, s_n] \in S_\Omega(A)$.

The first part of the definition essentially says that all objects of the algebra are structural descriptions, and the second part says that every n-ary operator combines with n already existing structural descriptions to generate a new structural description. (A reader already familiar with algebras will no doubt recognize that the class of structural descriptions of $\langle A, \Omega \rangle$ is nothing but the Ω-word algebra over A [Cohn 1981, p. 116].) Notice the square braces '[' and ']': they serve a different purpose than parentheses '(' and ')'. In fact, in showing structural descriptions graphically I often draw them as labeled and ordered directed acyclic graphs, as in Figure 6.6, and not use the square braces at all. In that case, a structural description simply becomes a labeled directed acyclic graph in which all the nodes that have no outgoing arcs ('leaf' nodes) are labeled with objects of the algebra and every intermediate node having n outgoing arcs (pointing to the 'children' nodes) is labeled with an n-ary operator of the algebra. The graphs are 'ordered' because the order in which the children of an intermediate node appear matters: different orders mean different structural descriptions. Note that every structural description has one and only one node that has no incoming arcs. We will call this node the 'root' node.

Next I define an *evaluation* function, which I abbreviate as *eval*, that assigns an object of $\langle A, \Omega \rangle$ to every structural description in $S_\Omega(A)$ as follows. For every $s \in S_\Omega(A)$,

1. if $s \in A$ then eval(s) = s, and

2. if s is of the form $\omega[s_1, \ldots, s_n]$, for some $\omega \in \Omega(n)$, then eval(s) = $\omega(\text{eval}(s_1), \ldots, \text{eval}(s_n))$.

Again the intuitive idea behind this is very simple, even though the definition may look somewhat complicated. If we consider structural descriptions as labeled ordered directed acyclic graphs then to evaluate a structural description we start with its leaf nodes. Since leaf nodes are labeled with objects of the algebra, they evaluate to themselves. Now we move one level up and consider all the nodes at level 1 (that is, all those intermediate nodes such that all their children are leaf nodes). Any node at this level will be labeled with an n-ary operator if, and only if, it contains n children. Moreover, since it is a level 1 node, all these children are in turn labeled with objects that have been evaluated to themselves in the previous step. In other words, each level 1 node is labeled with an n-ary operator and has n ordered objects as children, for some n. Each such node evaluates to the object obtained by applying the n-ary operator to the children objects, in that order. This process is repeated until the root, or the top level node, is evaluated. The resulting object is precisely the object assigned to the structural description by *eval*. This process is shown in Figure 6.7 for the structural description of Figure 6.6 (b).

Now a *(structural) description of an object* a of an algebra $\langle A, \Omega \rangle$ is simply a structural description $s \in S_\Omega(A)$ such that eval(s) = a. Note that an object may have more than one description. Also, every object is its own description. In fact, if an algebra has no operators (that is, $\Omega = \emptyset$) then this is the *only* description that an object has.

Given a description of an object, the class of objects that appear at the leaf nodes of the description are called the *components* of the description, and the description tree obtained by replacing every object at the leaf

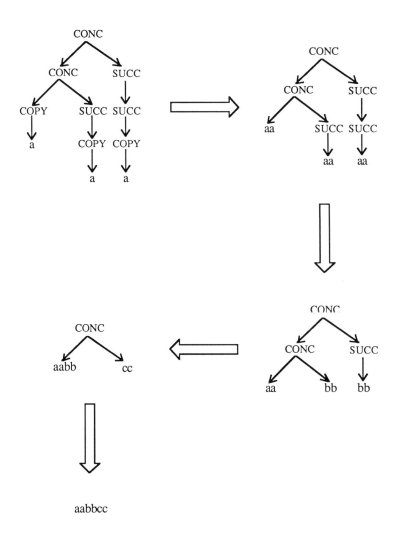

FIGURE 6.7: Evaluation of the description shown in Figure 6.6(b).

node of the description tree with a variable (one variable for each object) is called the *structure* of the description. For instance, the description of Figure 6.6 (c) has as its components the class {*aa, bb, cc*}, and its structure is conc[X, conc[Y, Z]], where X, Y, and Z are variables.

6.5.3 Closures and Generating Classes

The notions of closure and generating class are very closely related to that of description, and since they are both used later on, this is perhaps the best place to introduce them. Let $\langle A, \Omega \rangle$ be an algebra. Now given any subclass X of A, I define $S_\Omega(X)$ as above. It includes only those descriptions of $S_\Omega(A)$ that have their class of components included in the class X. Note, however, that these descriptions may evaluate to objects that are not in X. For example, consider the algebra STRING, and let $X = \{a\}$. The description in Figure 6.6 (b) is included in $S_\Omega(X)$, since its class of components is $\{a\}$, but that description evaluates to the string 'aabbcc' which is not in X.

Now if we take the class of all objects that can result from evaluating some description in $S_\Omega(X)$, it is called the *closure* of X, and is denoted by $J_\Omega(X)$. In other words, $x \in J_\Omega(X)$ if, and only if, there is some $s \in S_\Omega(X)$ such that eval(s) = x. Since every object is a description for itself, we have $X \subseteq J_\Omega(X)$. Also, whenever $X \subseteq Y$, we have $S_\Omega(X) \subseteq S_\Omega(Y)$, and consequently $J_\Omega(X) \subseteq J_\Omega(Y)$. In particular, since $J_\Omega(A) = A$, we have $J_\Omega(X) \subseteq A$.

Alternately, the notion of closure can also be defined as follows. Starting with $X \subseteq A$, we first inductively define a sequence of increasingly larger subclasses of A by:

$$X_0 \;=\; X$$
$$X_{k+1} \;=\; X_k \cup \{x \text{ where } x = \omega(x_1, \ldots, x_n) \text{ for some } x_1, \ldots, x_n \in X_k$$
$$\text{and } \omega \in \Omega(n)\}$$

For instance, if we carry out this construction for the class $X = \{a\}$ in the algebra STRING, we get:

$$X_0 \;=\; \{a\}$$
$$X_1 \;=\; \{a, b, z, aa\}$$
$$X_2 \;=\; \{a, b, z, aa, c, bb, y, zz, aaaa, ab, ba, az, za, aaa,$$
$$bz, zb, baa, aab, zaa, aaz\}$$
$$\vdots$$

etc.

It should be obvious that for all k, $X_k \subseteq X_{k+1}$; and also that $X_k \subseteq A$. Therefore, if we take the union of all X_k as k varies from 0 to infinity the resulting class will be a subclass of A. This is called the *closure* of X. That is:

$$J_\Omega(X) = \bigcup_{k=0}^{\infty} X_k$$

The concept of closure can be more easily explained intuitively by using the construction kit algebra example. Given a construction kit which has some of the construction pieces missing, one may not be able to make the complete model of the ocean liner, but there may still be several partial or complete models that can be constructed by using the available pieces. All such models form the class generated by the available construction pieces. Obviously since any such model can also be constructed with the complete kit, this generated class is a subclass of the algebra.

Any subclass X of A such that $J_\Omega(X) = A$ is called a *generating class* of $\langle A, \Omega \rangle$. Further, X is a *minimal generating class* if it is a generating class and no proper subclass of X is a generating class also. A minimal generating class for an algebra, if it exists, need not be unique. For instance, all the objects of the algebra INTEGER can be generated by the class $\{1\}$, and also by the class $\{-1\}$, both of which are minimal. The algebra STRING can be generated by any one of the twenty six classes: $\{a\}$, $\{b\}$,..., and $\{z\}$, all of which are minimal. In fact, it can be shown that if an algebra contains one pair of operations that are inverses of each other—meaning that if one of them applies to an object x, with possibly other objects, to yield another object y, then the other applies to y, with the same other objects, to yield x—as *addition* and *subtraction* are in INTEGER, and *succ* and *pred* are in STRING—then it does not have a unique minimal generating class. However, the condition that an algebra lacks any such pair of operations is not sufficient by itself to ensure the existence of a unique minimal generating class. This is easily seen by considering the algebra that has three objects $\{0, 1, 2\}$ and only one one-place operator *add1* which adds 1 to the argument number and then converts the result to modulo 3. Thus, add1(0) = 1, add1(1) = 2, and add1(2) = 0. This algebra has three minimal generating classes: $\{0\}$, $\{1\}$, and $\{2\}$.

In fact, the minimal generating classes of an algebra need not all be of the same size. For instance, two generating classes of the algebra INTEGER are $\{1\}$ and $\{2, 3\}$, both of which are minimal but one of them has only one element and the other two.

All this is to point out that most 'interesting' algebras, at least from my point of view, do not have a unique minimal generating class. This makes it so that a concept network, which is formalized as an algebra, need not have a unique class of primitives that generates it; and, moreover, an object-concept in a concept network may have several possible descriptions depending on which object-concepts are regarded as primitive. I believe that most of our concept networks do, indeed, exhibit these characteristics.

An algebra is said to be *finitely generated* if it has a finite generating class. Since its generating class must by definition be a subclass of its objects, every finite algebra is finitely generated. An infinite algebra may or may not be finitely generated. The algebras STRING and INTEGER are both finitely generated. In contrast, if we consider the algebra of all positive integers under the operation of multiplication, it is not finitely generated as there does not exist a largest prime number.

6.5.4   Closure Over Operators

Just as we defined closure over the objects of an algebra, we can also define closure over the operators. The result is called the class of *polynomial operations*. Given that $\langle A, \Omega \rangle$ is an algebra, the class of *polynomial operations* over $\langle A, \Omega \rangle$, written as $P_A(\Omega)$, is the smallest class that satisfies all the following four conditions:

1. Ω is a subclass of $P_A(\Omega)$.

2. For every $n > 0$, and every $i \leq n$, the identity operator $I_n^{(i)}$ is in $P_A(\Omega)$.

3. For every $n > 0$, and for every object a in A, the constant operator $C_n^{(a)}$ is in $P_A(\Omega)$.

4. For every n-ary operator β in $P_A(\Omega)$, and all sequences of m-ary operators $\alpha_1, \ldots, \alpha_n$ in $P_A(\Omega)$, the composition $\langle \alpha_1, \ldots, \alpha_n \rangle \circ \beta$ is also in $P_A(\Omega)$.

It follows from these conditions that for every α in $P_A(\Omega)$, all specializations of α are also in $P_A(\Omega)$.

6.5.5   Computability of Operators

So far I have not discussed how operators, which are functions, are specified. As with classes [see Section 1], an operator can be specified in two possible ways: by enumerating all its members, as I did with ALG1 and ALG2; or by providing a rule that determines how, given the argument objects to the operators, the resulting object is derived, as I did with STRING and INTEGER. Obviously, the former method can only work with finite classes, and for infinite classes the operators invariably have to be specified as rules. However, there may or may not exist some kind of procedure for carrying out the rule. This characteristic is captured precisely by the notion of computability. A computable function or rule is such that an effective procedure exists for implementing it. (See Kfoury, Moll, & Arbib [1982] or Rogers [1967] for a theory of computable functions.) We say that an algebra is *computable* if every one of its operators is computable. Notice that all finite algebras are computable by this criterion.

6.6 Subalgebras and Finite Generativity

Given that concept networks are formalized as finitely generated algebras, and that a concept network may be partially instantiated in an environment (as is typical in metaphorical interpretations), it is important to explore how finite generativity is effected when objects and/or operators of an algebra are dropped. This is exactly what I set out to do in this section.

The concept of subclass can be extended to algebras also. However, care must be exercised to ensure that the algebraic structure—that is, closure under the actions of the operators—is preserved. This requirement makes it so that only some subclasses are acceptable as subalgebras.

A *subalgebra* of an algebra $\langle A, \Omega \rangle$ is a pair $\langle B, \Sigma \rangle$ such that $B \subseteq A$, $\Sigma(n) \subseteq \Omega(n)$ for all n, and whenever $b_1, \ldots, b_n \in B$ and $\sigma \in \Sigma(n)$ then $\sigma(b_1, \ldots, b_n) \in B$. Thus, we see that there are two ways in which a subalgebra can be obtained from an algebra. The first way is by shedding its operators, thereby making it less structured (permitting fewer structures); and the other is by dropping some objects. However, when the objects are dropped, one has to make sure that the objects that are left over are closed under all those operators that are still there. In other words, one has to ensure that the remaining objects do not generate an object that was dropped out by any combination of the remaining operators.

An example would make this clear. Consider the class of all even integers and zero. This is a subclass of the class of objects of INTEGER. It is also closed under all the operators of INTEGER. In particular, the negation of an even number is another even number, and addition, subtraction, and multiplication of two even numbers also yield an even number. Therefore, the class of all even integers, together with all the operators of INTEGER, form a subalgebra of INTEGER. However the class of all odd numbers, also a subclass of the class of objects of INTEGER, does not form a subalgebra of INTEGER if all the operators are kept. This is because the addition, subtraction, and multiplication of odd numbers all result in even numbers, which have been dropped out. If these three operators are dropped, and only the *neg* operator is kept, we then end up with a subalgebra of INTEGER.

Though both the changes—of dropping operators and dropping objects—can be carried out at once in forming a subalgebra, it is often useful to consider changing one at a time. When a subalgebra is formed by shedding some of its operators, I refer to it as an *S-subalgebra,* and when a sub-algebra is formed by dropping some objects, I refer to it as an *O-subalgebra.* Thus, the objects of an algebra are maintained in its S-subalgebras; and all the operators appear in its O-subalgebras.

Notice also that in forming subalgebras of an algebra—whether by dropping objects, or by dropping operators, or by both—the structural descriptions of its objects, and consequently its generating classes, are altered. For S-subalgebras, formed by dropping some operators but keeping all the objects, their class of structural descriptions becomes smaller, and the size of minimal generating classes can only grow. This is because if $\langle A, \Omega \rangle$ is an algebra and $\langle A, \Sigma \rangle$ is its S-subalgebra, meaning that $\Sigma(n) \subseteq \Omega(n)$ for all n, then every generating class of $\langle A, \Sigma \rangle$ is also a generating class of $\langle A, \Omega \rangle$. In other words, if X is a minimal generating class of $\langle A, \Sigma \rangle$ then there is a minimal generating class Y of $\langle A, \Omega \rangle$ such that $Y \subseteq X$.

However, no such simple trend can be observed for O-subalgebras. One might expect the size of minimal generating classes to become smaller as objects are dropped out, but such is not always the case. For instance consider a simple algebra formed by the three positions of a wedge as shown in Figure 6.8. Two positions, *rest-left* and *rest-right* are stable but the third one corresponding to the wedge balanced on its edge, called *on-edge,* is unstable. The algebra has two unary operators: *push-left* and *push-right.* A push is very gentle and the weight of the wedge is such that it is not possible to move it from one stable position to the other by using any of the operators. That is, though *push-left* and *push-right* applied to *on-edge* result in *rest-left* and *rest-right* respectively, neither operator produces any change when applied to *rest-left* or *rest-right.* Now this algebra can be generated by the unstable position alone, since the other two can be obtained from this by applying the appropriate operators. However, the O-subalgebra of two stable positions re-

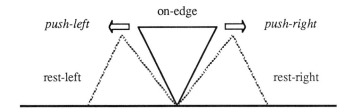

FIGURE 6.8: A simple algebra of a wedge. The objects of the algebra are three positions of the wedge. The two unary operators correspond to pushing the wedge left or right. The algebra can be generated by the unstable position 'on-edge,' but its subalgebra containing the two stable positions requires both of them to be in the generating class.

quires both of them to be there in the minimal generating class, since neither of them can be generated from the other.

Since concept networks are defined to be finitely generated algebras, it is worth exploring to see if subalgebras of a finitely generated algebra are also finitely generated. Let us start with S-subalgebras. We have already seen that the size of a minimal generating class of an S-subalgebra can only grow. But does it always remain finite? The algebra INTEGER easily provides a counterexample. INTEGER is finitely generated, as one of its generating class is $\{1\}$. Now let us consider an S-subalgebra of INTEGER that has only one operator $\times$. Clearly, this subalgebra is not finitely generated since there does not exist a largest prime number. In fact, many trivial counter examples can be found by starting with any finitely generated infinite algebra, such as INTEGER or STRING, and forming an S-subalgebra by dropping all its operators.

How about O-subalgebras? Is it true that the O-subalgebra of any finitely generated algebra is also finitely generated? The answer here is again negative. A counter example is provided by considering the algebra of positive non-zero integers under a binary operator *add1* which is defined as follows:

$$\mathrm{add1}(x, y) = \begin{cases} (x+1) & \text{if } y = 1 \\ 2 & \text{otherwise} \end{cases}$$

Clearly, this algebra is generated by the class $\{1\}$, and is therefore finitely generated. However, an O-subalgebra of it that is formed by dropping 1—

that is, with the class of objects being $\{2, 3, \ldots\}$—is not finitely generated.

6.7 Groupings on Algebras: Algebras of Classes

Before introducing the concept of a relation between two algebras, it will be useful to extend the concept of groupings to algebras, for a relation between two algebras also induces groupings over the algebras. In doing so, one must, as with subalgebras, ensure that the algebraic structure is preserved. However, before that, one needs to specify how an operator, which was defined to act only on objects, acts on classes of objects; what it means to have a group of operators; and how a group of operators acts on groups of objects.

Given a grouping G on A (G is a class of subclasses of A) and an operator $\omega \in \Omega(n)$, we say that G *admits* ω if whenever $X_1, \ldots, X_n \in G$, then there exists some $X \in G$ such that the class $\{x$ such that there exist $x_1 \in X_1$ and $\ldots$ and $x_n \in X_n$ and $x = \omega(x_1, \ldots, x_n)\}$ is a subclass of X. If for every $X_1, \ldots, X_n$, there is a unique such X, then we say that G admits ω *uniquely*. For instance, consider the algebra INTEGER. A grouping $G = \{A_0, A_1, A_2\}$ on its objects is given below:

$$A_0 = \{\ldots, -3, 0, 3, 6, 9, 12, \ldots\}$$
$$A_1 = \{\ldots, -2, 1, 4, 7, 10, 13, \ldots\}$$
$$A_2 = \{\ldots, -1, 2, 5, 8, 11, 14, \ldots\}$$

All the numbers that yield the same remainder when divided by 3—that is, the numbers that are equal modulo 3—are grouped together. It can verified that this grouping admits—in fact, admits uniquely—each operator of INTEGER (*add, mult,* etc.)

On the other hand, consider a grouping $G = \{A, B, \ldots, Z\}$ of the objects of STRING shown below:

$$A = \{a, aa, aaa, aaaa, \ldots\}$$
$$B = \{b, bb, bbb, bbbb, \ldots\}$$
$$\vdots$$
$$Z = \{z, zz, zzz, zzzz, \ldots\}$$

There are twenty six classes, each corresponding to a character. The class corresponding to a character contains only those strings that are formed by one or more occurrences of that character only. This grouping admits each of the one-place operators of STRING (*reverse, succ,* etc.)—and admits it uniquely—but does not admit the two-place operator *conc*. The result of applying *conc* to A and B results in the class $\{ab, aab, abbbb, \ldots\}$, which is not included in any of the $A, \ldots, Z$.

When a grouping admits an operator, what it means is that it is possible to define the action of the operator, which was defined to act only on objects, over the grouping. If G admits ω then for any $X_1, \ldots, X_n \in G$ we can simply define the operation ω on the grouping, $\omega(X_1, \ldots, X_n)$, as any $X \in G$ such that the class $\{x$ such that there exist $x_1 \in X_1$ and $\ldots$ and $x_n \in X_n$ and $x = \omega(x_1, \ldots, x_n)\}$ is a subclass of X. The definition of admissibility makes sure that at least one such X exists for every $X_1, \ldots, X_n \in G$. However, there may be more than one such X for some $X_1, \ldots, X_n \in G$, and this allows one to define the action of ω on the grouping in more than one way. For instance consider the grouping $\{B_1, B_2\}$ over the objects of algebra ALG2, where $B_1 = \{b_1, b_3\}$ and $B_2 = \{b_2, b_3\}$. This grouping clearly admits the operator g_1 but does not admit it uniquely, since the class $\{x$ such that $x = g_1(y, z)$ for any y in B_1 and z in $B_2\}$ equals $\{b_3\}$, which is a subclass of both B_1 and B_2. For this reason, we could set $g_1(B_1, B_2)$ to be either B_1 or B_2. Of course, if G admits ω uniquely, then there is no such ambiguity. There is one other condition under which we can define the action of ω on G uniquely, but before considering it I would like to extend the concept of admissibility to classes (groups) of operators.

Clearly, in order to meaningfully consider the action of a class of operators on a grouping of objects, all operators in the class must have the same arity. In other words, the class of operators cannot contain an m-ary operator and an n-ary operator, with $m \neq n$, at the same time. Now given an algebra $\langle A, \Omega \rangle$, a grouping G on A, and a class of operators of the same arity $\Delta \subseteq \Omega(n)$, we say that G *admits* Δ if whenever $X_1, \ldots, X_n \in G$, then there is a class $X \in G$ such that the class $\{x$ such that there exist $x_1 \in X_1, \ldots, x_n \in X_n, \delta \in \Delta$ and $x = \delta(x_1, \ldots, x_n)\}$ is a subclass of X. If for every $X_1, \ldots, X_n \in G$ there is a unique such X then we say that G admits Δ *uniquely.*

Fact: 6.6 *If G admits Δ then G admits every $\delta \in \Delta$.*

The proof of this fact is very simple and omitted here. Notice, however, that the converse of this fact is not true. The grouping $\{A_0, A_1, A_2\}$ on INTEGER that was introduced earlier admits *add* and *mult* individually, but does not admit the class $\{add, mult\}$. Also G may admit Δ uniquely, but may not admit every $\delta \in \Delta$ uniquely.

When a grouping admits a class of operators, it means that it is possible to define the action of the class of operators, as if it were one operator, on the members of the grouping, as if they were objects. Here again, an ambiguity would exist unless the class of operators is admitted uniquely by the grouping. We, of course, have the following fact that ensures uniqueness under certain conditions:

Fact: 6.7 *If a grouping is pairwise disjoint—meaning that the intersection of any two members of it is always the empty class—then all operators, and non-empty classes of operators admitted by it are admitted uniquely.*

The proof is again easy and is not mentioned here. Since all partitions are pairwise disjoint by definition, it follows that any partition, if it admits an operator (or a class of operators), admits it uniquely.

It is interesting to see if we can come up with some other way to define the action of a class of operators Δ on a grouping G uniquely even when G does not admit Δ uniquely (given that G admits Δ.) One possibility is to see if there is a unique minimal $X \in G$ for every $X_1, \ldots, X_n \in G$ such that the class $\{x$ such that there exist $x_1 \in X_1, \ldots, x_n \in X_n, \delta \in \Delta$ and $x = \delta(x_1, \ldots, x_n)\}$ is a subclass of X, and moreover, if any other $Y \in G$ satisfies this condition then $X \subseteq Y$. If this is the case, then we can simply set $\Delta(X_1, \ldots, X_n)$ to be this unique X for every $X_1, \ldots, X_n \in G$.

Of course, the existence of a unique minimal such X cannot be guaranteed in the general case. But when the grouping G is closed under intersection—meaning that if any two classes M and N are in G then their intersection $M \cap N$ is also in G—then we can prove the existence of a unique minimal such X for every $X_1, \ldots, X_n \in G$.

Fact: 6.8 *Given that $\langle A, \Omega \rangle$ is an algebra, G a grouping on A that is closed under intersection, and $\Delta \subseteq \Omega(n)$ for some n such that G admits Δ, then for any $X_1, \ldots, X_n \in G$, there is a unique minimal $X \in G$ such that the class $\{x$ such that there exist $x_1 \in X_1, \ldots, x_n \in X_n, \delta \in \Delta$ and $x = \delta(x_1, \ldots, x_n)\}$ is a subclass of X.*

Proof: Let us refer to the class $\{x$ such that there exist $x_1 \in X_1, \ldots, x_n \in X_n, \delta \in \Delta$ and $x = \delta(x_1, \ldots, x_n)\}$ as Z. Now since G admits Δ there exists some $X \in G$ such that $Z \subseteq X$ by definition.

Clearly, if X is the only class in G such that $Z \subseteq X$ then there is no problem. However, suppose that there are a number of such classes in G, say a family $Y = \{Y_i\}_{i>1}$, such that $Z \subseteq Y_i$ for all i. We must now show that this family has a unique minimal element.

First we eliminate all non-minimal members from Y. That is, whenever

$Y_j \subset Y_k$, for any j and k, we eliminate Y_k as clearly it is not minimal. At the end of this process, if we are left with only one member in Y, then it is the unique minimal element.

But, what if we are left with two or more classes in Y at the end of last step? We will now show that this cannot be the case.

Let us assume the contrary. Say that there are two minimal classes that we end up with: Y_1 and Y_2. Since they are both minimal (and distinct) neither $Y_1 \subseteq Y_2$ nor $Y_2 \subseteq Y_1$. Moreover, because they were both initially included in Y, $Z \subseteq Y_1$ and $Z \subseteq Y_2$.

Now G is closed under intersection. So we have $Y_1 \cap Y_2 \in G$. Also, since $Z \subseteq Y_1$ and $Z \subseteq Y_2$, we have $Z \subseteq Y_1 \cap Y_2$.

This means $Y_1 \cap Y_2$ must be included in Y also. And since $Y_1 \cap Y_2 \subseteq Y_1$ and $Y_1 \cap Y_2 \subseteq Y_2$, we know that neither Y_1 nor Y_2 is minimal, contradicting our assumption.

Thus, there cannot exist two minimal classes in Y, proving our result. $\square$

Given an algebra $\langle A, \Omega \rangle$, a *grouping on* $\langle A, \Omega \rangle$ is a pair $\langle G, \Upsilon \rangle$, such that G is a grouping on A, Υ is a grouping on Ω that respects arity of operators— meaning that every member of Υ is a subclass of $\Omega(n)$ for some n—and G admits every member of Υ. If, in addition, G admits every member of Υ uniquely we say that $\langle G, \Upsilon \rangle$ is an *algebra of classes* over $\langle A, \Omega \rangle$.

Again, it would be interesting to ascertain whether an algebra of classes of any finitely generated algebra is also finitely generated. I do not yet have a proof, or a counter example, to settle this issue one way or another, but my intuition is that it is not true; that is, a finitely generated algebra might have an algebra of classes that is not finitely generated.

6.8 Relations Between Algebras: Correspondences

We are now in a position to consider relations between two algebras, which is how cognitive relations are formalized in this framework. If one discounts the operational structures of algebras, and regards them as mere classes, the concept of relations can easily be extended to cover them. However, what is of interest is the case when the relations between two algebras preserve their algebraic structures, for such relations correspond to coherent cognitive relations. I refer to the relations (between two algebras) with this structure preserving property as *correspondences*. I start by introducing products of algebras and correspondences; then I consider groupings induced over algebras by correspondences; and, finally, I discuss some characteristics of difunctional correspondences and extend Theorem 6.1 to correspondences.

6.8.1 Products of Algebras and Correspondences

Given two algebras $\langle A, \Omega \rangle$ and $\langle B, \Sigma \rangle$ their *product* $\langle A, \Omega \rangle \times \langle B, \Sigma \rangle = \langle C, \Gamma \rangle$ is such that $C = A \times B$; for any n, whenever $\langle \omega, \sigma \rangle \in \Omega(n) \times \Sigma(n)$ and $\langle a_1, b_1 \rangle, \ldots, \langle a_n, b_n \rangle \in C$ then $\langle \omega, \sigma \rangle$ is defined to be an n-ary operation over C with the value $\langle \omega(a_1, \ldots, a_n), \sigma(b_1, \ldots, b_n) \rangle$ (this is written as $\langle \omega, \sigma \rangle(\langle a_1, b_1 \rangle, \ldots, \langle a_n, b_n \rangle)$); and $\Gamma(n) = \Omega(n) \times \Sigma(n)$ for all n.

A *correspondence* over two algebras $\langle A, \Omega \rangle$ and $\langle B, \Sigma \rangle$ is a relation between them that preserves the algebraic structure. In other words, a pair $\langle R, \Psi \rangle$ is a correspondence between $\langle A, \Omega \rangle$ and $\langle B, \Sigma \rangle$ when:

1. $R \subseteq A \times B$;

2. $\Psi(n) \subseteq (\Omega(n) \times \Sigma(n))$ for all n; and

3. whenever $\langle a_1, b_1 \rangle, \ldots, \langle a_n, b_n \rangle \in R$ and $\langle \omega, \sigma \rangle \in \Psi(n)$ then $\langle \omega(a_1 \ldots a_n), \sigma(b_1 \ldots b_n) \rangle \in R$

An example of a correspondence from ALG1 to ALG2 is shown in Figure 6.9 (a). In 6.9 (b) I also show a relation from ALG1 to ALG2 that is not a correspondence because $\langle a_1, b_1 \rangle$ and $\langle f_2, g_2 \rangle$ are both in the relation but $\langle f_2(a_1, a_1), g_2(b_1, b_1) \rangle$ is not in it.

There are two correspondences between INTEGER and STRING that are interesting and I mention them here. The first one, which I call MODULO, is from STRING to INTEGER and relates all those strings that contain one or more occurrences of character 'a' only, with all the numbers that are 0 modulo 26; all those strings that contain one or more occurrences of character 'b' only, with all the numbers that are 1 modulo 26; etc.; and operator *succ* with *next*. This relationship is graphically shown below:

$$\{a, aa, aaa, \ldots\} \longleftrightarrow \{\ldots, -26, 0, 26, 52, \ldots\}$$
$$\{b, bb, bbb, \ldots\} \longleftrightarrow \{\ldots, -25, 1, 27, 53, \ldots\}$$
$$\vdots \quad \vdots \quad \vdots$$
$$\{z, zz, zzz, \ldots\} \longleftrightarrow \{\ldots, -1, 25, 51, 77, \ldots\}$$
$$succ \longleftrightarrow next$$

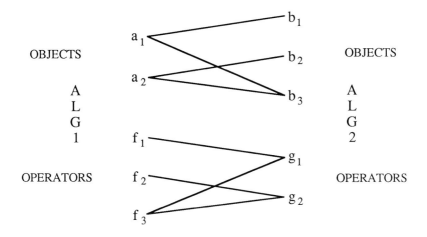

(a) A correspondence from ALG1 to ALG2.

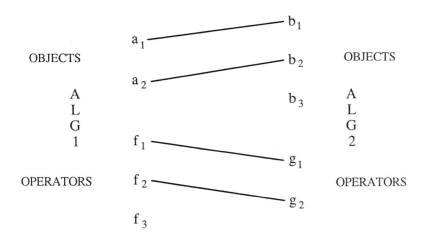

(b) A relation from ALG1 to ALG2 that is not a correspondence.

FIGURE 6.9: Examples of a correspondence and a non-correspondence.

Where every member of the class at one end of the arrow is related to every member of the class at the other end of the arrow. It is simple to verify that this relation is, indeed, a correspondence.

The second correspondence, called LENGTH, is from INTEGER to STRING. It relates every positive non-zero integer with a string containing that many characters; and operator *add* with *conc*. Using the same notation as above, this relationship is depicted below:

$$\{1\} \longleftrightarrow \{a, b, \ldots, z\}$$
$$\{2\} \longleftrightarrow \{aa, ab, \ldots, zz\}$$
$$\vdots \quad \vdots \quad \vdots$$
$$\text{add} \longleftrightarrow \text{conc}$$

Here, again, it is easy to verify that this relationship preserves the algebraic structure and is, therefore, a correspondence.

By condition (3) in the definition of a correspondence, we know that a correspondence is closed under pairwise operations (as defined for products of algebras). This directly leads to the following fact:

Fact: 6.9 *A correspondence* $\langle R, \Psi \rangle$ *over* $\langle A, \Omega \rangle$ *and* $\langle B, \Sigma \rangle$ *is an algebra under pairwise operations. In particular, it is a subalgebra of* $\langle A, \Omega \rangle \times \langle B, \Sigma \rangle$.

Often, I would like to assert that some x is an element of an algebra $\langle A, \Omega \rangle$ without specifying whether x is an object ($x \in A$) or an operator ($x \in \Omega$). In those situations I write $x \in \langle A, \Omega \rangle$ to mean $x \in A$ or $x \in \Omega$. Thus, if $\langle R, \Psi \rangle$ is a correspondence then $\langle x, y \rangle \in \langle R, \Psi \rangle$ means that $\langle x, y \rangle \in R$ or $\langle x, y \rangle \in \Psi$. Since the class of objects of any algebra is disjoint from its class of operators, there is no ambiguity in this notation.

The inverse of a correspondence and the composition of two correspondences are defined in a way similar to relations. Given a correspondence $\langle R, \Psi \rangle$ over $\langle A, \Omega \rangle$ and $\langle B, \Sigma \rangle$ its *inverse* $\langle R, \Psi \rangle^{-1}$ is defined to be $\langle R^{-1}, \Psi^{-1} \rangle$; or in other words for all $x \in \langle A, \Omega \rangle$ and for all $y \in \langle B, \Sigma \rangle$, $\langle y, x \rangle \in \langle R, \Psi \rangle^{-1}$ if and only if $\langle x, y \rangle \in \langle R, \Psi \rangle$. Similarly, given another correspondence $\langle S, \Phi \rangle$ over $\langle B, \Sigma \rangle$ and $\langle C, \Gamma \rangle$, the *composition* of $\langle R, \Psi \rangle$ with $\langle S, \Phi \rangle$, written as $\langle R, \Psi \rangle \circ \langle S, \Phi \rangle$, is defined as $\langle R \circ S, \Psi \circ \Phi \rangle$; or in other words for all $x \in \langle A, \Omega \rangle$ and all $y \in \langle C, \Gamma \rangle$, $\langle x, y \rangle \in \langle R, \Psi \rangle \circ \langle S, \Phi \rangle$ if and only if there is some $z \in \langle B, \Sigma \rangle$ such that $\langle x, z \rangle \in \langle R, \Psi \rangle$ and $\langle z, y \rangle \in \langle S, \Phi \rangle$. It is easy to see that the inverse of a correspondence and the composition of two correspondences are themselves correspondences. In particular, $\langle R, \Psi \rangle^{-1}$ is a correspondence over $\langle B, \Sigma \rangle$ and $\langle A, \Omega \rangle$ and $\langle R, \Psi \rangle \circ \langle S, \Phi \rangle$ is a correspondence over $\langle A, \Omega \rangle$ and $\langle C, \Gamma \rangle$.

6.8.2 Groupings Induced by Correspondences

Like relations, correspondences also induce groupings on the objects and operators of their domain and codomain algebras. We have already seen the groupings induced by MODULO and LENGTH. In Figure 6.10, I show the groupings induced on ALG1 and ALG2 by the correspondence of Figure 6.9 (a). Notice that these groupings are algebraic in that groupings on the objects admit the groupings on the operators of their respective algebras. This raises the interesting question whether this is always the case. The following theorem provides the answer:

Theorem: 6.2 *Let $\langle A, \Omega \rangle$ and $\langle B, \Sigma \rangle$ be algebras, and let $\langle R, \Psi \rangle$ be a correspondence over them. Let C be the grouping induced by R over B, and Γ be the grouping induced by Ψ over Σ. Then C admits every member of Γ. In other words, $\langle C, \Gamma \rangle$ forms a grouping over $\langle B, \Sigma \rangle$.*

Proof: Let $\Delta \in \Gamma$. Then by definition of correspondence, Δ is a class of n-ary operators of Σ, for some n. Moreover, by definition of induced groupings, Δ is the image of some $\alpha \in \Omega(n)$ under Ψ. That is, $\Psi(\alpha) = \Delta$.

Now take any $Y_1, \ldots, Y_n \in C$. By definition of induced grouping again, each of $Y_1, \ldots, Y_n$ is the image of some object in A under R. Let these objects be $a_1, \ldots, a_n$ respectively. Thus, $R(a_1) = Y_1, \ldots,$ and $R(a_n) = Y_n$.

I must now show that the class $\{y$ such that $y = \delta(y_1, \ldots, y_n)$ for some $\delta \in \Delta, y_1 \in Y_1, \ldots, y_n \in Y_n\}$, which we will refer to as Y, is a subclass of some member of C.

Consider any $b \in Y$. Now $b = \beta(b_1, \ldots, b_n)$, for some $\beta \in \Delta$, $b_1 \in Y_1, \ldots,$ and $b_n \in Y_n$. But since $\Psi(\alpha) = \Delta$, $R(a_1) = Y_1, \ldots,$ and $R(a_n) = Y_n$, we get $\langle \alpha, \beta \rangle \in \Psi$, $\langle a_1, b_1 \rangle \in R, \ldots,$ and $\langle a_n, b_n \rangle \in R$.

From the definition of correspondence, we conclude that $\langle \alpha(a_1, \ldots, a_n), \beta(b_1, \ldots, b_n) \rangle \in R$; or $\langle a, b \rangle \in R$ where $a = \alpha(a_1, \ldots, a_n)$. Now since for every $b \in Y$ it is the case that $\langle a, b \rangle \in R$, we get $Y \subseteq R(a)$.

Given that C is a grouping on B induced by R, we know that $R(a)$ must be in C. Thus we have proved the theorem. $\square$

Notice however, that $\langle C, \Gamma \rangle$ may not necessarily form an algebra of classes over $\langle B, \Sigma \rangle$; the reason being that though C admits every member of Γ, it may not admit it uniquely. For instance, the grouping induced by the correspondence of 6.9 (a) on its codomain algebra (ALG2) is not an algebra of classes. In particular, the grouping on the objects of ALG2 does not admit the group of operators $\{g_2\}$ uniquely, as I pointed out earlier.

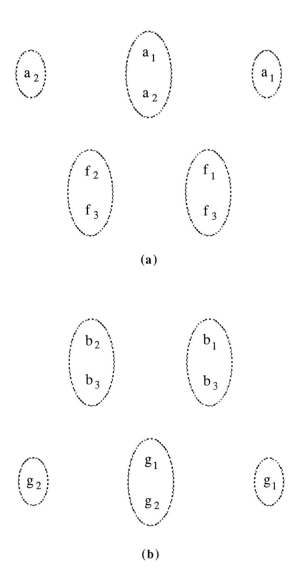

FIGURE 6.10: Groupings induced by the correspondence of 6.9(a) on (a) its domain ALG1, and (b) its codomain ALG2.

Since the inverse of a correspondence is also a correspondence, this theorem also shows that the grouping induced by $\langle R, \Psi \rangle$ on $\langle A, \Omega \rangle$ is also algebraic.

6.8.3 Difunctional Correspondences

A correspondence is said to be *functional* if the grouping induced by it on its domain algebra is a partition; *cofunctional* if the grouping induced by it on its codomain algebra is a partition; and *difunctional* if it is functional as well as cofunctional.

Similar to relations, correspondences also give rise to chains of subalgebras in their domain and codomain. All the results that were derived for relations would extend to correspondences provided one can show that correspondences preserve algebraic closure—meaning that the image of a subalgebra is another subalgebra. This is easily proved in the following theorem:

Theorem: 6.3 *Given that $\langle R, \Psi \rangle$ is a correspondence over algebras $\langle A, \Omega \rangle$ and $\langle B, \Sigma \rangle$, and $\langle X, \Delta \rangle$ is a subalgebra of $\langle A, \Omega \rangle$, then $\langle R, \Psi \rangle (\langle X, \Delta \rangle)$ is a subalgebra of $\langle B, \Sigma \rangle$.*

Proof: Let us denote $\langle R, \Psi \rangle (\langle X, \Delta \rangle)$ by $\langle Y, \Lambda \rangle$. Clearly, $Y \subseteq B$ and $\Lambda \subseteq \Sigma$. So we only need to show that Y is closed under Λ. In other words, given any $\lambda \in \Lambda(n)$, and $y_1, \ldots, y_n \in Y$ we must show that $\lambda(y_1, \ldots, y_n)$ is also in Y.

Since $Y = R(X)$ we know that there are $x_1, \ldots, x_n \in X$ such that $\langle x_1, y_1 \rangle, \ldots, \langle x_n, y_n \rangle \in R$. Similarly, we know that there exists $\delta \in \Delta(n)$ such that $\langle \delta, \lambda \rangle \in \Psi$.

From the definition of correspondence, we infer that $\langle \delta(x_1, \ldots, x_n), \lambda(y_1, \ldots, y_n) \rangle$ is also in R. But since $\langle X, \Delta \rangle$ is a subalgebra, $\delta(x_1, \ldots, x_n)$ is in X. Therefore, it follows that $\lambda(y_1, \ldots, y_n)$ must be in Y. $\square$

We can now generalize Theorem 6.1 to algebras. However, before doing that I would like to introduce the concepts of homomorphism and isomorphism.

An Aside: Homomorphisms and Isomorphisms

Given a correspondence $\langle f, \alpha \rangle$ over $\langle A, \Omega \rangle$ and $\langle B, \Sigma \rangle$ we say that it is a *homomorphism* from $\langle A, \Omega \rangle$ to $\langle B, \Sigma \rangle$ if and only if for every x in $\langle A, \Omega \rangle$ there is exactly one y in $\langle B, \Sigma \rangle$ such that $\langle x, y \rangle$ is in $\langle f, \alpha \rangle$. Thus, homomorphisms are functions that preserve algebraic structure. The pair $\langle B_1, \Sigma_1 \rangle$ such that $y \in \langle B_1, \Sigma_1 \rangle$ if and only if there is some $x \in \langle A, \Omega \rangle$ such that $\langle x, y \rangle \in \langle f, \alpha \rangle$

is said to be the *image* of $\langle f, \alpha \rangle$. From Theorem 6.3 we infer that the image of any homomorphism is a subalgebra of its codomain algebra.

Clearly, it follows from the definition that every homomorphism is functional. In particular, the grouping induced by a homomorphism on its domain algebra is a partition. Using Theorem 6.2 and Fact 6.7 we can infer that this grouping is an algebra of classes. It is called the *kernel* of the homomorphism. I denote the kernel of a homomorphism $\langle f, \alpha \rangle$ by $ker(\langle f, \alpha \rangle)$.

When a homomorphism is cofunctional also (meaning that it is difunctional) we say that it is an *epimorphism*.

Composition and inverse of homomorphisms are defined similarly. It is easily shown that the composition of two homomorphism is another homomorphism. The inverse of a homomorphism, though undoubtably a correspondence, may not be a homomorphism. Whenever $\langle f, \alpha \rangle$ is a homomorphism such that $\langle f, \alpha \rangle^{-1}$ is also a homomorphism, we say that it is an *isomorphism*.

Resumption: Difunctional Correspondences

We can now transport Theorem 6.1 to algebras.

Theorem: 6.4 *Let $\langle R, \Psi \rangle$ be a difunctional correspondence from $\langle A, \Omega \rangle$ to $\langle B, \Sigma \rangle$, and $\langle F, \Delta \rangle$ and $\langle G, \Lambda \rangle$ be groupings induced by $\langle R, \Psi \rangle$ on $\langle A, \Omega \rangle$ and $\langle B, \Sigma \rangle$ respectively. Then:*

1. *$\langle F, \Delta \rangle$ and $\langle G, \Lambda \rangle$ are algebras of classes, and*

2. *there exists a unique isomorphism, say $\langle R, \Psi \rangle^{\star}$, from $\langle F, \Delta \rangle$ to $\langle G, \Lambda \rangle$ such that the pair $\langle X, Y \rangle$ is in $\langle R, \Psi \rangle^{\star}$ if, and only if, $\langle R, \Psi \rangle(X) = Y$ and $\langle R, \Psi \rangle^{-1}(Y) = X$.*

Proof: The first part follows directly from Theorem 6.2 and Fact 6.7. For the second part, we infer from Theorem 6.1 that there is a bijection from $\langle F, \Delta \rangle$ to $\langle G, \Lambda \rangle$ that assigns to every X in $\langle F, \Delta \rangle$ the unique non-empty Y in $\langle G, \Lambda \rangle$ such that $\langle R, \Psi \rangle(X) = Y$ and $\langle R, \Psi \rangle^{-1}(Y) = X$. We only need to show that this bijection preserves the algebraic structure—or, what is the same, is an isomorphism.

Let $X_1, \ldots, X_n$ be in F and Π be in $\Delta(n)$. Also, let the class $\{x$ such that $x = \pi(x_1, \ldots, x_n)$ for some $x_1 \in X_1, \ldots, x_n \in X_n$ and $\pi \in \Pi\}$ be denoted by U. Since $\langle F, \Delta \rangle$ is an algebra of classes, there must be a unique class in F, say M, such that U is a subclass of M.

Similarly, let $Y_1 = R(X_1), \ldots, Y_n = R(X_n)$ be in G $\Gamma = \Psi(\Pi)$ be in $\Lambda(n)$. Note that Theorem 6.1 guarantees the existence of unique such $Y_1, \ldots, Y_n$ and Γ. Also let us denote the class $\{y$ such that $y = \gamma(y_1, \ldots, y_n)$ for some $y_1 \in Y_1, \ldots, y_n \in Y_n$ and $\gamma \in \Gamma\}$ by V. Since $\langle G, \Lambda \rangle$ is an algebra of classes, there is a unique N in G such that V is a subclass of N.

We must now show that $R(M) = N$ and $R^{-1}(N) = M$.

To show $R(M) = N$, since N is the unique member of G that includes V, it is sufficient to show that V is a subclass of $R(M)$.

Since R is a difunctional relation from A to B and M is in the grouping induced by R on A, we know that M is not empty and for any m in M, $R(m) = R(M)$ (see the proof of Theorem 6.1). From this, and knowing that U is a subclass of M, we conclude that $R(U) = R(M)$. Thus, we must now show that V is a subclass of $R(U)$.

Take any v in V. By the definition of V, there must be $v_1 \in Y_1, \ldots, v_n \in Y_n$ and $\gamma \in \Gamma$ such that $\gamma(v_1, \ldots, v_n) = v$. But since $Y_1 = R(X_1)$, etc., we must have $u_1 \in X_1, \ldots, u_n \in X_n$ and $\pi \in \Pi$ such that $\langle u_1, v_1 \rangle, \ldots, \langle u_n, v_n \rangle$ are all in R and $\langle \pi, \gamma \rangle$ is in Ψ. By the definition of correspondence this in turn implies that $\langle \pi(u_1, \ldots, u_n), \gamma(v_1, \ldots, v_n) \rangle$ is in R also. In other words, if we write $\pi(u_1, \ldots, u_n)$ as u, then $\langle u, v \rangle$ is in R. But by definition of U, u is U also. So we have proved that v is in $R(U)$, or that V is a subclass of $R(U)$.

The other half of the proof, that $R^{-1}(N) = M$, is similar. $\square$

There are two special cases of this theorem that are more familiar. The first of them concerns homomorphisms. Notice first that epimorphisms are difunctional by definition and so the theorem directly applies to them. But then any homomorphism can be made an epimorphism by replacing the codomain with its subalgebra that is the image of the domain under the homomorphism. Thus, every homomorphism generates a unique isomorphism between the groupings on its domain and codomain. This result is commonly known as the *first isomorphism theorem*. (See Mal'cev [1973], pp. 47–48; and Cohn [1981], p. 60.)

The second case concerns those correspondences over an algebra and itself that are also equivalence relations. Such correspondences are called *congruences*. Thus, a *congruence* is a correspondence $\langle R, \Psi \rangle$ of an algebra $\langle A, \Omega \rangle$ over itself such that for all $x, y, z \in \langle A, \Omega \rangle$:

1. $\langle x, x \rangle \in \langle R, \Psi \rangle$,

2. $\langle y, x \rangle \in \langle R, \Psi \rangle$ whenever $\langle x, y \rangle \in \langle R, \Psi \rangle$, and

3. $\langle x, z \rangle \in \langle R, \Psi \rangle$ whenever $\langle x, y \rangle \in \langle R, \Psi \rangle$ and $\langle y, z \rangle \in \langle R, \Psi \rangle$.

Since Fact 6.1 applies to all equivalence relations, we know that every congruence is difunctional, though the converse is not the case. From Theorem 6.4 we can then infer that the grouping induced by a congruence is an algebra of classes.

6.9 Cognitive Models

A cognitive model, as you may recall from the last chapter, has three components: a concept network, an environment, and a cognitive relation between the two. I had also indicated that the concept network and the environment are formalized as algebras, and the cognitive relation as a correspondence between the two algebras. Now that I have introduced algebras, I can present the three components of a cognitive model more formally. I start out this section by giving a formal definition of cognitive models. Then I introduce the concepts of local coherency and coherency. Finally, I define some of the terms like 'complete' and 'full' that can be applied to cognitive models and that were informally introduced in the last chapter [Section 5.7.4], and relate them to the characteristics of cognitive relations.

6.9.1 Basic Definition

A *concept network* is an algebra $\langle A, \Omega \rangle$ with the following characteristics:

1. The class of operators Ω is either finite, or is included in the class of polynomial operations generated by a finite subclass of Ω. In other words, there is a finite subclass $\Omega_1 \subseteq \Omega$ such that $\Omega \subseteq P_A(\Omega_1)$.

2. Every operator in Ω is a computable function.

3. The algebra is finitely generated. That is, there is some finite $X \subseteq A$ such that $J_\Omega(X) = A$.

All these requirements on concept networks have to do with finite representability. That is, assuming that our minds are finite, and concept networks are mental structures that we can access and manipulate, it should be possible to represent concept networks with finite means. A concept network is said to be finite if the class of objects A is finite, and infinite otherwise.

I should note here that the conditions of computability and finite generativity are rather weak. Consequently, the above characterization of concept network is quite broad. Depending on what this framework is being used for, one might wish to impose stronger constraints on concept networks. For instance, an upper bound on the complexity of the operators in Ω can be specified, though this would exclude certain scientific theories from being regarded as concept networks. Or, one might put an upper bound on the arity of operators. This latter condition seems quite appealing for two reasons. One is that any algebra having operators of arity greater than 3 can be embedded in an algebra with at most binary operators. [Cohn 1981, Chap. III, Theorem 7.1 (p. 147)]. Secondly, Halford and Wilson [1980] have demonstrated that a child's ability to use unary operators, binary operators, and the composition of operators—which is needed to get the effect of ternary and quaternary operators—can be linked to the stages of the child's cognitive development.

A *cognitive model* is a triple $\langle\langle A, \Omega\rangle, \langle R, \Psi\rangle, \langle B, \Sigma\rangle\rangle$ such that all of the following conditions are satisfied:

- $\langle A, \Omega\rangle$ is a *concept network* as defined above.

- $\langle B, \Sigma\rangle$ is any algebra, representing what I have been referring to as the *environment*.

- $\langle R, \Psi\rangle$ is a relation (representing a *cognitive relation*) from $\langle A, \Omega\rangle$ to $\langle B, \Sigma\rangle$—that is, $R \subseteq A \times B$ and $\Psi(n) \subseteq \Omega(n) \times \Sigma(n)$ for all n—with the following characteristics:

  1. Every operator in Σ is related to some operator in Ω. In other words, for all σ in Σ, $\Psi^{-1}(\sigma) \neq \emptyset$.

  2. The subalgebra of $\langle A, \Omega\rangle$ that is related to the environment algebra $\langle B, \Sigma\rangle$ by $\langle R, \Psi\rangle$—that is, $\langle R, \Psi\rangle^{-1}(\langle B, \Sigma\rangle) \subseteq \langle A, \Omega\rangle$—is also a concept network as defined above. In particular, $\langle R, \Psi\rangle^{-1}(\langle B, \Sigma\rangle)$ is a finitely generated algebra.

These conditions call for a few words of explanation. The first condition comes from one of the underlying assumptions of my framework, namely that *the objects in the environment acquire a structure only via the operational structure of the concept network*. In other words, the operators in the environment, or transformations as I called them in the last chapter, cannot exist without being related to some operator in the concept network.

The second condition is merely to make sure that though I allow for a concept network to be partially interpreted—meaning that only a part of the network has been instantiated in the environment—the part that is related must be a proper concept network, since otherwise, finite representability of the cognitive model can no longer be assured. Note that of all the requirements on a concept network, the only ones that might not be met in $\langle R, \Psi \rangle^{-1}(\langle B, \Sigma \rangle)$ are those of being an algebra and being finitely generated.

A cognitive model is *finite* if its concept network is finite—meaning that the class A is finite—and is *infinite* otherwise.

6.9.2   Local Coherency and Coherency

Notice that I defined a cognitive relation to be a relation and not a correspondence. It is the coherency condition that turns a cognitive relation into a correspondence. However, first I would like to introduce the notion of local coherency, and then use it to define coherency.

Given a cognitive model $\mathcal{C} = \langle \langle A, \Omega \rangle, \langle R, \Psi \rangle, \langle B, \Sigma \rangle \rangle$, and a class $X \subseteq A$, we say that $\mathcal{C}$ (or $\langle R, \Psi \rangle$) is *locally coherent* in X if and only if whenever $x_1, \ldots, x_n$ are all in X, ω is in $\Omega(n)$, and $\omega(x_1, \ldots, x_n)$ is in X then for any $y_1, \ldots, y_n$ in B and σ in $\Sigma(n)$ such that $\langle x_1, y_1 \rangle, \ldots, \langle x_n, y_n \rangle \in R$ and $\langle \omega, \sigma \rangle \in \Psi(n)$ it is the case that $\langle \omega(x_1, \ldots, x_n), \sigma(y_1, \ldots, y_n) \rangle$ is also in R. Similarly, given a class $Y \subseteq B$, we say that $\mathcal{C}$ (or $\langle R, \Psi \rangle$) is *locally coherent* in Y if and only if whenever $y_1, \ldots, y_n$ are all in Y, σ is in $\Sigma(n)$, and $\sigma(y_1, \ldots, y_n)$ is in Y then for any $x_1, \ldots, x_n$ in A and ω in $\Omega(n)$ such that $\langle x_1, y_1 \rangle, \ldots, \langle x_n, y_n \rangle \in R$ and $\langle \omega, \sigma \rangle \in \Psi(n)$ it is the case that $\langle \omega(x_1, \ldots, x_n), \sigma(y_1, \ldots, y_n) \rangle$ is also in R. The following fact can now be easily derived from these definitions:

Fact: 6.10 *A cognitive model* $\mathcal{C} = \langle \langle A, \Omega \rangle, \langle R, \Psi \rangle, \langle B, \Sigma \rangle \rangle$ *is locally coherent in A if, and only if, it is locally coherent in B.*

When $\mathcal{C}$ (or $\langle R, \Psi \rangle$) is locally coherent in A (or B) we say that it is *fully coherent* or simply *coherent*. Thus, the cognitive relation of a fully coherent cognitive model is a correspondence between the algebras of the concept network and the environment.

The coherency condition ensures that in a cognitive model the concept network and the environment preserve the structures of each other *via* the cognitive relation. As I emphasized in the last chapter, this is necessary if the cognitive model is to provide a reasonable basis for predicting changes in the environment, and for planning one's actions. Obviously, since we interact with a small chunk of our environment at any given time, and since, with our minds being finite, we can access only a finite portion of a concept network at any time, the concept of local coherency is much more important and useful than full coherency. However, for mathematical simplicity I limit myself to fully coherent cognitive models from here to the end of Section 11. The question of how the coherency of infinite models may be established by finite minds is addressed in Section 12.

6.9.3   Some Characteristics of Cognitive Models

Let $\mathcal{C} = \langle\langle A,\Omega\rangle, \langle R,\Psi\rangle, \langle B,\Sigma\rangle\rangle$ be a cognitive model. Any element x of its cognitive model $\langle A,\Omega\rangle$ is said to be *relevant* if $\langle R,\Psi\rangle(x) \neq \emptyset$, and *irrelevant* otherwise. If every x in $\langle A,\Omega\rangle$ is relevant then the cognitive model $\mathcal{C}$ is said to be *full*. Another way of defining fullness of a cognitive model is to say that the grouping induced by it on the environment does not contain the empty class.

For any pair of elements of the cognitive model $\langle A,\Omega\rangle$, say x and y, we say that x is *synonymous* with y if $\langle R,\Psi\rangle(x) = \langle R,\Psi\rangle(y)$. If there are no synonymous pairs of distinct x and y in the cognitive model $\langle A,\Omega\rangle$, then we say that the cognitive model $\mathcal{C}$ is *optimal*.

Any element y of the environment $\langle B,\Sigma\rangle$ is said to be *visible* if $\langle R,\Psi\rangle^{-1}(y) \neq \emptyset$ and *invisible* otherwise. If every element of the environment $\langle B,\Sigma\rangle$ is visible, we say that the cognitive model $\mathcal{C}$ is *complete*. Another way to specify completeness of a cognitive model is to say that the grouping induced by it on the environment is full.

If the grouping induced by the cognitive relation $\langle R,\Psi\rangle$ on the environment $\langle B,\Sigma\rangle$ is pairwise disjoint, we say that the cognitive model $\mathcal{C}$ is *unambiguous*. Two elements x and y in the environment $\langle B,\Sigma\rangle$ are *indistinguishable* if $\langle R,\Psi\rangle^{-1}(x) = \langle R,\Psi\rangle^{-1}(y)$. If the environment $\langle B,\Sigma\rangle$ has no pair of indistinguishable elements, the cognitive model $\mathcal{C}$ is *fully resolved*. Notice that these two characteristics are independent: that is, a fully resolved model need not be unambiguous, and an unambiguous model need not be fully resolved.

The following facts can now be derived that show how these characteristics of cognitive models depend on their cognitive relations:

Fact: 6.11

1. *A cognitive model is full, complete, and unambiguous if, and only if, its cognitive relation is difunctional.*

2. *A cognitive model is full, complete, unambiguous, and fully resolved if,*

and only if, its cognitive relation is an epimorphism from the cognitive model to the environment.

3. *A cognitive model is full, complete, optimal, and unambiguous if, and only if, its cognitive relation is an epimorphism from the environment to the cognitive model.*

4. *A cognitive model is full, complete, optimal, unambiguous, and fully resolved if, and only if, its cognitive relation is an isomorphism.*

The proofs of all these facts are simple, and I leave them for you to work them out. They are merely an exercise in recalling the definitions and using the facts that were derived earlier in this chapter.

For any element y in the environment of a cognitive model, whenever there is some element of its concept betwork x such that $\langle x, y \rangle$ is in the cognitive relation, we say that x is a *representation* of y. Moreover, any structural description of x is then said to be a *description* of y.

A cognitive model can *induce* operators in its environment. Here is an example. Consider the correspondence LENGTH from INTEGER to STRING, which was introduced earlier in this chapter [§6.8.2], to be a cognitive relation. Technically, there is a slight problem here, since not every operator of STRING is related to something in INTEGER. But we can remedy it by taking an S-subalgebra of STRING containing only the operator *conc* to be the codomain of LENGTH. The algebra INTEGER is then the concept network. Now notice that the operator *next* in INTEGER is a specialization of *add*. Since *add* is related to *conc*, it suggests that we can induce operators like *next* in STRING that are specializations of *conc*, as shown in Figure 6.11. Similarly, the correspondence MODULO [§6.8.2] can induce an operator like *pred* in INTEGER that is the inverse of *next*. (This process of inducing operators is similar to the *augmentation* of Indurkhya [1986].)

6.10   Cognitive Models Over an Environment

Often one would like to compare cognitive models that share the same environment. Are they equivalent? Does one of them provide more detailed information about the environment? Does one of them give more complete information about the environment? And so on. In this section, I characterize these notions formally, and then derive a fact that is used in the next

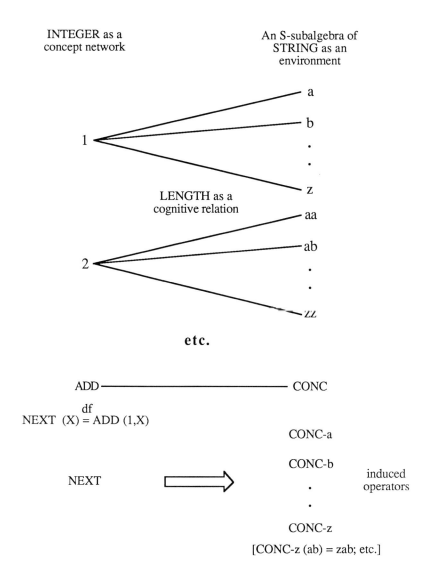

FIGURE 6.11: An example to show how a cognitive relation can induce operators in the environment.

chapter to show why certain kinds of metaphors are incapable of generating any new information about the environment.

First consider the notion of equivalence. We would like to say that two cognitive models over the same environment are *equivalent* when they both induce the same grouping on the environment. If, in addition, their concept networks are also isomorphic, then they are said to be *strongly equivalent*.

Now consider the relations of extension and restriction, which are the inverse of each other. Intuitively, a restriction of a cognitive model makes the environment less visible while keeping the structure of the environment that is still visible the same as before. To define it formally, let $\mathcal{C} = \langle\langle A_1, \Omega_1\rangle, \langle R, \Psi\rangle, \langle B, \Sigma\rangle\rangle$ and $\mathcal{D} = \langle\langle A_2, \Omega_2\rangle, \langle S, \Phi\rangle, \langle B, \Sigma\rangle\rangle$ be two cognitive models over the environment $\langle B, \Sigma\rangle$. Now we would like to formally state the conditions under which $\mathcal{D}$ is a restriction of $\mathcal{C}$. Clearly, the first condition is that less of the environment $\langle B, \Sigma\rangle$ should be visible under $\mathcal{D}$ than under $\mathcal{C}$. This is easily formalized by saying that $\langle S, \Phi\rangle(\langle A_2, \Omega_2\rangle) \subset \langle R, \Psi\rangle(\langle A_1, \Omega_1\rangle)$. For the other condition, which says that the environment that is visible under $\mathcal{D}$ should be structured the same way as under $\mathcal{C}$, we can use the notion of equivalence. Let us use the notation $\langle R, \Psi\rangle/\langle B_1, \Sigma_1\rangle$, where $\langle B_1, \Sigma_1\rangle$ is a subalgebra of $\langle B, \Sigma\rangle$, to mean $\langle R, \Psi\rangle$ *restricted* to $\langle B_1, \Sigma_1\rangle$, where $\langle x, y\rangle$ is in $\langle R, \Psi\rangle/\langle B_1, \Sigma_1\rangle$ if, and only if, $\langle x, y\rangle$ is in $\langle R, \Psi\rangle$ and y is in $\langle B_1, \Sigma_1\rangle$. Now we can define the relation of restriction between two cognitive models over the same environment as follows. $\mathcal{D}$ is a *restriction* of $\mathcal{C}$ provided:

1. $\langle S, \Phi\rangle(\langle A_2, \Omega_2\rangle) \subset \langle R, \Psi\rangle(\langle A_1, \Omega_1\rangle)$; and

2. the cognitive models $\langle\langle A_2, \Omega_2\rangle, \langle S, \Phi\rangle, \langle S, \Phi\rangle(\langle A_2, \Omega_2\rangle)\rangle$ and $\langle\langle A_1, \Omega_1\rangle, \langle R, \Psi\rangle/\langle S, \Phi\rangle(\langle A_2, \Omega_2\rangle), \langle S, \Phi\rangle(\langle A_2, \Omega_2\rangle)\rangle$ are equivalent.

The relation of extension is the reciprocal of restriction. That is, $\mathcal{C}$ is an *extension* of $\mathcal{D}$ if $\mathcal{D}$ is a restriction of $\mathcal{C}$.

Finally, I introduce the concept of refinement. Intuitively a refinement of a cognitive model makes the environment more resolved without restructuring it otherwise. To define it formally, we first define a relation of *indistinguishability* over the environment of a cognitive model. Given a cognitive model $\mathcal{C} = \langle\langle A, \Omega\rangle, \langle R, \Psi\rangle, \langle B, \Sigma\rangle\rangle$, the *indistinguishability* relation induced by $\mathcal{C}$ over the environment $\langle B, \Sigma\rangle$, written as $\iota_{\mathcal{C}}$, is a relation such that for any x and y in $\langle B, \Sigma\rangle$, the pair $\langle x, y\rangle$ is in $\iota_{\mathcal{C}}$ if, and only if, x and y are indistinguishable in $\mathcal{C}$; or in other words, if, and only if, $\langle R, \Psi\rangle^{-1}(x) = \langle R, \Psi\rangle^{-1}(y)$. It is easy to see that $\iota_{\mathcal{C}}$ is an equivalence relation, though it is not necessarily a congruence.

Now let $\mathcal{C} = \langle\langle A_1, \Omega_1\rangle, \langle R, \Psi\rangle, \langle B, \Sigma\rangle\rangle$ and $\mathcal{D} = \langle\langle A_2, \Omega_2\rangle, \langle S, \Phi\rangle, \langle B, \Sigma\rangle\rangle$ be two cognitive models over the same environment $\langle B, \Sigma\rangle$. Then we say that $\mathcal{C}$ is a *refinement* of $\mathcal{D}$ provided:

1. They both make exactly the same parts of the environment visible: that is, $\langle R, \Psi\rangle(\langle A_1, \Omega_1\rangle) = \langle S, \Phi\rangle(\langle A_2, \Omega_2\rangle)$; and

2. $\mathcal{C}$ structures the environment in the same way as $\mathcal{D}$ except for making it more resolved: in other words, $\iota_\mathcal{C} \subset \iota_\mathcal{D}$.

We can now prove the following fact that is used in the next chapter:

Fact: 6.12 *Let $\mathcal{C} = \langle\langle A, \Omega\rangle, \langle R, \Psi\rangle, \langle B, \Sigma\rangle\rangle$ be a cognitive model, and let $\langle A_1, \Omega_1\rangle$ be some concept network. Given a correspondence, say $\langle S, \Phi\rangle$, from $\langle A_1, \Omega_1\rangle$ to $\langle A, \Omega\rangle$ we can form another cognitive model, say $\mathcal{D}$, over $\langle B, \Sigma\rangle$ as $\mathcal{D} = \langle\langle A_1, \Omega_1\rangle, \langle S, \Phi\rangle \circ \langle R, \Psi\rangle, \langle B, \Sigma\rangle\rangle$. Then $\mathcal{D}$ can neither be an extension of $\mathcal{C}$ nor a refinement of $\mathcal{C}$.*

Proof: To show that $\mathcal{D}$ cannot be an extension of $\mathcal{C}$ we merely note that $\langle S, \Phi\rangle \circ \langle R, \Psi\rangle(\langle A_1, \Omega_1\rangle)$ is the same as $\langle R, \Psi\rangle(\langle S, \Phi\rangle(\langle A_1, \Omega_1\rangle))$; and since $\langle S, \Phi\rangle(\langle A_1, \Omega_1\rangle)$ is a subclass of (or is equal to) $\subseteq \langle A, \Omega\rangle$, it follows that $\langle S, \Phi\rangle \circ \langle R, \Psi\rangle(\langle A_1, \Omega_1\rangle)$ is a subclass of (or is equal to) $\langle R, \Psi\rangle(\langle A, \Omega\rangle)$. Thus, it cannot be the case that $\langle R, \Psi\rangle(\langle A, \Omega\rangle)$ is a proper subclass of $\langle S, \Phi\rangle \circ \langle R, \Psi\rangle(\langle A_1, \Omega_1\rangle)$

To show that $\mathcal{D}$ cannot be a refinement of $\mathcal{C}$, we will assume the contrary and derive a contradiction. So assume that $\mathcal{D}$ is a refinement of $\mathcal{C}$. It means that there are at least two distinct elements in the environment $\langle B, \Sigma\rangle$, say y_1 and y_2, that are distinguishable under $\mathcal{D}$ but not under $\mathcal{C}$. In other words, $\langle R, \Psi\rangle^{-1}(y_1) = \langle R, \Psi\rangle^{-1}(y_2)$; but $(\langle S, \Phi\rangle \circ \langle R, \Psi\rangle)^{-1}(y_1) \neq (\langle S, \Phi\rangle \circ \langle R, \Psi\rangle)^{-1}(y_2)$.

But $(\langle S, \Phi\rangle \circ \langle R, \Psi\rangle)^{-1}(y_1) = \langle S, \Phi\rangle^{-1}(\langle R, \Psi\rangle^{-1}(y_1))$, and the same for y_2. Thus, we have $\langle S, \Phi\rangle^{-1}(\langle R, \Psi\rangle^{-1}(y_1))$ is not equal to $\langle S, \Phi\rangle^{-1}(\langle R, \Psi\rangle^{-1}(y_2))$; and from $\langle R, \Psi\rangle^{-1}(y_1)$ equals $\langle R, \Psi\rangle^{-1}(y_2)$ we get $\langle S, \Phi\rangle^{-1}(\langle R, \Psi\rangle^{-1}(y_1))$ is not equal to $\langle S, \Phi\rangle^{-1}(\langle R, \Psi\rangle^{-1}(y_1))$ which is clearly a contradiction. $\square$

6.11   Projective and Accommodating Models

In the previous chapter we saw that the coherency of cognitive models is maintained essentially from an interplay of two different mechanisms: projection and accommodation. In projection the structure of the concept network is kept invariant and the cognitive relation of the model is altered to maintain coherency. In accommodation, the cognitive relation is kept fixed, and it is the structure of the concept network that is altered. We also saw that though in most cases projection and accommodation act in consort, there are situations in which one or the other plays a dominating role, giving rise to projective or accommodating models. The question I would like to address in this section is whether there are any distinctive formal characteristics of projective and accommodating models.

Let us begin by considering projective or concept driven models. As mentioned above, in projection, the cognitive agent starts out with a concept network, and then varies the correspondence between the concepts and parts of the environment to find a coherent fit. (See Figure 5.15.) The result is that the grouped environment appears as an isomorphic copy of the concept network to the cognitive agent.

This suggests that a projective model may be characterized by the fact that the grouping induced by it on the environment is an algebra of classes that is isomorphic to the concept network. However, that would preclude the possibility that the concept network may contain synonyms. But this is easily remedied by requiring that the correspondence from the concept network to the algebra of classes (that is induced by the cognitive relation of the cognitive model) on the environment be a homomorphism.

Now when a cognitive agent views the environment through the concept network, what it sees is the algebra of classes in the environment that is induced by the concept network. So we might as well take this algebra of classes to be the environment of the cognitive model. In that case, the cognitive relation itself becomes a homomorphism from the concept network to the environment. Thus, *a cognitive model is projective when its cognitive relation is a homomorphism from the concept network to the environment.*

Now consider accommodation. It works by keeping the correspondence between the concepts and parts of the environment fixed, and then adapting the structure of the concept network to reflect the structure of the environment (See Figure 5.14). In other words, we start with a fixed grouping on the environment. This grouping then reveals a structure consisting of those operators, and classes of operators, of the environment that are admitted by the grouping. The structure of the concept network is adapted till it becomes an isomorphic copy of the visible structure of the environment.

In order for a cognitive agent to adapt its concept network to the structure of the environment, the grouping on the environment must be unambiguous; or, what is the same, pairwise disjoint. Otherwise, if there is some ambiguous object in the environment that belongs to two different groups, the cognitive agent would not know which group is present whenever it sees the ambiguous object. Moreover, since the grouping on the environment is determined by the bias of the cognitive and perceptual apparatus of the cognitive agent, which is kept fixed in accommodating models, we may assume that the grouping extends to cover all the environment. In other words, accommodating models are also complete.

Both these observations are incorporated by saying that *a cognitive model is accommodating if its cognitive relation is a homomorphism from the environment to the concept network.* (It is interesting to note here that Q-morphisms of Holland *et al.* [1986] become, in my framework, accommodating cognitive models over the same environment, with successive layers being refinements of previous layers.)

6.12   Finite Representability and Coherency

Earlier, I emphasized that coherency is an important condition on cognitive models. It is coherency that ensures that the result of a long sequence of reasoning or construction carried out in the concept network will also hold in the environment. However, with my emphasis on finite representability, this immediately raises a major question: How can we establish coherency with our finite minds? Notice that the problem exists not only for infinite models but also for finite ones, since even though the concept network of a cognitive model may be finite the environment is still potentially infinite and coherency involves both the concept network and the environment.

Of course, it is precisely to address this problem that I introduced the concept of *local coherency,* which is coherency limited to a part of the concept network or the environment. Local coherency is finitely representable and, consequently, a more useful concept than full coherency. However, for certain cognitive activities—and science comes immediately to mind as a prime example—local coherency is not enough. A scientist is usually not interested in theories that are locally true, but seeks universal theories that are fully coherent. At least that remains an ideal to which the scientific community aspires. And therefore, the problem of the finite representability of full coherency is an important one, and must be addressed in this framework.

It turns out that by using algebras, with finitary operators, to formalize concept networks and environments, and by requiring the concept network to have computable operators and to be finitely generated, we have made full coherency—of even infinite cognitive models—finitely representable in some cases.

For instance, incoherency of any cognitive model, whether finite or infinite, is always detectable by finite means. Recall that a cognitive model $\mathcal{C} = \langle\langle A, \Omega\rangle, \langle R, \Psi\rangle, \langle B, \Sigma\rangle\rangle$ is said to be fully coherent if, and only if, its cognitive relation $\langle R, \Psi\rangle$ is such that whenever $\langle x_1, y_1\rangle, \ldots, \langle x_n, y_n\rangle$ are all in R ($x_1, \ldots, x_n$ are in A and $y_1, \ldots, y_n$ are in B), and $\langle\omega, \sigma\rangle$ is in $\Psi(n)$ ($\omega \in \Omega(n)$ and $\sigma \in \Sigma(n)$), then the pair $\langle\omega(x_1, \ldots, x_n), \sigma(y_1, \ldots, y_n)\rangle$ is also in R. It means that if $\mathcal{C}$ is incoherent, then there exist, for some finite n, n objects in A, say $a_1, \ldots, a_n$, an n-ary operator in Ω, say α, n objects in B, say $b_1, \ldots, b_n$, and an n-ary operator in Σ, say β, such that $\langle a_1, b_1\rangle, \ldots, \langle a_n, b_n\rangle$ are all in R, $\langle\alpha, \beta\rangle$ is in Ψ, but $\langle\alpha(a_1, \ldots, a_n), \beta(b_1, \ldots, b_n)\rangle$ is not in R. Since α is a computable function, by the definition of concept networks, and n is finite, this shows that the incoherency of any cognitive model is always finitely representable.

This characteristic of cognitive models is well known in the philosophy of science: a scientific theory is required to be refutable by some kind of experimentation and/or empirical observations. (See Popper [1959; 1962].)

There is one other way in which full coherency is finitely representable—this time for projective models. I show how any concept network (which is required to be finitely generated) can be projected coherently onto an environment by finite means. This result is derived from a slight adaptation of a well-known theorem in algebra that says that given an algebra $\langle A, \Omega\rangle$, a subclass X of A, and any other algebra $\langle B, \Omega\rangle$; any function from X into B extends to a unique homomorphism from the algebra $\langle S_\Omega(X), \Omega\rangle$ to $\langle B, \Omega\rangle$. [Cohn 1981, Chap. III, Theorem 2.6 (p. 120)]. The adapted version of this theorem that is useful for my purpose here is presented below:

Theorem: 6.5 *Given a concept network $\langle A, \Omega\rangle$; a finite generating class X of $\langle A, \Omega\rangle$ ($X \subseteq A$), an environment $\langle B, \Sigma\rangle$; and a relation $\langle R, \Psi\rangle$ between $\langle A, \Omega\rangle$ and the environment such that $R \subseteq X \times B$, R is full in X (meaning that every x in X is related to at least one y in B by R), $\Psi(n) \subseteq \Omega(n) \times \Sigma(n)$ for all n, Ψ is full in both Ω and Σ, and $\langle R, \Psi\rangle$ is locally coherent in X; then there is a cognitive relation $\langle R', \Psi\rangle$ between $\langle A, \Omega\rangle$ and $\langle B, \Sigma\rangle$ such that $R \subseteq R' \subseteq A \times B$ and $\langle R', \Psi\rangle$ is fully coherent.*

Proof: To prove that $\langle R', \Psi\rangle$ exists with the said properties, I show here how to construct it.

Consider the class of all structural descriptions in $\langle A, \Omega\rangle$ that are rooted in X: in other words, the class of all those structural descriptions over $\langle A, \Omega\rangle$ that have all their leaf nodes in X. This class is denoted by $S_\Omega(X)$.

Now form a relation, say Φ, from $S_\Omega(X)$ to $S_\Sigma(B)$ as follows. For every s in $S_\Omega(X)$, relate it to all those structures in $S_\Sigma(B)$ that can be obtained from s by replacing every leaf node x in s by some element of $R(x)$, and every intermediate node ω in s by some element of $\Psi(\omega)$. The fullness of R and Ψ in X and Ω, respectively, guarantees that every s in $S_\Omega(X)$ will be related to at least one structure in $S_\Sigma(B)$.

Now define R' as follows. For any x in A and y in B, $\langle x, y \rangle$ is in R' if, and only if, there exist some s in $S_\Omega(X)$ and t in $S_\Sigma(B)$ with $\langle s, t \rangle$ in Φ, eval$(s) = x$, and eval$(t) = y$.

From the construction, it should be clear that $\langle R', \Psi \rangle$ is, indeed, a correspondence from $\langle A, \Omega \rangle$ to $\langle B, \Sigma \rangle$. Moreover, since X is a generating class of $\langle A, \Omega \rangle$, $\langle R', \Psi \rangle$ is full in $\langle A, \Omega \rangle$: that is, $\langle R', \Psi \rangle^{-1}(\langle B, \Sigma \rangle) = \langle A, \Omega \rangle$. Given that $\langle A, \Omega \rangle$ is a concept network, we have proved that $\langle R', \Psi \rangle$ is a fully coherent cognitive relation. $\square$

I should note a few things regarding this theorem. First of all, though the construction of $\langle R', \Psi \rangle$ in the proof of the theorem is deterministic, and therefore yields a unique cognitive relation, there may well be other cognitive relations from $\langle A, \Omega \rangle$ to $\langle B, \Sigma \rangle$ that are an extension of $\langle R, \Psi \rangle$. Secondly, this construction does not preserve functionality: that is, if $\langle R, \Psi \rangle$ is taken to be a function from $\langle X, \Omega \rangle$ to $\langle B, \Sigma \rangle$, then $\langle R', \Psi \rangle$ need not come out as a homomorphism. In fact, in certain cases it may be impossible to extend a locally coherent function, from $\langle X, \Omega \rangle$ to $\langle B, \Sigma \rangle$, to a homomorphism from $\langle A, \Omega \rangle$ to $\langle B, \Sigma \rangle$.

Theorem 6.5 makes coherency of projective models finitely representable as follows. Since every concept network has a finite generating class, we can start out by forming a relation between a finite generating class of the concept network and the environment, and over the class of operators. We then ensure the local coherency of this finite relation over the generating class. Now we can extend this relation, by the procedure explained in the proof of the theorem, to cover the whole concept network. Of course, it is not necessary to carry out the full extension at any one time—if the concept network is infinite it simply cannot be done—but as long as the proper procedure is followed in extending the relation to the relevant part of the concept network, the coherency will be guaranteed. This mechanism is often used in projecting mathematical concept networks to the real-world situations.

Chapter 7

An Interaction Theory of Metaphor

7.1 Introduction

In my framework of cognition, the paradox of interactionism is resolved by pointing out that while it is the cognitive agent who gives an ontology to the external world by instantiating concept networks, the structure of the world, as seen from this ontology, is determined by reality. Thus, it is only by instantiating different concept networks that the cognitive agent can 'see' different structures in reality. In other words, any reorganization and restructuring of the world view is essentially the process of reinstantiating the concept networks—a process I have been calling *projection*.

My main objective is to extend this approach to give an account of similarity-creating metaphors and resolve the paradox of creation of similarity. However, I would like to do so by developing a general theory of metaphor which addresses similarity-based metaphors and certain other issues related to metaphor such as the thesis "All knowledge is metaphorical," and the aptness and correctness of metaphors. In this chapter I am concerned with laying out my account of metaphor. The metaphor-related issues are discussed in the next chapter.

This chapter is organized as follows. In Section 2, I present arguments leading to the conclusion that a metaphor is essentially a projective cognitive relation. As this conclusion might not be obvious, (what is the 'environment' of a metaphor?), and given that it is the keystone of my account of metaphor, I take special care in laying down my arguments, using the examples introduced in Chapters 1 and 2.

Then, in Section 3, I introduce nomenclature associated with metaphor that is used in articulating my theory. The important thing there is to incorporate the distinction between the concept network and the environment orthogonally to the dichotomy between the source and the target that is used in the traditional characterization of metaphor. Most existing theories of metaphor do not make any distinction analogous to concept network-environment, but it is crucial to the ability of my framework to explain similarity-creating metaphors.

In Section 4, I analyze similarity-based and similarity-creating metaphors, comparing and contrasting the two with respect to the role each kind plays in cognition. I classify similarity-based metaphors further into *syntactic* and *suggestive* metaphors depending on whether or not they are open-ended, since these two kinds of metaphor aid cognition in different ways. I also resolve the paradox of creation of similarity here by discussing, with some examples, how a metaphor can create similarities, without the creation being arbitrary. Finally, Section 5 summarizes the main theses of this chapter.

7.2 Metaphor as Projection

Earlier in Chapter 1, you may recall, I characterized metaphor as an unconventional way of describing (or representing) some object, event or situation (real or imagined). The object of description is the target, and the object that is being used to unconventionally describe the target is the source. We also saw that the source participates in the process as a structured set of symbols that have to be applied to the target in unconventional ways in order to render the description meaningful.

In the interactionist approach to cognition I have outlined in the last two chapters, a structured set of symbols is referred to as a concept network, an object of description is referred to as an environment, and an interpretation is referred to as a cognitive relation. While regarding the source of a metaphor as a concept network seems quite reasonable, some of you might find it quite odd to think of the target as an environment. Considering some examples might make it seem even more strange. What is the environment in Boland's 'wild flowers as water' metaphor? Or in Spender's 'ocean as a harp' metaphor? Or in Mondrian's *Composition with Blue and Yellow?* Or in Antonioni's 'Giuliana's emotional state as blotches of paint' metaphor? (The first three of these four examples are presented in Chapter 2 [§2.2], and the fourth one is presented in Chapter 1 [§1.5].) The problem is that an environment, in my framework of cognition, is the external world that has been given an ontology by instantiating a concept network in it. But in understanding each of these metaphors, the external world does not seem to be directly involved. (You can understand each of these metaphors even though you are not experiencing the corresponding sensory stimuli at that time—the sunlight playing on the waves, in the case of Spender's metaphor.)

The key to harmonizing this apparently discordant note is to use the notion of multi-layered cognitive systems [§5.8], which are a more realistic way of describing human cognition. In a layered cognitive system, you may recall, a cognitive relation may be formed between any two adjacent layers. Thus, the target becomes an autonomous structure in the layer below the concept network layer.

Even this conclusion might seem baffling. What is the autonomous structure in the layer below the concept network layer for Boland's 'wild flowers as water' metaphor? In fact, it might not even be clear what the concept network layer is for this metaphor. The other three metaphors mentioned above face a similar problem.

To clarify these issues, let us backtrack a little and reconsider some of the identifying characteristics of metaphor that were articulated in Chapter 1 [§1.2, §1.3 and §1.5]. We observed there that every metaphor (and non-metaphor) involves a description and an object or situation to which the description is intended to apply. In applying the description to the object, the target, parts of the description might not apply to the target using the conventional interpretations. It is the concepts occurring in these part of the description (and related concepts) that forms the source of the metaphor.

Consider Boland's poem now. It is a description of wild flowers growing on a hill in the Irish countryside, which become the target. The text of the poem, the description, becomes the potential source.

There should be no problem in regarding the text of the poem as a concept network. The words are essentially concepts that are structurally interrelated in a certain way in the poem. Moreover, words, by virtue of their 'meaning' (as in 'dictionary meaning'), are related to each other in certain ways. Both these interrelations give the text of the poem an autonomous structure.

The situation is not so simple with regard to the target, because it could be a real or imaginary object. Let us focus on the easier case first, when the target is a real object. Consider the scenario where the poem was conceived while observing wild flowers in the Irish countryside. Or, considering Spender's *Seascape,* suppose that you are reading it while sitting on a beach and observing the sunlight playing on the waves. In such situations, the external world is providing a set of stimuli (sensorimotor data set) to the cognitive agent, of which the poem is a description. Moreover, this set of stimuli is structured independently of any descriptions that might be attached to it. (You might recall here my earlier discussions in Chapter 2 [§2.4.2] about creation of similarity in the context of perceptual proportional analogies, and in Chapter 3 [§3.2] about the Star of David example of Black.)

The process of giving descriptions (in terms of concept networks) is essentially what I have referred to as conceptualization (or instantiating a cognitive relation) in my framework of cognition. The process involves interaction between two structured levels—the level of concept networks and the level of the sensorimotor data set. As the words in any language are related to each other in certain ways and the set of stimuli has its own independent characteristics, not just any arbitrary description will qualify as a description of the stimuli.

Now whether we focus on the process of coming up with a description (as in conceiving the poem) or interpreting a given description (as in trying to understand the poem while experiencing more or less the same set of stimuli as the poet), the important thing is that a cognitive relation between the concepts of the concept network and pieces of the sensorimotor data set needs to be established. Part of this cognitive relation might be conventional in the sense that the cognitive agent habitually interprets the concept in that way. For instance, the concepts 'from a distance,' 'sharp flowers,' and 'stirring on those hills' in Boland's poem would all have to be interpreted conventionally. However, there are other concepts, such as 'splashes,' 'shyness,' 'superstitious aura,' 'ivory, downhill rush,' and 'fluency only water has,' that cannot be connected to parts of the stimuli in a conventional way. It is these concepts, and other related concepts, that form the source of the metaphor.

At this point the person reading the poem has three options. She can discard the description as anomalous, since it cannot be made to fit the structured set of stimuli. This is something an unimaginative person might do. Or she can change the description to fit the stimuli, which would correspond to accommodation. This change can be affected in two ways, as there are two structural components to the source concept network. One is to change the text of the poem, so that it becomes a conventional description of the stimuli. The other is to redefine the words 'splashes,' 'superstitious,' etc. so that their dictionary meanings are changed in a way that makes them correspond to parts of the stimuli in a conventional way. Though the second of these two ways of accommodation may seem somewhat drastic, it can, nevertheless, be evidenced, albeit in a small way, in the phenomenon by which a novel metaphor, through repeated use, becomes a conventional metaphor, and eventually fades into polysemy.

The third option is to instantiate the troublesome concepts (words and phrases) in an unconventional way. Though the person (cognitive agent) is constrained by the autonomous structure of the concepts (in how they are related to other concepts in the text of the poem and through the dictionary 'meanings') and the independent structure of the set of stimuli, she has freedom in instantiating the concepts. It is this option that leads to a metaphorical interpretation. However, this is precisely what I have referred to as 'projection' in my framework of cognition. Thus, a metaphor becomes an instance of projection.

Now consider the case when there is no stimulus present. Obviously, one can read and understand Boland's and Spender's poems without being in the environments described in the poems. In fact, most poems, and other metaphors of language, are understood in this way. How is a metaphor an instance of projection in these situations?

The key to answering this question lies in analyzing what exactly goes into 'understanding' a metaphor. We can start by considering what goes on in 'understanding' a non-metaphorical description (piece of text). Suppose someone tells you "It is snowing outside." You 'understand' the utterance. But what exactly does that mean? There exist two schools of thoughts here. According to one school, which is dominant in much of the cognitive science and artificial intelligence research, to 'understand' is to represent internally, in the form of an appropriate network of concepts, the information contained in the utterance. As concepts are related to each other in certain ways (in the sense of encyclopedic and dictionary meanings), this internal representation can be used to infer a number of other things that are not explicitly mentioned in the utterance, such as it is cold outside, and it is not sunny outside.

According to the other school of thought—such as the one proposed in Neisser [1976, Chap. 8] and incorporated in a few accounts of metaphor (Johnson & Malgady [1980], and Verbrugge [1980])—'understanding' means imagining a perceptual experience that could have been described by the utterance. Of course, in this imagination some subjectivity is bound to occur. You might imagine big snow flakes falling gently, or a blizzard with gusty winds, depending on what else you know about the weather outside (or, if the sentence occurs in a novel, what else has been described about the weather). But the important thing is that certain characteristics remain invariant across the different ways in which one can imagine that it is snowing outside. Moreover, these invariant characteristics reflect the person's past perceptual experiences that were described as 'snowing.' (This process of imagination is the inverse of what Dretske [1981, Chap. 7] has referred to as 'digitalization.')

It is this second approach to 'understanding' that I adopt here. To fully justify this choice would be a distraction from the main line of argument. Suffice it to say that in the internal representation approach, 'understanding' can occur without experience, which, to me at least, is quite an unacceptable consequence. This is not to say that in order to 'understand' anything we must have experienced it at some time or another. We understand many fictitious words and descriptions such as 'unicorn,' 'a mountain of gold,' and 'it was raining milk and honey from the sky.' But in any such situation, the words and phrases are necessarily descriptive, and we have perceptual acquaintance with the individual terms making up the description. Further evidence of the limitation of the internal representation approach to understanding is provided by the failure of the the computational models of metaphor based on this approach to address similarity-creating metaphors. This issue is discussed at length in Chapter 10.

To incorporate the imagination approach to 'understanding' in my framework of cognition, I need to bring in the notion of the layered cognitive system that was introduced in Chapter 5 [§5.8]. In a layered cognitive system, the intermediate layers contain structures that are less abstract than the concepts, and yet they derive their structure (in part) from the autonomous structure of the sensorimotor data sets encountered in the past. Moreover, these structures can be combined to produce 'derived' structures in the intermediate layers. Given all this, the 'imagined' perceptual experience that reflects the understanding of the utterance (a concept network) can be placed in the intermediate layers.

In 'understanding' the utterance "It is snowing outside" the cognitive agent produces a derived structure in one of the intermediate layers. This structure would be an instantiation (conventional in this case) of the concepts like 'snowing' and 'outside.' However, this instantiation is constrained by the already existing structure of the intermediate layer, which reflects the cognitive agent's past experiences with falling snow, being outside, etc. Moreover, the instantiated structure of the intermediate layer is 'derived' in the sense that it is not rooted in the sensorimotor data set, but is made up by combining previously existing experiential structures in the layer. In other words, the cognitive relation terminates at the intermediate layer, and does not go all the way to the sensorimotor data set layer.

With this notion of 'understanding' in the background, it is easy to see how a metaphor can be seen as an instance of projection in the absence of sensory stimuli. When reading Boland's poem, one imagines the experience being described in the poem, and the description of the poem (the concept network) forms a cognitive relation with this imagined experience. While some of the concepts are interpreted conventionally in the context of the imagined experience; other concepts cannot be so interpreted. This is because one's previous experiences with watching wild flowers growing on a hill gives the imagined experience an autonomous structure that cannot be violated in the description. For instance, wild flowers are not 'fluid' and do not 'flow' like water. Faced with the given description and the autonomous structure of the imagined experience, the cognitive agent again has three choices: (1) consider the description anomalous, (2) use accommodation to change the description, or (3) instantiate the troublesome concepts in a non-conventional way. Exercising the third of these options leads to metaphor. And since the structure of the concept network is not altered in the process, it amounts to projection.

To take another example, consider Spender's poem. That the poem is about the ocean is signaled explicitly by the relevant concepts in the text. To understand the poem, one needs to imagine the ocean vividly, and it is this vivid imagination that becomes the domain in which the text of the poem is interpreted. The imagined scene of ocean must include the waves in the ocean, the wind making patterns on the waves, the sunlight reflecting on the waves in a certain way, and so on. All this information, which incorporates one's prior perceptual experiences with watching the ocean and the waves, gives the domain of ocean an autonomous structure that resists being described arbitrarily. Moreover, it is less abstract and more detailed than the textual descriptions. Otherwise, if one lets the concept networks of 'ocean' and 'harp' (as reflected in their dictionary meanings) interact, then the poem would have to be deemed anomalous, as there is no way to reconcile the two disparate concept networks. The poem is rendered meaningful by interpreting, through projection, some of the concepts in the text in a non-conventional way in the imagined domain of ocean. (This account of metaphor incorporates the observations of Ricoeur [1978], the 'vividness thesis' of Ortony [1980, p. 78], and the observations of Johnson [1987, Chap. 6] on the nature of imagination.)

A consequence of this account of metaphor is that a perceptual acquaintance with the domain of interpretation is necessary for understanding a metaphor, for it is this perceptual acquaintance that makes it possible to imagine the domain vividly. Of course, it is not necessary to actually have

seen the ocean in order to be perceptually acquainted with it. It is sufficient
to have seen it in a movie or on television. It is even sufficient to have read
descriptions of the ocean. But at some level, the terms of these descriptions
(including the images being seen on the movie or the television screen) must
be grounded perceptually, thereby making it possible for the cognitive agent
to imagine what the ocean might look like. I am sure that if someone has
never seen the sunlight playing on the waves and being reflected in the water
(or watched it on the television, or seen photographs of it, etc.), then she
would not be able to understand or appreciate Spender's poem at all.

In the examples discussed so far, the domain of interpretation was explicitly signaled by the concept networks. This, however, is not always the
case. In Antonioni's 'emotional state as blotches of paint' metaphor [§1.5],
the domain of interpretation is only hinted at in a subtle way. In the case of
Mondrian's *Composition with Blue and Yellow* [§2.2], the domain of interpretation is not even hinted at. One is left to one's own devices to find a suitable
domain, and carry out an interpretation. Clearly, whether the metaphor is
comprehended or not crucially depends on being able to find an appropriate
domain of interpretation. As quipped by Johnson and Malgady: "[I]t may be
that Metaphor comprehension *is* the invention of a context or circumstances
in which the metaphor might have been conceivably produced." (Johnson
& Malgady [1980], p. 266. Emphasis Johnson & Malgady's.) Not surprisingly, such metaphors are sometimes lost on the audience, just as the 'glass
telephone booth as the cage of misery' metaphor from Hitchcock's *The Birds*
[§1.5] was lost on Truffaut [Truffaut 1984, p. 288].

But once a domain of interpretation is selected, say the moral opposition
of good and evil for interpreting the Mondrian, as in the quote from Mondrian
in Chapter 2 [§2.2], the autonomous structure of the domain resists being described arbitrarily. And since the painting (the concept network) has its own
independent structure (the squares and the lines in the Mondrian are related
to each other in a certain way), the process of interpretation must respect
both these structures. As neither structure is altered, the only recourse is to
alter the cognitive relation by giving a new ontology to (new way of looking
at) the domain of interpretation so that its structure with respect to the new
ontology reflects the structure of the concept network. But this is nothing
but projection.

7.3 Nomenclature Associated with Metaphor

I now introduce some nomenclature to allow me to refer to the different components participating in a metaphorical projection. There is the domain of interpretation (the real or imagined experience of the sunlight playing on the waves of the ocean for Spender's metaphor), which is 'an autonomous structure in the layer below (less abstract than) the concept network layer.' To avoid using this awkward phrase every time, I borrow Goodman's term *realm* (Goodman [1976], II, 6, p. 72) to refer to the less abstract, but autonomous structure of the 'domain' layer, of which the environment is a special case. In fact, in doing so, I am not changing the sense of Goodman's 'realm' all that much. In keeping with the source-target dichotomy I have been using throughout this book, I refer to this realm as the *target realm*.

In order to identify the source, we must distinguish between two concepts networks in the given description. One concept network includes those concepts that have a conventional interpretation in the target realm (and related concepts). In Boland's poem, concepts such as 'from a distance' and 'stirring on those hills' belong to this first concept network. The other concept network includes those concepts that cannot be conventionally interpreted in the target realm (and related concepts). The water-related concepts in Boland's poem and harp-related concepts in Spender's poem constitute the second concept networks for their respective target realms. This second concept network that must be given a metaphorical interpretation, I refer to as the *source concept network*.

Often, there might exist a concept network that has a conventional interpretation in the target realm. In Boland's and Spender's poems, there exist conventional descriptions of the realm being described. (In fact, some of the conventional description is actually used in each poem.) In the examples of Antonioni's and Mondrian's metaphors, it is possible to describe the target realms (the emotional state of Giuliana, and the moral opposition of good and evil) using conventional terms. Of course, this might not always be possible, since certain realms cannot be adequately described using only conventional words and phrases. (In fact, as I argue in the next section, even in the metaphors of Boland, Spender, and Mondrian, where the target realm can be described conventionally, the conventional description is not equivalent to the metaphorical description, for each of these metaphors works by giving a new ontology to the target realm, and revealing a new structure there.) But whenever a conventional description of the target realm exists, whether it be equivalent to the metaphorical description or not, I refer to it as the *target concept network*.

Just as the target concept network, when it is explicitly mentioned, evokes the image of target realm, the source concept network might also sometimes evoke the image of a realm. For instance, in reading Boland's poem, you might imagine water flowing, rushing down the hill. Or in reading the Spender, you might imagine someone gently strumming a harp. (Again, this might not always be possible. In seeing the Mondrian, for example, there is no realm in which the concept network of the painting has a conventional interpretation.) Whenever such a realm exists, I refer to it as the *source realm*. It follows then that the source concept network has a conventional interpretation in the source realm.

A cognitive relation instantiated between the source concept network and the target realm as a result of the projection process is called a *metaphorical relation,* or simply a metaphor. Figure 7.1 shows all these terms graphically.

Thus, the 'interaction,' in my account of metaphor, is an interaction between the source concept network and the target realm. Besides the fact that each of them has an autonomous structure, there is also a difference in their degree of abstraction. Concept networks are more abstract, and realms are less abstract and more detailed. In instantiating the source concept network in the target realm, parts of the realm are 'grouped' together and made to correspond to the concepts of the concept network. In this process, the target realm is given a new ontology, and its structure, as seen from the more abstract concept network layer, is changed (with the new structure depending on the autonomous structure of the realm and how the grouping was carried out).

Most theories of metaphor do not make a distinction between what I have been calling the 'concept networks' and the 'realms.' In literature, when the terms 'source domain' and 'target domain' are used to refer to the two interacting components of a metaphor, each of them refers to the cognitive agent's conceptualization of the source and the target respectively. The same is true when other terms, such as 'vehicle' and 'tenor,' or 'secondary system' and 'primary system,' are used. This, in my opinion, has been the major hurdle for such theories of metaphor to satisfactorily explain the phenomenon of creation of similarity. As long as the interaction is limited to the source and the target concept networks, only similarity-based metaphors can be accounted for, as I show in the next section.

One should note here that the asymmetry of metaphor is rather obvious

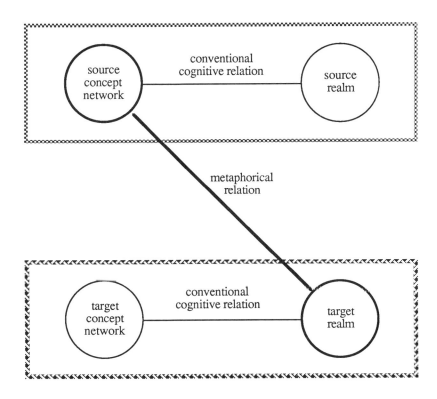

FIGURE 7.1: Nomenclature associated with Metaphor.

in my account. The source concept network and the source realm are two different structures; and so are the target concept network and the target realm. So, in reversing a metaphor, when the target concept network is used to describe the source realm, the interaction is between two different structures, and it should not be surprising at all if the result is different.

I should also make it explicit here that a metaphorical relation can be partial. In other words, it is not necessary that all of the source concept network be interpreted in the target realm in order to instantiate a metaphorical relation.

7.4   Modes of Metaphor

In Chapters 1 and 2, I identified two different modes of metaphor depending on whether there were similarities between the source and the target *before* the metaphor or not. Using the nomenclature introduced in the previous section, the similarities in question are similarities between the source concept network and the target concept network, since similarities are properties of conceptualizations. Thus, similarity-based metaphors become those metaphors in which there are similarities between the source and target concept networks, before the metaphorical relation is formed. In similarity-creating metaphor, on the other hand, there are no such similarities, and only *after* the metaphorical relation is formed are there similarities between the two concept networks. In this section I present an account of these two modes of metaphor, and distinguish between them on the basis of the role played by the target concept network in forming the metaphorical relation from the source concept network to the target realm. (See also Indurkhya [1991b].)

7.4.1   Similarity-Based (Comparative) Metaphors

In a similarity-based metaphor, the conventional description of the target realm (the target concept network) is used to mediate the process of projecting the source concept network onto the target realm. For example, consider Antonioni's metaphor of 'emotional state of Giuliana as blotches of paint.' Once the target realm is identified, the possible emotional states can all be conventionally described. (And, to emphasize the point once again, the metaphor can be completely missed if the target realm is not identified.) The source concept network is made meaningful in this realm by connecting the structural relationships between the blotches of paint, described as 'lacking any regular pattern' or 'haphazard,' with the conventional description of a possible emotional state, described as 'disturbed' or 'irrational.'

Or consider a more mundane example, "The sky is crying." Here, the target realm of possible weather conditions has conventional descriptions for each condition. In instantiating the source concept network in this realm, one looks for some condition that has a description similar to the description of 'crying.' 'Raining' becomes the obvious choice, and so the source concept network is instantiated accordingly. Of course, once a set of concepts from the source concept network has been instantiated, additional concepts can be instantiated in a way that does not correspond to anything in the target concept network (which does not have a conventional description). In this example, one can 'see' the sky in a sad mood, perhaps overwhelmed by some tragedy. This is certainly not a part of any conventional description of some weather condition. In this way, a similarity-based metaphor can be open-ended.

The open-endedness of similarity-based metaphors is often linked with the mode of analogy I have referred to as 'predictive' analogy (inferring further similarities based on existing similarities) in Chapter 1, a mode that is quite troublesome as I show in Chapter 9. In order to isolate this open-endedness, I break up similarity-based metaphors into two classes: *syntactic metaphors* and *suggestive metaphors*. Syntactic metaphors are not open-ended, but suggestive metaphors are. Of course, this division is somewhat artificial, and very much depends on how much of the source concept network one decides to instantiate in the target realm. The same metaphor can be a syntactic metaphor for one person and a suggestive metaphor for another. Or, a single metaphor could be a syntactic one to the same person at one time and suggestive one at another time. Nevertheless, it will be useful to make this distinction for my purpose here, so that I can refer to open-ended metaphors explicitly and note their characteristics, before contrasting them with predictive analogy in Chapter 9. I now discuss each of these classes of similarity-based metaphors individually.

Syntactic Metaphors

A syntactic metaphor is characterized by the fact that the cognitive relation from the source concept network to the target realm is completely mediated by the target concept network. Here, the cognitive agent is usually quite familiar with the target realm. In terms of its conceptualization, we might say that it has a sufficiently rich (structurally speaking) target concept network.

Syntactic metaphor works by first creating a correspondence from the source concept network to the target concept network, and then extending this correspondence to the target realm via the conventional interpretation of the target concept network.

This process is graphically shown in Figure 7.2. The nodes of the concept networks represent the symbols, and arcs represent the structure. Each arc can be thought of as a one-place operator such that, when applied to the symbol at one end, it generates the symbol at its other end, and remains an identity operator when applied to any other symbol. Since a cognitive relation can be many-to-many, if one considers all the objects in the realm that a symbol of the concept network is connected to, we will, in general, get a set of objects, which is the 'group' of the realm corresponding to the symbol. In Figure 7.2, the shaded areas represent such groups in the target realm, and the arcs between them represent the autonomous structure of the realm (as seen by the cognitive agent) with respect to the groupings.

In the figure, C_T is the conventional interpretation from the target concept network to the target realm, and the correspondence between the source and the target concept networks is C_{ST}. The cognitive relation instantiated by the syntactic metaphor is $C_{ST} \circ C_T$. Using the formalization of the previous chapter, it is easy to see that the cognitive relation $C_{ST} \circ C_T$ will be coherent provided that the correspondence C_{ST} preserves the structures of the source and the target concept networks. (This is assuming, of course, that the interpretation C_T is coherent. But since C_T is a conventional cognitive relation, it seems reasonable to assume that it is coherent as far as the cognitive agent is aware. To avoid having to state this explicitly every time, I assume, for the rest of this chapter, that all conventional interpretations are coherent.) (Syntactic metaphors correspond to the strongly coherent T-MAPs in the formalization of Indurkhya [1986].)

An example taken from Gentner & Gentner [1983] is helpful here in illustrating how syntactic metaphors work. Consider the theory of hydraulic systems as the source concept network, and the domain of electrical circuits as the target realm. The source concept network contains various concepts such as 'pipe,' 'pressure,' 'narrowness,' 'viscosity' and 'flow-rate,' as well as an operational structure in the form of laws that relate these concepts by making it possible to derive some concepts from other concepts. For instance, an operator 'JOIN' generates a 'simple-hydraulic-system' from a 'pump' and three 'pipes.' Similarly another operator F1 derives the value of the concept 'flow-rate,' given the value of 'pressure,' by multiplying pressure with a constant. A portion of the source concept network is shown in Figure 7.3.

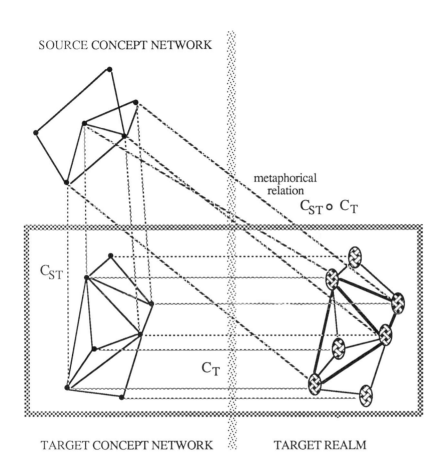

FIGURE 7.2: Syntactic Metaphor. The metaphorical relation is formed by making a correspondence between the source and the target concept networks, and then extending it to the target realm via the conventional cognitive relation of the target. The part of the target realm visible under the metaphorical relation is shown with dark lines.

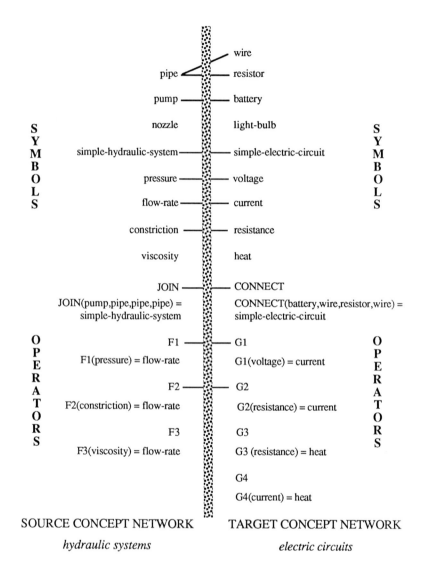

FIGURE 7.3: An example of a correspondence between the source and target concept networks.

The target realm consists of electric networks of resistors, wires and batteries, with currents flowing through them. Here, we also have a target concept network, which reflects the cognitive agent's knowledge of electricity. It contains various electrical concepts, such as 'current,' 'voltage' and 'battery'; and the laws, such as 'Ohm's law' and 'Kirchhoff's laws.' A small part of the target concept network is also shown in Figure 7.3. The conventional interpretation between the target concept network and the target realm connects concepts of the concept network with the appropriate physical objects. Clearly the cognitive relation is coherent, as far as we know, since the realm respects the 'laws' of the concept network.

Now one could construct a correspondence between the concepts of the source and the target concept network, as shown in Figure 7.3. Thus, 'pressure' is associated with 'voltage,' 'flow-rate' is associated with 'current,' etc. Coherence of this correspondence can be established with ease since both concept networks are accessible to the cognitive agent. Once this correspondence is instantiated, the hydraulic concept network can be applied to electrical networks of batteries, wires, and resistors coherently—meaning in such a way that it makes correct predictions about the behavior of the electrical network.

At this point it is natural to ask an important question: What possible advantage might a syntactic metaphor have, since obviously any prediction about the target realm that one might derive by using the source concept network can as well be derived by using the target concept network without doing the extra work of having to construct the coherent correspondence between the two concept networks? It turns out that there are four different ways in which a syntactic metaphor can lend itself to cognition.

- **Easier Cognitive Access to the Target Realm:** One use of a syntactic metaphor is that if the cognitive agent is more familiar and consequently more at ease with accessing and manipulating the source concept network, then it would prefer interacting with the target realm by using the source concept network as much as possible. The coherent correspondence between the source and target concept networks needs to be constructed only once, and after that the source concept network—or at least a part of it—becomes useful in interacting with the target realm.

  I must emphasize here that this role of syntactic metaphors does not include providing an increased understanding of some unfamiliar and poorly understood realm and creative problem solving. These roles of metaphors are explained later. In a syntactic metaphor, the cognitive agent has an adequate understanding of the target realm via the target concept network; or, in other words, the metaphor adds nothing new, at least as far as understanding about the target realm is concerned. It does, however, bring in new information, since noticing that two concept networks are similar has cognitive value.

An example might perhaps illustrate this point better. I recall that when I was an undergraduate student in electrical engineering, we would often analyze mechanical systems by converting them to their electrical analogs, solving the equations of the resulting circuits, and then converting the results back to the mechanical systems. Now in doing that, we fully knew the properties of the mechanical systems, how to write their equations, how to solve them, etc. In fact, it is this knowledge that made us confident that we could analyze them as electrical systems, and the results would still be correct. However, we preferred using the electrical analogs because we were much more used to dealing with electrical quantities than mechanical quantities.

- **Highlighting and Downplaying:** A syntactic metaphor can make a part of the target realm invisible. For instance, to take an example from Black [1979], the metaphor "Nixon is a halo surrounding a vaccum" hides the significance of whatever former U.S. president Nixon might have achieved in his political career. (See also Black[1962], p. 41; and Lakoff & Johnson [1980].)

  This phenomenon is explained in my account as follows. In forming the correspondence between the source and the target concept networks, it is possible that some parts of the target concept network are not related to anything in the source concept network. Consequently, any part of the target realm that was related—by the conventional interpretation C_T—only to those parts of the target concept network that are not included in C_{ST}, will not be visible under the metaphorical relation $C_{ST} \circ C_T$. Thus, the highlighted parts of the target realm are those parts of it that are still visible under the source concept network via the metaphorical relation. The downplayed parts are those that were visible under the target concept network but are no longer visible under the source concept network. In Figure 7.2, the highlighted portion of the target realm is shown with darker lines.

  The example of the hydraulic model of electricity is again helpful in elaborating this explanation. Note that the electrical concept network contains the concept-networks corresponding to magnetic, heating, and lighting effects of electricity which are not related to anything in the hydraulic concept network. (The partial depiction of the electrical concept network shown in Figure 7.3 does not contain all the information pertaining to these effects.) Therefore, these effects become invisible when the hydraulic concept network is applied metaphorically to the electrical realm. For example, the hydraulic concept network cannot be used to predict the current through a solenoid when an alternating voltage is applied across it.

Thus, a syntactic metaphor provides a mechanism by which attention can be focussed on a part of the target realm. This, obviously, makes it a double-edged sword that can be used to advantage as well as abused. For instance, Miller [1976] observed: "...[I]n educational writing metaphors are typically used to *gloss over* matters which cannot be well explained or clearly specified...[and] metaphors are often used in a misleading way to play upon the emotions or carry an argument by means of distortions and over emphasis." [p.174]. Numerous misuses of metaphor can often be found in political rhetoric and propaganda. (See, for instance, Lakoff [1991].)

- **Abstraction:** The third way in which a syntactic metaphor makes itself useful is by making it possible for the cognitive agent to construct new concept networks that are abstracted from the source and target concept networks based on the similarities between them as represented in the correspondence C_{ST}. After the correspondence C_{ST} is formed, the structure carried by it—that is the structure that the source and the target concept networks have in common and that is the basis for C_{ST}—can be broken free from both concept networks and given the status of a concept network itself. In the example of Figure 7.3 this process can be carried out by starting out with either the source concept network or the target concept network, discarding all those concepts of the network that are not included in the correspondence C_{ST}, and replacing every concept that is left, with an appropriate abstract concept. The resulting concept network, in this example, will be a graph theoretic 'network-flow' concept network.

The process of abstraction is illustrated graphically in Figure 7.4. (It should be noted that my abstraction corresponds to *schema-induction* of Gick & Holyoak [1983].) One of the ways in which abstraction plays an important role in cognition is by allowing us to create hierarchies of concept networks. It is the process of abstraction that makes mathematics possible. The abstracted concept network might have no conventional interpretation in any realm, and its structure can be studied

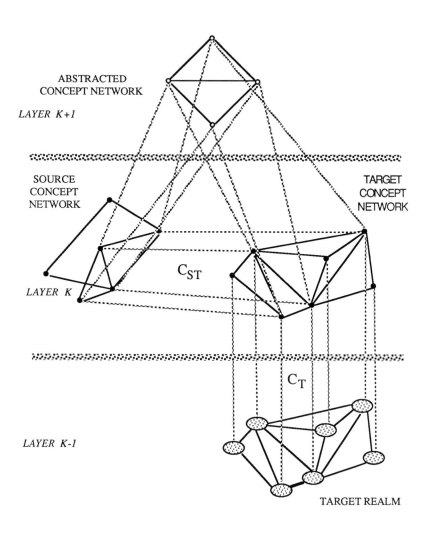

FIGURE 7.4: Abstraction by Syntactic Metaphor

non-referentially. Any insights into its structure can then be used ref-
erentially, by projecting the concept network to any realm into which
it seems to fit (as in applying the method of triangulation to mark a
certain location; see also Mac Lane [1986].)

Thus we see that syntactic metaphors are quite a valuable asset to cognition.
Let us now examine their limits. Obviously, since the metaphorical relation
is formed by composing the correspondence C_{ST} between the source and the
target concept networks with the conventional interpretation C_T between
the target concept network and the target realm, the metaphorical relation
is always a *restriction* [§6.10] of C_T. This condition can be better stated
in terms of the following two characteristics of syntactic metaphors, which
reveal their limitations.

1. A syntactic metaphor can never increase the visibility of the target
   realm. To do this would require that parts of the target realm not
   represented in the target concept network be related to some concepts
   of the source concept network. This would be impossible to achieve
   with a syntactic metaphor. Thus, if the cognitive agent was not aware
   of the magnetic and heating affects of currents, the syntactic metaphor
   of Figure 7.3 would not reveal them.

2. A syntactic metaphor can never increase the resolution of the target realm. That is, if a part of the target realm was grouped under
   one concept by the conventional interpretation from the target concept
   network, then it cannot be broken into two or more concepts by the
   metaphorical relation. For instance, the syntactic metaphor of Figure 7.3 can never introduce a distinction between the solar batteries
   and alkaline batteries, or between carbon resistors and metal resistors.

   A formal proof of this was presented in the previous chapter [Fact 6.12
   in §6.10] and here I make an intuitive argument. Suppose that a syntactic metaphor does increase the rsolution of the target realm. This
   would mean that there are at least two objects (or transformations) in
   the target realm that are related to non-identical sets of symbols (or
   operators) in the source concept network but to a single set of symbols
   (or operators) in the target concept network. Without any loss of generality, let us take them to be objects. As these objects are related to
   two non-identical sets of symbols in the source concept network, it implies that there is at least one symbol there that is related to one object
   and not the other. However, since the metaphorical relation is formed

by composing the correspondence between the two concept networks
with the conventional interpretation of the target system, the symbol
in the source concept network must be related to at least one symbol
in the target concept network that is related to one object but not
the other. Such a symbol cannot exist in the target concept network
because, as the two objects are indistinguishable in the target concept
network, every symbol in the target concept network is either related
to both the objects or to neither of them. Therefore, our premise must
be false.

A syntactic metaphor results essentially from an interaction between the
source and the target concept networks. The target realm plays a completely passive role in receiving the source concept network. The coherency
of metaphorical relation is guaranteed if the correspondence between the two
concept networks is coherent. In other words, a metaphorical relation is
established between the source concept network and the target realm by examining the structures of the source and the target concept networks alone.
Because these structures are syntactic objects from the point of view of the
cognitive agent, I have chosen to call such metaphors syntactic metaphors.
(Note that syntactic metaphors correspond to simple analogies [§1.6.2].)

Suggestive (Open-Ended) Metaphors

Once a metaphorical relation is formed by a syntactic metaphor, it can be extended by instantiating other related concepts of the source concept network
that are instantiated in the target realm. The extension, however, can be carried out without the aid of the target concept network. When this happens,
the syntactic metaphor turns into a suggestive metaphor. The metaphor
"The sky is crying" discussed above, which heightens the interpretation of
the metaphor to include an aura of tragedy and sadness attributed to the
sky, provides a simple example of how a syntactic metaphor can turn into a
suggestive metaphor.

Thus, the target concept network plays a partial role in forming the
metaphorical relation; it provides an initial footing for the source concept
network, based on which further interaction between the source concept network and the target realm can take place. Many suggestive metaphors are
also characterized by the fact that the cognitive agent is not very familiar with the target realm. That is, the target concept network (which is a
conventional description of the target realm) has very little structure to it.
(Intuitively, 'little structure' means that there are very few laws relating con-

cepts to one another: so that it has little potential to provide predictability with respect to the target realm.) Another typical characteristic of many suggestive metaphors is that the target realm is really the 'environment.' In other words, the cognitive agent, in instantiating new concepts from the source concept network, interacts with the external world by carrying out experiments, since the questions about what is 'possible' in the target realm cannot always be answered by consulting the structure of the intermediate cognitive layers.

This process is graphically demonstrated in Figure 7.5, though an example I discuss at length later may help to understand it better. The cognitive agent first creates an initial correspondence between the source and the target concept networks, resulting in a syntactic metaphor. Obviously, this correspondence will be sparse since the target concept network has little structure. The correspondence C_{ST} in the figure gives rise to the metaphorical relation $C_M = C_{ST} \circ C_T$ from the source concept network to the target realm. This metaphorical relation C_M will always be a restriction of the relation C_T between the target concept network and the target realm, as we have seen before. However, since the source concept network is structurally richer, there is a potential for inducing more structure in the target realm based on the initial relation C_M and subject to maintaining coherency. Thus begins the process of extending the relation C_M.

I illustrate this process with an example discussed in Gick and Holyoak [1980]. (See also Holland *et al.* [1986], Section 10.1.1.) Gick and Holyoak studied how an analogy from army maneuvers helped many subjects (cognitive agents) solve the problem of how to use electromagnetic radiation to destroy a tumor without destroying the surrounding healthy tissue. The target realm of electromagnetic rays and their effects on tissue was conventionally understood to some extent. The target concept network gave it a clearly defined ontology (terms like 'rays,' 'tumor,' 'healthy tissue,' etc.) but it had very little structure. In their experiment they presented the subjects with a source concept network of army maneuvers that can be used to capture an enemy fortress. This source concept network was richer—compared to the target concept network—in that it had several operators, like divide the army into several smaller units, look for an unguarded approach to the fortress, etc. (Actually Gick and Holyoak divided the subjects into groups and each group was presented with a story highlighting one of the operators of the source concept network. On being presented with the target realm, the subjects, as would be expected, tried to apply the operator from the source concept network to the target realm.) On encountering the problem, the subjects had little trouble in making an initial correspondence between the

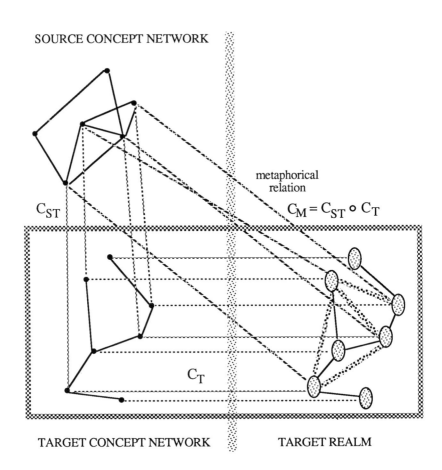

FIGURE 7.5: Suggestive Metaphor. The target concept network has very little structure to it. Based on an initial correspondence between the source and the target concept networks, the structurally rich source concept network suggests possible ways of adding structure to the target realm (shown by heavy shaded lines.) The imported structure must, of course, be verified in the target realm.

source and the target concept networks. The fortress was identified with the tumor, electromagnetic rays were identified with the army, healthy tissues were identified with the mines lying around the fortress, and so on.

Notice that there is some structure in the target concept network that is preserved by this initial correspondence. In identifying healthy tissues with mines, one is preserving the fact that a contact between healthy tissues and radiation is disastrous, and to be avoided. The fact that the mines are a nuisance, and that their elimination makes the goal of occupying the fortress is easier to achieve, is incoherent with the structure of the target concept network, which requires that the healthy tissue be preserved. It is for this reason that an operator in the source concept network that works by exploding all the mines, and then sending the army, is not even considered for testing operationally in the target realm.

However, the other operators that are not incoherent with the initial mapping form a rich source of heuristics in suggesting new operators in the target realm. These operators, of course, must be operationally tested to determine their coherency. The fact that a part of the source concept network is analogous to the target concept network, and thereby applicable to the target realm, does not imply that the rest of the source concept network can also be applied to the target realm without further investigation. Much of the abuse of metaphors and analogies originates from people exploiting the illusory plausibility of this faulty reasoning—political rhetoric being a rich source of examples. (See Chapter 9.)

Often, some fine tuning is necessary to make the operator workable in the target realm. For example, in Gick and Holyoak's experiments, some subjects tried to apply the operator illuminated by a scenario in which the general discovers an unguarded and unmined road to the fortress and decides to send the entire army along it. Because there was nothing corresponding to 'an unguarded and unmined road to the fortress' in the target concept network they had to make up something for it before the operator can be applied. This was not merely a matter of coming up with a concept in the target concept network; the concept had to correspond to something in the target realm. Moreover, because 'mines' and 'fortress' were already made to correspond to 'healthy tissues' and 'tumor,' respectively, of the target concept network, and to the chunks of target realm via the conventional interpretation, any part of the target realm that was made to correspond to 'an unguarded and unmined road to the fortress' (via some concept in the target concept network) had to be 'a path to the tumor, free from intervening healthy tissues and along which electromagnetic rays can travel.' Some of the subjects, in fact, came up with the idea of a ray-proof flexible tube that could be inserted in the body of the ill patient until making contact with the tumor. Electromagnetic rays could then be sent along it. This process of fine tuning obviously requires ingenuity and originality.

Several researchers have noted the characteristics of suggestive metaphors and the important role played by them in cognition. For instance, in Gordon's empirical research on creative problem solving, some of the examples of what he characterized as *making the strange familiar* [Gordon, 1961, p. 35] are instances of suggestive metaphor. (The use of the horse's anal sphincter analogy in solving the dispenser problem mentioned in Chapter 2 [§2.5.1] is a case in point.) As the name suggests, in 'making the familiar strange' one tries to understand an unfamiliar problem or situation by applying some familiar conceptual system. This conceptual system gives an ontology to the unfamiliar situation that allows the structure of the system to be transported to the problem by *suggesting* possible solutions. These suggestions must, of course, be operationally tested to see if they really work.

Suggestive metaphors are also evidenced in Hesse's account of material models as an indispensable aid in the growth of science. [Hesse 1966, 1974, 1980.] Material models can often be seen at work behind scientific theories when they are at an exploratory stage. Often the subject of the scientific theory, the target realm, is not well understood, and scanty knowledge of it might suggest an initial correspondence with some other theory or well-understood phenomenon. Based on this correspondence, further hypotheses can be made about the target realm. Attempting to operationally verify these hypotheses results in an increased knowledge of the target realm, which is reflected in a larger and more comprehensive target concept network. It is in this sense that material models can be said to determine the direction of growth of our knowledge by affecting the questions that are posed about the target realm.

Finally, I should emphasize once again that the mechanism underlying suggestive metaphors should not be confused with predictive analogy. In predictive analogy, the existing similarities between the source and the target concept networks are seen as somehow *justifying* that there might be other similarities as well. This, in turn, suggests that in trying to solve some problem about a realm, one's best bet may be to find a concept network that is most similar to whatever is known about the target realm, and use that concept network to form hypotheses about how the problem might be addressed. Suggestive metaphors, on the other hand, carry no such justification. The fact that certain parts of the source concept network have been successfully interpreted in the target realm, says nothing whatsoever about whether other parts of the concept network might also be so interpreted. In particular, it does not carry even a hint of the suggestion that a concept network that is very similar to the target concept network is likely to lead to the solution of whatever problem one might be facing with the target realm.

7.4.2   Similarity-Creating (Projective) Metaphors

I presented several examples of similarity-creating metaphors in Chapter 2. They all had the characteristic of having no similarities between the source and the target concept networks prior to the metaphor. Only after the metaphor was understood, if it was understood at all, were there similarities between the two concept networks. I refer to such metaphors, which are known to be the hallmark of a truly creative genius, as *projective metaphors.* (The term 'projective' is actually borrowed from Schön [1963], but also fits naturally with the sense in which I have been using the term 'projection' in my framework of cognition.)

Projective metaphors work by completely disregarding the structuring of the target realm under the target concept network, and projecting the source concept network on it anew, as if the target realm were being encountered for the first time. In the process, the structure of the source concept network is kept more or less invariant, but the ontology of the target realm is varied so that its structure, as seen from the concept network layer, is isomorphic (as far it can be) to the structure of the source concept network. Whatever part of the source concept network has been instantiated in this fashion is now considered the new description of the target realm. Therefore, it follows naturally that the new description of the target realm will be similar to the source concept network. Thus, though there might be no similarities between the old target concept network and the source network, there will always be similarities between the source concept network and the new description of the target realm (which will be a subnetwork of the source concept network). The only time this cannot happen is when the projection attempt fails, causing the metaphor to be dubbed meaningless or anomalous. Creation of similarities by a projective metaphor in this fashion is shown graphically in Figures 7.6(a) and 7.6(b).

Let us now consider a few examples and analyze how the similarities are created in them. First let us focus on those projective metaphors that require an interaction with the environment—that is, the target realm is actually the target environment. Such metaphors can be found in the history of science

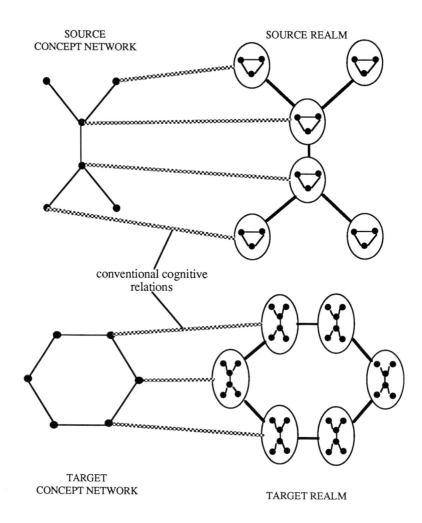

FIGURE 7.6 (a): Projective (similarity-creating) metaphor: Before. The source and the target concept networks group their respective realms quite differently. There are no existing similarities between the two concept networks

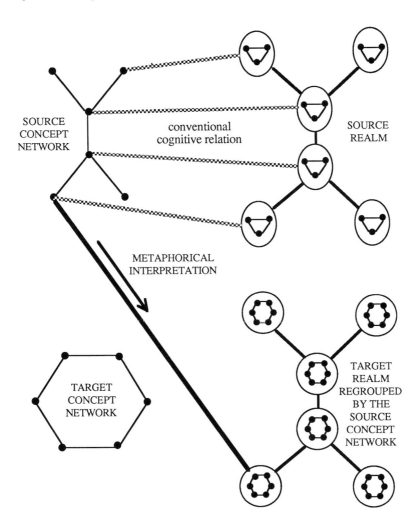

FIGURE 7.6 (b): Projective (similarity-creating) metaphor: After. The stucture of the target realm is regrouped so as to reflect the structure of the source concept network. Now there are similarities between the source and the target (as seen through the new groupings.)

and creative problem solving. (They can also be found in perceptual domains, such as the domain of geometric figures discussed in Chapter 2 [§2.4.2]. See Indurkhya [1991a] for an explanation of the creation of similarity using the example of the figure of the Star of David in this domain.) To start with, consider Schön's example of 'paintbrush as a pump' metaphor that was introduced in Chapter 2 [§2.5.2]. You might recall that a product-development team came up with this metaphor in trying to develop an improved synthetic-fiber paintbrush. It was already emphasized in Chapter 2 that the metaphor did not result from noticing some existing similarities between painting and pumping. Moreover, the metaphor gave a totally different ontology to the process of painting, and the role of a paintbrush in the process was radically transformed. It is not that the source concept network of 'pump' and 'pumping' was *mapped* onto the initial target concept network of 'paintbrush' and 'painting,' but rather the chunks of the target environment were regrouped and renamed, thereby acquiring a new ontology in the process of projection. This point was very aptly emphasized by Schön [1979, pp. 259–60]. This new ontology of the target environment was by no means a mere extension of the initial target concept network, as was the case with Holyoak and Gick's radiation problem.

Let me elucidate how projection might have worked in this example by considering the human visual system as a layered cognitive system. Let us say that a cognitive agent views some situation and a corresponding image is formed on its retina. The research on the human visual system in this century has conclusively demonstrated that the situation as 'seen' by the cognitive agent at a higher perceptual level is not simply derived from the retinal image by progressive refinement, but rather that the retinal image is integrated into some concept at a higher level. In other words, the operation of lower-level perceptual apparatus is not epistemically neutral, but is heavily biased by the organization of the higher layers. Of course, some of this organization is hard-wired. In the visual system, for instance, the retinal cells are so connected with the next perceptual layer that the eye is actually looking for contrast, straight edges, corners, lines with fixed orientation, and so on. The hard-wired nature of this organization is revealed in numerous paradoxes of vision. (See *The Mind's Eye*, readings from *Scientific American*, W.H. Freeman & Co. (1986), New York, NY, for a very readable collection of articles on the human visual system.)

However, not all the organization is hard-wired—at least not in humans—and this fact is the key to metaphor. This makes projective metaphor possible and also accounts for its usefulness in cognition, especially in creating new perspective. To see this let us elaborate our example a little more. Say that a cognitive agent is painting a wall by using a paintbrush, or watching someone else do it. A pattern of images is formed in the cognitive agent's eye as the paintbrush is dipped into paint, given a few shakes to shed the excess paint off, and then moved in uniform, broad strokes across the wall. If the cognitive agent believes that the paintbrush works by smearing paint on the wall, then this pattern of images is divided into groups accordingly and a causal structure imposed upon it (or 'seen' in it). On being presented the 'paintbrush as a pump' metaphor, the cognitive agent regroups the pattern of images—which it has to, in order to make sense of the metaphor. The main thing to note here is that the pattern of images on the cognitive agent's eye has not changed. The process of painting has not changed. It is the cognitive agent's perception of it that has changed, and changed considerably. If we keep in mind that perception is not epistemically neutral then we can say that the process of painting, as seen by the cognitive agent, has changed as a result of the metaphor. It is in this sense that it can be said that the metaphor *created* a new perspective.

Several other instances of projective metaphor are noted by Kuhn in the history of science. Though most of the time science proceeds in a widening spiral, with new hypotheses consistent with the current theory constantly being explored a process in which suggestive metaphor plays a crucial role. However, there are occasions when a totally new theory, with a radically different ontology, is called for; an extension of the existing theory just will not do. Kuhn mentioned at least three such occasions: (1) the replacement of Ptolemaic astronomy with Copernicus' astronomy, (2) the replacement of the phlogiston theory of chemistry with Lavoisier's oxygen theory of combustion, and (3) the replacement of Newtonian mechanics with Einstein's theory of relativity. (See Kuhn [1962], Ch. VII; and also Kuhn [1957].) On all these occasions, a scientific revolution took place; the scientific community threw away the existing paradigm in favor of a new and radically different one. (Of course, this process is not as abrupt and sudden as this statement implies. There is invariably a period of adjustment when various attempts are made to stretch the existing paradigm to assimilate the anomalous data, and the new paradigm is subjected to a harsh criticism and stringent tests. See Kuhn [1962] for a detailed discussion of the process of adjustment to the new paradigm.)

In fact, a truly creative or revolutionary metaphor almost invariably works by disregarding the existing ontology of the target environment as seen from the target concept network. Projective metaphors are often necessary because the structure of the target environment, as seen through the target concept network, reflects the earlier goals and preferences of the cognitive agent, and it might not be possible to extend it in any way to explain some unusual phenomenon or to solve a different type of problem. Kuhn's scientific revolutions, Schön's [1963] generative metaphors, and Gordon's [1961] 'making the familiar strange' are prime examples.

How does a projective metaphor create a new perspective? Obviously, projecting different source concept networks leads to different organizations of the target environment, which might or might not be useful for solving a certain problem. For example, in the paintbrush example discussed above, Schön remarked that the researchers also considered the 'painting as masking a surface' metaphor but it did not result in any useful insight. What then makes a source concept network more successful than others?

For an answer, we must look at the environment in which the source concept network has a conventional interpretation; that is, the source environment. It is the only thing that can provide a link between the source concept network and the target environment (given that we do not wish to use the target concept network as a possible link).

Reality, the Kantian things-in-themselves, is richly connected. We might even say that it is totally connected: given any two objects, one can always find some way of relating them to each other, and find something that they have in common. It is only our perceptual and cognitive apparatus that groups the 'real-world' into chunks and imposes the structure of our cognitive concept networks on them. However, in carving up two environments in this fashion—that is, in imposing a conceptual structure on each of them—this connectivity is lost. The environments, viewed through their respective concept networks, are no longer seen as similar. However, in projecting the source concept network, which might have originated through an interaction with the source environment, onto the target environment, this connectivity is partially recovered, as the cognitive agent is forced to regroup the ontology of the target environment to create one that is isomorphic to the source concept network. This is what Schön may have had in mind when he wrote in connection with the 'paintbrush as a pump' metaphor:

> "It is important to note that the researchers were able to see painting as similar to pumping before they were able to say 'similar with respect to what.' At first, they had only an unarticulated perception of similarity which they could express by doing the painting and inviting others to see it as they did, or by using the terms like 'squeezing' or 'forcing' to convey the pumplike quality of the action. Only later, and in an effort to account for their earlier perception of similarity, did they develop an explicit

account of similarity, an account which later still became part of
a general theory of 'pumpoids,' according to which they could regard paintbrushes and pumps, along with wash-cloths and mops,
as instances of a single technological category." [1979, p. 260]

In other words, there are potential similarities between the process of painting
and the action of a pump—potential similarities that are discarded in grouping the process of painting as a smearing process. And it is these potential
similarities that are made real by the metaphor 'paintbrush as a pump.'

This account of projective metaphor also explains why it is such an invaluable asset to cognition. Cognition typically involves grouping. Various
objects and transformations, in the world that is made available to us by
our perceptual and motor apparatus, are further grouped into categories and
operations. Thus, the world as seen from the cognitive layers is considerably
more simplified and structured than the one seen from the lower perceptual
layers. This simplification is necessary to make us survive in an infinitely
complex world of things-in-themselves with our finite and limited minds.
However, an act of grouping invariably involves loss of information. (See also
Hesse [1974], p. 48–51, for arguments leading to the conclusion that any classification necessarily results in a loss of verbalizable empirical information.)
When a bunch of objects are placed in a category, their potential differences
are overlooked; one might say that they are discarded by the process of cognition. Similarly, in putting two objects in different categories their potential
common grounds are discarded as well. In grouping the world in one way—
though the resulting simplified world view makes it easier for the cognitive
agent to interact with the world—the cognitive agent is deprived of a horde
of alternate world views.

If the cognitive relations between all layers were predetermined for each
cognitive agent—whether biologically or culturally—then the lost worlds
would be lost forever. The parts of the world that are indistinguishable in the
cognitive model would remain indistinguishable permanently. The cognitive
agent could never recover the information lost in cognition and reorganize its
world views.

However, if the cognitive agent can project different concept networks
onto the same environment, it can partially recover these lost worlds. Some of
the potential distinctions between different parts of the environment that are
discarded in grouping it conventionally can be made visible under the unconventional grouping induced by another concept network. Thus, a projective
metaphor allows the cognitive agent to partially reclaim the lost information
that inevitably results from cognition.

A similar explanation can be given to those similarity-creating metaphors that do not require a direct interaction with the environment—as in Boland's 'wild flowers as water' and Spender's 'ocean as a harp' metaphors. The target is really a target realm here, which is an imagined target environment in the intermediate cognitive layers. (That is, if the cognitive agent were experiencing the stimuli that are being described in the poem, then it might result in the imagined structure in the intermediate cognitive layers.) Moreover, this imagined scenario is based on the cognitive agent's past experiences, which endow it with a structure that is independent of how it might be described. It is this autonomous structure that constrains which source concept networks can be instantiated in the target realm, and how they can be be instantiated, thereby ruling out arbitrary metaphors. I have already emphasized all these points in Section 2.

In understanding Boland's poem, the target realm of 'wild flowers growing in a hilly countryside' is given a new ontology by instantiating the source concept network of 'bodies of water (lakes, waterfalls, etc.) and related concepts.' Notice that while the target realm has a conventional description, the conventional description is not equivalent to the metaphorical description. In instantiating concepts like 'water rushing downhill' and 'fluidity,' the imagined target realm becomes alive in a way that it cannot under any conventional description. As hawthorns start blooming, one can imagine the effect as that of flowing water. It is as if one took a film of the hilly countryside over a period of several days (or even weeks), and were now viewing the film very fast. Of course, the details of imagery are quite subjective, and different people may experience the metaphor in different ways. But my point is that the ontology of the imagined experience is quite different from what it would be in a conventional description. (Otherwise, one should be able to see similarities between wild flowers and water before having read the poem.)

After the poem is understood, the structure of the target realm with respect to this new ontology is bound to be similar to the source concept network, as the ontology is created by instantiating the source concept network. This is exactly how the similarities are created between wild flowers and water in the cognitive agent's mind.

The same explanation can be put forward for Mondrian's interpretation of his paintings as the dynamic opposition between good and evil. Mondrian's interpretation, for instance, gives a completely new ontology to the moral opposition of good and evil. Evil is no longer something that must be destroyed. Rather, it becomes an essential ingredient of life and order in the world. Unless the dynamic opposition of good and evil is seen from this new ontology, Mondrian's interpretation would not be meaningful, even after the target realm is explicitly pointed out. And it is creating this new ontology that the metaphor creates the similarities between the painting and the moral opposition of good and evil.

Where do the created similarities come from? As with the 'paintbrush as a pump' metaphor, we again look at the source realm. In reading Boland's poem, the metaphor evokes the image of water rushing downhill, splashing, creating puddles, and so on. This image is seen as similar to the target realm. (In fact, this is why the source concept can be instantiated as it is.) However, these similarities are not present in the conventional descriptions of 'water rushing downhill' and 'wild flowers growing on a hill.' If one tried to understand the metaphor by processing the concept networks alone, the metaphor would be considered anomalous. But once the realms are evoked, the potential similarities are partially recovered. Moreover, these similarities can now (after the metaphor is understood) be seen from the concept network layer, since the target realm has been given a new ontology and a new structure by the metaphor.

Of course, one can counter here by saying that it all depends on what one takes to be the conventional description of 'wild flowers growing on a hill' (the target realm). It is certainly possible to include the relevant information so that the metaphor can be understood from a comparison of the source and the target concept networks, thereby turning it into a similarity-based metaphor. I do not deny this at all. In fact, every similarity-creating metaphor, *after* it is understood and the new ontology for the target realm has been seen, can be presented as a similarity-based metaphor. But then, for any given conventional description of the target realm, no matter how detailed, there are always other metaphors that cannot be analyzed on the basis of that description. I have already emphasized this point in connection with proportional analogies involving geometric figures [§2.4.2]. Thus, there will always be similarity-creating metaphors as long as *some* information is lost in conceptualization.

7.5 Summary

In this chapter, I began by arguing that the process underlying metaphors is essentially that of projection. This argument rests on three separate points. The first is that the 'source' of a metaphor is a system of symbols (for example, the text) that has its autonomous structure (the words in the text are arranged in a certain order, and the words are related to other words in certain ways, as in dictionary meanings.) Using the terminology of my framework of cognition, this is referred to as the 'source concept network.'

The second point is that the domain of interpretation (the 'target') either is some object in the external world that has been converted into an autonomously structured sensorimotor data set by our sensory apparatus, or is an imagined experience of the object that is more detailed than a concept network, and has an autonomous structure that reflects the cognitive agent's prior perceptual experiences with the object. This is referred to as the 'target realm.'

The third point is that the structure of the source concept network is not altered in interpreting a metaphor, but the concepts are given a new interpretation, thereby giving a new ontology to the target realm. The autonomous structure of the target realm endows this new ontology with a new structure. Thus, a metaphor becomes an instance of an unconventional cognitive relation formed by projection.

A main novelty of this account is the introduction of a distinction between an object or an experience (whether actual or imagined) and its representation. Making this distinction has been crucial to the account's ability to resolve the paradox of creation of similarity.

I then argued that there are three different modes of metaphor, each with its own set of characteristics that make it useful to cognition in certain ways but not in others. These modes must be distinguished to make sense of the different characteristics of metaphor, and the many diverse roles it plays in cognition. The modes are distinguished on the basis of the degree of participation of the target concept network (a conventional representation of the target realm) and the source realm (the object or experience, real or imagined, that is conventionally represented in the source concept network) in the process of instantiating the metaphorical relation.

Syntactic and suggestive metaphors fall under what I have been calling similarity-based metaphors. In syntactic metaphors, the process of interpretation is completely mediated by the target concept network. Even though syntactic metaphors do not provide any new information about the target realm (information that is not already present in the target concept network), they are, nonetheless, useful to cognition is several ways. For instance, they can provide an easier access to the target realm, if the cognitive agent finds it easier to manipulate the source concept network. Or, they can be used to draw attention to certain parts of the target realm by highlighting them.

In suggestive (open-ended) metaphors the target concept network is used only to provide an initial ontology for the target realm, on which the initial interpretation of the source concept network is anchored. After the initial interpretation, however, additional structure can be imported from the source concept network to enhance the structure of the target realm (enhanced from what is already there in the target concept network), as long as the imported structure is coherent with the autonomous structure of the target realm.

As suggestive metaphors come close to what I have termed as 'predictive analogy' (the process of inferring further similarities between two objects or situations given some existing similarities) in Chapter 1, great care must be taken to distinguish the two. In suggestive metaphor, there is no 'justi-fication' attached, so that the fact that certain parts of the source concept network have been successfully interpreted in the target realm does not in any way justify that other parts can be interpreted as well. Predictive analogy, on the other hand, carries precisely such a justification. (I discuss predictive analogy in Chapter 9.)

In projective (similarity-creating) metaphors, the target concept network is competely discarded, and the source concept network is interpreted in the target realm, as if the target realm is being encountered for the first time. Here, it is the source realm that ends up playing a role by deter-mining (indirectly) the result of projecting the source concept network onto the target realm. It is the potential similarities between the source and the target realms—potential similarities that were discarded in the conventional conceptualization—that are discovered in the process of projection.

Of these three modes, projective metaphors might well be considered the *pneuma* of metaphors. While syntactic metaphors and suggestive metaphors also involve some originality in making correspondences between the source and the target concept networks, and in importing structure from the source concept networks; it is projective metaphors that require the ability to break the shackles of one's language and culture, and to be able to ungroup and regroup the sensorimotor data set into different meaningful patterns. If the primary role of cognition is to braid the kaleidoscopic flux of impressions we get from our senses into a meaningful pattern, it is projective metaphors that make it possible for different patterns to be woven into the braid, thereby creating different modes of reality.

Part III

The Implications

Chapter 8

Some Metaphor-Related Issues

8.1 Introduction

Now that I have articulated my account of metaphor, and have addressed the phenomenon of creation of similarity within it, it would be useful to examine what consequences it has for some other issues related to metaphor. For instance, there is the thesis "All knowledge is metaphorical," which is as vehemently supported by some scholars as it is opposed by others. Since I have characterized the metaphorical in contrast with the conventional, it might seem that my account of metaphor implicitly rejects this thesis. On the contrary, I show in Section 2 that proponents of this thesis do not use the term 'metaphor' in the same sense as I have been using it; and with their sense of metaphor, my account comes out strongly favoring the thesis. I also show in this section how using the term metaphor in different senses has created a needless debate over literal-metaphorical dichotomy.

So far I have characterized metaphor as a *meaningful* interpretation. However, this is a rather broad characterization, Often, one wishes to apply the stricter criteria of *correctness* (or truth) and *aptness*. For instance, consider the metaphor "Nixon is a halo surrounding the vacuum." An admirer of the former United States president Richard Nixon might consider this statement quite incorrect (or false) even though she clearly understands the metaphor (since otherwise, she would not be able to declare it incorrect). How is the understanding (meaningfulness) to be distinguished from correctness? Then there is also the problem of distinguishing between literal and metaphorical correctness, for a very literal-minded critic of Nixon might also declare the above statement false, but obviously for a different reason. These issues are discussed in Section 3.

Finally, there is the quality of metaphor. Some metaphors seem more compelling than others. For instance, Quinn [1986, Chap. 3] recounts how disgruntled the attendants at a wedding were, when the sermon compared marriage to an ice cream cone: you can eat it up all at once, or make it last a long time. One can certainly make some sort of coherent interpretation of marriage as an ice cream cone (you can eat it up all at once, or make it last a long time), so the metaphor can be dubbed meaningful, and even correct. Yet it would be considered not very compelling and of poor quality by most people. What makes a metaphor better than another? I discuss this issue in Section 4.

8.2   The Thesis 'All Knowledge is Metaphorical'

A certain thesis, which I refer to as the *strong thesis of metaphor,* is often advanced, according to which the process of metaphor is not only an indispensable tool to cognition, but is the very basis of cognition. Then all knowledge—essentially a product of cognition—is metaphorical too. Proponents of the strong thesis include Arbib & Hesse [1986], Berggren [1962–63], Black [1962, 1979], Cassirer [1955], Emmett [1945], Hesse [1974], Richards [1936], Ricoeur [1976, 1977, 1978], Sewell [1964], Turbayne [1962] and Wheeler [1987]. At least two schools of thought, led by Mac Cormac [1985, Chap. 3] and Lakoff and his colleagues [Lakoff & Turner 1989, Chap. 2] respectively, have articulated detailed arguments, citing empirical evidence, to reject the strong thesis. Given this state of affairs, it is important to clarify where my account of metaphor stands with respect to the strong thesis.

It might seem at first that my account of metaphor automatically rejects the strong thesis, for I have characterized the metaphorical in contrast with the conventional, thereby incorporating a conventional-metaphorical dichotomy right from the start. However, it turns out that the proponents of the strong thesis do not use the term 'metaphor' in the same sense as I have been using it. Actually, there are significant variations, in how the term 'metaphor' is used, even amongst the proponents of the strong thesis. To add to the confusion, the opponents of the strong thesis have articulated their arguments based on *their* definitions of 'metaphor.' For instance, though Mac Cormac and Lakoff have both rejected the strong thesis, they have harshly criticized each other for using the term 'metaphor' in a confused manner, to say the least. In fact, the debate over the strong thesis of metaphor provides an excellent example of the unnecessary confusion and the needless controversy that is created when different people use a term with different, but related meanings. For metaphors, this confusion has served only to draw the researchers' attention away from some of the key issues.

It is my objective in this section to lift this fog by identifying the different senses of the strong thesis, and exposing the unnecessary controversy over the strong thesis created by the Lakoff-Mac Cormac debate. I start by discerning three versions of the strong thesis that I consider to be prominent. One version maintains that all knowledge is metaphorical in the sense that it involves an element of projection. The second version holds that all thought is metaphoric and proceeds by comparison. The third version argues that all language is, or once was, metaphorical. I analyze each of these versions in turn, and then go on to discuss the Lakoff-Mac Cormac debate on literal-metaphorical dichotomy.

8.2.1 Version 1: All Knowledge is Projective

The first version of the strong thesis, embraced by Cassirer, Emmett, Turbayne, Berggren, and Sewell, starts out by emphasizing the creative role played by the human mind in any conceptualization—or, which is the same, in forming systems of symbols. It is argued that there are no pre-existing mind-independent and objective structures to which our concepts must conform. Rather, it is the cognitive agent itself who gives an ontology to its experiences with the external world by instantiating symbols. In other words, cognition works by *creating* structures in the world, and not by adapting to some preexisting ones. Cassirer, as I acknowledged in Chapter 4 [§4.3], was a champion of this view.

Then, it is pointed out that metaphor is the primary process by which structures are created in the external world. In other words, it is metaphor that makes a correspondence between the symbols and parts of the world, thereby creating structures in the world that the cognitive agent sees. Thus, metaphor becomes the key to cognition. From 'all knowledge is inherently symbolic' and 'symbols are necessarily interpreted by metaphor,' one arrives at the conclusion: 'all knowledge is necessarily metaphorical.'

This thesis, however, raises an interesting metaphysical problem. If all our knowledge is metaphorical, how can we ever be aware of it? If the only mode of interaction with the external world available to us is by using symbols that are created by us, what difference does it make if we assume those symbols to be rooted in the structure of the external world?

An answer to these questions is provided by Turbayne in his fascinating essay *The Myth of Metaphor*. He argues, with a very elaborate example, that the external world is inaccessible to us, and we can only view it through some metaphor. Yet, we can view it through *different* metaphors, and only by doing so can we gain awareness of the metaphorical nature of our knowledge. Moreover, in refusing to do so, and in taking the structure of one's conceptual system to be a reflection of the structure of the external world, the metaphor turns into a myth. (Turbayne's sense of the term 'myth' here may be better understood as 'one-track mind.')

Obviously, this version of the strong thesis is fully incorporated in my framework. Recall that in Chapter 5, I emphasized repeatedly how the ontology of the external world is determined by the cognitive agent via its perceptual and cognitive apparatus. The process, which I refer to as projection, works by the cognitive agent grouping parts of the environment together and associating them with concepts. Later, in Chapter 7 [§7.2], I also argued that metaphor is nothing but projection. Thus, we can say that all knowledge is metaphorical in that the ontology of the external world—and any form of knowledge presupposes an ontology of some kind—is not predetermined, but is established by the cognitive agent through metaphor.

Of course, the projection might be partially or fully encoded biologically in the cognitive agent, and the strong thesis—this version of it—loses its force when the cognitive agent has no freedom in carrying out the projection. Since if the projection is fully encoded biologically, then as far as the cognitive agent is concerned, the ontology of its world is fixed by its biological nature, and it can never be aware of the metaphorical nature of its knowledge: The ontology of its world could not be otherwise.

In my account of human cognition, the world view of a cognitive agent is first determined by its perceptual apparatus interacting with reality (the Kantian things-in-themselves), resulting in the sensorimotor data set. The sensorimotor data set is then further reorganized, one might say 'simplified,' by the higher perceptual layers and the cognitive layers. Viewed through a concept network in a higher (more abstract) cognitive layer, what the cognitive agent sees in reality is an isomorphic copy of the concept network. This is made possible by the mechanism of projection working through all the lower cognitive and perceptual layers—a process which also underlies metaphor. Moreover, by projecting different concept networks, the cognitive agent can see different structures in reality, and thereby become aware of the metaphorical nature of its knowledge.

8.2.2   Version 2: All Thought is Comparative

Let us now examine another version of the strong thesis, perhaps best summarized by Richards [1936]: "*Thought* is metaphoric, and proceeds by comparison, and the metaphors of language derive therefrom." (From p. 51 in Johnson [1981a].) A similar thought is echoed by Black [1979]. The suggestion here is that metaphor is fundamental to thought processes, and the comparative aspect of metaphor underlies all cognition, with the term 'comparative' not merely refering to noticing pre-existing similarities, but also to the creation of similarities.

This version of the strong thesis is somewhat vaguely stated, but it can be articulated within my framework so that it captures the essence of what Richards and Black may have had in mind. Recall that in Chapter 7 [§7.4.2], I pointed out how cognition typically induces groupings which leads to a loss of information. In a purely accommodating cognitive system—one in which the projection mechanism is fully encoded biologically or culturally—this information loss is permanent and irrecoverable. The worlds lost are lost forever.

I also argued there how projective metaphors make it possible for the cognitive agent to recover some of the lost worlds. The process works by projecting a different concept network onto the environment (different than the one that is conventionally used with that environment). Or, to use a metaphor from Turbayne, if we are always viewing the world through a pair of green glasses, our perception is very much biased. However, within the constraint that we can view the world not with the naked eye but only through a pair of glasses, the capability of putting on different colored glasses extends our cognitive abilities a great deal. It is precisely in this sense that our abilities to create and understand metaphors are an invaluable asset to cognition.

I also noted (in §7.4.2) that in projecting a source concept network onto a target realm, the cognitive agent is, in effect, realizing the potential similarities between the source and target realms. This process can be thought of *as if* the cognitive agent were comparing the source realm with the target realm. The 'as if' part is emphasized because the realms are not always directly accessible for comparison. When the source and target realms are actual objects in the external worlds, then we cannot compare the two objects because they belong to the world of things-in-themselves that is not accessible. However, in projecting the concept network that is the conventional description of one object onto the other object, we are partially getting some information about their 'comparative aspects.' This is the comparative aspect of metaphor that is responsible for creating new insights about the target realm, and for making metaphor a key player in cognition. I believe it is this comparative aspect of metaphor to which Black and Richards were alluding.

An analogy can be drawn here with the functioning of our perceptual system. In past years, research into the physiology of our sensory system has established beyond doubt that our senses are geared towards detecting *differences* rather than absolute levels. For instance, the eye is more sensitive to contrasts and to changes in illumination levels, than to absolute illumination levels. I conjecture that this very same principle is also the basis of cognition, and metaphor is a manifestation of this principle in cognition. (See Bateson [1979] also for a discussion of the role played by 'differences' in cognition.)

8.2.3   Version 3: All Conventional Meanings Arise By Way of Metaphor

The third sense of the strong thesis—which can be discerned in Arbib & Hesse [1986], Cassirer [1955], Ricoeur [1976] and Wegener [1885]—is derived from an empirical fact. Linguists have known for a long time that metaphors play a key role in the process of meaning change. (I am using the term 'metaphor' in my sense here to refer to non-conventional interpretations.) Metaphors that are considered novel at one time, lose their novelty through frequent usage and become a part of the conventional language. Mac Cormac [1985, p. 59] cites 'war' as an example. The current dictionary meaning of the word includes 'mental hostility,' which was absent from Samuel Johnson's *A Dictionary of the English Language* in 1775. Lakoff [1987a] offers many other examples to show that this process of meaning change caused by metaphors takes place in several stages. For instance, the origin of the word 'pedigree' can be traced back to *pie de grue* of Old French, meaning 'foot of a crane.' Initially, this term was metaphorical, evoking the image of a crane's foot to refer to a family-tree diagram. However, now the use of 'pedigree' does not evoke any such image in most people. They might not even be aware that it has anything to do with a crane's foot, though the New College Edition (1975) of *The American Heritage Dictionary of the English Language* still records the origin of the term. One might say that, when one now uses the word 'pedigree' to refer to one's ancestry, it is being used conventionally, or even literally. On the other hand, the use of 'fight' in "The presidential candidates fought bitterly in the debate" may still evoke the image of 'war' in some people, even though the dictionary meaning of 'fight' now includes 'a verbal disagreement.'

Given that *some* conventional meanings originate as metaphors, this version of the strong thesis generalizes it to conclude that *all* conventional meanings must have been metaphorical once.

Even with this clarification, it is possible to misinterpret this version of the strong thesis. One might take it to mean that it is impossible to have a concept network (system of symbols), ever, that has a conventional interpretation right from the start. Taken in this sense, this version of the strong thesis is easily refuted. Consider the process of making a scale model of a ship. One starts by choosing an appropriate scale and what aspects of the ship are being modeled. For instance, the features included in a model to be used by a travel agent for showing prospective travelers the types of available accommodations will be different from those included in a marine engineer's model to test the ship's seaworthiness. Once these choices are made, it is the structure of the ship that determines the structure of the model. (A coherent cognitive relation is being formed by accommodation here.) When the model is completed, there is only one intended interpretation of it that allows it to refer to the ship modeled. This interpretation is conventional right from the start.

Several other examples can be suggested along this line. In developing a mathematical theory of electricity that uses otherwise meaningless symbols like R for resistance, I for current, etc., and explains the relationship between these symbols by mathematical equations, there is no initial metaphorical interpretation of the theory. Basically, any cognitive relation that is being formed by accommodation will have a conventional interpretation right from the start. This is because in an accommodating cognitive relation, the concepts of the concept network are given a meaning *before* the concept network is given a structure.

However, the interesting thing is that in all such examples, the system being modeled or studied is given an initial ontology by using other concepts and concept networks that have conventional interpretations. For instance, in deciding what aspects of the ship are being modeled, one has to use concepts like 'cabin,' 'deck,' 'hull,' and so on. Before studying the relationship between resistance and current, one must describe what 'resistance' is and what 'current' is, and these descriptions (which must include the ways in which currents and resistances might be measured) make use of other concepts that have conventional interpretations.

Thus, if there are already concepts with conventional meanings, it is certainly possible to define other concepts and generate concept networks that start out with conventional meanings. But this is not what the third version of the strong thesis is trying to say. Its main thrust is that *a system of symbols that is not rooted in pre-existing conventional symbols always starts out as a metaphor.*

I should emphasize that what is meant by 'metaphor' here is the process of giving a *new* ontology to the environment. The purport of this version of the strong thesis is that what we take to be the conventional description of the world is actually brought about by a process that was alive and vibrant once; a process that also makes metaphors meaningful. Thus, this version is actually quite close to the first version of the strong thesis, in spite of the fact that the term 'metaphor' is used with different meanings in the two versions.

There are two lines of argument supporting this version of the strong thesis. One comes from anthropology by considering different stages through which symbols evolve in a culture. These arguments are best articulated by Cassirer [1955]. (See also my brief discussion of Cassirer's three types of symbols in §4.3.) The other line of argument comes from considering the development of concepts in a child. Though Piaget did not explicitly address the strong thesis of metaphor, his numerous experiments with children to demonstrate his constructivism [§4.4] provide indirect support to this version of the strong thesis. (See, for instance, Piaget [1945] and Piaget [1975].)

I find this version of the strong thesis quite appealing, though, technically speaking, my account of metaphor is neutral with respect to it, because I do not take sides on how the conventional interpretations come about. The arguments of Cassirer and Piaget convince me that all that we regard as conventional and literal was once as vibrant as the metaphors of Boland and Spender; and you need not study other languages and cultures in order to convince yourself of this, but only need to remember your childhood experiences and joy of figuring out what a word means.

8.2.4   Lakoff-Mac Cormac Debate

As I noted before, the strong thesis of metaphor has been criticized by Lakoff and his colleagues, and by Mac Cormac. Since I endorse each of the three versions of strong thesis, it would only be appropriate to address the points raised in both their criticisms. However, before doing that, I would like to discuss Mac Cormac's criticism of Lakoff, and Lakoff's rebuttal to Mac Cormac, for two reasons. One is to demonstrate how using the term 'metaphor' in different senses can create a needless controversy. I feel that this issue must be brought out, since each of them is an influential scholar. The second is that in discussing their criticism of each other first, my task of refuting the arguments raised by each of them against the strong thesis of metaphor will be made short, since each exposes the weaknesses of other's arguments rather well.

Lakoff and Johnson [1980] put forth the following theses to suggest that most of our conventional language is inherently metaphorical:

LJ1: Many of our everyday concepts are metaphorical in the sense that they organize one thing in terms of another: 'love as a journey,' 'arguments as war,' and so on.

LJ2: Even the conceptual organizations that we take for granted and use in our day to day lives reveal hidden metaphors. (For example, 'time is money.') Since the metaphorical nature of these concepts is taken for granted, these might be thought of as literal or conventional metaphors.

LJ3: If one assumes an 'objective theory of meaning,' implying that words and phrases correspond to some 'natural' categories of reality, and if one provides no mechanisms for violating this correspondence, then several characteristics of metaphor cannot be explained, including how so many of our concepts happen to be metaphorically structured in terms of another concept.

LJ4: Our conceptual structure does not reflect some *natural* structure of reality.

LJ5: Many of our concepts are metaphorically structured in terms of the concepts we acquire from 'direct bodily experience.' The term 'direct bodily experience' does not merely refer to the fact of our having a certain body, but also includes the bias of our experience due to our cultural and social background.

Mac Cormac [1985, Chap. 3] raised several objections to Lakoff and Johnson's theses, and argued for maintaining a literal-metaphorical distinction. The main points of his counterattack are summarized below:

M1: The characterization of metaphor as experiencing, understanding, and organizing one thing in terms of another is too lose and fits any semantic process involving symbols and their meanings.

M2: Most of the examples presented by Lakoff and Johnson are so called 'dead metaphors,' that is, metaphors that have faded into polysemy through frequent usage. (Mac Cormac cites the example of 'war' mentioned above.) Thus, he argues, Lakoff and Johnson are merely redefining the terms literal and metaphorical to be literal metaphor and figurative metaphor.

M3: While it cannot be denied that metaphors give rise to literal meanings—for as the use of a metaphor becomes more frequent, its novelty wears off and it gradually acquires the status of literal meaning—this recognition does not necessarily force one to accept the conclusion that all language is metaphorical.

M4: If one takes literal meanings as given, and assumes they correspond to some *natural* categories of the external world, it does not necessarily preclude any theory that allows category violations under certain conditions. In fact, Mac Cormac's theory attempts to do just that.

M5: There are several problems with Lakoff and Johnson's account of how many of our concepts are structured in terms of the concepts acquired from 'direct bodily experience.' The most weighty objection is that Lakoff and Johnson do not clearly explain how the 'directly acquired concepts' are formed. For instance, citing Lakoff and Johnson's own example of front-back orientation which some cultures express using 'in front of' and others express with 'in back of,' he writes, "If some spatial concepts vary from culture to culture, how can we have any certainty that spatial concepts emerge directly?" [Mac Cormac 1985, p. 68.]

M6: There is the empirical research of Berlin and Kay [1969] that shows how color terms in various languages share a common structure. This shows that there are certain *natural* boundaries in the external world that all conceptual systems reflect.

M7: Conclusion: The distinction between the literal and the metaphorical is prerequisite to any theory of metaphor, though the boundary between the two is not a sharp one but fuzzy.

Lakoff responded to these objections by pointing out that there are no less than four different senses of 'literal' [Lakoff 1986] and no less than four different senses of 'dead metaphor' [Lakoff 1987a]. Lakoff and Turner [1989, pp. 114–131] also argued that the 'literal meaning theory' and the 'dead metaphor theory' are inconsistent with the empirical findings. Let us focus here on Lakoff's objection to what he called the literal meaning theory, which is based on distinguishing between the following four senses of 'literal':

literal1: Refers to conventional literality, as opposed to poetic language, exaggeration, irony, indirect speech acts, etc.

literal2: Refers to the language ordinarily used to talk about some subject matter. Thus, when one normally talks about ideas as plants [Lakoff and Johnson 1980, p. 47], as in "Her ideas finally came to fruit," it is seen as literal usage in this sense.

literal3: Refers to the usage of language that is directly meaningful: that is, it does not present one thing as something else. Thus, "Her ideas finally came to fruit" would not be literal in this sense, whereas "The car moved forward" would be considered literal.

literal4: Refers to the language capable of describing the objective world, and therefore capable of being objectively true or false.

Based on this distinction, Lakoff argued that Mac Cormac's arguments are ill-founded since they muddle the four senses. In particular, Lakoff claimed, Mac Cormac has combined *literal1, literal2,* and *literal3* in his use of the term 'literal,' thereby introducing "an important theoretical assumption— an assumption that has, as a consequence, the conclusion that conventional metaphor cannot exist." [Lakoff 1986, p. 296.] (This is because only *literal3* is defined in contrast with the metaphorical, and metaphorical is consistent with *literal1* and with *literal2*.)

In their later elaboration, Lakoff and Turner [1989, pp. 114–128], characterize the 'literal meaning theory' as having the following characteristics:

- "If an expression of a language is (1) conventional and ordinary, then it is also (2) semantically autonomous and (3) capable of making reference to objective reality.

- "Such a linguistic expression is called 'literal,'

- "No metaphors are literal." [Lakoff & Turner 1989, pp 114–115].

They refute this theory by empirically showing that it is possible to have condition (1) but not (2)—conventional expressions might not be semantically autonomous, as in "Her ideas came to fruit," and that it is possible to have condition (1) and not (3)—conventional language does not reflect the objective reality. In fact, Lakoff and his colleagues have consistently argued that there is no *natural* structure in reality that our concepts must reflect; that is, condition (3) is not satisfied by any expression, literal or metaphorical.

This debate reveals a great deal of confusion and misunderstanding of each other's positions, and clouds what are the essential points of differences between them. In fact, once the fog is lifted, it turns out that the two schools of thought are closer than either one might be willing to admit, for they both take the same side on an important issue, and that issue is not the strong thesis of metaphor.

To see all this, let us analyze the points raised by each camp. The main objective of Lakoff and Johnson's study was to show that metaphor is a powerful tool in shaping the cognitive world that we experience. For this objective, conventional metaphors, even 'dead' metaphors, are quite important, since they bring evidence that even what we take to be the conventional and ordinary description of the world is actually brought about by a metaphor, even though the metaphor might not be alive and vibrant today. It is the conventional metaphors that demonstrate that metaphors are not something that occur only in the domains of poetry, art, and flowery language, but are an indispensable part of everyday language and concepts. Given that, it seems quite logical that Lakoff and Johnson would include conventional metaphors under the rubric of 'metaphor.'

Mac Cormac's criticism of Lakoff and Johnson utterly fails to appreciate this important point. He regards metaphors to be non-conventional use of language that results in new meanings, and, from this point of view, he is vehemently arguing that what Lakoff and Johnson are calling metaphors are not metaphors at all.

Interestingly, however, Mac Cormac's use of the term 'metaphor' is quite reasonable for what he is trying to achieve in his theory. He is interested in showing how novel metaphors derive their meanings. He would agree with thesis LJ3 as it is. However, he correctly emphasized in M4 that in a theory that assumes literal meanings as given and predetermined, it is not necessarily true that *no mechanism can ever be provided* for violating the categorical structure imposed on the world by the literal meanings. His own theory starts from such an assumption and then provides mechanisms by which metaphorical meanings are created. In fact, he is not the only one; others have tried in the similar vein. [Levin 1977; Searle 1979.] These theories attempt to explain metaphor as a process of relaxing semantic constraints on literal-conventional meanings. Now one might disagree whether this is the right way to formulate a theory of metaphor, but the enterprise certainly makes sense. The proponents of this approach, including Mac Cormac, argue that when we understand a new metaphor, we are already familiar with the conventional meanings of the words and phrases. Therefore, it seems reasonable that a theory of metaphor should try to do the same: take the conventional meanings as given, and explain how new meanings are derived from the conventional meanings. With this objective in mind, one can see why conventional metaphors and literal usage is lumped together under the banner of 'non-metaphorical.'

Lakoff's criticism of Mac Cormac, in turn, completely disregards all these points. In characterizing the four senses of literals, and pointing out that only one of them is defined in contrast to metaphorical, Lakoff is assuming that the meaning of 'metaphorical' itself is unequivocal. The same implicit assumption underlies Lakoff's four senses of 'dead metaphor,' where it is further assumed that being 'dead' refers to a certain fixed characteristic of metaphor. This assumption finds its way unscathed into Lakoff and Turner's later rebuttals of the literal meaning theory and the dead metaphor theory.

That the basis of this debate is a misunderstanding of the word 'metaphor' is clearly seen in how each of them defines metaphor. Lakoff takes 'metaphor' to mean "understanding and experiencing one kind of thing in terms of another." [Lakoff & Johnson 1980, p. 5.] Mac Cormac, on the other hand, defines a metaphor to be "a cognitive process by which new concepts are expressed and suggested [and a] cultural process by which language itself changes." [Mac Cormac 1985, pp. 5–6.] As long as we use their intended sense of 'metaphor' in interpreting the arguments from each camp, there is no problem, for each line of argument seems quite reasonable—they do not contradict at all.

The unnecessary controversy in their debate stems from the implicit assumption each of them makes that his is the correct usage of the term metaphor. In making all their arguments, neither of them ever questions his own definition of 'metaphor.' Lakoff, while he distinguishes four senses of literal, does not consider even once the possibility that someone else might use the term 'metaphor' differently from him.

The fact is that two senses of 'metaphor' can be clearly distinguished in common usage. One of them, let us say *metaphor1,* applies only to novel metaphors. I noted in Chapter 1 that one of the reviewers of this manuscript objected to my characterizing "The chairperson of the meeting plowed through the agenda" as a metaphor. This was a conventional usage of 'plow,' as far as she was concerned, and, therefore, not a metaphor. Though I am not aware of any such study, I conjecture that if one were to present a number of what Lakoff calls conventional metaphors together with some poetic metaphors and some examples of what Lakoff calls *literal3* to a group of subjects (without giving them any definition of metaphor), and were to ask them to sort out the examples into metaphors and non-metaphors, many of the conventional metaphors, such as 'time is money,' would be classified as non-metaphors. This merely reflects the conventional way in which people use the word 'metaphor.'

The second sense of metaphor, let us call it *metaphor2*, corresponds to Lakoff's definition of 'metaphor' and includes conventional metaphors. It is *metaphor2* that is defined in contrast with *literal3*, but it is not the only sense of metaphor.

In fact, the concept of *metaphor2* is somewhat problematic, and this is where Mac Cormac's criticism of Lakoff is most effective. For instance, Mac Cormac is right in pointing out [M1] that any symbolic process can be characterized as experiencing one kind of thing in terms of another. (More persuasive arguments supporting this claim can be found in Cassirer [1955], who argued that it is the process of forming a symbol itself that gives an experiential ontology to the environment, and the symbol essentially works by representing the experience as something else.) And, therefore, Lakoff's definition seems to lead to the conclusion that all language is metaphorical.

Lakoff, of course, vehemently denies this, and points out that certain concepts are non-metaphorical in that they are understood 'directly,' that is, not as something else. This separation of *metaphor2* with *literal3* is also not without problems—I already mentioned some in Chapter 4 [§4.5]. For instance, consider the point raised by Mac Cormac in thesis M5: Why is it that the front-back orientation is considered a non-metaphorical concept when it is really a result of projecting a conceptual system? When the very same situation is experienced as "the ball is in front of the rock" by one person and as "the rock is in back of the ball" by another person, could we not say that one of them is experiencing it in terms of 'in front of' and the other in terms of 'in back of'? But in each case, they are experiencing the situation as *something else*. Or, consider when someone decides to 'save' time by being more organized. Why is she experiencing the time as something else? If the person grew up in a culture where the 'time is money' metaphor *(metaphor2)* is prevalent, this might well be her direct experience of time. In many of the conventional metaphors cited by Lakoff, it is questionable how many of them really fit the category "experiencing one kind of thing as another." All this reveals is that the concept of *metaphor2* is not as straightforward·as Lakoff takes it to be.

Lakoff's criticism of Mac Cormac is most effective against theses [M4] and [M6], where Mac Cormac attempts to identify the literal (literal2) meanings with natural boundaries in the external world. In fact, in the attempt to refute the 'literal meaning theory,' it is only these theses that Lakoff succeeds in refuting, once the two senses of metaphor are clarified. (For, in refuting that all conventional language is not semantically autonomous, the term 'semantically autonomous' is used in contrast with *metaphor2,* which faces all the problems mentioned above. For instance, why is it that 'time is money' is not semantically autonomous, if that is how one experiences time?)

However, taking conventional meanings as given, and regarding them as non-metaphorical does not necessarily lead one to assume that the conventional meanings correspond to some natural preexisting boundaries in reality. Mac Cormac takes this position, but Kittay [1987], who also uses the term metaphor in the sense of *metaphor1,* and articulates a theory of metaphor that explains the emergence of new metaphorical meanings as a function of already existing literal-conventional meanings, does not. It is perfectly reasonable to maintain, as I have been doing throughout my framework, that conventional meanings are also a result of projection, so that they do not reflect some transcendental structure in reality. Thus, the 'objective meaning' condition in Lakoff's characterization of the literal meaning theory is not a necessary condition of using the term metaphor in the sense of *metaphor1.*

Let us now examine Lakoff and Mac Cormac's arguments as far as they constitute a rejection of the strong thesis of metaphor. Mac Cormac clearly stands in opposition to the strong thesis—all three versions of it. This results from his wanting to maintain that there are natural categories in the world that our literal-conventional concepts reflect. There is no evidence for this though. The Berlin and Kay studies cited by Mac Cormac is quite troublesome, as I have discussed earlier in Chapter 4 [§4.2.4]. Given that, Mac Cormac's arguments do not constitute a serious threat to the strong thesis.

Given my clarification of the different senses in which the term 'metaphor' is used in the strong thesis, I believe that Lakoff would agree with Version 1. He might not agree with Version 3 though, and might continue to maintain that certain concepts are understood 'directly.' But my discussion in this section, taking note of Mac Cormac's criticism of Lakoff, shows that Lakoff has not convincingly demonstrated that these 'direct' concepts are not understood as anything else. So, Lakoff's arguments do not pose a serious challenge to the strong thesis either.

Ironically, Lakoff's insistence on maintaining that certain concepts are understood directly puts him and Mac Cormac on the same side of an important issue. Notice that in Lakoff's characterization of a metaphor as experiencing one *kind* of thing in terms of another, there is an implicit assumption that

things can be sorted out into different 'kinds,' *before being conceptualized.*
Otherwise, what makes 'time' a different kind of thing than 'money'? What
makes 'life' a different kind of thing than 'journey'? If no categorization
exists prior to conceptualization, as Lakoff staunchly maintains, then how do
we know that something is being experienced as something else? To have his
cake and eat it too, Lakoff implies at other places that one can sort out different experiential domains into kinds before conceptualization. For instance,
Lakoff and Turner argue: "[M]etaphor can provide structure and attributes
not inherent in the target domain, as, for example, when dying is understood
as departure to a final destination or death is understood as a reaper. *The
phenomenon of death is not objectively similar to a reaper.*" [Lakoff & Turner
1989, p. 123; emphasis mine.] How can one conclude that the phenomenon of
death is not objectively similar to a reaper unless there exist some objective
natural kinds. But then this can be considered the *natural* structure of the
pre-conceptual world in the sense of Mac Cormac.

There is another way in which Lakoff's 'directly emergent concepts' nudge
him closer to Mac Cormac. In claiming that some of these concepts are
derived from our having bodies of certain sorts, it follows that these concepts
ought to be the same for all those with similar bodies. (This is a point I
emphasized earlier in Chapter 4 [§4.5] as a weakness of the Lakoffian approach
to cognition.) However, this immediately gives such concepts the status of
'universals.' Then, the only difference between Lakoff and Mac Cormac seems
to be that Lakoff would maintain that the source of these 'universals' is in
our bodies, and Mac Cormac would argue that it is in the structure of reality.

Of course, they might both be correct to a certain extent. It cannot be
denied that all humans have certain physiological and anatomical features in
common. We all have certain sensory and motor organs that share many characteristics. It is also true that we inhabit a world with an autonomous structure that, while exhibiting wide variations from one geographical location to
another, nevertheless has many features that do not change. For instance,
the cycle of light and darkness recurs with great stubbornness, though their
relative lengths vary a great deal depending on the latitude, time of the year,
and the atmospheric conditions. With so much common ground, it is certainly possible in principle that widely different cultures might share certain
conceptual structures. However, the complexity of the human brain, which
defies a simple-minded way of rooting the source of our conceptual structures
into the physiological structure of the brain [§4.2.4], and the creativity of the
human mind, which keeps coming up with newer ways of conceptualizing
even the most mundane objects and experiences, makes me quite sceptical
of whether any such 'universal' structures will ever be empirically found to

lend support to either Lakoff's or Mac Cormac's hypothesis.

8.3 Metaphor and Correctness

So far I have characterized metaphor as a 'meaningful interpretation.' Obviously, though, an interpretation can be meaningful, and yet be deemed 'false' or 'incorrect.' For instance, on a bright and sunny day, if someone says "The sky is crying," you would understand the statement, but would consider it false. Then, of course, a literal-minded person might consider the statement false even if the sky were grey and it were raining, but still maintain that she understands it. Consider again the example that was introduced at the beginning of the chapter: "Nixon is a halo surrounding a vacuum." An admirer of the former Unites States president, and an ardent critic of Nixon, both might understand what is meant by the statement, though bitterly disagree on whether the statement is correct or incorrect. Moreover, each of them could quite reasonably argue that the correctness (or incorrectness) of the metaphor is a matter of historical fact, something that could be objectively verified. To add to the confusion, a literal-minded person could again claim that the statement is incorrect objectively speaking.

These examples raise a number of important questions with which any comprehensive theory of metaphor must grapple. What does it mean for something to be correct? What is the difference between correctness and truth? What is the difference between understanding and correctness? What is the difference between literal (conventional) and metaphorical correctness? In this section I address these questions within my framework of metaphor and cognition.

8.3.1 Correctness, Truth and Coherency

In the example of the scale model of a ship that I introduced in the previous section, there is an obvious criterion to determine whether or not the model is correct. The correspondence between the parts of the model (concept network) and the parts of the ship is fixed and cannot be varied. For this reason, one merely needs to ask if the structure of the model respects the structure of the object being modeled in order to determine the correctness of the model. However, this characteristic is called 'coherency' in my framework. This suggests that correctness can be identified with coherency.

Let us look at another example. Say that someone is learning to do parallel parking. The person has some feel for driving and the maneuvers necessary for parallel parking. She carries out the maneuvers, and hits the curb. Obviously, one would say, the maneuvers were 'incorrect.' Now from the point of view of the person attempting the task, she was carrying out 'actions' that *she thought* would make the car end up in the desired position. However, on actually carrying out the actions, she discovered that the car did not end up in the desired position. We could say that the result of actually carrying out the action corresponding to the 'mental action' (operator in my framework) did not result in the situation (parallel parked car) that corresponds to the 'mental image' (symbol) that the 'mental action' predicted. In other words, the environment did not respect the actions of the driver as she expected, based on her concept network. In short, the cognitive relation between the driver's mental concept network of parallel parking and the environment was incoherent.

There are many other examples as well. Consider skiing, swimming, or any other activity that requires coordination and planning. Come to think of it, all activities, even walking and sitting, require coordination and planning, except that we are so habituated to some of them that we are not consciously aware of it. In each of these cases, it can easily be seen that the notions of correctness and coherency coincide.

It must be emphasized here that coherency here invariably means *local coherency*. In the example of parallel parking, if the driver managed to do a perfect maneuver we cannot say that her concept network of driving is correct for all situations and at all times. In fact, the question of correctness can be raised with respect to any *description*. You might recall from Chapter 5 [§5.7.3] that the term 'description' applies to any object or situation in the environment via its representation in the concept network. In the context of the parallel parking example, the situation of a parallel parked car is represented internally in the driver's concept network of driving, and any sequence of operations that results in this representation is a description of parallel parking. However, in interpreting this description in the environment, by actually performing the actions corresponding to the operators, it might reveal incoherency. In that case we would say that the description was incorrect. Otherwise, if the interpretation of the description did result in the object described, we would say that the description was correct, irrespective of whether the interpretation of the rest of the concept network is coherent or not.

So if coherency is correctness, what is truth? Observe that had I defined my concept networks in terms of relations, instead of operators, coherency would have come out as the Tarskian model theoretic notion of truth as correspondence. This suggests that *truth is to relations as correctness is to operations.* In other words, if the underlying algebraic structure of a cognitive system is a boolean algebra, then a 'description' becomes a 'statement,' and 'coherency' is 'truth.' As with correctness, I mean local coherency here also. That is, we can ask whether a statement is true or not, without considering whether the interpretation of the whole concept network is coherent.

Several interesting observations can be made here. Firstly, notice that the concept of correctness is more fundamental than the concept of truth in that the concept of truth does not apply, or becomes meaningless, in many situations where correctness is still applicable. For instance, in the example of the scale model, or that of parallel parking, one cannot say that the model is false or the driver's parallel parking maneuvers were false, without unduly stretching the meaning of false. On the other hand, the use of "The sky is crying" to describe a clear sunny day could be described either as false or incorrect. Considerations such as these have led some other researchers, including Hesse [1974, 2.IV.3, pp. 56–61] and Black [1979, p. 41], to argue that the concept of correctness is broader, more useful, and encompasses the narrower concept of truth; and therefore, when talking about cognition, one should use the terms correct and incorrect rather than true and false. This conclusion, in the light of the analogy 'truth is to relations as correctness is to operations,' reinforces my Piagetian assumption that in cognition, the notion of operations is more fundamental than the notion of relations. [Piaget 1953.]

Secondly, it must be emphasized here that coherency in my account *does not mean internal consistency of a system of symbols.* In fact, my notion of coherency is defined only for cognitive relations, and not for systems of symbols (concept networks). This is to say that my coherency invariably involves a correspondence between elements of the concept network and parts of the environment. It is only an interpretation of a concept network in an environment that can be coherent or incoherent. The concept cannot be applied to a concept network by itself. For this reason, my use of the term 'coherency' is more along the lines of Hesse [1974, Chap. 2], and not at all as Mac Cormac [1985, pp. 211–212] views it.

Finally, though my view of truth also involves a correspondence with parts of the environment, there is a key difference between it and the Tarskian model theoretic view of truth based on correspondence. In the model theoretic view of truth, though the symbols are allowed to be *interpreted* different-ly—indeed, the classical model theory was developed expressly to study the

characteristics of systems of symbols under different interpretations—the process of carrying out the interpretation is not taken into consideration at all.
This, in my opinion, is the major factor behind the inadequacies of all the
attempts made so far to come up with a complete and satisfactory theory of
truth and reference that start out with a Tarskian model theoretic approach.
This, of course, is not to fault the model theory—it was developed for a different purpose and has a different role to play—but only its use in cognitive
theories of reference and truth.

In my account, on the other hand, *the process of making a correspondence between the concept network and the environment is seen as an act of
cognition itself.* This difference has two very important consequences. One
is that every meaningful statement is capable of being objectively correct or
incorrect. This is a point I shall elaborate upon in a moment. The other
consequence is that the referent of any concept cannot be determined without changing the meaning of the concept in the process. For instance, in
determining the referent of 'water' the cognitive agent must make causal
connections with certain stuff in the environment based on the available description of water. Since some of this stuff that tastes and feels like water
might later turn out to have a different chemical composition, the meaning
'water' has been changed, unbeknownst to the cognitive agent, in determining
its referent. (See Indurkhya [in preparation] for elaboration of this point.)

It is interesting to point out that the concept of 'truth' itself does not have
an unequivocal meaning in everyday language, as the fascinating study by
Sweetser [1987] clearly demonstrates. She investigated the concept of 'lie'—
which, one might simply say, means a false statement—only to discover the
complex of one's cultural background, concept networks of information and
communication, concept networks of morality, etc., that underlie its use in
normal everyday discourse. (For instance, is it 'lying' to tell the host how
wonderful the dinner was, even if one thought it was awful?) This accentu-
ates the fact that there is no fixed correspondence between our concepts and
the external world, based on which all coherency (and truth) must be determined. A framework such as mine is more eager to incorporate Sweetser's
observations by noting that truth depends on the correspondence between
parts of the concept network and parts of the environment, and this correspondence is determined by the cognitive agent itself, which would naturally
reflect its cultural and individual background.

8.3.2 Understanding vs. Correctness

The difference between understanding a description (or a statement) and judging it as correct or incorrect is easily settled. Recall that in Section 2, I articulated the view that to understand a description is to imagine an experience in the intermediate cognitive layers to which the description could have been applied. Moreover, the cognitive relation formed in understanding a description respects the autonomous structure of the intermediate layer (which reflects the cognitive agent's past perceptual experiences)—that is, the cognitive relation is coherent. (Otherwise, the description is dubbed anomalous.) When the experience is no longer imaginary but real, then the notions of understanding and correctness begin to coincide. In other words, if the process of interpretation does not stop at an intermediate cognitive layer, but goes all the way to the environment through the sensorimotor data set, then in understanding a description, we are actually determining its correctness.

Considering some examples will elucidate the difference between understanding and correctness. Take the statement "It is snowing outside." To understand this statement, you might imagine a scenario of snowy weather. To say that it is correct, however, you would need to look outside, and see if the statement describes the stimuli you are receiving from the environment. Notice that the correctness is not established by matching the imagined scene against the stimuli. You might have imagined a blizzard, whereas there is only a light snow and no wind outside. So, the process of interpretation must begin all over, taking into account the information being received from the environment, in determining the correctness of a description.

Take another example now. In understanding "The sky is crying," you might imagine a perceptual experience that could have been described by the statement, giving an unconventional interpretation to the concept 'cry' in the process. However, in determining whether the statement is correct or not, you look out of the window, and see if the description can be applied to the stimuli received from the environment. Again, the concept 'cry' must be interpreted unconventionally. A literal-minded person, on the other hand, unwilling to interpret 'crying' unconventionally, might declare the statement anomalous; or she might fantasize a realm in which the sky is literally crying, and thus 'understand' the statement, but, looking out the window when it is grey and raining outside, declare it incorrect.

This account of determining correctness is somewhat simplistic. Many of the things we take to be 'correct' are not based on direct observation, as I implied above. For instance, you might correctly know that it is raining outside because someone just came through the door with a dripping umbrella. Much of our knowledge comes indirectly from books, newspapers, and other media.

This feature can be incorporated into my account by noticing that certain realms in an intermediate layer can be dubbed 'correct.' We read a description, say in a newspaper story, a historic account, or an encyclopedia, and understand it by creating a derived realm in an intermediate cognitive layer. This derived realm can then be labeled 'correct,' if we have reasons to believe that the author of the description has verified the descriptions in the environment. Now any interpretation that is coherent in this realm would be considered correct, as if it were coherent with respect to the environment.

8.3.3   Conventional and Metaphorical Correctness

With the difference between understanding and correctness cleared away, let me recapitulate what it means to say that a description or a statement, literal-conventional or metaphorical, is correct or incorrect. A part of the concept network that contains the description is interpreted in the realm via all the intermediate layers. This interpretation can be literal-conventional or metaphorical; this is not crucial. Once the interpretation has been decided on, then one can test to see whether the description is coherent with respect to the interpretation or not. This is what determines the correctness.

Simple as this account of correctness is, it incorporates many of the observations made on the nature of truth and correctness, both literal-conventional and metaphorical, by previous scholars. I would like to note a few important connections here.

My view of correctness, and we have seen that truth is a special case of correctness, sees the same mechanism underlying literal-conventional and metaphorical descriptions. In this respect I am in complete agreement with Binkley [1974], Goodman [1976, p. 79], Lakoff & Johnson [1980, Ch. 24], and Hintikka & Sandu [1990, p. 72]. As this is also a major point of difference between my view and that of many other scholars, such as Mac Cormac, it would be useful to elaborate upon it some more.

Notions of truth and correctness presuppose an ontology. Something can be true or false, correct or incorrect, only with respect to some perspective. And this perspective is determined by the cognitive agent in establishing a correspondence between parts of the concept network and parts of the environment, thereby giving an ontology to the environment. This correspondence might be composed of only the conventional interpretations that the cognitive agent is habituated to (as in interpreting "It is snowing outside,") only the novel metaphorical interpretations that are derived by using the mechanisms described in Chapter 7 [§7.4] (as in interpreting the Mondrian), or some conventional and some metaphorical interpretations (as in interpreting Boland's and Spender's poems). A description or statement is made *referential* in making such a correspondence. And it is only after making a description referential that we can determine whether it is correct or not.

However, once the correspondence is established, by whatever means, the mechanism for determining coherency does not depend on whether the interpretation is conventional or metaphorical. In other words, the mechanism for determining correctness is the same for metaphorical descriptions as for conventional descriptions, echoing the thoughts of Binkley: "[I]t is necessary to keep separate the two different activities of establishing the truth and establishing the meaning of an expression. Although literal and metaphorical sentences have different types of meaning, when they are used to make claims those claims can be true or false in roughly the same way, i.e., without the mediation of an additional expression of their meanings." (From p. 150 in Johnson [1981a].)

Of course, in interpreting a concept network metaphorically in an environment, since there is no generally accepted interpretation of the concept network in that environment—it would not be metaphorical otherwise—there is plenty of room for vagueness and wide variations among individual interpretations. It is this characteristic that causes metaphors sometimes to miscommunicate and their meanings to be vague. However, this happens to literal interpretations as well. (See Kamp [1981] and Scheffler [1979] for a discussion of some issues surrounding 'vagueness' in literal use of the language.) Therefore, any attempt to distinguish the literal from the metaphorical on the basis of vagueness—and I am alluding to Mac Cormac's use of fuzzy set theory to characterize metaphors here—is not likely to be very fruitful.

The final point to be highlighted here is that in my account all meaningful statements are capable of *objectively* being correct or incorrect—or true or false, if one is working with a concept network having a relational structure. Here, by the term 'objective' I mean referring to the external world—something that could be verified intersubjectively. Of course, the correctness must be decided with respect to the ontology created by instantiating the theory or the concept network itself. For instance, Gentner and Gentner [1983] studied two models, *teeming crowd* and *flowing water,* that people use to understand and reason about electricity. They noted that the teeming crowd model is correct for making certain predictions about electrical systems, and the flowing water model is correct for some other predictions. Of course, there are characteristics of electricity that both models predict correctly and characteristics that neither one does. However, this correctness or incorrectness is an objective matter. It is the autonomous structure of the external world, made visible by giving it an ontology with the concept network, that makes the model incorrect, if it does not respect the structure of the concept network.

Thus, my sense of 'objective' here is different from the way Lakoff uses it in *literal4* and in his characterization of the literal meaning theory (Section 2.4). Lakoff is using it to mean not just 'being able to be verified intersubjectively' but to also include 'the one and only correct way to describe reality.' For instance, he used the example from Gentner & Gentner [1983] to argue that these two models are not capable of being objectively true or false:

> "[B]ecause we have no objective way of knowing what electricity 'really is,' they are not literal4. In fact, the fluid metaphor and the crowd metaphor have inconsistent ontologies. Both metaphors could not both be objectively true, because fluids are continuous and crowds are individuated." [Lakoff 1986, p. 295]

I, on the other hand, would argue that both the models are capable of objectively being true or false. This, of course, is merely a terminological difference, for Lakoff would quite agree with me on the objectivity of metaphors—with the term 'objective' being used in my sense. Still, I feel that it is important to clarify this point, lest a needless controversy like the literal-metaphorical dichotomy ensue.

From this perspective, it is easy to see how two persons might disagree about whether "Nixon is a halo surrounding a vacuum" is correct or not, with each maintaining that the matter is an objective one. (And each of them would be understanding the statement metaphorically, since declaring it incorrect based on a literal understanding of it would be explained as in the previous section.) The difference between the two lies in the ontology given to Nixon's actions during his political career by grouping them in order of their significance. To one. theses actions are all insignificant, so she sees a vacuum there. To the other person, many of his actions were quite significant, so, although she understands the vacuum metaphor, it does not agree with what she sees as the actual state of the environment. Both persons are objectively correct, and there is no contradiction there, because each of them is viewing the world with a different ontology, even if they use the same word—perhaps

not unlike Lakoff and Mac Cormac. Indeed, it is only when one forgets
that words do not have an intrinsic meaning that they become tyrannical, as
Chase [1938] has argued so well.

8.4   Aptness (Quality) of Metaphor

There is another characteristic of metaphor—variously referred to as aptness,
compellingness, or quality—that characterizes the fact that certain metaphors seem more compelling than others. In the beginning of the chapter,
I mentioned Quinn's example of the ice cream metaphor for marriage (you
can eat it all at once, or make it last a long time) that is meaningful (might
even be considered correct) but would be considered a very poor metaphor
by most people.

What makes a metaphor more compelling than another? Many psychologists have studied this question empirically, and have come up with different ways of characterizing metaphoric quality. For instance, Ortony [1979;
1979a] characterized metaphoric quality in terms of the salience of the attributes transferred from the source to the target: a good metaphor uses
highly salient attributes of the source to highlight less salient attributes of
the target. Johnson and Malgady [1980] concluded that a metaphor is judged
good when it is easily interpretable and when there are many interpretations.

Though I consider the quality of metaphor essentially a pragmatic issue—
whether a metaphor is judged good or bad depends on what the intent of the
metaphor is, I would like to make some general observations regarding how
different factors affect the quality of a metaphor in my account, and how these
factors are related to others' characterizations of aptness. Before undertaking
this task, I must point out that the quality of a metaphor has nothing to
do with whether the metaphor is correct (or true) or not. The ice cream
metaphor for marriage may well be correct under a certain interpretation,
but it still remains a poor metaphor. On the other hand, an admirer of
Nixon might give high marks for the quality of "Nixon is a halo surrounding
a vacuum" metaphor (the idea that a person can be 'a halo surrounding
a vacuum' is certainly quite interesting and novel), but still deny that the
metaphorical description applies correctly to Richard Nixon.

Let me now list some factors that can affect the quality of a metaphor:

1. *The degree of conventionality of the interpretation:* I have characterized
   metaphor as an unconventional interpretation of a concept network in a
   realm. Clearly, if the interpretation is conventional, it is not metaphor-

ical. As conventionality is not an all or none affair—there are degrees
of it—the degree of conventionality of an interpretation ought to be
inversely related to its metaphoricity. Thus, conventional metaphors
("I have decided to be more organized so as to save time") are seen
as less metaphorical than novel metaphors ('wild flowers as water' in
Boland's poem).

2. *The degree to which the target is made to look similar by the source:*
   Clearly, a metaphor is much better if a larger part of the source concept
   network can be interpreted in the target realm. As any interpretation
   results in making the target realm look similar to the source, it means
   that the more the similarities there are between the source and the
   target (these are similarities *after the metaphor has been understood*)
   the better the metaphor.

   While this role of similarities in affecting metaphoric quality has been
   demonstrated by many scholars (see Malgady & Johnson [1980]; Mc-
   Cabe [1983]; and 'within-domain' similarity criterion of Tourangeau
   and Sternberg [1982]), most of these studies do not distinguish between
   similarities before and after the metaphor. In fact, with the exception
   of McCabe, they all take a static view of metaphor in that the given
   representations of the source and the target never change as a result of
   understanding the metaphor. Not surprisingly then, such studies conclude that the source and the target (concept networks) must be similar
   prior to the metaphor, in order for the metaphor to be compelling.

   McCabe, who did make a distinction between similarities before and after the metaphor, found that when metaphors are presented in isolated
   formulaic contexts (which is how most other studies presented metaphors), then the quality of metaphor is significantly related to 'before
   similarities' between the source and the target. However, when metaphors were presented in an extended context (included in a larger body
   of text), there was little or no correlation between 'before similarities'
   and metaphoric quality. (See also the discussion in Chapter 2 [§2.3].)

3. *The degree of difficulty in interpreting the metaphor:* It has been proposed that the easier it is to interpret the metaphor, the better the
   metaphor. [Johnson & Malgady 1980; Katz, Paivio & Marschark 1985.]
   However, what makes a metaphor easier to interpret? Or, to use my
   terminology, when is a concept network easy to interpret in a realm?

   There are two things that can affect the ease of interpretation. One
   is that if the target realm is such that no matter how it is described,

and how its ontology is changed, it just does not fit the structure of the source concept network, then the metaphor will be difficult to interpret. (Recall that the target realm has its own autonomous structure.) Such might be the case with Johnson and Malgady's examples like "Hair is a ship."

The other thing affecting the ease of interpretation is that, assuming that different parts of the source concept network have different saliences, and that the cognitive agent starts out by trying to interpret the highly salient parts first, it follows that if the highly salient parts of the concept network are getting interpreted, then the metaphor is easier to interpret. Thus, the "Billboards are warts" metaphor ends up being easier to interpret (ugliness being a highly salient property of warts), than "The highway is a rope" (with the intended meaning that the winding highway is like a coiled rope), for being coiled is a less salient property of the rope. (See Ortony [1979; 1979a]; and the 'extreme value of the transferred attribute of the vehicle' criterion of Tourangeau & Sternberg [1982].)

4. *The open-endedness of the metaphor:* A metaphor is considered more compelling, if it can be interpreted in more than one way (as in the metaphor of Boland). And when there is an unambiguous core interpretation of the metaphor (as in "The sky is crying"), then a metaphor is more compelling if there is ample room for extending the core interpretation by subjectively interpreting other parts of the concept network in various ways. This is because different people have different perceptual experiences with the target, and choosing a concept network that allows different people to interpret the concept network in their own ways heightens the emotional and personal value of the metaphor. Moreover, if the same person can interpret the metaphor in different ways, then the meaning of the metaphor is enriched, for the metaphor seems to be saying all those different things at once.

   If the target realm is not explicitly supplied by the metaphor (as in Mondrian's painting), then the metaphor becomes even more appealing (if it is understood at all), since now different people can choose their own realms, and interpret the metaphor in these realms in their own way (or the same person can interpret the metaphor in different realms in different ways). Thus, the more interpretations a metaphor has, the better it seems. [Johnson & Malgady 1980.]

5. *The structural richness of that part of the source concept network that is interpreted by the metaphor:* I noted in the last chapter [§7.4.1] that

a syntactic metaphor allows the cognitive agent to reason about the less familiar target realm by using the more familiar source concept network (as in analyzing the mechanical systems as electrical circuits). Since it is the operational structure of a concept network that provides an ability to reason and make predictions about the environment, this suggests that the more structurally rich the source concept network is (actually, the part of it that is interpreted in the target realm), the better the metaphor. [Gentner 1983.]

Here I am strictly referring to the role of metaphor in which one already has sufficient knowledge of the target realm in the target concept network, for it is this knowledge that is used in ascertaining which part of the source concept network can be successfully applied to the target realm. (This knowledge, of course, might reside in the teacher, who decides to explain a new concept to the students by using an analogy from a concept familiar to the student.)

6. *The cognitive information generated by the metaphor:* The most important role of metaphor in cognition might well be to reclaim (partially, of course) some of the information that was lost in cognitization (in reducing the detailed world of sensorimotor data set to a handful of concepts and categories). From this perspective, it seems that the more new information generated by the metaphor, the better the metaphor. Thus, 'painting as pumping' is a better metaphor than 'painting is a masking surface.' Or 'jacking mechanism as the Indian rope trick' is a better metaphor than 'jacking mechanism as a biological system.' [§2.6]

Even when the metaphor does not generate any new information about the target (as in syntactic metaphors), it can still have cognitive value in highlighting subtle features of the target realm (features that are, nevertheless, included in the target concept network). For instance, Ortony [1979; 1979a] noted that a metaphor works by highlighting less salient attributes of the target, as in "Highways are snakes." If the attribute of the target highlighted by the metaphor is already highly salient, as in "Encyclopedias are dictionaries," then the statement becomes what Ortony referred to as 'literal comparison.'

Tourangeau and Sternberg [1982] have also suggested a related factor, called the 'between-domains' similarity between the source and the target, that is inversely related to the quality of a metaphor. Between-domains similarity is taken to be a measure of how semantically distant the domains are. The more distant the domains, the better the metaphor. Thus, "The shark is the hawk among fish" would be considered a less compelling metaphor than "Nixon is the submarine of world leaders," because the domains of 'birds' and 'fish' are less distant than the domains of 'world leaders' and 'ocean vessels.' One can view the between-domains distance between the domains as the semantic distance created by our cognitive apparatus in categorizing the environment. When a metaphor successfully links two distant domains, then it effectively amounts to suggesting an alternate semantic metric in which the two domains are actually quite close. Thus, the more distant the two domains, the more is the surprise in realizing that they could be represented as much closer, and the more is the cognitive information generated by the metaphor.

A point must be emphasized with respect to the last factor listed above— namely that what (and how much) cognitive information is generated by a metaphor (and hence the quality of the metaphor) can be determined only *after the metaphor* has been assimilated. There is no way to tell from looking at the source and the target concept networks before the metaphor is presented whether the metaphor will come out as insightful or mundane.

A number of scholars combine this factor affecting metaphoric quality with the one preceding it (structural richness of the source), leading them to conclude that if a metaphor transfers structurally richer parts of the source concept network to the target concept network, then it is also more likely to provide new cognitive information about the target realm. [Gentner 1983.] This immediately turns metaphor into what I have termed predictive analogy [§1.6.2]. While I discuss predictive analogy at length in Chapter 9, I must, once more, emphasize that my notion of metaphor does not cover predictive analogy in any way, and, therefore, I do not need to address the predictive ability that some scholars impute to metaphors.

As a parenthetic remark, let me add that my framework of cognition does include a notion of predictability, which should not be confused with predictive analogy. If you put two marbles in a box, and then put in three more, then you can predict that there are five marbles in the box without actually emptying out the box and counting the marbles. It is the operational structure of a concept network, the natural number system with the operation of addition in this case, that makes it possible to make this prediction under a certain interpretation. Of course, the prediction might or might not turn out to be true—it might be a magician's box with a false bottom— depending on whether the autonomous structure of the environment respects the structure of the concept network or not, a property that I have been calling 'coherency.' This sense of predictability, however, is quite different from the way predictive power is imputed to metaphors in predictive analogy. For, as I show in Chapter 9, in predictive analogy, a certain characteristic of concept networks—namely, that the source and the target concept networks are structurally similar—is tied to the structure of the environment, something that blatantly violates the structural autonomy of the environment that I have been emphasizing throughout my account.

Thus, as far as providing an answer to the question "Why do certain metaphors provide illuminating insights while others do not?" in terms of the characteristics of the source and the target concept networks, I must essentially concur with Black: "There is, in general, no simple 'ground' for the necessary shifts of meaning—no blanket reason why some metaphors work and others fail." [Black 1962, p. 45] Metaphor must, therefore, remain to us a reminder of the limits of cognition with our finite minds in an infinitely complex world.

Chapter 9

On Predictive Analogy and Induction

9.1 Introduction

In Chapter 1 [§1.6.2], I identified a sense of 'analogy' that is used to refer to the process of predicting further similarities between two objects or situations, given some existing similarities. I have been calling this mode of analogy *predictive analogy,* but it is also known as *analogical reasoning, analogical inference,* and *argument by analogy.* For instance, given that one has just bought a 1987 Toyota Celica for $6000, on hearing that a close friend is considering buying a 1987 Toyota Celica also, predictive analogy leads her to expect that the friend will spend around $6000. Or, on finding out that the planet Venus has several characteristics in common with Earth, predictive analogy would suggest that Venus is inhabited also.

In each of the above examples, predictive analogy imports features from a more familiar object or situation, usually referred to as *the source,* to a less familiar one, usually referred to as *the target.* In the first example, the subject's own automobile is the source, the automobile that the friend is considering to buy is the target, and the feature imported from the source to the target is the cost. Similarly, in the second example, Earth is the source, Venus is the target, and the state of being inhabited is the imported feature.

It ought to be clarified from the outset that a conclusion drawn from predictive analogy is seen as *justified* and not necessarily true. That is, in some psychological sense or probabilistic sense a conclusion from analogy is considered more rational or more likely. Justification is independent of truth—a true statement can be unjustified and a justified statement can be false—and the two should not be confused with each other. All through this chapter, I am only concerned with the justification of predictive analogy (and induction), and not at all with its truth.

Notice that a conclusion derived from predictive analogy is not a logical inference. In other words, an argument from predictive analogy cannot be logically deduced from the existing knowledge of the source and the target. Thus, predictive analogy makes possible *new* knowledge beyond the logical limits of the existing knowledge, and therein lies the lure of predictive analogy.

Indeed, philosophers, cognitive psychologists and artificial intelligence researchers have all taken the bait of predictive analogy. Philosophers have tried to formulate elaborate mathematical systems to show why an inference from predictive analogy is more probable. Cognitive psychologists have tried to provide empirical evidence to show how predictive analogy is a valuable problem-solving heuristic. Some artificial intelligence researchers have embraced predictive analogy whole-heartedly by designing computational systems that, on encountering a new problem, work by recalling some familiar problem (the solution of which is known) that is similar to the new problem, and then applying the solution of the familiar problem, as it is or in a modified form, to the new problem.

Given the prominence enjoyed by predictive analogy, and given my repeated emphasis that my characterization of metaphor does not cover predictive analogy in any way, it is necessary now to analyze predictive analogy in more detail, so that my reasons for distinguishing it from metaphor can become clear. This is my main objective in this chapter.

I begin, in Section 2, by articulating in more detail exactly how predictive analogy differs from each of the different modes of metaphor [§7.4]. I show here that it is the process of suggestive (open-ended) metaphor that comes closest to predictive analogy, but there is one big difference: predictive analogy carries the aura of 'justification,' whereas suggestive metaphor does not. I argue at the end of this section that this difference is quite significant because it is the 'justification' that adds luster to predictive analogy, and makes it an attractive problem-solving heuristic.

The next problem then is to provide some grounds for the justification of predictive analogy. This problem has been attacked on two fronts. One has been to provide some logical justification for predictive analogy by showing that an inference from predictive analogy is more probable than, say, a random inference. The other has been to show empirically that predictive analogy plays a significant role in creative problem solving, including scientific breakthroughs. In Sections 3 and 4, I take a critical look at both these lines of research, and show that neither one has succeeded in validating predictive analogy.

As the believers in predictive analogy only present those examples where an inference from predictive analogy is justified (for some other reason), the 'dark' side of predictive analogy is rarely seen. To put predictive analogy and its role in cognition in proper perspective, it is necessary that the dark side of predictive analogy be exposed also. I make an attempt to do so in Section 5 by presenting some arguments from predictive analogy that might seem psychologically compelling but are not rationally justified.

Having seen both sides of predictive analogy, I present, in Section 6, what I consider a balanced perspective on predictive analogy and its role in cognition. I argue here that predictive analogy is best seen as a cognitive process that is as likely to lead to illuminating insights as it is to 'close' our minds by blocking crucial information coming from the environment; and that it is as likely to be a liability as an asset to cognition.

The big brother of predictive analogy is the process of induction. On having encountered a certain regularity in the environment on numerous past occasions, induction allows one to justifiably conclude that the regularity will also be observed on all future occasions. Indeed, many scholars see predictive analogy as nothing but a particular manifestation of the more general process of induction. The significance of the role played by predictive analogy in cognition is overshadowed by the significance of induction. Theories that have attempted to provide a justification for predictive analogy have been far fewer than theories of induction. Moreover, many theories of analogy are, in fact, corollaries to more comprehensive theories of induction.

The close connection between predictive analogy and induction is, however, a two-way street. If it can be used to apply theories of induction to the problem of justification of predictive analogy, it can also be used in the reverse direction—to extend the insights into predictive analogy to the process of induction. This is exactly what I set out to achieve in the rest of this chapter.

To begin with, I briefly discuss the background to the problem of induction in Section 7. In the section following that, I argue that any attempt to provide a foundation for induction by using probability theory is vulnerable to a generalized version of Goodman's 'grue' paradox. Then, in Section 9, I present some examples of what I consider to be unjustified uses of induction, to show that induction, like predictive analogy, can also be abused. Finally, in Section 10, I extend my perspective on predictive analogy that was laid out in Section 6, to the process of induction.

9.2   Predictive Analogy and Metaphor

Before we can compare predictive analogy with my modes of metaphor, it is necessary to reformulate the process of predictive analogy in the context of my framework. This task is somewhat non-trivial because, with the exception of Holland *et al.* [1986, Chap. 10], nowhere, in all the literature on predictive analogy I have seen, is a distinction made between an object (environment) and its representation (concept network). As this distinction lies at the heart of my framework, in order to relate metaphor with predictive analogy we must first decide whether the 'source' in predictive analogy refers to a concept network or an environment, and the same for the target.

Recall that in predictive analogy, one notices that the source and the target have some properties in common and that the source has some additional properties; and from this one *concludes* that the target has these additional properties as well. Keeping in mind that, in my framework, an environment is not accessible to the cognitive agent except *via* some concept network, it becomes obvious that the source could not possibly be an environment. Since the contribution of the source to the process of predictive analogy is to supply properties, it must necessarily be the 'source concept network.'

The target, however, is another matter. It supplies properties to establish the preconditions of predictive analogy, and then 'receives additional properties' from the source. Though the former role must necessarily be played by the concept network, the latter function can equally well be carried out by the concept network or the environment.

An example might be helpful here. Consider the source as army maneuvers to capture a fortress, and the target as use of electromagnetic radiation to destroy a tumor: an example from Gick & Holyoak [1980] that I introduced in Chapter 7 [§7.4.1]. The precondition of predictive analogy—existing similarities between army maneuvers to capture a fortress and use of electromagnetic rays to destroy a tumor—is established by comparing the respective concept networks. One notices that in approaching the tumor by electromagnetic radiation, a contact with the surrounding healthy tissue should be avoided, just as in approaching the fortress the army should avoid any contact with land-mines. This similarity can be comprehended by examining the two concept networks, since the relevant facts must be there if the cognitive agent that is reasoning from predictive analogy knows them at all. Note that there are similarities as well as dissimilarities. The healthy tissue surrounding the tumor *must be preserved,* but the mines surrounding the fortress are to be destroyed or neutralized. However, it is the similarities that make the process of predictive analogy applicable.

Once the process of predictive analogy is evoked, based on the observed similarities between the source and the target concept networks, the cognitive agent concludes (or hypothesizes) that the source and the target might be similar in other respects as well. In the example above, the cognitive agent might conclude that given that the army can be divided into several small units and be made to converge on the fortress simultaneously in order to capture it, the same approach might also be used to destroy a tumor with electromagnetic radiation. Any property of the source that the cognitive agent selects to apply to the target must again be a part of the source concept network, since otherwise the cognitive agent cannot be said to have known the property at all.

In applying the additional source property to the target, there are two possibilities. The first is to merely check that that the property indeed holds in the target by examining one's knowledge of the target environment; that is, by checking to see if the property is either already implied by the target concept network or definitely contradicts it. In the above example, the source concept network suggests that it is possible to send decoys to detonate mines, after which the army can proceed to capture the fortress. However, the existing structure of the target concept network rules out transferring this property—the healthy tissue needs to be preserved and ought not to be destroyed. Notice that when the additional property of the source concept network is merely applied to the target concept network, the process produces nothing new beyond what is already included in the target concept network. For this reason, it can hardly be said to be 'predictive.'

The second—and more interesting—case is when it cannot be established by just looking at the target concept network whether the additional property from the source concept network is definitely present there, or definitely contradicts some known fact in the target concept network. In other words, the property transferred from the source concept network is consistent with, but not implied by, the structure of the target concept network. In this case, this property from the source concept network must be operationally tested in the target environment, which, by virtue of its autonomous structure, can accept or reject the property. In situations like these, the additional property gives us a new *prediction* about the target environment. It is precisely these cases that form instances of predictive analogy.

We can sum up the above discussion in the following definition of predictive analogy: it is the process by which, based on the knowledge that the source concept network and the target concept network have certain properties in common, it is concluded that some additional properties of the source concept network, that are not already included in or contradicted by the target concept network, can also be applied to the target environment. (This formulation of predictive analogy fully agrees with the 'analogy as a second-order Q-morphism' view of Holland *et al.* [1986, pp. 196–300]—the only other theory to make a distinction between representations and objects.)

Let us now see how predictive analogy differs from metaphor. I carry out this task by considering each mode of metaphor [§7.4] in turn, and noting similarities and points of difference between it and predictive analogy.

Consider projective (similarity-creating) metaphor first. One can easily see that projective metaphor differs from predictive analogy in two important respects. Firstly, predictive analogy is a process less often applicable than projective metaphor since it (predictive analogy) requires as a precondition that there be some similarities between the source and the target concept networks. But projective metaphor, as I argued in [§7.4.2], places no such requirements. It works by directly interpreting the source concept network in the target environment and often produces deep insights into situations when there were no existing similarities between the source and the target concept networks before the metaphor.

Secondly, predictive analogy carries more force. It *concludes* that the additional properties of the source concept network are also applicable to the target environment. Projective metaphor merely *interprets* the source concept network in the target environment coherently.

What is the difference between *interpreting* a concept network in an environment and *concluding* that the properties of a concept network are applicable to an environment? Well, in interpreting a concept network, one is free to carve up the environment in any possible way so long as coherency is maintained. In other words, the ontology of the environment is not predetermined and can be adjusted to suit the concept network. In concluding from predictive analogy, on the other hand, the conclusion is made with respect to the existing ontology of the target environment as seen from the target concept network. Thus, projective metaphor and predictive analogy are two entirely different processes.

The situation is somewhat different with syntactic and suggestive metaphors [§7.4.1]. Being similarity-based, both types of metaphors are triggered by the existing similarities between the source and the target concept networks, just as predictive analogies. But syntactic metaphor says nothing new about the target environment. (Recall that in a syntactic metaphor, the source concept network is interpreted only by comparing it with the existing conceptualization of the target environment in the target concept network, and there is no open-endedness to it.) Its usefulness lies exclusively in making it easier for the cognitive agent to reason about the target environment by using a more familiar concept network (even though the cognitive agent can reason with the target concept network) and in highlighting and downplaying parts of the target environment (that are already included in the target concept network). It is hardly predictive at all.

That leaves us with suggestive metaphor. Indeed, suggestive metaphor can be considered a close cousin of predictive analogy. They are both triggered by the existing similarities between the source and the target concept networks. They both make hypotheses about how additional structure can be imported from the source concept network to the target environment—structure that is not already present in the target concept network. Moreover, this imported structure is with respect to the existing ontology of the target environment as seen from the target concept network.

Yet, there is a seemingly small but crucial difference. In suggestive metaphor, given that a part of the source concept network has been meaningfully interpreted in the target environment by using the ontology given to it by the target concept network, there is no promise, no justification, that some additional structure can also be so interpreted by using the same ontology. The process might or might not succeed.

Predictive analogy, on the other hand, carries exactly such a justification with it. It suggests that if the source and the target concept networks are structurally similar in certain ways, it is very likely that some other structural features of the source concept network—those that are consistent with the structure of the target concept network—might also be found in the target environment.

Thus, suggestive metaphor is essentially predictive analogy minus the justification. Or, to put it the other way, when a suggestion from suggestive metaphor is seen as 'forceful' in any way, then it turns into predictive analogy.

If this justification business seems to be just a technical point, let me point out that without it, predictive analogy loses all its force as a problem-solving heuristic. Given a target environment on which one is trying to get some new insight (for problem solving, or any other reason), the fact that some metaphors can be open-ended does not tell you which source will bring in the interesting insights. On the other hand, predictive analogy, in connecting the existing similarities with would be similarities, immediately suggests that the source that is most similar is also the most likely one to lead to the sought after insights.

Thus, justification is very much the lifeblood of predictive analogy. This should also be obvious from the amount of effort various scholars have spent in trying to provide some logical or empirical grounds for this justification. It is these efforts that I discuss next.

9.3 The Search for Logical Justification of Predictive Analogy

Suppose that two objects S and T have a set of properties ϕ in common. In addition, suppose S has a set of properties ψ about which it is not known whether T has them or not. What justification is there, if any, in assuming that T has properties ψ also? This is the logical problem of justification of predictive analogy in its essence.

There are, of course, variations. It might be known that S and T are dissimilar in some respects also—say, S has some properties, α, that T does not have, and T has properties, β, that are absent from S. What effect, if any, do the dissimilarities have on the justification that T has ψ also? Then there is the question of *degree of similarity*. For instance, suppose that there is another object S' that has properties ϕ' in common with T such that properties ϕ are included in ϕ' ($\phi \subset \phi'$). But S' does not have properties ψ. Instead, it has the properties ψ' that are disjoint from ψ ($\psi \cap \psi' = \emptyset$), and of which it is also not known whether T has them or not. Then are we more justified in assuming that T has ψ' than we are assuming that T has ψ? And if so, why?

I leave such variations for you to muse upon (see also Hesse [1966], pp. 101–129) and focus exclusively on the central problem of the justification of predictive analogy, which is problematic enough as it is. In the past thirty years or so, many theories have been suggested that purported to show why the inference from predictive analogy—namely that T has ψ also—is justified. Needless to say, the justification is provided in a probabilistic sense, since the inference from predictive analogy is not considered true, but only *very likely*.

There are basically three approaches that have been taken to provide justification for the inference from predictive analogy. I discuss them each in turn now.

9.3.1 Predictive Analogy as an Inductive Process

A number of theories of predictive analogy see it essentially as a form of inductive reasoning. Recall that induction is the process which allows us to justifiably infer, on having noticed some regularity several times in the past, that the same regularity will be observed in the future as well. In the case of predictive analogy, the 'regularity' is the set of similarities between the source S and the target T. All the properties that are included in ϕ 'confirm' this regularity. From this, one inductively infers that the similarity will extend to the properties included in ψ as well. Thus, the problem of the justification of predictive analogy is easily solved by embedding it in a theory of induction.

Harrod [1956, pp. 123–127], for instance, used the sampling principle to justify analogical reasoning. The sampling principle, easily demonstrated by using simple combinatorics, asserts that if a *random* sample is drawn from a population then the probability that the population has the same characteristics as the sample is very high, provided that the sample is large enough. Since the known properties of an object can be considered a sample of all of its properties—known as well as unknown—Harrod argued that if it is known that two objects S and T have some properties in common then it is highly probable that they will have other properties in common as well. Intuitively, the argument proceeds as follows. Suppose that S and T have fifteen properties in common, and further, S has ten other properties of which we do not know if T has them or not. Now if S and T had exactly fifteen properties in common, and no more, it is highly improbable that we would get to know only those fifteen properties of T. In other words, if the properties of T that are known to us are considered a sample of all the properties of T then the probability of T sharing other properties with S is much higher than the probability of T not sharing any other properties—beyond the known fifteen—with S. Thus, Harrod concluded, "[T]he argument by analogy has the fundamental characteristic of a sampling argument." [Harrod 1956, p. 127].

In Harrod's framework, each known similarity between the source S and the target T provides a separate instance to confirm the hypothesis that S and T are alike. Thus, the more the known similarity between S and T, the higher is the probability that S and T are alike and, consequently, the more justified is the inference from predictive analogy. Following this reasoning,

Harrod wrote: "Argument by analogy has been shown not to be, as Keynes, for instance, supposed, an arm of empirical reasoning independent of, and to be contrasted with, induction by simple enumeration. Its principles are to be derived from the more fundamental principles of induction by simple enumeration." [Harrod 1956, p. 255].

Harrod's theory, since it considers the source and the target isolated from their context, can be easily shown to lead to a paradox, which I do a bit later. A minor flaw in it is that merely counting properties to lend strength to an argument from predictive analogy does not seem satisfactory. Carnap [1962], for example, noted that, based on the evidence that b and c have some properties in common and that, further, b has an additional property; some difficulty is involved in justifying the hypothesis that c has that property too. "It seems plausible to assume that the probability of the hypothesis is the higher the more properties b and c are known to have in common; on the other hand, it is felt that these common properties should not be simply be counted but weighted in some way." [Carnap 1962, p. 569].

One obvious reason for this is that if a property p subsumes (implies) another property q (as being a 'bachelor' subsumes being a 'male') then we should not count p and q twice. Even if two properties are independent in the sense that neither of them subsumes the other, they might still make different contributions to the argument from analogy because of their different *logical width;* where the logical width of a property measures, intuitively, the number of logically independent properties subsumed by it: the more the subsumed properties the logically narrower the predicate. (See Carnap [1962], pp. 124–130 for the formal definition of the logical width of a predicate.) Thus, if being red, being triangular, and having a smooth texture are all all logically independent properties, then the property of being a red triangle is logically wider than the property of being a smooth red triangle. If a property subsumes another property, then the former is logically narrower than the latter—the property of being red is logically narrower than the property of being colored.

Now given objects S and T such that ϕ is the conjunction of all the properties S and T are known to share, the width of ϕ is x, $\phi \wedge \psi$ is the conjunction of all known properties of S, and the width of $\phi \wedge \psi$ is y, the probability that the object T will have properties $\phi \wedge \psi$ as well is given in Carnap's system by [Carnap 1962, pp. 569–70]:

$$\frac{y+1}{x+1}$$

Obviously, since $\phi \wedge \psi$ subsumes ϕ, y is less than x. Therefore, Carnap's system captures the intuition that the more properties S and T are known to have in common, the more confidence can be placed in the inference by analogy (that T has properties ψ as well). Moreover, the relative increase in the confidence factor, as more shared properties are discovered between S and T—or as x approaches y, is very small and Carnap points out that "[T]his is in agreement with the general conception according to which reasoning by analogy, although admissible, can usually yield only rather weak results." [Carnap 1962, p. 569].

Criticisms and revisions of Carnap's system continued further in Achinstein [1963], Carnap [1963], and Hesse [1964]. However, one major characteristic of his original system, which was also present in Harrod's framework that used the sampling principle, remained untouched in all these revisions: namely that the source and the target are considered in isolation—devoid of any context. That is, if a less familiar object T is being compared with a more familiar object S, and many of the known properties of T are possessed by S, formal systems *a la* Carnap or Harrod would predict with a high probability that the object T has other properties of S as well. In this prediction only the overlap between properties of S and T is considered. The knowledge of other objects and their properties has no bearing on this prediction.

This, however, immediately leads to a paradox. For instance, suppose that the objects S_1 and S_2 are exactly alike except that S_1 has the color red and S_2 is black. Now, given a less familiar object T such that its color is not known and all of its known properties are possessed by both S_1 and S_2, contradictory predictions are made of T's color depending on whether it is compared with S_1 or S_2. This point was made astutely by Agassi [1964] who argued that analogies are either generalizations or are completely *ad hoc*.

9.3.2 Predictive Analogy as a First Order Generalization

A number of theories of predictive analogy see it as a first order generalization. That is, given that S and T have properties ϕ in common and, further, that S is known to have properties ψ, the inference that T has properties ψ also is seen as based on the generalization that all objects that have properties ϕ also have properties ψ. For example, knowing that one's own 1987 Toyota Celica cost about $6000, the inference that another 1987 Toyota Celica will also cost that much is nothing but the application of the general principle: "If an automobile has the make Toyota, model Celica, and was built in 1987, then it costs about $6000." Why I call this a first order generalization, as opposed to a second order one, will become clear in the next section.

From this viewpoint, the knowledge that there is some object S' that has properties ϕ but not the properties ψ—say, one knows about one's brother's 1987 Toyota Celica that it cost only \$4000—provides a counterexample to the generalization and renders the analogical inference from S to T mute. Thus, regarding predictive analogy as a generalization causes the source and the target to be considered in the context of the total state of knowledge and not in isolation.

Still, there remain two problems. The first problem is that this approach does not take into account the number of properties included in ϕ—weighted or not. In other words, it is not explained how and why the justification for the analogical inference depends on the amount of existing similarity between the source and the target. This is remedied by assigning probabilities to generalizations based on the scopes of their antecedents and consequents.

Keynes' [1921, Ch. XIX, pp. 222–232] was one of the early attempts—and a very thorough one—in analyzing the probabilities of generalizations. He, as Harrod observed, saw the argument by analogy as an empirical form of reasoning, which in conjunction with Pure Induction—the strength lent to an argument from the number of instances alone—comprises inductive reasoning that is rational though not conclusive. Thus, on having encountered and savored numerous eggs, when we expect the same taste and relish from yet another egg: "We argue from Analogy in so far as we depend upon the *likeness* of the eggs, and from Pure Induction when we trust the *number* of the experiments." (Keynes [1921], p. 218. Emphasis Keynes.') Thus, Keynes' theory of induction had two independent parts. In the first part, he assigned an a priori probability to the generalization $\phi \Rightarrow \psi$ depending on the scopes of its antecedent (ϕ) and consequent (ψ). In the second part, he showed how this a priori probability is affected by the number of instances confirming the generalization. It is the first part of his framework that is of relevance here.

Keynes' notion of the scope of a proposition is analogous to Carnap's notion of the width of a predicate. Intuitively, if a proposition f_1 implies another proposition f_2, then the former has a scope smaller than or equal to that of the latter. Based on this definition, Keynes showed that the probability of a generalization $\phi \Rightarrow \psi$ is in direct proportion to the scope of its consequent (ψ) and in inverse proportion to the scope of its antecedent (ϕ); and therefore "some generalizations stand *initially* in a stronger position than others." [Keynes 1921, p. 225.] Thus, if fewer additional properties are inferred about the target based on a large number of properties that the source and the target have in common, then the inference is more justified; if more additional properties are inferred based on fewer existing similarities, then the inference has less justification.

A very similar approach was taken by von Wright [1965, pp. 134–136] who argued that reasoning from analogy depends, "for its logical force, on simple ideas concerning the proportionality of scope and probability in generalizations." [p. 136].

The second—and fatal—problem with the 'predictive analogy as a first order generalization' approach is that it makes the existence of the source superfluous. Since the initial probability of the generalization 'all objects that have ϕ have ψ as well' is only dependent on the scopes of ϕ and ψ, we can make the inference 'the target T has ψ, given that T has ϕ' with the same degree of justification without using the source S, assuming, of course, that no counter-examples to this generalization are known. For this reason, it can hardly be said that an inference so derived is 'from analogy.'

Of course, the number of confirming instances does affect the probability of the generalization beyond its initial value—the major part of Keynes' and von Wright's theories were meant to showing just that. But in any of these accounts, the increase in the initial probability of the generalization caused by the knowledge of the source—merely one instance confirming the generalization—is extremely small. Therefore, in as far as the inference is from 'analogy,' its justification is almost non-existent.

9.3.3 Predictive Analogy as a Second Order Generalization

All these shortcomings of the existing approaches led Weitzenfeld [1984] to view the process of predictive analogy in a different light. First of all, he saw predictive analogy as a second order generalization—and not a first order one. Secondly, he argued that it is a deductive process—in the logical sense of the word—but one based on an assumed premise of the second order generalization.

Let us first clarify the difference between first order generalizations and second order ones. A first order generalization has the form: "If an automobile has the make Toyota, model Celica, and was built in 1987, then it costs about $6000." A second order generalization, on the other hand, says: "if two automobiles have the same make, same model, and were built in the same year, then they cost about the same." Though the existence of the source is superfluous with respect to a first order generalization, save for providing a single confirming instance, it is very crucial for a second order generalization. Given the above second order generalization, and a 1987 Toyota Celica, the cost of which is not known, nothing whatsoever can be inferred about its cost without an appropriate source.

Weitzenfeld referred to the second order generalizations as *determining structures*—the relations and properties in the antecedent are seen as *determining* the relations and properties in the consequent. The source and the target, which are instances of a second order generalization, he called *homeomorphs.*

(Weitzenfeld also discussed *paramorphs,* which are determining structures that are assumed to be isomorphic. I do not discuss them here because they do not provide any additional perspective on the logical problem of justification of predictive analogy beyond the one provided by homeomorphs.)

The second novelty in Weitzenfeld's approach to predictive analogy lay in that he saw it as a deductive process that *assumes* the premise of the second order generalization. The 'extra-logical' force of the inference from predictive analogy comes from this assumed premise, since it *cannot be deduced* from the background knowledge.

Now this might seem to be a mere technicality. I certainly sympathize if you fail to see any real difference between Weitzenfeld's approach and the traditional view, which puts the 'extra-logical' force in the *process* of deriving an analogical inference from logically true premises (existing similarities between the source and the target). Yet this technicality underlies a significant point of divergence. In the traditional view, the process of predictive analogy is given the existing similarities between the source and the target. From this, the process infers that it is very likely that there will be other similarities as well. Thus, the existing similarities alone are seen as justifying the analogical inference. Though no one has yet been able to explain satisfactorily what this justification is, I have already discussed the shortcomings of some of the attempts.

In Weitzenfeld's approach, on the other hand, predictive analogy is merely a deductive process that is given the existing similarities between the source and the target, and the second order generalization. Now the existing similarities are logically true, but the second order generalization is not. The problem of the justification of predictive analogy, then, becomes the problem of justifying the second order generalization from one's background knowledge. This latter problem is essentially a cognitive one, and the arena for tackling it is wide open. The main thing is that the existing similarities between the source and the target are no longer the only factor—or even a factor—affecting this justification process.

Thus, though Weitzenfeld does not solve the logical problem of justification of predictive analogy *per se,* he presents it in a different perspective—a perspective that is more likely to lead towards the resolution of the problem than the traditional view, as I will show shortly. Before doing so it will be illuminating to review the attempts that have been made to justify predictive analogy on empirical grounds.

9.4 The Search for Empirical Justification of Predictive Analogy

Various researchers, mostly psychologists, have tried to justify predictive analogy on empirical grounds. These attempts essentially provide supporting evidence for predictive analogy in two different ways. One set of supporting evidence comes from numerous classroom experiments that have been done to demonstrate that people do use predictive analogy to successfully solve problems and reason about an unfamiliar target domain. The other set of supporting evidence is provided by analyzing real-world problem solving activities that include scientific and technological breakthroughs. Let us consider each set of supporting evidence in turn, and see if it does, indeed, provide a justification for predictive analogy.

9.4.1 Evidence from Classroom Experiments

A number of psychologists have tried to show that predictive analogy is a useful problem solving heuristic by conducting classroom experiments in a somewhat artificial setting. (See Clement & Gentner [1991]; Gentner [1989]; Gick & Holyoak [1980; 1983].) For instance, in Gick and Holyoak's [1980] study, five different experiments were conducted to investigate how exactly people use analogy in problem solving. One of the problems that was used in their experimental set up was the radiation problem that I have discussed earlier [§7.4.1]. (You might recall that the problem in this domain was to come up with some way to use electromagnetic radiation to destroy a tumor without destroying the surrounding healthy tissue.)

In one of Gick and Holyoak's experiments, three groups of subjects were given an analog source (army maneuvers to capture an enemy fortress) and a way (different for each group) to solve the analogous problem in the source, while a fourth group was supplied with no such source. The results indicated that for the three groups who were given the analog source, the given solution to the source problem had a marked influence in their proposed solution to the target problem. Moreover, the fourth group did rather poorly: about half of the subjects ended up suggesting that the patient be operated upon to clear a path for the electromagnetic rays. None of the subjects in this group suggested what was considered to be the most creative solution: that weak electromagnetic rays be sent from different directions so as to converge on the tumor. The experiment was conducted both with the experimenter interacting with the subjects during problem solving, and without such interaction, which was found to have no significant effect on the results, except that more incomplete solutions were generated in the non-interactive version of the experiment. This, according to Gick and Holyoak, clearly demonstrated the power of predictive analogy in solving an unfamiliar problem.

In another experiment, it was found that even when the solution to the source problem was not explicitly given, and the subjects were allowed to develop their own solution to it, they were still able to use the solution of the source problem to solve the target problem. This is purported to show that even when the subject does not already know the solution of a similar problem in the source, making the analogy is still helpful because the subject can proceed by first solving the analogous source problem (which ought to be easier, as the subject is more familiar with it) and then transferring the solution to the target.

In yet another experiment, the subjects were divided into two groups. Both groups were presented with three stories, one of which was a potential source analog for the target problem. Then each group was given the target problem to solve. The subjects in one group were told that one of the stories presented earlier could provide a hint in solving the problem. The results of this experiment were that the a large fraction (92%) of subjects in the group that was given the hint were able to find the right source and apply it successfully to solve the target problem, whereas only a small fraction (20%) of subjects in the 'no-hint' group were able to solve the problem at all. This showed that predictive analogy is not an automatic problem-solving strategy, but needs to be consciously applied.

Before analyzing to see if these experiments do indeed provide an empirical justification for predictive analogy, let us review one more set of experiments that was published more recently [Clement & Gentner 1991]. In their experiments, Clement and Gentner made up a scenario about some hypothetical creatures called 'Tams' as the potential source (referred to as 'base' by Clement and Gentner). The scenario had two different causal structures in it that explained why Tams, which habitually grind and consume minerals through their underbellies, sometimes stop using their underbellies, and why they cannot work on a new terrain. One causal structure explained that when the mineral in one spot is all exhausted then Tams stop using their underbellies. The other causal structure explained that the underbelly of a Tam gets specialized to the texture of a particular rock through adaptation, and so it is unable to function on a rock with a different texture.

The subjects were given two different versions of a target scenario involving robots that gather data on planets using probes. In one version, the subjects were told that when robots exhaust data from one place, they must move to another place; and that the robots are designed with delicate probes that cannot survive flight to another planet. In the other version, the subjects were told that when the robots gather a lot of data, their internal computers overheat; and that the probes adapt and become specialized to one planet.

Then the subjects were asked to make predictions about the target scenario. Clement and Gentner argued that there are two potential predictions with respect to each version of the target. For instance, with respect to the first version, it might be predicted that the robots would stop using the probes at some point (when the data is exhausted) or that the robots cannot function on another planet (since they have delicate probes that cannot survive flight to another planet). Only one of these predictions (the first one) fits the systematicity model of Gentner [1983], which was shown to be the most favored prediction in the experiment. Thus, Clement and Gentner not only claimed to have demonstrated that people use predictive analogy for making predictions, but that the predictions are derived from a 'systematic' mapping (which means a mapping that includes higher order relations and not the attributes) between the source and the target are more likely ot occur.

Let us now see if any of these experiments do provide an empirical justification for predictive analogy. First consider Gick and Holyoak's experiments. Interestingly, one condition that was true in all of their experiments, and not mentioned explicitly at all by them, was that *the analog source did lead to the solution of the target problem.* Even when two other seemingly irrelevant sources were included, those two sources were not analogous to the target problem. In other words, that predictive analogy would work in this example was satisfied a priori. What the experiment did confirm was that whenever that is the case (that it is known a priori that predictive analogy would work), then the subjects were capable of using predictive analogy to arrive at the solution (as long as it was explicitly hinted).

To validate predictive analogy as a problem-solving heuristic, an issue must be addressed that Gick and Holyoak's experiments ignore altogether: How to select the source domain? To appreciate this, consider a real-world problem-solving situation. There is a problem that no one knows how to solve. Now if some source (similar to the target) provides a solution to the problem, then applying predictive analogy with that source would lead us to it (and we will know afterwards that the source is, in fact, the correct one). However, there are a large number of potential sources; how do we decide which one to use? There is no oracle here to point us to the correct source. Predictive analogy purports to fill this gap by suggesting that a source that is similar in certain respects (according to systematicity or some other such criterion) is more likely to be the correct one. But then it must be empirically demonstrated that this is the case, something that Gick and Holyoak's study fails to do.

Clement and Gentner's study is even weaker in providing an empirical justification for predictive analogy. The target domain is quite artificial, and there is no 'real' problem about it. What it does manage to show is that people tend to favor certain kinds of predictions based on analogy to certain others. But there is no correlation between what people might predict and the solution of a real-world problem. If the subjects in Clement and Gentner's study were to solve a real-world problem, and there was no oracle to give them the 'right' source, then it is not clear whether the kind of predictions they made in the experiments would be useful at all.

9.4.2   Evidence from Real-World Problem-Solving Activities

I faulted Gick and Holyoak's study above in its inability to provide an empirical justification for predictive analogy on the grounds that the success in their classroom experiments does not translate into success with real-world problem solving. This suggests that if one were to look at real-world problem-solving situations, and if it could be shown that predictive analogy is responsible for leading to the solutions of even some of these situations, then predictive analogy would have received some empirical justification.

Problem solving in the real world has not been extensively studied; but the few studies that have been done [Gordon 1961; Schön 1963] point away from predictive analogy by revealing that most creative insights are generated by using a source that is very dissimilar to the target—so much that the juxtaposition of the source and the target seems bizarre initially—a process that Gordon very aptly names *making the familiar strange*. I have already discussed this point at length in Chapter 2 [§2.5.2].

It must be emphasized with respect to these studies that when a 'strange' source is used to get a new perspective on the target, the process ends up creating similarities between the source and the target. That is, there are always similarities between the source and the target *after the fact*. Some scholars, not making any distinction between before-the-fact and after-the-fact states of affairs, cite these same studies as if they provide empirical justification for predictive analogy, when, in fact, they do not.

There are, nevertheless, a few examples of real-world problem solving studies that do provide some support for predictive analogy. There are the studies that I reviewed in [§2.5.1] where the source that is used to solve the problem about a target is initially similar to it. (See, for instance, Gordon's [1961, pp. 42–45] 'direct analogy.') Researchers who study creative problem solving, however, are cautious, and do not throw their weight behind predictive analogy for several reasons. One is that the insights obtained by the similarity-based approach are not always deep or insightful. For instance, Carnot's hypothesis "The rate of heat-flow is proportional to the temperature difference between two bodies," if it was derived as described in Gentner and Jeziorski [1989], seems rather obvious. On the contrary, in Schön's example of the 'paintbrush as a pump' metaphor, the hypothesis that how the fibers of a paintbrush bend in the process of painting affects the appearance of the painted surface contains a deep insight. Or, compare a theorem that is derived by predictive analogy from a similar known theorem about groups with Cantor's theorem that there are more real numbers than integers.

Secondly, most people who have had a first-hand experience with creative problem solving in the real world realize that truly creative insights require completely new and revolutionary perspectives. They are unwilling to suggest that when there is a problem about a target domain, one's best bet is to go looking for a similar source, and the more similar the source the better it is, which is exactly how predictive analogy is viewed in much of cognitive science and artificial intelligence. If predictive analogy is such a useful problem-solving heuristic as it is claimed to be, most of our economic, social, and scientific problem should be easily solvable—all we need to do is to find the most similar source. But the existing state of humanity seems to be quite far from such a blissful state.

Finally, scholars who have studied creative problem solving have a deep respect for the autonomous structure of the real world, which does not depend on the particular forms of our representations (concept networks). In particular, most of them never say that, in applying a similar source to solve a problem about a target, similarities (which are properties of representations) are more important in certain respects (such as structural similarities) than similarities in certain other respects. Nor do they impute any sort of 'justification' relation between similarities that are seen and similarities that might be lurking around the corner. For real-world problems, some sources work, and others do not, and the success and failure of a source just cannot be related to whatever similarities that source might have to the problematic situation.

To summarize this discussion, we see that the only empirical evidence for predictive analogy from problem solving in the real world is that occasionally using a source that is similar to the target can lead to a successful solution to the target problem. Moreover, the solution to the target problem suggested by predictive analogy in these cases is usually not a particularly deep or insightful one. Given that, for real-world problems, deep insights come from using 'strange' sources that do not seem similar to the target at all, a system that puts its faith in predictive analogy as a problem-solving strategy is sure to miss most such insights. Consequently, predictive analogy is not such a wonderful problem-solving heuristic as it is purported to be.

9.5   The 'Dark Side' of Predictive Analogy

Given that no one has been able to provide a reasonable justification for predictive analogy, either logically or empirically, one wonders if there are any examples of 'unjustified' instances of predictive analogy. Perhaps not surprisingly, all the research on predictive analogy only cites what one might consider as reasonable examples of predictive analogy. In fact, most of the predictive analogy examples used in the literature make correct predictions about their targets, and their sources are quite useful in understanding the unfamiliar targets. This only shows the careful attention these researchers give in selecting (or making up) their examples, so as to present predictive analogy in the best possible light. The 'dark side' of predictive analogy, which contains instances when an inference from predictive analogy is *not justified,* and when predictive analogy becomes a hindrance rather than an aid to cognition, is never seen at all.

To fill this vacuum, I provide some examples below that provide a glimpse of the dark side of predictive analogy. For each example, I argue why the suggestion from predictive analogy is not justified, or why predictive analogy becomes an obstacle to cognition by blocking the information that might otherwise be received from the environment.

- Suppose you are in a jury. The case being tried involves an accident between a Ford Escort and a Toyota pick-up. The drivers of both vehicles give completely contradictory accounts, putting each other at fault. The accounts given by both drivers are consistent with the known facts. The pictures of the scene of the accident taken by the police are no help in identifying who is at fault. There are no eyewitnesses either. However, you recall that several months ago you witnessed a very similar accident at an intersection similar to the one at which this accident took place. (There are many relational and causal ['systematic'] similarities involved here.) Is it justifiable for you to predict from this analogy that the fault for the accident that is being tried lies with the Toyota driver?

  I would say that there is no such justification there. The prediction might well be correct, but based on the available information, nothing whatsoever can be said about who was at fault in the accident being tried. All the 'systematic' similarities it might have with the accident you saw before are completely irrelevant.

- In a study of first-time users of computer text-editors, Allwood and Eliasson [1987] found that many of their difficulties emanate from the fact that they use the typewriter analogy to understand text-editors.[1] The subjects were familiar with using a typewriter, and they automatically formulated an analogy between it and the text-editor (there are many structural similarities between the two). They then proceeded to apply this analogy to understand the text-editor. Unfortunately, as documented by Allwood and Eliasson, this analogy became a stumbling block to their understanding. In particular, it led to a number of errors (keeping a key pressed too long so that multiple instances of a command were issued) and inefficiences (moving the cursor characterwise when it would have been more efficient to move wordwise) in their use of the text-editor. (See also Halasz & Moran [1982] for difficulties of using analogical models in explaining some computer-related concepts.)

  Here the fact that predictive analogy may hinder cognition is clearly seen. If it were not for analogy, these subjects would be open-minded

---

[1] I am grateful to Dr. Erica Melis for bringing this work to my attention.

about learning the text-editor. As it is, they rush into it thinking that they understand it through predictive analogy, and fail to realize the important differences and the vastly superior power of text-editors.

• Gentner and Jeziorski [1989] provide some examples of alchemists' use of analogies. For instance, they cite Stillman [1924] who noted that egg was used as a source of many analogies. In one such analogy, "[T]he shell, skin, white, and yolk of the egg were thought to be analogous to the four metals involved in transmutations—copper, tin, lead, and iron—although the pairings could vary between the components and the metal." [Gentner & Jeziorski 1989, p. 313.]

Such analogies amount to no more than fanciful whims that are not 'justified' in any sense of the word. In fact, they often hinder the true objective of scientific inquiry by making irrational arguments that refuse to acknowledge facts when the facts do not fit these whimsical analogies. (See, for instance, Francesco Sizzi's arguments against Galileo's discovery of the satellites of Jupiter that I cite in Section 9.)

• On January 14, 1991, as the multinational force allied against Iraq and led by the United States stood poised for attacking Iraq in a bid to liberate Kuwait, an article appeared in the *Wall Street Journal* [Robbins 1991] that made an analogy between the arguments used by the representatives of the U.S. congress during the debate to authorize the President the use of force against Iraq, and the arguments used in the congress during a similar debate in 1939, when Europe was standing on the brink of what was to become World War II. Besides a three sentence introduction, the article contained nothing else than pairs of quotations; one quotation of every pair was taken from the 1939 debate and the other from the 1991 debate, with an appropriate heading for each pair. Both arguments in each pair made essentially the same point. For instance, under the heading "To save democracy?" Senator Charles Tubey was quoted as arguing in 1939, "[This is] a war not to save democracy but to preserve territorial powers of certain Europen nations." And Representative William Gray was quoted as arguing in 1991, "Is [our policy] to defend democracy? Hardly! Kuwait is no democracy, neither is Saudi Arabia or Syria." Thus, there is a clear analogy between the debate of 1939 and the debate of 1991. (And since the arguments involve causal structure and higher order relations, there is an obvious 'systematicity' in the analogy.)

What is the point of analogy? Taken as it is (in the sense of what I refer to as syntactic metaphor), it merely shows that congress is cautious about rushing into war and committing billions of dollars and putting lives of hundreds of thousands of people in jeopardy when the security of the country is not directly threatened. But the author seems to be implying something more. In one of the three sentences preceding the quotations, the author claims that "The similarity is more than superficial," but no further explanation was offered as to how. Of course, if one uses predictive analogy, a number of other hypotheses are at once suggested. For instance, one might conclude that if we did not go to war right away, a World War would ensue with significantly greater loss of life, or that Iraqi war machinery was as formidable as Germany's was in 1939, or that all reservations put forward in the 1991 debate are meaningless because they turned out to be not valid in 1939. One can go on and on here. Perhaps the author, using predictive analogy as a psychological sleight of hand, meant people to draw all (or some) of these conclusions subconsciously. God forbid, if artificial intelligence systems that used the 'systematicity' principle to make predictions about the future had ever anything to do with political decision making, they would be easy prey to such sleight of hand.

Analogies like these are quite common in political rhetoric. They essentially work by hiding what is significantly different about two situations, and by presenting a distorted picture so that people may draw the conclusion that the politician wishes them to draw. Since the conclusion is not always stated explicitly (as in this example), it seems all the more convincing. (Everyone thinks that they arrived at it themselves!) By not questioning the basis of predictive analogy, we only make ourselves more vulnerable to such manipulation.

- Another example in the same vein is provided by Eleanor Clift's criticism of President George Bush's handling of the U.S. economy. She was quoted as saying, "The rhythm method is about as good in economic planning as it is in family planning."[2] (The comment was a response to President Bush's remark on waiting in the 'natural cycle' of the economy as a strategy to combat the recession.) This analogy makes a completely irrelevant comparison to support a conclusion. Of course, the conclusion (that waiting in the 'natural cycle' of the economy is not a successful strategy to combat recession) can be independently analyzed, and one can argue for or against it. But the analogy tries to give an aura of justification to the conclusion without bringing in a

---

[2]This appeared in "Quotes of Notes," (p. 27) in the *Boston Globe* on Saturday, November 30, 1991.

shred of evidence or considering a single fact about the economy.

- Finally, a historical example where predictive analogy, justified or not, would have been a grave liability. During the French revolution, the political situation was in such a state of flux that what was 'politically correct' at one point in time would become the reason for sending someone to the guillotine a little later. How predictive analogy would have led to disaster in this period might be best appreciated from Shurkin's [1984] description of a computer simulation of the French revolution designed by historian Michael Carter:

> "Students at Dartmouth can ... play a game that simulates the French revolution. The student assumes the role of a Jacobin who undergoes political interrogation. He or she must answer the questions according to the party line at a certain time during the revolution or be swept off to the guillotine. Given a second chance at the questions, they frequently find that what was right before is fatally wrong now; the rules have been changed and they are still doomed. A number of real Jacobins died that way." [Shurkin 1984, p. 317.]

Political revolutions provide an excellent source of examples where a cognitive agent reasoning from predictive analogy is doomed. Consider the recent failed coup in the Soviet Union. During the coup, the rules changed as to what was considered right. When the coup was overthrown, the rules changed again to the other extreme. In fact, even sitting on the fence in not opposing the coup was also punished in various ways. All this shows that predictive analogy is not such a great asset to cognition as it is purported to be, and an artificial system that uses it as a source of heuristic is not going to survive any revolutions.

I hope all these examples give you at least a cause for concern about predictive analogy: that an inference from predictive analogy (whether 'systematic' or not) is not always justified, and is not always useful to cognition. On the contrary, predictive analogy can become a major stumbling block to one's ability to be objective and see things as they are, with possibly fatal consequences.

9.6 Predictive Analogy and Cognition

Now that we have seen the dark side of predictive analogy, we can analyze it more objectively. Clearly, and this is what the psychological studies of Gentner and Holyoak have effectively demonstrated, people find arguments from predictive analogy psychologically compelling. I have no problem understanding this point. Also, from this point of view, predictive analogy seems an important cognitive phenomenon that ought to be researched, so that we can understand it better, and become aware of the pitfalls it creates in cognition. But this has not been the spirit of the cognitive science research on predictive analogy, where the attitude towards predictive analogy has been nothing short of awe and reverence: Predictive analogy is good. Predictive analogy works most of the time. Predictive analogy is the key to learning and problem solving. Predictive analogy is a key ingredient of intelligence. Predictive analogy must be incorporated in computational models of intelligence. And so on. Almost no effort has been spent to examine the negative effects of predictive analogy in cognition. The fact that an inference from predictive analogy appears psychologically convincing often prevents a person from seeing things as they are, some examples of which I presented above. In fact, my examples show only the tip of the iceberg. Once you become aware of the potential abuses of predictive analogy, you would be surprised to find how much more predictive analogy is abused than it is used. But the abuses are rarely, if at all, discussed in the literature about predictive analogy. This, what is essentially a negative contribution of predictive analogy to cognition, raises serious doubts as to whether it is useful to incorporate predictive analogy in an artificial intelligence system at all.

This point can be better understood by an analogy (used in an explanatory 'syntactic' sense and not in a predictive sense). Consider our visual system. Its structure makes it useful to us in certain ways, but also gives rise to certain hallucinations and paradoxes. (See Favreau & Corballis [1976]; Gillam [1980]; Kanizsa [1976]; Sekuler & Levinson [1977]; and Siegel [1977].) Now one can study these paradoxes so as to get a better understanding of how our visual system is structured. But it would be quite silly to insist that in order to design and build a smart machine vision system, we must somehow incorporate these paradoxes in the design. But this is precisely the approach taken by much of artificial intelligence research with respect to predictive analogy.

Looking at predictive analogy as a cognitive process, sometimes successful but often misleading, some observations can be made here. One is that there is no correlation between the existing similarities between the source and the target concept networks, and the likelihood of finding some additional structure of the source concept network in the target environment. Indeed, if this correlation were as assumed to be in predictive analogy, then most problems (whether they be proving a theorem, developing a new product, coming up with a new physical theory, or settling a political crisis) would be solved by merely finding a similar source. On the contrary, we find that in real world situations, predictive analogy often leads to mundane and trite observations. The key to creativity lies in bringing in a fresh perspective, in *creating* similarities where none existed before, and in noticing things that are hidden by the usual categories formed by our cognitive apparatus. All of this is accomplished by trying to interpret a source concept network that is *very dissimilar* to the target concept network in the target environment. However, there is no correlation here either between the dissimilarities between the source and the target concept network, and what fresh perspective, if any at all, would be provided by interpreting the source concept network in the target environment. Given a problematic target, many dissimilar sources fail to create any insights at all, let alone useful ones. Thus, the fact remains that some source concept networks work—in terms of creating a useful perspective on the target environment that results in getting the problem solved—whereas many others do not, and this difference cannot be explained on the basis of the existing similarities between the source and the target concept networks

This conclusion can be better appreciated in my framework, as I alluded in Section 2. The thesis that an argument derived solely from some existing similarities between the source and the target concept networks is justified, essentially says that if parts of the source concept network have been meaningfully interpreted in the target environment, then other parts can also be so interpreted with respect to the same ontology. This, in turn, amounts to saying that the cognitive agent can determine the ontology of the environment *and* its structure. But I have emphasized in Chapter 5 that the cognitive agent can determine either the ontology of the environment, (as in accommodation, when the environment constrains the structure), or the cognitive agent can opt to impose the structure of a concept network on an environment, (as in projection, when the environment constrains the possible ontologies), but cannot do both. In other words, predictive analogy effectively denies the fact that an environment is *autonomous and external to the cognitive agent*—thereby reverting to an extreme form of subjectivism.

The second observation is that even though an inference from predictive analogy does not have an increased likelihood of success in the environment, one could still use the term 'justified' in a psychological sense to distinguish reasonable inferences based on predictive analogy (such as inferring the cost of an automobile from the cost of another automobile with the same make, model, year, and mileage) from unreasonable ones (such as the examples presented above). This is where Weitzenfeld's [1984] approach is most illuminating. You might recall from Section 3.3 that he saw predictive analogy as a deductive process that *assumes* a second order generalization as a premise; and, in his account, the justification for an argument from predictive analogy comes from the assumed second order generalization. At that time it might have seemed a technicality, but now we can appreciate the full significance of Weitzenfeld's insights.

Weitzenfeld's account contains two key insights. One is that if an inference from predictive analogy is based *only on existing similarity* between the source and the target concept networks, then there is absolutely no justification for it. In fact, an inference derived only from some syntactic properties (such as systematicity) of the source and the target concept networks is not justified at all. However compelling such an inference may seem, the compellingness is really a result of implicitly assuming that an argument from predictive analogy is always justified, an assumption that is easily refuted by the examples of Section 5. It is this implicit but false assumption that makes an argument from predictive analogy cast a spell that is exploited in various abuses of analogy and suggestive metaphor. Certain similarities are pointed out between the source and the target concept networks as a justification for reaching an erroneous conclusion about the target environment—a technique all too often employed in propaganda and political rhetoric. It is this spell which undermines the educational and explanatory usage of metaphor and analogy. [Miller 1976.]

Once the spell is broken, we realize that an argument that is based only on some existing similarity between the source and the target concept networks, and nothing else, is utterly unjustified. We learn to exercise extreme caution in trusting an argument based solely on some existing similarities. Every such argument is a potential snare. It must be operationally tested in the target environment. And if that is not possible, one must find some other piece of knowledge, some other fact—besides the existing similarities between the source and the target concept networks—that justifies the argument from predictive analogy. And if no such justification can be found, the so called argument from analogy ought to be properly discarded.

The second insight of Weitzenfeld is that the justification of an inference from predictive analogy lies in how far the second order generalization that is assumed in the predictive analogy is justified from the background knowledge. This, however, introduces a semantic component to predictive analogy; because the justification to predictive analogy comes from the background 'knowledge,' which is interpreted concept networks (cognitive models) that are coherent (as far as the cognitive agent has been able to ascertain). For instance, in the example of inferring the cost of an automobile from the cost of a similar automobile, it is the background knowledge that automobiles of the same make and model cost approximately the same in any given year, and that they depreciate at roughly the same rate with years and mileage, that makes the inference justified.

I must emphasize that I am talking about justification in a psychological sense here. Given the autonomous structure of the external world, one's background knowledge is fallible, and, therefore, there is no guarantee, even in a probabilistic sense, that a justified inference will turn out to be correct. The psychological nature of this justification can be better appreciated by emphasizing its subjectivity. Different people can have different conceptual systems, with different types of causal links and different ways of giving ontologies to the world by instantiating these concepts. Yet, all these conceptual systems can quite reasonably be considered background 'knowledge.' For instance, to a believer in astrology, there is a causal relationship between the positions of the stars and the planets in the sky and certain events taking place on Earth. This relationship might well be coherent with the actual experiences of such a person. To her, the generalization that two people, if they were born when the planet Mars was in the same position would have certain character traits in common would be perfectly justified. Yet, to a non-believer in astrology, this is about as justified as saying that two cars of the same make, model, and year are of the same color.

Taken in this sense, predictive analogy can be more fruitfully studied along with its justification. For instance, we might find out what it is that makes unjustified inferences psychologically compelling to people. Is it that they subconsciously, as in the phenomenon of apparent motion [§4.2.1], fill in the requisite second order generalization needed to make the inference from predictive analogy justified? Or is it that they have some background knowledge that is being made overt by the inference from predictive analogy. Focusing on issues such as these is bound to increase our understanding of predictive analogy, prepare us better to counter the negative role it plays in cognition, and heighten our awareness of its potential abuses so that we are less vulnerable to it.

9.7 The Problem of Induction

Predictive analogy, as I mentioned in the introduction, is often seen as an instance of the more general process of induction. On having encountered a certain regularity in the environment on numerous past occasions, induction allows one to 'justifiably' conclude that the regularity will be observed in the future as well. The problem of the justification of induction was first discussed at length by David Hume, a leading eighteenth century philosopher, in his celebrated work, *A Treatise on Human Nature*. After some deliberation, Hume concluded that all our observations and experiences give us absolutely no logical basis for concluding anything about the unobserved. This later came to be known as the *sceptical* thesis about induction.

Since most, perhaps even all, of our cognitive activity consists in making predictions about the future based on the past experiences and observations, Hume's sceptical thesis conveys a chilling sense of insecurity. Is there no logical basis for any of our knowledge? Is the outcome of any event predicted by a scientific theory that is supported by several previous observations no better than a random guess? Of course, in practice, we do continue to put our faith in predictions based on our past experiences; even an act as simple as walking requires many such predictions which we instinctively carry out. Hume, despite his scepticism, had no problem granting this. But this pragmatic success of induction in certain cases is not an issue here—since even the most ardent inductivist would acknowledge that induction can, at times, lead to false conclusions from true premises. The issue is to provide some 'logical foundation' for induction such that an inductive inference is seen as rational, even if occasionally fallible. And it is precisely this project that is undermined by the Humean thesis.

As you might be aware of, there have been many attempts since Hume to refute his sceptical thesis and provide a logical foundation for induction. Most of them have taken the form of designing some mathematical framework, almost always based on probability theory, that made inductive inferences come out to be more probable than any other inferences; and, further, the probability of an inductive inference increased with the number of confirming instances. An excellent account of some of these theories of induction can be found in Salmon [1966].

So close is the relationship between predictive analogy and induction, that many theories of predictive analogy—including those of Carnap, Harrod, and Von Wright that I discussed earlier—are, in fact, corollaries to more comprehensive theories of induction. However, given the paradoxes and problems facing these theories of predictive analogy, should we not expect a similar fate for the theories of induction?

Indeed, the problem of the justification of induction is riddled with paradoxes. For instance, there is the Raven's paradox. Consider the hypothesis "All ravens are black." Intuitively, we expect this hypothesis to be confirmed whenever we find a black raven, strengthened as the number of observed black ravens increases, and refuted whenever we find a non-black raven. Finding any other object that is not a raven should have no effect on this hypothesis. However, this hypothesis is logically equivalent to its contrapositive "All non-black things are non-ravens," which is confirmed by finding a non-black non-raven, such as a white handkerchief.

There are several other paradoxes as well, one of which I discuss in some detail in the next section. Undaunted by them, inductivists kept on devising more complex theories and coming up with newer arguments to justify induction. One such recent attempt has been made by David Stove in his book *The Rationality of Induction.* He advanced very rigorous arguments to justify inductive reasoning by presenting four 'proofs' to refute what he calls "the sceptical thesis about induction." However, I have shown elsewhere [Indurkhya 1990] that none of Stove's four 'proofs' succeed in this task. Three of his proofs do not refute the sceptical thesis at all, but an altogether different thesis. Stove's fourth 'proof' uses the sampling principle to justify—in a probabilistic sense—one particular inductive inference. Having one justified inductive inference, of course, refutes the sceptical thesis that no inductive inference is justified. However, I have shown that Stove's 'proof' makes a crucial unstated assumption regarding the randomness of a sample. The particular inductive inference is not justified at all, once this unstated assumption is brought to light. Since many theories of induction seek to justify it by using the sampling principle, I review my critique of Stove's fourth 'proof' [Stove 1986, pp. 55–75] in the next section.

9.8 The Sampling Principle, Randomness, and the Generalized Grue Paradox

The sampling principle states that when a sample is drawn randomly from a population, the probability that the sample is representative of the population is very high provided that the sample is 'reasonably large.' The interesting thing about it is that 'reasonably large' is measured on an absolute scale, and not as in 'reasonably large fraction of the total population.' In fact, the sampling principle holds even when the sample is a very small fraction of the total population, as long as it is reasonably large on an absolute scale. For instance, as Stove showed by using simple combinatorics, in a population of one million ravens composed of just 50 percent black ravens, more than 99 percent of the 3000-fold samples match the blackness frequency of the population within 3 percent. That is, of all the possible samples containing 3000 ravens that can be drawn from this population, more than 99 percent of them have a proportion of black ravens between 47 and 53 percent. Clearly, 3000 is a small fraction of one million. Moreover, the probability that the random sample will nearly match the distribution of the population shows an almost negligible decrease, as the size of the population grows while the size of the sample is kept constant.

Based on this sampling principle, Stove very carefully constructed an argument to show that from the hypotheses A and D given below, where 'Pop' stands for "the population of ravens, each at least 100 cc in volume and no overlapping, on earth between 10,000 B.C. and A.D. 10,000," the inductive inference E has a very high probability.

A: S is a 3000-fold sample of Pop.

D: Just 95 percent of the ravens in S are black.

E: The proportion of black ravens in Pop is near 95 per cent.

The gist of Stove's argument is very simple, though he took great pains to lay down each and every step very elaborately. Since by the sampling principle, most of the 3000-or-more-fold samples of Pop contain nearly the same proportion of black ravens as Pop, it follows that the probability that S contains the same proportion of black ravens as Pop is very high. Consequently, the probability of E given A and D is also very high. As the inference from A and D to E is inductive, Stove concluded that this amounts to a refutation of the sceptical thesis about induction by means of a counterexample.

The above arguments, however, make a very crucial hidden assumption. In order to highlight this underlying assumption, consider the following scenario. You are standing outside a sealed room which is known to contain a large number of balls, say a million. The balls, all of the same size, maybe all black, all white, or any proportion in between. There is a slot in the room from which a person inside the room passes you a ball. You examine the ball, determine its color, and then return it back through the slot, at which point the person passes you another ball, and so forth. After going through this procedure 3000 times and having found that 95 percent of the balls were black, would you say confidently—or with a high degree of probability—that 95 percent of the balls in the room are black? I claim that in the absence of any other information, any rational person will be very much reluctant to make such sweeping generalization. For instance, there seems to be no reason to suppose that the person is giving a new ball to be examined each time, instead of using just one black and one white ball.

One might object here that it is the presence of a person, a free agent, that makes all the difference. But suppose that you replace the person with a machine; in the absence of any knowledge about how the machine operates one would still be reluctant to conclude anything about the balls in the room. Even if you were not required to return the balls, having examined 3000 balls, and having no knowledge whatsoever about the mechanism responsible for ejecting balls out of the slot, I maintain that a rational person will have no 'grounds' to make any conclusions about the balls inside the room. However, arguments similar to Stove's can be made for all these situations, leading one to infer with a high probability that 95 percent of the balls in the room are black.

The fallacy in Stove's argument, as should be apparent by now, stems from illegitimately assimilating two distinct cases. One case is of an urn containing one million balls such that 95 percent of the 3020 balls *randomly* drawn from it are black. The other situation is that of the 3020 ravens observed so far 95 percent are black. In the first case there is a very high probability that 95 percent of the balls in the urn are black. In the second case, in the absence of any other information, nothing whatsoever can be said about the colors of all the ravens (except that 2869 of them are black). (The confusion emanating from ignoring the relevant distinction in these two cases has also been noted by Keynes [1921], ch. XXIV:4, p. 284.)

However, let us concentrate on the specifics of Stove's arguments. Stove's argument does indeed show that one can infer E from A and D with high probability provided that sample S is taken at random. But if the sample examined is not random, the inference to E from A and D has no credibility. Thus, in order to vindicate induction, Stove must show that it is possible to infer E from A and D where S is a 3020-fold sample of ravens examined so far. In order for his arguments to lead to this end he must also show that this sample S is random with respect to Pop. Since Pop extends over space ('on Earth') as well as time ('between 10,000 B.C. and A.D. 10,000'), the randomness of S must be demonstrated with respect to space and time.

First consider randomness of S over space. For A and D to justify E, with a high degree of probability, the sample S must be chosen randomly from the surface of Earth, or else the hypothesis E must be restricted accordingly. It is very easy to imagine that due to environmental differences, ravens in different geographic regions have different colors (as is indeed the case with several other species—bears, for instance). Having drawn one's sample all from Australia it would be unreasonable to conclude that 95 percent of the ravens are black all over Earth. Even when an attempt has been made to seek ravens from *most* places on Earth and examine their color, a reasonable person will not rule out—in the absence of any other grounds, the possibility of a large population of ravens existing in some underexplored region, say the South Pole, and of predominantly white color. The confidence in the randomness of S, and consequently in the hypothesis that is inductively derived from it, will, and should, depend a great deal on how the sample S was collected. One cannot rule out the possibility of Mother Nature playing a trick, in spite of our best efforts to ensure the randomness of S.

So it seems that in order for Stove's arguments to save induction's face, the sample S in hypothesis A must be randomly drawn from all over Earth. Though this criterion is by no means easy to satisfy, let us grant it to Stove. But what about randomness with respect to time? It is conceivable, again due to environmental differences, that ravens at different time spans show variations in their plumage color. If this sounds farfetched to you, consider the following case that the biologists found puzzling at one time. Around 1850, previously unrecorded dark forms of several species of moths were observed in the industrial areas of Manchester and Birmingham, England. Later work by Dr. H.B.D. Kettlewell showed that the change of color resulted from the adaptation of moth species to environmental alterations caused by industrialization. Vast quantities of soot, released from factories and home chimneys, had deposited on tree trunks in the surrounding areas and made the bark uniformly black. Moth species adapted by developing the dark form so that they were more effectively concealed on the black tree trunks from the predator birds.[3] [Wallace & Srb 1964, pp. 40–42]. This example, of course, is presented merely to point out the possibility that, for reasons unforeseeable at present, all the ravens after year A.D. 3000 could turn out to be white.

Thus, in order to conclude E justifiably from A and D, the sample S must be drawn randomly over 20,000 Earth years. One specimen from 5000 B.C., another from A.D. 12000, and so on. In this case it is impossible to make S random unless one admits the possibility of time travel. One can include in S random samples of ravens from 10,000 B.C. to the present time, though some ancient ones might be hard to find. (Here, by including a raven in sample S, I

---

[3]I am grateful to Beryl Nelson for bringing this example to my attention.

do not require that a single person must go examine each of the ravens. This, of course, is impossible. It is sufficient that someone has seen the raven and recorded its color—and that there is no reason to suspect that this person was color-blind or was lying.) But how would you include samples of future ravens in S?

This is the real problem with Stove's final attempt at vindicating induction. The best we can do is obtain a sample S that is random with respect to the surface of Earth and between 10,000 B.C. and the present. On the basis of such a sample, one might conclude, with a high probability, that the proportion of black ravens in the population of ravens on Earth between 10,000 B.C. and the present time is 95 percent, notwithstanding Mother Nature playing a trick. But as this sample is anything but random as far as Pop is concerned, nothing whatsoever can be concluded about Pop with any degree of probability. At least to me, this is what the sceptical thesis on induction is all about.

The form of Stove's argument, as well as any other that uses the sampling principle to justify induction, is fatally vulnerable to Goodman's *grue* paradox. [Goodman 1955, pp. 72–81.] Goodman put forth a riddle for theories justifying induction by introducing a predicate *grue*. Grue is defined as follows: an object is grue if, and only if, it is green and is examined before the year A.D. 2000 or is blue and is not examined before the year A.D. 2000. Based on this definition, a large sample of objects of a kind E, say emeralds, if all taken before the year A.D. 2000 and all green is also all grue. Consequently, on the basis of this sample, if one feels justified, à la Stove, in concluding that all Es are green, one should also feel justified in concluding all Es are grue. But both these hypotheses lead to contradictory expectations for Es observed after the year A.D. 2000.

The first thing to notice about the grue paradox is that it exposes the flaw in any argument that attempts to justify an inference spanning all times based on a sample restricted over a smaller time span. Since, in the absence of any further assumptions, a sample restricted over a specific time span (small or large) is not random with respect to a population spanning a larger time span, any attempt to justify probabilistically a hypothesis covering the whole population based on the sample will be vulnerable to the grue paradox. The reason is that if we know a priori that the sample is restricted to a time span T_s, where the population has a time span T_p and $T_p > T_s$, then it is always possible to introduce a predicate like grue that applies to the objects that are examined inside the time span T_s and are green; and the objects examined outside the time span T_s, i.e. in the time span $(T_p - T_s)$, that are blue. As far as I am aware, the debate on the grue paradox has failed to note this simple crucial point. (See Barker & Achinstein [1960]; Goodman [1972, pp. 398–412]; Rescher [1976]; Bunch [1980]; Shirley [1981].) If we admit the possibility of time travel, which makes it possible to have a sample that is random with respect to time span of the whole population, then an argument based on the sampling theorem will be irrefutable and, moreover, impervious to the grue paradox. The reason the grue paradox cannot be raised against such an argument is that the sample, being random, is as likely to contain objects that are examined before the year A.D. 2000 as objects examined after the year A.D. 2000.

From here it is only one more step to see how the grue paradox can be generalized so that it can be used against any argument that tries to justify a conclusion about a whole population based on a sample drawn from a small section of the population. Consider a population P that spans an interval D_p in some dimension. The dimension could be space, time, or a combination of both. Now let S be a sample of P, i.e. a proper subset of P, that spans a smaller interval D_s across the same dimension. The problem of induction in this context is: What justification is there to admit a statement about the characteristics of the unsampled population $(P - S)$ based on the characteristics of sample S? The sceptical thesis, of course, says 'none!.' The non-sceptic might try to argue that by the sampling principle that if S has a certain characteristic R it is highly probable that P has characteristic R as well. I am deliberately using a vague word 'characteristic' to cover a wide range of inductive statements like 'all Xs are Ys,' 'most Xs are Ys,' '95 percent of Xs are Ys,' etc. For our purpose here, let R be the statement 'all Xs are Ys,' where X and Y are two independent predicates. Now an argument based on the sampling principle to justify induction will be valid only when one of the following two conditions is satisfied:

1. The sample S is random with respect to D_p. Since the issue of randomness is a controversial one [Keynes 1921, Ch. XXIV; Burks 1977, pp. 585–603], let me say at least say that D_s must not be knowable a priori.

2. It is known a priori that the objects satisfying predicates X and Y are uniformly distributed in the interval D_p. In this case one would qualify the argument justifying induction by saying that it only applies to predicates that are uniformly distributed.

If neither of these conditions is satisfied, then the argument based on the sampling principle can easily be shown to be paradoxical by introducing a new predicate Z, where Z applies to objects that lie in the span G_s and are Y, or that do not lie in the span G_s and are not Y. The sample S, obviously, also has the characteristic 'all Xs are Zs' setting up an expectation in the unsampled population $(P - S)$ that contradicts the one predicted by 'all Xs are Ys.' If the first of the above conditions is satisfied, then the paradox cannot be raised, as G_s is not known beforehand. If the second condition is true, then again the paradox fails because now Z is not uniformly distributed across D_p by virtue of its definition. This demonstrates that the sampling principle cannot be used to rescue induction without making further assumptions about randomness or uniform distribution.

9.9   The 'Dark Side' of Induction

Given that the problem of justification of induction is as open as the problem of justification of predictive analogy, one wonders if induction also has a dark side, containing inductive inferences that are not justified. Indeed, there are plenty of unjustified inductive inferences. Some examples are presented below.

- 1 is less than 1000, 2 is less than 1000,. . . ,999 is less than 1000, therefore all numbers are less than 1000.

- It has been reported that Francesco Sizzi used the following argument against Galileo's discovery of the satellites of Jupiter:[4]

    "There are seven windows in the head, two nostrils, two eyes, two ears, and a mouth; so in the heavens there are two favorable stars, two unpropitious, two luminaries, and Mercury alone undecided and indifferent. From which and many other similar phenomena of nature, such as the seven metals, etc., which it were tedious to enumerate, we gather that the number of planets is necessarily seven." (This is quoted on page 822 in Newman [1956].)

- During 1988, which was a presidential election year in the US, I was amused to find, in several newspapers, statistical analyses of the past elections. Several patterns were noted by reporters and presented as suggestive of this year's outcome. For instance, in one such news story,[5]

---

[4]I am grateful to Prof. Peter Gacs for bringing this example to my attention.

[5]As I recall, this story appeared in *Boston Globe* around the middle of February 1988.

it was noted that in the past, whenever the Democratic party nominee was the one who had won the Iowa caucus (the first caucus to be held), he lost to the Republican opponent in the main election. On the other hand, whenever a Democratic nominee was the one who had won the New Hampshire primary (the first primary to be held, which follows the Iowa caucus) then he won the presidential election. Would this justify an inference that the winner of the Iowa caucus (who was Richard Gephardt) would lose the presidential election, if nominated? Perhaps the point of including this analysis in the new story was to weakly suggest it, but this is a prime example of what I would consider totally unjustified inference from induction.[6]

- Sports is another area that is rife with analyses like this. Past statistics are often put forward, with no justification whatsoever, suggestive of what might happen now. For instance, during the baseball world series in 1991, the two contending teams (Minnesota Twins and Atlanta Braves) were tied 3-3 going into the seventh and the final game. The seventh game was taking place in Minnesota so that the Twins had the home-team advantage. Before the game, many sportswriters recalled a similar situation four years ago when Minnesota entered the seventh game with a 3-3 tie against St. Louis, and won the game, and the world championship, by beating St. Louis at home. Predictive analogy would surely suggest that they would do the same again in 1991.

During the telecast of the seventh game between the Twins and the Braves, the commentator pointed out that in the history of baseball, only five times before it has happened that in the first six games of the world series, the home team always won. (This would result in a 3-3 tie, because three of the six games are played at the home of one team, and the rest are played at the home of the other team.) And in four of these situations, the home team lost the seventh game. (The exception was the 1987 world series.) Applying inductive inference to this data would suggest that Minnesota has a 20% chance of winning the game. This contradicts the inference from predictive analogy using the 1987 world series as the source.

I am sure there are some of you who find such statistics compelling would disagree, but I consider such use of induction quite unjustified. What is the connection between the world series that was played in

---

[6]Incidentally, the inductive inference suggested by this analysis turned out to be false. Michael Dukakis, the Democratic nominee and the winner of New Hampshire primary, lost the presidential election to George Bush.

1955 (when Brooklyn won at New York Yankees) and the one being played now? And why should anything that happened in 1955 have any relevance to what may happen now? (Of course, such statistics might be quite interesting for its own sake. I am only objecting to their use in generating inductive inferences.)

- In investigating the *Challenger* space shuttle disaster with the Presidential commission, famous physicist and Nobel laureate Richard Feynman noted the gross abuse of induction as one of the factors contributing to the tragic mishap:

> "...[T]he phenomenon of accepting seals that had shown erosion and blowby in previous flights is very clear. The *Challenger* flight is an excellent example: there are several references to previous flights; the acceptance and success of these flights are taken as evidence of safety. But erosion and blowby are not what the design expected. They are warning that something is wrong. The equipment is not operating as expected, and therefore there is a danger that it can operate with even wider deviations in this unexpected and not thoroughly understood way. The fact that this danger did not lead to a catastrophe before is no guarantee that it will not the next time, unless it is completely understood. When playing Russian roulette, the fact that the first shot got off safely is of little comfort for the next." (See Feynman [1986]. The quote here is from p. 223 of the reprint in *What do you care....*)

There are many other examples like these. In fact, one can inductively infer from them that induction is not justified. But, attractive as this trivial refutation of induction is, it is not the point here. The point is that the justification for an inductive hypothesis is not to be found in the number of instances confirming the hypothesis alone, and a hypothesis based solely on some regularity observed in the past is not justified at all.

9.10 Induction in Cognition

There remain two facts concerning induction that cannot be ignored. Firstly, *some* inductive inferences are justified, as our scientific and technological progress clearly attests. Secondly, induction carries a psychological force that makes an inference derived from it almost compelling, even when it is not justified, as the last two examples above testify. Any reasonable theory of induction must be able to explain both these factors.

Regarding the first factor, we ask: What justifies an inductive inference? We have just seen that it cannot be the number of instances encountered in the past alone. Well, then we need to look in some other place. But where?

Weitzenfeld's perspective on predictive analogy illuminates the way to an answer here. Recall that Weitzenfeld argued that it is not the observed similarities between the source and the target that provide a justification for an argument from predictive analogy, but instead, it is the background knowledge that justifies (or does not justify) the second order generalization which says that the observed similarities determine the inferred ones. In the same spirit, we can perhaps seek the justification for an argument from induction in terms of background knowledge.

Indeed, when we reconsider the justified inductive arguments, we find that almost always there is some underlying theory that gives some *explanation* for why finding the confirming instances of the inductive hypothesis should increase one's confidence in the hypothesis. Thus, the number of instances encountered in the past lends strength to an inductive hypothesis only when there already exists some theoretical framework providing the justification.

This observation, trite as it might seem to some, has several major consequences. Firstly, since 'theories' are cognitive constructs, it immediately makes the justification of an inductive hypothesis a subjective notion. People have different theories and, therefore, what is a justified inductive argument for one is humbug for another. Various kinds of superstitious beliefs, astrology, etc. provide examples to illustrate this point. It might well be the case that whenever a total lunar eclipse has occurred, some misfortune has befallen John. This provides compelling evidence to John, a believer in astrology, that total lunar eclipses cause misfortune. However to Peter, a close friend of John and an unimaginative but bright aeronautics engineer, they are merely coincidences. On the other hand, Peter has never been able to convince John, who has a fear of flying, about the safety of air travel. All the evidence that Peter points out, John dismisses with a wave of hand as coincidences.

The second consequence of this observation is that it identifies two independent dimensions of the problem of induction: cognitive and metaphysical. Understanding the difference between them would help a great deal to get a better perspective on induction, and to avoid some of the needless controversy over it.

The cognitive dimension comes from considering the question: How does our background knowledge justify some inductive hypotheses but not others? A study of this problem can be undertaken within a framework of beliefs and cognitive mechanisms that allow our beliefs to affect our perception of the world, and the world to modify our beliefs—within frameworks such as those of Goodman [§4.3], Piaget [§4.4] and the one developed here. For instance, in the framework of interactionism developed here, it can be argued (in a very general sense, of course) that it is the process of *projection*—or assimilation, to use the more general Piagetian term—that underlies induction. The only way we can interact with an object or a situation, and perceive it, is by assimilating it to a pre-existing concept network or schema. It is this assimilation that gives rise to certain expectations from the object based on the concept network; and it is the process of having expectations about the object, based on past experiences, that is formally known as induction. If we realize that the concept network, to which the object is being assimilated, incorporates, in some way, the structures of the objects and situations encountered in the past, then there is no difficulty in seeing how induction can arise from assimilation.

Thus, induction is not seen as providing justification to certain cognitive processes, but rather it is viewed as arising out of cognition. That is, instead of taking the position that external reality is such that an inductive inference is justified in a probabilistic sense, we reverse our stand, and view induction as a human cognitive process—all too fallible. With this approach, the problem of induction lies in studying the underlying cognitive mechanisms, and to explain the characteristics of induction in terms of these mechanisms. (An effort in this spirit has been carried out by Holland *et al.* [1986].) Admittedly, this problem is still too complex, given our existing knowledge of cognition, to be addressed fully here. Yet, it seems promising to me in that I foresee considerable progress being made towards unraveling it in the next few years or so.

Interestingly, viewing induction from this vantage point also explains why arguments from induction appear psychologically compelling. This point might be better appreciated by comparing induction with some other cognitive process, say vision. When a dot is flashed in the visual field of a person followed by another dot a short distance away from the first one, the person sees a continuous motion—as if one dot moved smoothly from the position of the first dot to the position of the second. (See Kolers [1972], and also §4.2.1.) The imaginative mind seems to fill in the gaps of the perceptual data to create a pattern of its own liking. Perhaps, in the same way, when a repeated pattern is presented, as in the examples above, the mind seems to fill in the theory needed to make the argument justified.

The metaphysical dimension to the problem of induction comes from considering the question: What is it about the nature of the external world that makes some (many?) inductive inferences valid, and consequently justifies the process of induction? (The reason I refer to it as the metaphysical dimension is because of its intimate relationship to the questions like: Why do we exist? Why are we the way we are? Why is the world the way it is? etc., the pursuit of which is equally futile.) Notice that this formulation, by taking 'justification' to mean 'increased likelihood of succeeding in the external world,' immediately places the problem of justification in the structure of the external world. For this very reason, however, any approach to addressing this problem essentially leads us to a dead end.

The key point of difference between the two dimensions of induction, and the futility of pursuing the metaphysical dimension, can be better appreciated by considering our visual system again. Visual perception and cognition in humans are of a complex character with many 'illusions' like subjective contours, apparent motion, figural aftereffects etc. Studying these characteristics of vision from a cognitive point of view amounts to studying them empirically, and formulating functional and structural theories to integrate the empirical observations in a framework. For instance, take the characteristic of the eye that causes it to 'fill in' the edges and contours in the visual field. What justification is there for it? The cognitive approach seeks justification in the structure and function of the eye. In this case, it is explained from the connections between the cells in the lateral geniculate nucleus and the visual cortex. Significant advances in our understanding of the human visual system that have been made in this century clearly attest to the success of this approach. (See Hubel [1988].)

The metaphysical approach, however, begins by taking the nature of the vision as given, and asking: What is it about the structure of the external world that makes our visual system succeed? Why do we have two eyes? What is it about the external world (and ourselves) such that our visual system's characteristic of filling the edges and contours in the visual field increases our survivability? The utter hopelessness of even trying to address these questions should be obvious. Of course, one could partially answer these questions from an evolutionary and genetic standpoint, but then induction can also be explained in a similar way. However, an ardent inductivist, seeking the solution to the metaphysical problem, is not happy with that. For her, to say that induction is justified because it has been successful in the past is itself an inductive argument. The only way to avoid circularity is to show somehow why it is likely to be successful in the future as well. But since this cannot be done without violating the autonomy of the external world: this road leads nowhere. Of course, it does not prevent one from hypothesizing elaborate theories that justify induction metaphysically, but any such theory must remain essentially a conjecture.

To sum up, induction is a cognitive mechanism, and, in this respect, no different from other cognitive mechanisms like vision. While these cognitive mechanisms are a valuable asset to cognition, they can nevertheless, lead to serious judgmental errors. The best we can do is to understand them fully, and make ourselves less vulnerable to the erroneous judgments caused by them. This project, however, can only be addressed from a cognitive point of view.

As far as the metaphysical dimension to the problem of justification of induction is concerned, it can no more be justified than we can justify the fact that we have two eyes. The fact that we are the way we are, and that it has worked well for us so far in terms of our survival, does not guarantee that our perceptual and cognitive mechanisms will continue to work well for us in the future also. It is not hard to imagine environments, in which induction becomes a liability rather than an asset. Dinosaurs, bowheads, Mayans— and there are numerous other examples—have all become extinct or nearly extinct for not being able to counteract properly the disturbances in their environments, whether the disturbances were natural or caused by other, or even their own, species. We may prove to be no exception.

Chapter 10

On Computational Approaches to Metaphor and Analogy

10.1   Introduction

The field of Artificial Intelligence (AI), which concerns itself with designing and building machines—usually in the form of computer programs—capable of exhibiting 'intelligent' behavior, has not been oblivious to the role of metaphor and analogy in creativity and problem solving, two of the major processes requiring intelligence. But its focus has not exactly been on similarity-creating metaphors and creative analogies. The term 'metaphor' in the AI literature is almost always used restrictively to refer to the instances of metaphor in language. In this narrower sense, metaphor has received rather scanty attention in AI. Moreover, the few attempts that have been made to model metaphors have all been comparison-theoretic in spirit. That is, they all assume that the basis of any metaphor is some underlying similarity between the source and the target, and then they either set out to compute the similarity, or take the similarity as explicitly given and set out to use this information to determine the meaning of a metaphorical phrase. Clearly, while such approaches address the mode of similarity-based metaphor, and to some extent suggestive metaphor, they leave similarity-creating metaphors completely out in the cold. Perhaps, this should not be surprising given the state-of-the-art of Natural Language Processing (NLP), which still remains in its infancy in spite of all the advances of the past thirty years. There are many key issues surrounding literal and conventional meanings that have not yet been fully and satisfactorily incorporated in any NLP system. Similarity-creating metaphors, having to do with novel and creative uses of words and phrases, have remained an unreachable and unrealistic goal. I present a brief overview of the NLP approaches to metaphor in Section 2.

It is in the area of analogy that we find much more activity. In the short history of AI, analogy has recurred with great stubbornness as a theme underlying AI models, and even as the subject of investigation through these models. In the last few years this recurrence has intensified a great deal. However, the hub of almost all this activity has been predictive analogy—the process of predicting further similarities between the source and the target based on some existing similarities. Now we have already noted in the last chapter that predictive analogy is related to only one mode of metaphor, namely suggestive metaphor, and even that only somewhat obliquely, since suggestive metaphor does not carry the force of justification that predictive analogy does. Consequently, all these models of analogy have little relevance to metaphor. To be more specific, while all these models address some issues concerning similarity-based and suggestive metaphors, they fail to throw any light on the process underlying creative analogies and similarity-creating metaphors. I discuss this issue in more detail in Section 3.

Though, for the most part, predictive analogy has kept the limelight focused on itself, and away from the other modes of analogy, a few (three, to be precise) computational approaches to analogy have sought to focus on proportional analogy relations—that is, relations of the form "A is to B as C is to D." First, there is the little known work of Mary Hesse [1959a, 1959b], where she developed an algorithm for computing the fourth term, given the other three terms, of a proportional analogy relation involving context-free verbal analogies, as in "what is to fish as nose is to man?." Then, there is the widely known work of Evans [1963], where he designed and implemented an algorithm for choosing the fourth term from a given set of five alternatives, given the other three terms of a proportional analogy relation involving configurations of geometric figures. Finally, there is the recent work of Douglas Hofstadter and Melanie Mitchell [1991], where they designed and implemented an algorithm for generating the fourth term, given the other three, of a proportional analogy relation involving strings of characters.

While only three models of proportional analogy have been studied, given the intensity of research effort that has been spent in modeling predictive analogy and given that proportional analogy relations seem quite artificial compared to the 'real-world' domains that have been used for predictive analogy, it is quite ironic that the most innovative approach to modeling the process of redescription that underlies all truly creative metaphors and analogies should be made in the context of proportional analogies. Evans was quite aware of the need for a redescription component in his architecture, and did include a primitive version of one in his program. However, it was over twenty years before the genius of Douglas Hofstadter tackled the problem head on.

From the outset of his research on analogy, Hofstadter has exclusively focused on the process of redescription and change of representation that accompanies all creative analogies and metaphors. To study the cognitive processes underlying this creativity, he designed an elegantly simple, and yet astonishingly rich, microworld of character strings in which proportional analogy relations can be formulated that require a process of redescription that is quite similar to the one that underlies creative analogies and similarity-creating metaphors. Then he and his colleagues developed a probabilistic computer program to generate the fourth term of a proportional analogy relation, given the other three. Unlike Evans' system, in which the descriptions of the terms A, B, and C were generated in the first stage and were kept fixed thereafter, coming up with the appropriate descriptions of the terms A, B, and C was the main task of Hofstadter's system. The description of each of the terms A, B, and C was affected by the descriptions of the other two terms, and it in turn affected the description of each of them. I briefly discuss how Evans incorporated the context-dependency of descriptions in his architecture, and then present Hofstadter's system in greater detail in Section 4.

Once we realize that there is an element of redescription underneath every creative metaphor or analogy, and if we stop relying on the keywords 'metaphor' and 'analogy' to lead us to the computational systems that can model the cognitive processes underlying creative analogies and projective metaphors, an interesting, and somewhat surprising, perspective emerges. We find that there are, in fact, many computational systems that are capable of generating creative analogies and metaphors—without calling them explicitly by these names—and bring about the creation of similarity in the process. I argue this point in Section 5. Following that, I outline an architecture for modeling similarity-creating metaphors in Section 6. Finally, Section 7 summarizes the main points of this chapter.

10.2   Computational Approaches to Linguistic Metaphors

As I mentioned above, there have been few computational models of linguistic metaphors. These models can be divided into two broad classes based on their approaches. The models in one class explicitly represent the meanings of all metaphorical usages a word can have, and then address the problem of deciding which is the correct meaning in a given context. Thus, the problem they address is essentially that of word sense disambiguation. I should perhaps emphasize here that the problem is not as trivial as it may sound, given the existing state of the art of NLP systems.

Two notable models in this class are those of Carbonell [1982] and Martin [1988]. Both these models address the task of providing an NLP system with an ability to handle 'conventional' metaphors, that is, metaphors that are so much a part of the accepted everyday speech as to almost become a part of the literal language, as in 'prices are soaring' or 'I want to kill this process.' Also, both these models are largely motivated by the work of Lakoff & Johnson [1980], in which the authors have shown that a large number of the conventional metaphors of language are derived from a few general metaphor schemas such as 'more is up, less is down,' 'personification' etc. Given this, Carbonell and Martin each felt that if an NLP system can be given explicit knowledge of these general metaphor schemas, and an ability to use this knowledge, then the user would be able to interact with the system using a large number of conventional metaphors. Since the speakers of any language usually have an explicit knowledge of the conventional metaphor schemas of their language, there seems to be no reason to not provide this information to an NLP system. Though such an approach is clearly justified from an engineering standpoint, it is not very interesting from a cognitive point of view, if what we are interested in is how metaphors get their meanings in the first place. It is like being given the multiplication table when one is interested in figuring out the multiplication algorithm.

The models in the second class actually undertake to compute, in some fashion, the meaning of a given metaphor. Notable among these are the systems proposed or implemented by Sylvia Russell, Jerry Hobbs, Eileen Way, Judith Weiner, Yorick Wilks and Dan Fass. As one would probably expect, there are wide variations in what is considered to be the 'meaning' of a metaphor, what 'background knowledge' is provided to the model from which the meaning is computed, and how exactly this computation is done. The brief discussion below should give you some idea of the various approaches.

Russell [1976], who was perhaps the first computational linguist to venture into the treacherous terrain of metaphors, implemented a system to figure out the meanings of metaphorically used verbs, as in "the country leapt to prosperity," or "the ship plowed the sea." The background knowledge of her system was provided in two forms. First, there was a multi-dimensional matrix that represented the structural similarities (and differences) between different verbal concepts. For instance, the concepts 'land' and 'sea' both had the features 'fixed' and 'two-dimensional,' though 'land' lacked the feature 'fluid' that 'sea' had. Second, there was additional information provided for the verbs that gave explicit 'narrow' and 'broad' constraints on what features the verb expects from its objects. For example, the verb 'plow' expected its object to be 'land' on a 'narrow' reading and 'two-dimensional' on a 'broad' reading. Her algorithm then specified a number of heuristics to resolve any clashes among the features of the verbal concepts constituting the metaphorical sentence. (If there are no clashes, then the sentence is not metaphorical.) For instance, one rule was that if the object of a verb lacks the 'narrow' feature expected by the verb, see if it has the 'broad' feature. The 'meaning' of the metaphor was then constituted as a cluster of features taken from the features of the concepts involved. Her program finally searched for a verbal concept that best corresponded to this cluster of features, and used this concept in paraphrasing the metaphorical sentence.

Weiner [1984; 1985] proposed a system that relied on salience, prototypicality, and epitomization to arrive at the meanings of the metaphors of the form "X is Y," as in "John's hands are ice." The main idea was to use the most salient attributes of Y (the attribute 'temperature' of 'ice' in the example) to see if they are applicable to X ('John's hands'), and when they were, those attributes applied to X constituted the meaning of the metaphor. The background knowledge was a hierarchy of concepts, with the attributes and value restrictions for each attribute specified for each concept using a KL-ONE network. Further, the attributes of each concept, as well as the ranges of their values, were graded in the order of their salience. (See Iwayama, Tokunaga, and Tanaka [1990] for an algorithm for computing the salience.) Prototypicality was used here so that the attributes attached to a concept were the attributes that a prototypical instance of that concept might have. Thus, attributes of the concept 'person' would include 'has two hands,' even though there are persons who have, through some unfortunate accident, lost one or both of their hands. Epitomization was used in the sense that if the typical value of the transferred attribute represented an extreme value for the target concept (X), then it would be considered a better metaphor. For instance, the range of temperature for 'ice' is much lower than the range of temperature for 'John's hands,' and hence there is all the more reason for transferring the temperature attribute to John's hands. Lastly, she uses the distance between X and Y in the abstraction hierarchy to decide whether the statement "X is Y" is literal, literal similarity, or metaphor: If X and Y were distant, then the statement was deemed to be a metaphor.

Wilks [1975] started out by proposing a 'preference semantics' framework in which, while agreement between the semantic features of the concepts used together in a sentence was preferred, it was not absolutely necessary. Thus, in "my car drinks gasoline," though the concept 'drink' preferred to have its subject be 'animate,' when this feature was absent from the concept 'car,' the utterance was still accepted but flagged as metaphorical. Later on, Wilks suggested that the system be provided the background knowledge about the workings of the car, and then an interpretation for 'drink' be found by matching its meaning against the background knowledge about the car. In this example, the system would find that 'drink' best matches 'use,' and the utterance would correspond to "my car uses gasoline." (See also the discussion in Fass and Wilks [1983].)

Fass [1989] extended this approach. In his system Met*, when an utterance could not be understood literally or metonymically, then an attempt was made to find an underlying analogy between the relevant concepts and, if one was found, it became the basis of the metaphorical meaning of the utterance. The background knowledge for his system was provided in the form of sense-frames, which contained an abstraction hierarchy of concepts, as well as other expectations associated with the concepts. For instance, the sense-frame for 'drink$_1$' contained the information that it is a subtype of concepts 'ingest$_1$' and 'expend$_1$,' and that it prefers its agent to be 'animal$_1$' and the object to be 'drink$_2$' (which is the noun sense of drink). On encountering "my car drinks gasoline," Met*, after failing to understand it literally or metonymically, would find an analogy between the parts of the sense-frames 'animal$_1$' and 'car$_1$,' namely that the animal drinks$_1$ drink$_2$, and the car uses$_2$ gasoline. The key to finding this analogy was the fact that both 'drink$_1$' and 'use$_2$' are subtypes of 'expend$_1$' and both 'drink$_2$' and 'gasoline$_1$' are subtypes of 'liquid$_1$.' (See also Helmreich, Iverson and Laroche [1990] for further extensions and a parallel implementation of Met*.)

Hobbs [1979, 1990] proposed an axiomatic approach to be able to draw proper inferences from a metaphor. He suggested that for simple metaphors, such as "John is a pig," the context would rule out certain inferences that could be drawn from the utterance—for example that John has a tail. For certain conventional metaphor schemas, such as the spatial schema to talk about variables in math (as in "the variable N is at zero"), one needs to provide an appropriate axiom to the inference generating system. In the above example, the axiom could be "if X is a variable and W is the condition of Y being its value, then W is also the condition of X being at Y." For more complex novel metaphors involving structural analogies between different schemas, as in "we insist on serving up these veto pitches that come over the plate the size of a pumpkin" (said by a Democratic congressman during the Ford administration in 1975), Hobbs, while acknowledging that no natural language processing system existing today can interpret it [1990, p. 68], suggested that if the schemas were represented as complex sets of axioms that were interrelated, within each schema, by the co-occurrences of the same predicates, then the schemas could be linked by assuming identity between corresponding conditions, as in the condition of being the Congress being identical to the condition of being the pitcher, with the text and the schemas providing valuable clues for making this identification.

Notice that all the models of metaphors discussed so far are 'syntactic' in the sense that they try to derive the meaning of the metaphor from syntactic objects: from the given representations of the words or concepts. Even when one talks about keeping 'semantic' information, it ends up being manipulated in a purely syntactic way. Russell's system does not really know what two-dimensional is, nor does Met* know what gasoline is. For instance, Met* would probably find the utterance "my car eats coca-cola" as acceptable as "my car drinks gasoline." The syntactic approach of these models is the main reason for their being limited to conventional metaphors, or similarity-based metaphors at the very best, for the creativity of metaphor comes from incorporating new information from the environment, and the syntactic approach provides no mechanism to handle this. The key to modeling creative metaphors, as we see later in this chapter, comes from bringing into the picture the objects to which the concepts refer.

There is one interesting approach though, which, while it is also syntactic in a sense, tries to model creative metaphors. It is the dynamic type hierarchy system of Way [1991]. This system is almost entirely based on the notion of an abstraction hierarchy. However, the abstraction hierarchy here contains *all possible ways of arranging the concepts hierarchically,* and not merely some canonical way of doing it that reflects the cultural norm. In fact, this is how Way's system incorporates the information from the environment, for one may view this global abstraction hierarchy as representing the state of the world as it actually is, and not as it appears through the structure of our language. Concepts 'Nixon' and 'submarine' have a superconcept 'things that behave in a secret or hidden manner,' even though this superconcept is not explicitly represented in our language and culture.

Clearly, this global hierarchy is almost useless due to its enormous size and the computational complexity of having to traverse it. So, Way introduced the notion of 'masks' which present only a small part of the global hierarchy. Masks organize the global hierarchy by showing certain links and hiding other links. For instance, the hierarchy imposed by our language can be thought of as a 'literal' mask placed over the global hierarchy. A metaphor, then, works by replacing the literal mask with another mask that shows a different organization of the concept. If the new organization reveals new concept nodes and new links, then the metaphor is novel. For instance, the literal mask for our language and culture organizes the concepts so that concepts 'Nixon' and 'submarine' are very far apart in the hierarchy—their lowest common superconcept may be 'things.' However, when the metaphor "Nixon is the submarine of world leaders" is presented, a different mask is put on the global hierarchy. The concept 'things that behave in a secret or hidden manner' becomes visible, and so do the links connecting it with the concepts 'Nixon' and 'submarine' as its immediates subconcepts.

Way's approach is interesting and original, though it amounts to determining in advance all possible similarities between all the concepts. With the idea of masks, her model shows how literal and conventional language can hide crucial cognitive information that is revealed by metaphors. Presented in this way, her account is not very different from the one I presented in Chapter 7. However, her actual implementation of the model slides back into the rut of syntactic approaches. To implement her ideas computationally, Way developed an algorithm for interpreting metaphors that uses the formalism of conceptual graph theory developed by Sowa [1984]. Her algorithm did not actually use the global hierarchical network, but worked by *creating* a new concept node that is closer to the source and the target concepts. For instance, in trying to interpret "the car is thirsty," the system created a new concept node that is the immediate superconcept of 'car' and 'animal' but a subconcept of 'mobile-entity,' which is the least common superconcept of 'car' and 'animal' before the metaphor. A definition of this concept was then created by specializing the definition of its superconcept ('mobile-entity') with respect to the vehicle concept ('thirst'). The result, for this example, was the concept 'mobile-entity that requires liquid.'

Implemented in this way, Way's approach has two major drawbacks. First of all, *anything* can be considered metaphorical, for the new concept can always be created—there is nothing to constrain it. Second, and more importantly, the definition of the new concept, as well as which attributes transfer from the source concept to the target concept, are determined entirely by the information in the definition and schema fields of the relevant concepts, which are all syntactic items.

To sum up, we see that the natural language processing approaches to metaphor have all relied on the given representations of word meanings, with some additional so called semantic information, to compute the meanings of metaphorical utterances. The result is that their ability to correctly interpret metaphors depends a great deal on the technical details of their representation formalism. Also, in most cases, the representations are tailored to suit the few examples that their systems can process, thereby raising questions about the extensibility of the general principles that they claim to embody. Again, this is not to belittle the intensity of the effort that these scholars have spent in trying to incorporate metaphors into their computational systems, but only to highlight the immensity of the task, and to suggest that the best avenue for approaching similarity-creating metaphor computationally may not be language after all.

10.3 Computational Approaches to Predictive Analogy

Predictive analogy has received considerable attention in the short history of AI. In fact, in AI, when people use the term 'analogy,' they almost always mean predictive analogy. It is perhaps understandable. It is predictive analogy that lures us into thinking that the existing similarities between two objects or situations constitute a reason to posit that there might be other similarities as well. And once we bite the bait, predictive analogy at once appears as a powerful heuristic for problem solving. Lured by this glitter of promise, several AI systems have been designed and implemented over the years that incorporate predictive analogy in some form or another. Since Kedar-Cabelli [1988] and Hall [1989] provide a detailed overview of various AI models of predictive analogy, I mention only a few models here to give you a flavor of their approaches, and to point out their inadequacy in modeling creative analogies.

Robert Kling [1971a, 1971b] implemented a system ZORBA-I for proving theorems by analogy. Given the proof of a theorem in one domain (say, abelian groups), ZORBA-I would use the proof to prove an analogous theorem in another domain (say, commutative rings). Assuming that the proof of the new theorem T' is analogous to the proof of the known theorem T,

ZORBA-I would first produce a mapping between the statements of T and T'. Then, starting with this initial mapping, ZORBA-I would extend the mapping, applying it to the axioms used in the proof of T, and identify analogous axioms in the domain of T'. These analogous axioms are used by a logic theorem prover to attempt a proof of T'. Thus, ZORBA-I drastically cuts down the search space of the theorem prover by focusing attention on a set of axioms that is much smaller than the set of all axioms in the domain of T'.

Notice here that the success of any such approach very much depends on whether the proof of the unknown theorem is, in fact, analogous to the given proof. That is, one needs to make the assumption—or determination, to use Weitzenfeld's term—that similarity in the statements of the theorems implies similarities in the proofs of the theorem. If this assumption does not hold for some pair of theorems, then analogy can actually be a hindrance. Given that the proofs of two theorems that look similar are in fact not similar, a system based on analogy is sure to waste much effort in computing the analogy, and then focusing on all the wrong axioms picked out by the analogy. A system that picks out axioms randomly would easily outperform the analogical system in this case.

My point is simply that the implicit meta-level assumption that might make the analogical system useful in some cases, severely limits its usefulness as a general heuristic. For instance, given the proof that there are as many perfect squares (1, 4, 9, etc.) as integers, an analogical system would have a very tough time trying to prove (or disprove) if there are as many real numbers as integers. To arrive at Cantor's diagonalization argument that proves there are more real numbers than integers requires a completely new way of looking at the numbers, possibly even coming up with a different set of axioms. Thus, any general purpose theorem prover that always tries to prove new theorems by analogy from past theorems is bound to discover only mundane theorems, and would never come up with anything creative. This is evident in the fact that no new and interesting theorem has ever been proven by any theorem prover based on analogy. (By 'new' I mean that the truth or falsity of the theorem is not yet known to mathematicians at large, and by 'interesting' I mean that the statement of the theorem is considered a research problem worth studying at least by some mathematicians.)

This argument can be extended to other computational systems that use analogy as a heuristic for generating supposedly better hypotheses [Carbonell 1986; Falkenhainer, Forbus and Gentner 1989; Holyoak and Thagard 1989], though different examples need to be considered for each system. I consider two recently developed systems here that try to put predictive analogy to work. Falkenhainer, Forbus and Gentner implemented a program called Structure Mapping Engine (SME) that computes similarities between the given representations of a source and a target. Now, since there can be many similarities between two given representations, SME focuses only on those similarities that are supported by Gentner's structure-mapping theory [1983]. According to this theory, which represents the source and the target as sets of predicate calculus formulas, it is 'good' to map two- or more-place relations (as opposed to one-place predicates called 'attributes'), and even 'better' to map those relations that are interrelated by higher-order relations (that is, relations that occur as arguments to other relations). Thus, in mapping the source situation 'water-flow' to the target situation 'heat-flow' in Figure 10.1, 'pressure,' rather than 'diameter,' is mapped onto 'temperature.' The 'goodness' of a mapping refers to its predictability, of course. That is, a mapping is better if it is more likely to make correct predictions about the target.

The problem here is that predictability depends on the autonomous structure of the external environment, and cannot be determined from the internal structure of a theory or a representation alone. I have already belabored this point in the last chapter. Systematicity, however, is a syntactic characteristic of a mapping between two representations. In equating the two, one commits the grave epistemological error of not only affirming that one's representations are always the 'right' ones and are 'complete,' but also that the external world is bound to conform to certain artificial features of these representations. Or, to look at it from another perspective, the reason systematicity works for this small and artificial example as it does is because the representations of the source and the target are specifically tailored to it. The background assumption needed for the analogy to be useful, namely that systematicity determines predictability, is blatantly made true in the given representations of the source and the target. As long as representations are tailored this way, systematicity would continue to give an illusion of success. However, if the representations are altered even slightly, systematicity fails miserably.

This point can be best appreciated by the examples provided by Hofstadter and Mitchell [1991, pp. 30–36.] Suppose the representation of the target included the information about the fact that the volume of the coffee in the beaker is greater than the volume of the ice cube [Figure 10.2]. Then systematicity alone would have no reason to prefer mapping 'pressure' to 'temperature' than to 'volume.' Or suppose that rate of flow was included in the representation of 'flow,' so that it became a five-place relation:

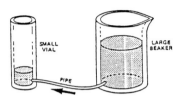

SOURCE SITUATION
(Water Flow)

TARGET SITUATION
(Heat Flow)

FIGURE 10.1 (a): Two physical situations involving flow. (From Falkenhainer et. al. [1989].)

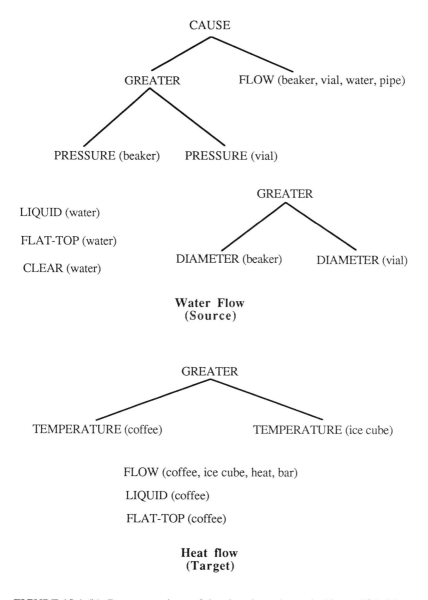

FIGURE 10.1 (b): Representations of the situations shown in Figure 10.1 (a). (From Falkenhainer et. al. [1989].)

GREATER

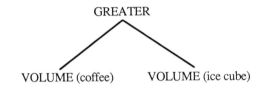

VOLUME (coffee)   VOLUME (ice cube)

GREATER

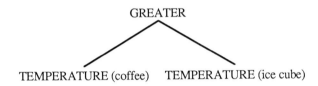

TEMPERATURE (coffee)   TEMPERATURE (ice cube)

FLOW (coffee, ice cube, heat, bar)

LIQUID (coffee)

FLAT-TOP (coffee)

**Heat flow
(Target)**

FIGURE 10.2: A different representation of the target situation.
(From Hofstadter and Mitchell [1990].)

'flow(beaker, vial, water, pipe, 10 cc/second).' One can go on and on here; it is quite easy to generate hordes of examples for which systematicity either does not pick the 'right' mapping, or picks the wrong one. (See also Carroll & Mack [1985, pp. 41–45], for further criticism of the structure mapping theory.)

The program Analogical Constraint Mapping Engine (ACME) designed by Holyoak and Thagard [1989] uses a slightly different approach and its authors argue that it does not have the same problems as SME. Like SME, ACME works with the given representations of the source and the target and tries to find a set of pairings between the terms of the two representations. Unlike SME, however, ACME uses a connectionist data structure and a spreading-activation relaxation algorithm to compute the analogical mapping. But since my criticism is not directed at how the mappings are computed, the details of the algorithm are irrelevant here.

ACME uses three criteria to evaluate which mappings are the 'right' ones: isomorphism, semantic similarity, and pragmatic centrality. While isomorphism and semantic similarity taken together amount somewhat loosely to Gentner's systematicity principle, it is the pragmatic centrality that is the main point of divergence between ACME and SME. The idea behind the pragmatism of ACME is to keep the search focused on those mappings that are of most interest to the user of the system. For instance, in the example of 'heat-flow' and 'water-flow,' suppose the representation of 'water-flow' included the facts that the volume of the water in the beaker is greater than the volume of the water in the vial, and this difference in volume is caused by the fact that the diameter of the beaker is greater than the diameter of the vial [Figure 10.3]. Now with the representation of 'heat-flow' containing the fact that the volume of the coffee is greater than the volume of the ice cube [Figure 10.2], ACME still does not try to map 'diameter' to 'temperature' and infer that the higher temperature of the coffee is caused by its greater volume because this is irrelevant to the goal of understanding the heat flow. This relevancy information, however, is supplied by the user, who assigns a higher weight to certain mappings.

Thus, we see that ACME is not all that much different from SME. It also constructs certain mappings—taking into account user preference besides systematicity—between the source and the target. The mappings are, however, still syntactic properties of the given representations of source and the target, and as such are no more than mirages as far as their ability to make predictions about the target is concerned.

The apparent success of SME and ACME has been demonstrated only in

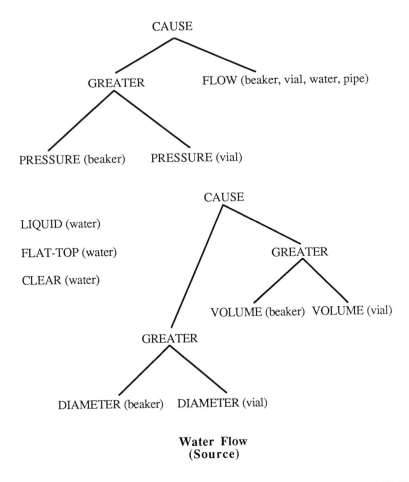

Water Flow
(Source)

FIGURE 10.3: Extended representation of the source situation used by ACME. (Based on Table 10 in Holyoak and Thagard [1989].)

small toy domains where the representations are all hand tailored, and where a solution to the target problem or a theory for the target phenomenon is already known to the person or persons who are coming up with the representations. In a real-world situation, when there is a real problem, the solution of which is not known but which it would be interesting to solve. (For example, a problem like the ones discussed in Gordon [1961] and Schön [1963]. See also §2.5.2). An approach based on SME and ACME would produce either only mundane theories and hypotheses, or none at all, for it would all depend on how the target is represented. And when one does not have a theory to explain the target phenomenon, or know how to solve the problem, it is hard to come up with the right representation in the first place: in fact, the key to problem solving lies in coming up with just such a representation.

To sum up, we see that predictability cannot be captured in the syntactic properties of the representations. Therefore, the use of predictive analogy—which essentially makes a hypothesis about the external environment based on some syntactic properties of the representations—as a general purpose heuristic in any domain depends crucially on whether the assumption that similarities between the given representations determine predictability is satisfied or not. To this end, perhaps the best approach to predictive analogy might be the one taken by Russell [1987]. Following Weitzenfeld's theory of analogy, which we discussed in the last chapter, Russell provided an explicit mechanism in his system for the user to add determinations. For example, if one wanted to say that analogies with respect to nationalities are relevant in determining the languages people speak, then one could put in a 'determination rule' saying that if two persons have the same nationality then they speak the same language. These determination rules were then used as logical axioms in generating analogical inferences. Thus, Weitzenfeld's second-order generalizations—the background assumptions of an analogical inference—were made explicit here. The resulting architecture is much cleaner, more efficient, less prone to erroneous inferences, and easier to adapt as background assumptions are changed in varying contexts.

Besides problem-solving, there is one other area in AI which has often used predictive analogy, namely learning [Winston 1978; 1981; Carbonell 1983; Greiner 1985]. There are two ways in which predictive analogy is associated with learning. One is as 'single-instance generalization,' and the other is as 'schema induction.' In single-instance generalization, one imputes a causal structure on a given representation of the source, thereby hypothesizing that certain properties imply certain other properties. Thus, a law seems to have been learned from an example. Clearly, this corresponds to the view of predictive analogy that justifies it as a first-order generalization, which we critically examined in the last chapter. The schema induction approach is somewhat more conservative. Here, after an analogy has been successfully used to predict something about the target, the analogy is abstracted to a general 'law-like' schema. It also sees predictive analogy as a first-order generalization, except that two confirming instances are required, one of which must be an experimental verification.

Before we address these uses of predictive analogy, we must distinguish between two forms of learning. One type of learning occurs when new information is gained from the environment. Examples of this type of learning are: learning that fluids tend to flow from a higher to a lower level, [a child] acquiring the notion of object permanence, learning one's way to the grocery store upon moving to a new town, noticing for the first time that the familiar figure of the Star of David has three parallelograms in it, etc. The other type of learning occurs when one notices some new connection between the pieces of knowledge that one already has, as in discovering a new theorem. Here all the relevant information is provided by the knowledge structures—or concept networks in our terminology—that the cognitive agent already had. There is no interaction with the environment, and no new information is gleaned from it. (Though, of course, if we take into account the cognitive relations of the concept networks, then the new information might be applicable to the environment in such a way that seems like the cognitive agent is getting new information from the environment. For instance, once I discover Pythagoras' theorem, then having the knowledge that John's farm is 4 miles due east from my place, and Bill's restaurant is 3 miles due north from John's farm, I can conclude that Bill's restaurant is 5 miles from my place. However, discovering the Pythagorean theorem itself—and by 'discovering' I mean coming up with the proof of it—does not require any new information from the environment.)

Now as far as learning of the first type is concerned, where new information is gained from the environment, learning by predictive analogy is no more than a myth. This point is made quite clearly and astutely by Russell [1987, pp. 96–97]. Whether the supposedly learned law is derived from single instance generalization, or from schema induction, its status remains essentially that of a conjecture, and since it does not say anything about the environment, there is nothing learned.

One might well argue here—an argument that is often advanced to justify the role of predictive analogy in learning—that the learning lies not in coming up with the generalization or the induced schema, but in using it to make a hypothesis about some unknown domain, and in trying to verify the hypothesis, for whether the hypothesis is confirmed or refuted, we end up learning something new about the unknown target. This verification step is incorporated in the schema induction approach even in generating the schema in the first place, for there must be at least one successful application of the analogy from the source to an unknown target before the schema is formed.

Notice, however, that by this argument any process that makes any kind of prediction about the target environment would qualify as an aid to learning. For example, consider generating random hypotheses. Even a random hypothesis, on being experimentally verified, would tell us something about the target environment. Or consider 'predictive disanalogy,' which works by noticing some existing similarities between the source and the target, and then, based on these similarities, it predicts that a certain characteristic of the source domain, about which it is not known if it exists in the target environment or not, *does not exist* in the target environment. The point here is simply that predictive analogy is no better tool in this sense of learning than any other process that also makes predictions about the target object, unless, of course, it can be shown that the real world is structured in such a way that the predictions made by predictive analogy are a better source of hypotheses than any other predictive process (such as predictive disanalogy). However, the search for any such blanket reason that shows why a hypothesis from predictive analogy is justified has been nothing but futile as I have discussed at length in the last chapter.

There remains one more sense of learning to consider, namely when learning involves noticing novel connections between existing knowledge structures. This is where we find that the AI approaches to analogy are most germane. One of the goals of cognition is clearly to strive for a certain economy of representation [Rosch 1978]. In this respect, the significance of noticing that two knowledge structures, acquired in quite different contexts, have similarities cannot be overemphasized, since one can replace the two structures with a single more abstract structure. Gentner's systematicity principle might serve well here to focus attention on highly structured similarities. Schema induction comes in handy to generate an abstracted model that unifies the source and target concept networks—all mathematical objects start out this way.

To sum up, we see that the main contribution of AI approaches to predictive analogy has been to develop techniques for computing existing similarities between the source and the target from their given representations—that is, syntactic analogy. Thus, while these approaches model some of the cognitive processes related to analogy and metaphor—such as highlighting and downplaying, generalization, abstraction [§7.4.1]—they leave creative analogies and similarity-creating projective metaphors completely out in the cold. These approaches to syntactic analogy can also model the cognitive process underlying suggestive metaphor, as long as the existing similarities are not seen as justifying the hypotheses generated by suggestive metaphor, and the metric of similarity is not used as a reflection of the potential of the source (as in picking the most similar source, because it is more likely to succeed).

10.4   A Computational Model of Creative Analogies: Douglas Hofstadter

In sharp contrast to all these approaches to analogy that have sought to focus on computing similarities between the existing descriptions of the source and the target, it was Douglas Hofstadter who realized that the crux of creativity lies in coming up with the right descriptions in the first place [Hofstadter 1981-85]. To study the cognitive process that generates different descriptions of the same object in different contexts, Hofstadter designed an elegantly simple, and yet surprisingly rich, microworld [Hofstadter 1984].

The objects of Hofstadter's microworld were strings of characters 'a' through 'z,' such as 'xyz,' 'abc,' and 'w.' Only a few concepts, such as 'copy' ('a' is a copy of 'a'), 'successor' ('d' is the successor of 'c'), and 'predecessor' ('w' is the predecessor of 'x') were allowed for describing the objects in this microworld. Yet, there were surprisingly many ways of describing any given object in this microworld. For instance, a seemingly simple object 'abc' could be described as "a three-character right-moving successor group starting with 'a'," "a three-character left-moving predecessor group starting with 'c'," "a (two-character) successor group followed by the successor of the last character of the group," and so on.

To model the effect of different contexts in selecting different descriptions of objects in the character-string microworld, Hofstadter considered proportional analogy relations of the form 'A is to B as C is to D' [§1.6.2]. Take the proportional analogy relations shown in Figure 10.4. Though the terms A, B and C are the same in all three analogies shown there, they need to be described differently for each analogy (or else the analogy cannot be comprehended). For instance, in 10.4(a), the term C is taken to be "a three-element right-moving successor group starting with 'i', the last element of which is a two-element copy group 'kk'." In 10.4(b), it is considered to be "a three-element left-moving predecessor group the first element of which is a two-element copy group 'kk' and the other two elements are single letters."

	A	**B**	**C**	**D**
(a)	aabc	aabd	ijkk	ijll
(b)	aabc	aabd	ijkk	hjkk
(c)	aabc	aabd	ijkk	ijkl

FIGURE 10.4: Proportional analogies in Hofstadter's micoworld of character strings. Even though the terms A, B and C are the same in each of the three analogies, they require different descriptions .

And in 10.4(c), the same term is described as "a four-character group with its last character as 'k'." In each case, it is the other terms of analogy relations (A, B and D) that affect which description of C is 'proper,' which, in turn, affects which descriptions of A, B and D are seen as 'proper.' Thus, the process of generating descriptions requires complex interactions between the descriptions of the four terms, for the description of each term affects the description of the other three terms, while, at the same time, being affected by them.

Hofstadter and his colleague Melanie Mitchell designed and implemented a computational system called Copycat that solves proportional analogy relations (produces the fourth term, given the other three) in this microworld of character strings. Copycat provides an excellent model of analogies that are not based on existing similarities but that create the similarities. Before examining this system, however, it would be useful to take a quick look at Evans' system for solving proportional analogies that was implemented in the early sixties [Evans 1963, 1968]. There is a special reason for taking this detour. Evans' system is very widely known, and is heralded for its success in solving the geometric analogy problems of intelligence tests. In fact, the perception of its success has been so complete that, until Hofstadter came up with his microworld, proportional analogies had ceased to be a domain for AI and cognitive modeling. Given this general feeling, it is necessary to highlight the limitations of Evans' system with respect to proportional analogy relations requiring redescription, in order to fully appreciate the significance of Hofstadter and Mitchell's work. This is, of course, not meant to devalue Evans' immense contribution in any way, which was quite remarkable, given the existing state of the art at the time, but only to point out that the interesting aspects of the proportional analogy relation were not even close to exhausted by Evans.

In fact, Evans himself was quite aware of the need for context sensitivity in generating the descriptions of the terms of the analogy relation. He even tried to incorporate context-sensitivity in his description-generating module in a somewhat primitive way. Seeing the need for redescription in the context of examples like those used by Evans, and understanding Evans' approach might help you to better appreciate the complexity of the task undertaken by Hofstadter and Mitchell.

10.4.1   An Aside: Context-Sensitivity of Descriptions in Evans' Approach

Evans was interested in building a computer program to solve proportional analogy relations involving configurations of geometric figures, such as the ones shown earlier in Chapter 1 (Figure 1.1). Specifically, the problem he had his program address was: given the three terms A, B, and C of a proportional analogy relation 'A is to B as C is to D,' choose the fourth term from a given set of five alternatives (Figure 10.5).

Evans' approach was to break this task into two stages. In the first stage, the objects A, B, C, and each of the five alternatives were broken into their respective components, and the relationships between these components were computed. For instance, in Figure 10.5, the object A would be decomposed as a triangle T1 and a triangle T2. The relationships between these two components would express the fact that T1 is inside T2. In our terminology of Chapter 5, this process can be seen as that of generating a *description* of each object A, B, C, etc. There is one other thing that Evans had his program do in the first stage, which was to figure out which of the component figures in each pair of objects are 'similar.' For instance, considering the pair (A, B) in Figure 10.5, it would compute that T2 and T3 are similar, and T1 and T3 are similar albeit of different sizes. In determining 'similarity,' the transformations that were factored out, besides a change of scale, included reflection and rotation.

In the second stage, Evans' program generated rules—there could be more than one—that convert object A into object B, taking into account the descriptions of A and B, and the similarity between their components, that were

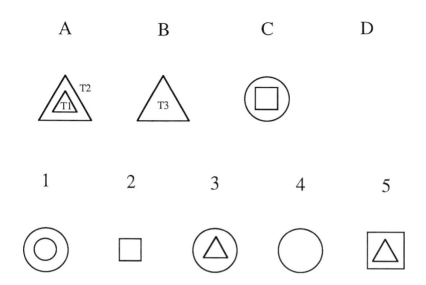

FIGURE 10.5: An example of the kind of geometric analogy problems solved by Evans' ANALOGY program. Given figures A, B and C, the program picks out the fourth figure D (from the five given alternatives, numbered 1 through 5) that best completes the analogy 'A is to B as C is to D'. The program picks out figure (4) in this exmple.

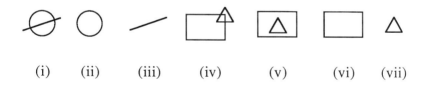

FIGURE 10.6: Figures for the quotation from Evans [1968].

(i)   (ii)   (iii)   (iv)   (v)

FIGURE 10.7: Figures for the quotation from Evans [1968].

produced in the first stage. Thus, for Figure 10.5, a rule would be to remove the inner triangle, while keeping the outer triangle the same. Another rule, for the same example, would be to remove the outer triangle, while making the inner triangle larger. Evans' next step was to generalize these rules, if necessary, so that they apply to the object C and convert it to one of the five given alternatives. For instance, a generalization of the first of the two rules mentioned above would be to remove the inner figure while keeping the outer figure the same. Finally, his program selected the most appropriate rule generalization based on a heuristic, and chose the alternative (from the given set of five) that resulted from applying this generalized rule to the object C.

Because his algorithm does not change the descriptions of the objects once they are derived in the first stage, it might appear at first that Evans overlooked the context-sensitivity of descriptions that is responsible for the creation of similarity in proportional analogies, such as the ones we discussed in Chapter 2 [§2.4.2, see also Figures 2.2 and 2.3]. However, on taking a closer look at his decomposition algorithm,[1] we find that Evans was acutely aware of this problem: to understand certain proportional analogy relations, the figures in which the objects A, B, C, and D are decomposed depend on one another. For instance, he wrote:

> "There appear to be two distinct approaches to the decomposition process: one can attempt to break up a figure on *Gestalt* criteria, such as some formalization of 'good continuation,' to separate, say, [Figure 10.6 (i)] into [Figure 10.6 (ii)] and [Figure 10.6 (iii)]. Alternatively one can perform the decomposition on the basis of information external to the figure itself, as in our case, from the other problem figures. ... [I]f Figure A consists of [Figure 10.6 (iv)] and Figure B of [Figure 10.6 (v)], it would be

---

[1]See Evans [1968], Sec. 5.3.3, pp. 302–306.

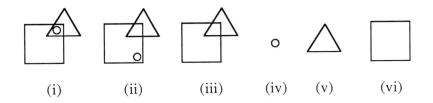

(i)   (ii)   (iii)   (iv)   (v)   (vi)

FIGURE 10.8: Figures for the quotation from Evans [1968].

natural, having found, trivially, that Figure B consists of two distinct pieces, [Figure 10.6 (vi)] and [Figure 10.6 (vii)], to attempt
to find one or both of these subfigures, up to similarity transformation, in Figure A. Some combination of these 'intrinsic' and
'context' heuristics should be suitable as the basis for a quite
useful decomposition program..."[Evans 1968, p. 303].

And later...

"A figure may of course be susceptible to various decompositions.
Which, if any, of these is appropriate depends on the other figures
of the problem. In the terms we have used, 'intrinsic' decomposition is inadequate and 'context' decomposition methods, on which
we have based our decomposition program, must be used. For example, Figure A = [Figure 10.7 (i)] and Figure B = [Figure 10.7
(ii)] require a decomposition of A into [Figure 10.7 (ii)] and [Fig-
ure 10.7 (iii)] (thus the rule generated will involve the removal
of the [Figure 10.7 (iii)]), whereas with the same Figure A, Figure B = [Figure 10.7 (iv)] will require decomposition of A into
[Figure 10.7 (iv)] and [Figure 10.7 (v)]" [Evans 1968, p. 305].

Since the description of any object very much depends on the figures into
which it is decomposed, Evans' program did have some capability to handle
redescription in proportional analogy relations, where the description of an
object is not kept fixed, but allowed to change based on the context provided
by the other figures.

Yet, Evans' program had this capability in a very limited way. First of all,
even though 'contextual' decomposition is highly desirable, Evans observed
that context alone is insufficient in certain situations to provide the right
decomposition.

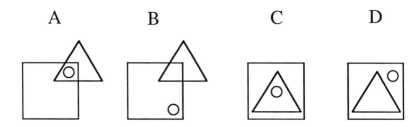

FIGURE 10.9: A proportional analogy relation for which 'context' decomposition fails. To understand this analogy requires that each of the Figures A and B be decomposed in terms of a triangle, a square, and a circle.

"If Figure A is [Figure 10.8 (i)] and Figure B is [Figure 10.8 (ii)], then viewing these figures as each consisting of the parts [Figure 10.8 (iii)] and [Figure 10.8 (iv)] will fail if the desired rule involves, say, removing the [Figure 10.8 (iv)] from inside the [Figure 10.8 (v)] but leaving it inside the [Figure 10.8 (vi)]." [Evans 1968, p. 306].

The proportional analogy relation shown in Figure 10.9 involves such a rule. Evans' proposed solution to this limitation was to incorporate into the decomposition program some 'intrinsic' criteria, such as 'look at all decompositions into simple-closed-curve subfigures.' However, the 'intrinsic' criteria necessary to 'correctly' decompose the figures would vary quite a bit from case to case. For instance, the intrinsic criterion would not work for the proportional analogy relation shown in Figure 10.10 (or those shown in Figures 2.2 and 2.3 of Chapter 2), where there are just too many ways to break each of

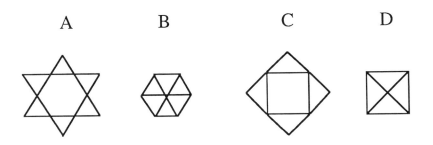

FIGURE 10.10: A proportional analogy relation for which both 'intrinsic' and 'context' decompositions fail. Context decomposition fails because none of the figures breaks easily into 'simple' figures that can be used as contextual clues for decomposing other figures. Intrinsic decomposition fails because there are too many ways to break each figure into simply-closed-curve subfigures.

the figures into simply-closed-curve subfigures. Moreover, for this example, Evans' 'context' decomposition would not work either, because he required that at least one of the objects A and B can be decomposed simply in a 'natural' way. (His program would decompose the simpler of the objects A and B into subfigures, and then look for occurrences of these subfigures in the more complex of the two objects.)

A second major limitation of Evans' approach comes from the fact that the primitive relations and properties in terms of which a figure can be described are all decided beforehand. Thus, Evans' program cannot solve the proportional analogy relation of Figure 10.11 (or that of Figure 2.2 of Chapter 2) because it lacks the primitives to describe eccentricity and its orientation. Of course, one can correct this by adding the required primitives, but then there are always more examples that involve still new primitives.

One might quite reasonably argue here that, in a computational setting at least, the primitives of the description must be provided to the system explicitly. (Since, otherwise, where would they come from?) But my point is simply that if one wants to admit richness of descriptions, and the ability to describe a figure using different sets of primitives, the set of all possible primitives may become so large that even simple figures would end up having a great many descriptions. Then it would be quite inefficient to precompute them all, in Evans' style, especially since most of them would not be needed

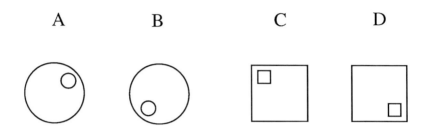

FIGURE 10.11: A proportional analogy relation which shows the limitation placed by choosing a priori the relations and attributes in terms of which the figures can be described. Evans' program cannot handle this analogy because it is not provided with relations to represent eccentricity and its orientation.

in any given context.

The problem these examples bring out is the need to use the relations and properties of the other figures, besides their subfigures, as contextual clues to the decomposition process, and even to choose the relations and properties in terms of which the figures would be described after looking at all the figures. The architecture of Evans' program is ill suited to have this flexibility because the process of decomposing a figure, and that of computing the properties and relations between its subfigures are done in separate stages; and each figure is processed separately. What is needed is some way of making the figures A, B, and C *interact,* and making the subfigures into which they are decomposed— as well as the properties and relations between these subfigures—depend on the result of this interaction. This is exactly how Douglas Hofstadter approached the problem about twenty years later.

10.4.2   Resumption: Hofstadter and Mitchell's Copycat

Let us now return to Hofstadter's microworld of character strings. We have already seen some examples of proportional analogy relations in this domain [Figure 10.4] that showed that the descriptions of the objects of an analogy need to be dynamically generated. Some other interesting examples given by Hofstadter might provide a glimpse of the subtlety of this innocent looking domain. Consider the three examples shown in Figure 10.12. In 10.12(a),

	A	**B**	**C**	**D**
(a)	abc	abd	xyz	wyz
(b)	abc	abd	mrrjjj	mrrjjjj
(c)	abc	abd	mrrjjj	mrrkkk

FIGURE 10.12: More examples of proportional analogies in Hofstadter's microworld of character strings that require redescriptions.

the concepts 'first' and 'successor' in A are connected with the concepts 'last' and 'predecessor,' respectively, in C; a phenomenon that Hofstadter refers to as *slipping*. (In going from A to C, 'successor' *slips* into 'predecessor.') In 10.12(b), the succession order of a character in A (described as a successor group starting with 'a') is slipped into the length of the corresponding copy group in C (described as three copy groups of increasing lengths). In 10.12(c), where the terms A, B and C are the same as in (b), A and C are described as three-element sequences each, and the individual elements (characters) in A are equated with the elements (copy groups) in the corresponding positions in C. These examples reveal a surprising degree of conceptual depth that can be attained in this microworld.

Hofstadter and Mitchell's Copycat program is designed to generate the fourth term of the proportional analogy relation given the other three. Unlike Evans' approach, Copycat does not compute descriptions of the objects of the proportional analogy in a separate initial module. Instead, the task of generating the descriptions is seen as an inseparable part of comprehending the analogy. A detailed account of Copycat's design, implementation, and several examples of analogies solved by it can be found in Hofstadter [1984], Mitchell and Hofstadter [1989; 1990a; 1990b], and Hofstadter and Mitchell [1991]. Here, I only summarize some of its key features and then discuss its significance in modeling creative analogies.

The architecture of Copycat is inspired by the biological processes that take place inside a cell, where the seemingly random activities of various simple enzymes end up building quite complex products such as proteins.

Inside the cell there is no central process or main enzyme that oversees or controls the final product. Nor is there any kind of built-in hierarchy that makes certain enzymes more influential than others. Thus, the contribution of each individual enzyme taken by itself is insignificant. Yet, a large number of cooperating individual enzymes can collectively assemble a complex biomolecule.

There are two key features of Copycat that reflect this underlying biological metaphor. One is its distributed architecture, where the whole process of generating descriptions and creating mappings between the descriptions is carried out by small simple agents called *codelets*. For example, a codelet might notice that there is a 'successor' relation between the neighboring characters 'a' and 'b,' an observation that might or might not turn out to be of significance eventually. Thus, codelets can be seen as counterparts of enzymes, where the action of each codelet by itself is insignificant, but a bunch of codelets together can lead to a complex and insightful description of the object. In this respect, Copycat is similar to the Hearsay II speech-understanding system [Erman *et al.* 1980].

The other key feature that Copycat borrows from its biological source is the probabilistic interaction of the processes. The enzymes inside a cell all seem to act randomly, if we look at them microscopically. Yet, a macroscopic order emerges from this apparent random interaction. A similar approach is taken in Copycat by incorporating probabilistic parameters at various places. This probabilistic approach of Copycat makes it quite unique and unlike other distributed AI systems like Hearsay II; and, as we see later, it is a crucial factor in Copycat's ability to model human creativity.

There are three major components of Copycat. There is the *slipnet,* a network of Platonic concepts, which is somewhat analogous to our notion of a concept network. The slipnet contains nodes representing various Platonic concepts such as 'opposite,' 'successor,' etc. and links between the nodes that capture the relationships between the concepts. The length of a link between two nodes reflects their conceptual proximity.

The slipnet is dynamic in the sense that the nodes acquire different levels of activation, which decay over time, and they spread their activation to neighboring nodes, where neighborhood is defined in terms of conceptual proximity (length of the link). Moreover, the lengths of the links themselves can also change, since every link has some label associated with it that corresponds to a node of the slipnet, and when that node is activated, all the links that have that label get shortened. For instance, the nodes 'successor' and 'predecessor' are connected by a link that has the label 'opposite.' When the node representing the concept 'opposite' is activated, the nodes 'successor' and 'predecessor' are brought in closer proximity (as well as other nodes, such as 'leftmost' and 'rightmost,' that are linked by 'opposite' too).

There is also a degree of depth associated with each concept in the slipnet. For instance, the concept 'opposite' is deemed deeper than the concept 'successor,' which in turn is considered 'deeper' than the concept 'a.' Depth is a static notion and reflects the abstractness of a concept. In a somewhat crude comparison, it can be likened to the order of a relation in logic—the second-order relation is deeper than the first-order relation, which in turn is deeper than the objects. Depth is used to constrain the conceptual slippage (a term Hofstadter uses to refer to the temporary and context-dependent identification of two distinct concepts as one, such as identifying 'successor' with 'predecessor' in comprehending the analogy " 'abc' is to 'abd' as 'xyz' is to 'wyz' "), so that a deeper concept is more likely to maintain its identity and less likely to slip into another concept.

The second major component of Copycat is the *workspace,* which initially contains the actual raw data (the terms of the analogy) but later ends up containing instances of the slipnet concepts that form the descriptions of the terms. Loosely speaking, the initial state of the workspace can be identified with our sensory motor data set that is being organized by a concept network (the slipnet) via a cognitive relation (instances). It is the codelets that organize the data in the workspace into various descriptions. For instance, in solving the analogy " 'aabc' is to 'aabd' as 'ijkk' is to what?" a codelet might notice that the neighboring objects 'a' and 'a' in 'aabd' are the same, and chunk them together in a 'sameness' group.

Each object in the workspace is assigned a measure of salience that determines how likely it is that the object would attract the attention of codelets. The salience is a dynamic property that depends on the extent to which the current descriptions of the object are built out of the highly activated nodes of the slipnet, and on how isolated that object is with respect to the other objects in the Workspace. Both these factors tend to increase the salience. The idea here is that if an object is currently being described in terms of highly active nodes, it should have a high salience. Also, an isolated object is given a high salience because, given the goal of integrating all objects into instances of slipnet concepts, if an object is isolated, then it needs more attention.

Finally, there is the *coderack,* which is a pool of codelets that are waiting to be run. Each codelet in the coderack is assigned a measure of urgency that determines how likely that codelet is to be chosen to be executed in the near future. At each time step, a codelet is picked up from the coderack and executed. The decision which codelet to run depends on the urgencies of the codelets. However, this decision is made on a probabilistic basis, and not in the strict order of decreasing urgencies. That is, while a low urgency codelet is less likely to be picked up in favor of a higher urgency codelet, it is possible nonetheless.

Codelets are the agents actually responsible for organizing the workspace, bringing concepts from the slipnet to bear on the items and structures in the workspace, and for changing the activation levels of concepts in the slipnet depending on how things stand in the workspace. There are top-down codelets, which are activated in response to the activation levels in the slipnet, that look for particular features in the objects in the workspace; and there are bottom-up codelets that look around for anything interesting in the character strings.

As codelets are being removed from the coderack and executed, new codelets are constantly being added to the coderack in three ways. First, bottom-up codelets are always being added to the coderack. Second, as the slipnet activation pattern changes, new top-down codelets are added to the pool of waiting codelets in response. Finally, some codelets, when they are executed, create follow-up codelets, which are added to the coderack.

All Copycat runs start out with a preassigned set of bottom-up codelets in the coderack and the three given terms of the proportional analogy in the workspace. This situation quickly changes, though, as the objects in the workspace influence the activation levels of the slipnet, which in turn influence the descriptions being generated in the workspace. The system as a whole strives for a unified structure in which—given the terms A, B, and C of the analogy relation "A is to B as C is to what?"—the descriptions of A, B and C are such that there is a rule for changing A into B, and a mapping (set of 'bridges') is built between A and C. The fourth term is then arrived at by applying the translated (or 'slipped') rule, given the A-to-C bridges, to the description of C, while extending the mapping between A and C to B and the fourth term.

The probabilistic approach of Copycat is evident in two of its three components. In the workspace, it is incorporated in the salience of the objects, which makes some objects more *likely* to receive attention than others. In the coderack, it is evidenced in the urgency levels of the codelets, which make some codelets more *likely* to be executed than others. There is an overall controlling parameter called *temperature* that controls how these likelihoods are actually determined from the length of the links, salience of the objects, or the urgency levels, with low temperatures resulting in large variations in the probabilities, and vice-versa. For instance, if a codelet X in the coderack has twice as high an urgency level as another codelet Y, then if the temperature is high the ratio of the probability that X will be chosen to the probability that Y will be chosen would be much less than two. On the other hand, if the temperature is low, the ratio would be much larger than two. Intuitively, at higher temperatures the system is more random (that is, unbiased) and at lower temperature it is more biased (that is, non-random). The temperature is computed from the degree of overall structure seen in the workspace. (In the original design, the slipnet was also supposed to be probabilistic in the sense that if any concept node were activated, its activation level would be *likely* to propagate to the neighboring nodes, with the likelihood depending on the length of the link connecting the activated node to the neighboring node. In the Copycat implementation, however, spreading of activation was kept deterministic. Activation levels themselves, though, make the slipnet probabilistic in two ways. One is that they are used probabilistically by codelets—a slipnet node with a high activation level is more likely to be used by a codelet in an actual description. The other is that the activation of a node in the slipnet affects the lengths of all those links that are labeled by that node, thereby affecting slippage).

At the macro level, the nondeterminism of Copycat is felt in that, given the three terms of the analogy, the program does not always come up with the same fourth term. For example, in a thousand runs of the program with the analogy " 'abc' is to 'abd' as 'mrrjjj' is to what?", the answer 'mrrkkk' was given 705 times, 'mrrjjk' 203 times, 'mrrjkk' 45 times, 'mrrjjjj' 39 times, 'mrrddd' six times, and 'mrrjjd' two times. Notice that each answer involves a different set of descriptions for the three given terms, and different ways of slipping the descriptions and making bridges. Thus, though the program shows a clear statistical preference for certain descriptions and structural organization, it is nonetheless capable of coming up with radically new ways of looking at the terms, which might or might not turn out to be insightful and creative.

It is this nondeterminism of Copycat that makes it such an attractive model of human creativity, and specifically of creative analogies. The research on human creativity has shown—and the history of our civilization clearly and unambiguously attests to it—that all insightful ideas are initially felt to be radical, offbeat, and shocking. We have already discussed in earlier chapters Schön's study of how the innovation in the synthetic-fiber paintbrush came about [Schön 1963]. One is also reminded of Gordon's *making the familiar strange* [1961] where it is suggested that in order to solve some particularly intriguing problem about a familiar situation or product, one must view it in a strange way—a suggestion that was based on observing several brain-storming sessions where a group of people was trying to solve some real problem about some real product. In the history of science and mathematics also we find that all creative insights were considered radical at the time they were first proposed. One is reminded here of Kepler's idea that the Sun might be the object around which the Earth revolves rather than vice-versa, Huygen's idea that light might be a wave, the quantum mechanical notion that particles behave like waves, Einstein's concept that mass and energy are interconvertible, etc.

One interesting thing about this aspect of creativity is that it defies a deterministic characterization. While seeking the most similar source, which is the basis of predictive analogy, offers a clear criterion for ordering the prospective source domains, seeking a 'strange' source domain presents no such clear choice. Given a certain representation of the target domain, there might be many possible source domains that are radically different from it, and each one might be different in a different way. Moreover, most of these source domains are likely to result in little or no creative insight into the target environment. This is precisely why creativity is so hard to teach even to humans, let alone to model computationally.

So while it is the radical ideas that might lead to creative insights, one cannot encourage them indiscriminately, since otherwise much wasted effort would be incurred. However, if a radical idea seems to be promising, it should be allowed to persist at least long enough so that its full impact can be assessed before a decision is made to accept or reject it. Interestingly, the history of humanity itself shows a manifestation of this principle. While people and institutions are generally conservative, revolutionary ideas do emerge and become accepted from time to time.

Thus, a deterministic approach faces a no-win situation. If it tries all 'strange' ways of looking at the target, then there may be a great deal of wasted effort, for most of these would lead to nothing interesting. If it sticks to 'familiar' ways, then no creative insights would be possible. If one tries to 'mix,' or 'dovetail,' the familiar ways with the strange ways, the problem is that there are so many strange ways, and one cannot know a priori which of them are going to be promising.

This problem is beautifully solved by Hofstadter and Mitchell by incorporating nondeterminism in their architecture, which results in an effect they refer to as a *parallel terraced scan*. Many ways of looking at the target are explored simultaneously. When a path looks promising, the probabilities are changed to reflect that, and it is more likely that the path will be explored further. On the other hand, when a pattern seems to be emerging, even less likely paths that fit that pattern are explored. This is akin to the situation when, once the idea that the paintbrush might work like a pump begins to take hold, even those hypotheses that would be considered totally offbeat by themselves—such as that the spaces between the fibers might hold the paint—become candidates for experimentation and verification.

At the macro level, this effect is visible in the fact that, while most of the time the program produces somewhat conservative—reasonable but not always very imaginative or insightful—answers, it does come up with deeply insightful answers sometimes. (And, of course, it also comes up with some very mundane and literal answers. Perhaps this only goes to show that creativity and extreme literal mindedness might be two sides of the same coin.)[2]

To sum up this discussion, Hofstadter and Mitchell's Copycat remains the only computational system to date that models creative analogies in a real sense. What now remains to be seen is how these ideas can be applied to some real-world domain. Hofstadter and his colleague Robert French have already embarked on a new project, called Tabletop, where the Copycat architecture is being applied to solving interpretive analogies in a different microworld [French and Hofstadter 1991]. The Tabletop microworld consists of the top of a table on which several objects (like cups, saucers, glasses, salt shakers, and so on) are placed. Two subjects, Henry and Eliza, sit on opposite ends of the table. Henry reaches out and touches an object on the table. Eliza is now asked to do the same thing as Henry. Thus, the problem for Eliza is to interpret Henry's action from her own point of view and carry it out. This microworld has more of a real-world flavor, and does not have the artificial aura that always surrounds proportional analogies no matter

---

[2]I am reminded here of an anecdote recounted by Hofstadter: "[W]hen I gave a lecture on analogies in the Physics Department at the California Institute of Technology several years ago, one Richard Feynman sat in the front row and bantered with me all the way through the lecture... [H]e would reliably answer each question 'What is to X as 4 is to A?' [as in 'What is to 151 as 4 is to 141'] with the same answer '4!,' and insist that it was good answer, probably the best. It seemed to me that Feynman not only was acting the part of the 'village-idiot' but even was relishing it. It was hard to tell how much he was playing devil's advocate and how much he was sincere... [After three years,] I ran into Richard Feynman at a conference. I reminded him of my lecture at CalTech three years earlier; his somewhat vague recollection of it was that it was 'silly.' I took that as a charitable way of saying that he hadn't seen any point in it. Which made me think that maybe his 'village-idiot' stance was due to genuine puzzlement, and not just an act." [Hofstadter 1985, p. 574 and p. 603]

what their domain.

One still wonders if the process of redescription and creation of similarity cannot be studied directly in a real-world domain. I believe that it can be, and with the existing state of technology in AI. This, precisely, is the subject of our discussion in the next section.

10.5   Projective (Similarity-Creating) Metaphor in Artificial Intelligence

We have seen that all computational approaches to metaphor and analogy have remained focused on syntactic metaphors and analogies. Hofstadter and Mitchell's Copycat provides a notable exception, but it is confined to an artificial microworld. Does this mean that the advent of a computational system that can model similarity-creating metaphors and analogies in a real-world domain must await many more years of theoretical research?

On the contrary, I would like to argue in this section that the AI technology for modeling projective metaphors and creative analogies already exists. In fact, once we stop using the terms 'metaphor' and 'analogy' to seek out AI systems that are capable of displaying the creation of similarity, and look for the actual process of redescription that underlies creative metaphors and analogies, we find, perhaps somewhat surprisingly, that there are already many computational systems that are capable of producing creative instances of metaphor or analogy, though the creativity of these computational systems has not been studied as such.

To make this argument, I start by arguing that the process of projection, which brings about the redescription that is required by creative metaphors and analogies, can best be seen as 'top-down' grouping, something that is quite commonplace in computational systems. Then, I discuss the issue of novel projection *vs.* conventional projection, since only the former can give rise to creative metaphors and analogies. Finally, I show how the creation of similarity can be explained from this perspective.

10.5.1   Projection as 'Top-Down' Grouping

Recall from our discussion in Chapter 5 that projection is the process of integrating the sensorimotor data set, which is the perceptual encoding of the environment, into a given concept network, such that the structure of the concept network is kept invariant, but the correspondence between the concepts and the chunks of the sensorimotor data set—or, in other words, the grouping or ontology of the sensorimotor data set—is altered. Now in order to find an equivalent mechanism, if one exists, in the domain of existing computational systems we must first determine what a concept network and a sensorimotor data set mean in the context of such systems.

As emphasized in Chapter 5, a sensorimotor data set is the input that forms the raw material for conceptualization, and concept networks provide abstract symbols that are used for structuring the sensorimotor data set. For instance, when we see a birch tree, the sensory stimuli that our eyes receive form the sensorimotor data set, which is categorized as a 'birch tree' in the conceptualization process.

Now there are many computational systems in which the input data forms the raw material that is organized in terms of abstract symbols in the course of processing. For instance, consider a parser for a formal language—a very commonplace computational system. The input to the parser is a string of characters. Assuming that the string is well-formed in the formal language, the parser will end up representing it as a parse tree. Here, the input string can be thought of as a sensorimotor data set. Also, the words (terminals) and syntactic categories (non terminals) appearing in a parse tree can be likened to the symbols of a concept network—the grammar of the formal language relates the terminals and non-terminals in specific ways like the operational structure of a concept network. Thus, the process of parsing becomes essentially that of integrating the sensorimotor data set (the input string) into the abstract structure of the concept network (the grammar of the language). But this is precisely what we have called the process of conceptualization—a process that works by forming a cognitive relation between a concept network and a sensorimotor data set.

Indeed, as simple and commonplace as the example of a parser is, it helps to illustrate many, if not all, aspects of the conceptualization process in a computational setting. For instance, notice that the input string, the sensorimotor data set, is independently structured. The order of the symbols in the string is something that the parser cannot alter. At the same time, the structure of the language, the concept network, is also autonomous. It does not depend on the input string. The interactive nature of the conceptualization process is also clearly brought out in this example, since the parse-tree corresponding to any given input string is truly determined in part by the structure of the language and in part by the structure of the string.

This example also helps to highlight the difference between the mechanisms of projection and accommodation. Consider projection first. It corresponds to the 'top-down' grouping in which the rules of the grammar (the structure of the concept network) are kept invariant but the grouping of the input string—which groups of symbols are assigned to which non-terminals—is altered to maintain coherency. Note here that coherency refers to matching the structure of the grammar to the structure of the string; or, in other words, to the condition that the string can be parsed in the grammar.

It must be emphasized that my use of the term 'top-down' here is quite different, hence the quotation marks, from its traditional usage in the context of parsing as well as many other computational systems. In parsing, for instance, the terms top-down and bottom-up refer to two different strategies that can be used to determine whether the input string can be made to correspond to the grammar of the formal language. In the top-down strategy, one applies the rules of the grammar in a certain order to enumerate parse-trees, checking at each step to see if the current parse-tree corresponds to the input string. In the bottom-up strategy, on the other hand, one starts with the input string, and produces all possible partial parses of it until a complete parse-tree is produced. However, in our sense, both these strategies would be called 'top-down' processes, the reason being that even in the bottom-up parsing, the input string is being integrated into the structure of the grammar, or in other words the sensorimotor data set is being organized in terms of the concept network.

A 'bottom-up' approach in my sense corresponds to the mechanism of accommodation. Recall that in accommodation, the ontology and the grouping of the sensorimotor data set is fixed, and it is the structure of the concept network that must conform. In the context of the parser, it means that the input string is already grouped in certain ways, and the goal is to modify the structure of the grammar so that the input-string can be parsed. This is precisely what grammar learning algorithms attempt to achieve. The process of accommodation, thus, is manifested in various machine learning systems.

My focus of interest here being the mechanism of projection, it must be noted that the corresponding 'top-down' grouping is performed by many computational systems. A scene-analysis system that produces a verbal description or a semantic-net-like representation of an image on the basis of its representation in the form of an array of pixels, is essentially carrying out a projection by grouping the pixels and making the 'groups' correspond to abstract concepts such as 'house' and 'roof.' A medical diagnosis expert system, in producing a diagnosis from the symptoms, is projecting the concept network of diseases onto the set of given symptoms. When a story-understanding system organizes the narrative information in the story as a frame or a script, it is essentially projecting the concept network that is the frame or the script onto the input sensorimotor data set that is the text of the story.

10.5.2   Novel vs. Conventional Projection

Given that many computational systems are capable of projection, coupled with the thesis that projection is the process underlying metaphors, we naturally ask: Can a computational system capable of projection also produce creative metaphors? To answer this question, we have to remind ourselves that not all projections produce metaphors, but only novel projections. That is, to recognize a body of clouds in the sky as 'clouds' also involves projection, since one has to group the perceptual field appropriately and link it with the concept 'clouds' in order to make the recognition. This act of recognition, however, is not metaphorical since the grouping, as well as the association of the grouping with the concept, is conventional. But to recognize in the body of clouds a 'kangaroo' is a novel projection, and might be considered metaphorical.

So to answer the question above, we first must distinguish between conventional and novel projections in the context of computational systems. Notice that this distinction cannot be made on the basis of familiarity with the stimulus. That is, we cannot say that the first time a parser encounters a sentence, its recognition amounts to a novel projection. This would be like arguing that the first time I see a cow I have never seen before, and recognize it as a 'cow,' I produce a creative metaphor.

Before addressing this issue in a computational setting, let us see how the corresponding problem of separating the metaphorical from the conventional is addressed in the context of human cognition. One approach is to assign 'conventional' referents (which are parts of the external world) to all the concepts. Indeed, we automatically assign most objects and events in the world (which we access through the sensorimotor data set) to certain concepts for biological or cultural reasons, as in recognizing an object as a 'cow' almost effortlessly. It merely reflects the intersubjective everyday usage of the concepts in any given society. Given the conventional referents of the concepts, any projection that associates a concept with an object in the world that is not the conventional referent of the concept can be dubbed 'novel.' Indeed, this dual or split reference—one conventional and one sustained by the novel projection—is sometimes touted as the most characteristic feature of metaphors [Ricoeur 1976].

Notice, however, that this method of distinguishing between conventional and novel projections requires the God's-eye view of the external world and the cognitive agent. This is because when I see something and recognize it as a 'horse,' to determine whether this projection is conventional or novel I need to know that the object I see is really a horse; in other words, whether the object is included in the conventional referent of 'horse' or not. But how can I know that, unless I have some way of accessing the conventional referent of 'horse'? Though for computational systems the designer or the user of the system has the necessary God's-eye view, for cognitive modeling of similarity-creating metaphors one must be able to characterize novel projections without resorting to the God's-eye view.

While I have discussed this problem elsewhere at length [Indurkhya, in preparation], for my purpose here I only need to note that since concepts are internal and fully accessible to the cognitive agent, if the notion of 'conventional' is introduced from the point of view of conceptualization, then no God's-eye view is required. Thus, given some object (part of the sensorimotor data set), a certain conceptualization of it is viewed as 'conventional' by the cognitive agent, and any other conceptualization of it would then be called 'novel.' For instance, when I look at clouds and see a kangaroo there, what makes it a novel projection is the fact that I am aware, at the same time, that it is a group of clouds, which is the conventional conceptualization of what I am seeing. In this way, the split-reference characteristic of metaphors is turned into split-conceptualization.

This however, only covers those novel projections that have been termed by Gordon [1961, pp. 35–36] as 'making the familiar strange.' There is the familiar (conventional) conceptualization of the object or event. Then in making a novel projection with another concept network, the familiar object or event is made to appear strange. There is another class of novel projections, corresponding to Gordon's 'making the strange familiar,' in which there does not exist any conventional conceptualization of the object or event, and therefore any projection is novel. For instance, on looking at aurora borealis or riding a roller coaster for the first time, one may feel completely at a loss for words to describe the sensations that one is experiencing. In such situation, any conceptualization (description) that one can come up with is going to be metaphorical. To identify such projections as 'novel,' the cognitive agent needs to be able to deem certain sensorimotor data sets as non-conceptual. *Any* conceptualization of a non-conceptual sensorimotor data set would be a novel projection, and hence metaphorical.

Let us now apply these insights to computational systems, so that we can see which systems are capable of making novel projections, or metaphors, and which are not. Since we have already talked a bit about parsers, let me begin by considering the example of a parser for Natural Language, say a fragment of English. I have already noted that when the parser produces a parse-tree (or a set of parse-trees) when presented with a well-formed expression or sentence of the fragment, it is essentially projecting the concept network that is the grammar of the fragment onto the sensorimotor data set that is the input expression. Now each of these projections must be dubbed conventional, whether we consider it from the God's eye-view or the parser's eye-view, because the correspondence between the parts of the input expression and the syntactic categories of the grammar is both something intended by the designer of the parser and something that the parser naturally comes up with.

We then ask: Can such a parser ever produce a novel projection? Let us see. Consider first the possibility of 'making the familiar strange.' That is, for an input expression that can be parsed by the parser, we ask whether it can be parsed in a non-conventional way. The answer is negative because the groupings of the input expression and their correspondence with the non-terminals of the grammar are fixed by the grammar and built into the parser. It is as if the projection mechanism is hard-wired in the parser, since given any expression there is only one unique way to integrate it into the concept network of the grammar.

I must emphasize that I am not talking about ambiguities here. Any reasonable parser for a natural language is bound to have ambiguities—in fact, this is why I chose the example of a parser for a natural language rather than a formal language. But all the ambiguities are already a part of the grammar, at least in the way I am envisioning this parser. The word 'deep' might enter into different combinations with the other words of the sentence, but it would not correspond to the word 'peep.' This point can be appreciated in another way by considering the fact that in everyday language, we often use ambiguous expressions but their dual or multi-fold conceptualizations are not termed metaphorical. For instance, 'Can you drive?' can be a genuine query or an indirect request, but both these conceptualizations of it would be called conventional.

Given that there is no possibility of having a dual conceptualization here, let us explore the other alternative for creating novel projections, which is to have the parser project its concept network onto those sensorimotor data sets for which no conventional conceptualization exists. This amounts to parsing a sentence outside the fragment for which the grammar was written, by using the same grammar rules. But any such attempt would result in an abrupt 'illegal syntax' or 'word not in the lexicon' response. Thus, we find our parser quite incapable of producing novel projections.

The reason for this failure is that a parser works in a noise-free and definitive domain. A word is either a member of the lexicon, or is not—there is no in-between. And when it is a member, there is no doubt as to what it is (notwithstanding ambiguities, of course). Does this mean that if we modify our example to work in a noisy and uncertain domain, it would be able to generate novel projections? Let us see.

There are several examples of AI systems that typically work on a noisy domain: speech understanding systems, machine vision systems, handwriting recognition systems, just to mention a few. Since I started with the parser, let me choose a speech understanding system, say Hearsay-II [Erman *et al.* 1980],[3] as the example of a computational system that has a 'top-down' mechanism and that works in a noisy domain. Hearsay-II is an AI system that recognizes a small subset of spoken English. A person speaks in front of a microphone and Hearsay-II produces a written version of the speech. The environment is typically noisy: there are individual variations, accents, presence of other sources of sound, reflected sound from the surrounding objects etc. to contaminate the speech. To recognize speech amidst all this noise, the system makes several assumptions about what the speech is likely to be. This bias is reflected in the organization and the rules of the system. The important thing to note with this example is that there is no pre-established correspondence between the acoustic pattern received from the microphone and the lexicon of the system.

Now to give the system a capability of producing novel projections, suppose that the speech recognition system has two modules: one containing the rules for recognizing a subset of English and the other containing the rules for recognizing a subset of French. Each of these sets of rules forms a concept network. Now suppose that the system is presented with an acoustic pattern from the microphone, which it recognizes as some sentence in French. That, then, becomes the conventional conceptualization of the input pattern. But what if we were to force the system to recognize the input pattern using the rules of English. While in most instances the system would probably fail, it is

---

[3]In what follows, I am idealizing Hearsay-II for the sake of my argument. The idealization, however, is not unrealistic. In fact speech understanding systems have matured quite a bit since Hearsay-II, and there is nothing in my arguments that attributes a non-existing capability to speech understanding systems.

possible that at least in some instances, especially when there is much noise contaminating the utterances, something meaningful might result. When it does, it amounts to a novel projection since the English conceptualization of the French utterance is non-conventional.

If this scenario seems a bit far-fetched to you, consider the humerous book *Mots D'Heures: Gousses Rames* by Luis d'Antin Van Rooten.[4] It contains text in French (which is somewhat nonsensical, but meaningful) that, when read aloud, sounds like Mother Goose's Nursery Rhymes.

You might also consider two other modules, one for recognizing conversation pertaining to real-estate business and the other about the stock market, instead. It is not an uncommon experience that in a noisy environment, such as a party, on catching fragments of a conversation what we make of it very much depends on what we think is being talked about. On being informed otherwise, there is invariably a 'regrouping' of the same perceptual data. To my mind, this is no different from the 'regrouping' of the pattern received from the microphone that takes place when a system such as Hearsay-II decides to use English rules instead of French; or the 'regrouping' that takes place in our perceptual apparatus when we try to 'see' the process of painting as pumping instead of smearing.

The obvious conclusion to be reached here is that there exist computational systems that are capable of producing novel projections and instances of creative metaphors. A handwriting recognition system that interprets a child's doodling as characters is producing a creative metaphor. A machine vision system, designed to recognize houses, if on being presented with a picture of camel interprets it as some sort of house is essentially carrying out a novel or metaphorical projection. Note that all these novel projections are not arbitrary; that is, the sensorimotor data set is not a passive receptor of projections, but constrains the possible conceptualizations. In recognizing a child's doodling, the system would invariably zoom in on various 'objective' features of the doodling and 'see' them not only as relevant, but as a key to the identification process. In this way, a well-designed system of sufficient complexity can quite impress its human designers by producing interesting conceptualizations when operated in domains other than the ones for which it was intended. What is needed is a systematic study of this creativity.

---

[4]I am grateful to Dr. Melanie Mitchell for bringing this interesting and unusual book to my attention.

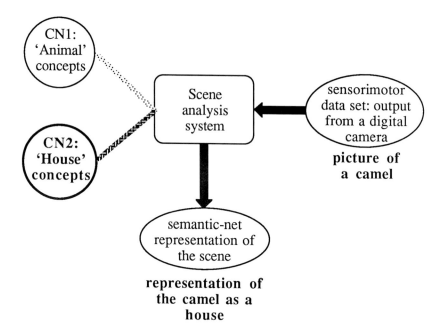

FIGURE 10.13: An example of novel projection in a computational setting. The scene analysis system would have normally represented the camel as an animal concept. But forced to use the house concepts, it could meaningfully represent it as a house, thereby creating similarities between a camel and a house.

10.5.3   The Creation of Similarity

In the light of our previous discussion, let us now see how the creation of similarity might take place in a computational setting. Consider a machine vision system that accepts a digitized image of a scene and produces a semantic-net-like representation of it [Figure 10.13]. This computational system is clearly carrying out a process of conceptualization. The sensorimotor data set for this system is the digitized image, which has its own autonomous structure, and the concept network is the language of the semantic net. Accommodation, in this context, corresponds to the situation in which the digitized image is already grouped into regions, and the structure of the semantic net is adapted to represent the grouped image. Projection corresponds to the situation in which the system is given a semantic net representation, and tries to determine if any part of the semantic net is, indeed, present in the digitized image.

In order to give the machine vision system a capability for novel projection, suppose that it has two concept networks: one for representing house scenes with concepts like 'roof,' 'chimney,' 'wall,' 'door,' 'yard,' etc., and the other for representing animals with concepts such as 'horse,' 'camel,' 'trunk,' 'hump,' 'legs,' 'tail,' etc. On being presented with the digitized image of, say, a camel, the system would recognize it as such, and represent it as a semantic net from the 'animal' concept network. This would be the conventional representation of the input image.

Now if one compares this representation with some previously stored representation of a house, there would be no similarities between the two. One reason is that the animal concepts are largely disjoint with the house concepts. And also structurally, one uses very different regioning and labeling techniques for identifying an animal than for identifying a house. However, if the system is forced to 'see' the image of the camel through the 'house' concept network, then the same digitized image is completely reorganized. Different regioning (regrouping) and labeling (remapping) routines would take over and try to identify the image as a house. The hump of the animal might be labeled as 'roof,' the neck as 'chimney,' etc. This regrouping would create the similarities between the image of the camel and a house, similarities that were not there between their 'conventional' representations.

Thus, we see that it is quite possible to model the creation of similarity with existing AI systems. With this background I now outline an architecture for modeling similarity-creating metaphors and discuss the research issues posed by it.

10.6   Modeling Metaphor as Change of Representation

The central idea is to model the process underlying similarity-creating metaphors as *change of representation*. The model would have concept networks that *represent* sensorimotor data sets. The concept networks would contain high-level concepts—in a semantic net or some similar formalism—that provide the primitives for representation. Sensorimotor data sets would contain raw sense data (output from a microphone or a digital camera) that needs to be organized by using the concepts from concept networks.

When the model would encounter any sensorimotor data set, it would immediately seek to represent it in some way in terms of its concepts; just as we are automatically organizing and filtering our sense-impressions to see instantiations of the concepts in our environment. The representation of a sensorimotor data set that the model would settle on, without any outside factor affecting it, we would call the 'conventional' representation of the sensorimotor data set. Now similarity-creating metaphors can be produced by forcing the model to change the representation of the sensorimotor data set from the 'conventional' to a 'novel' one. The model can be forced to do this by limiting the set of concepts and concept networks it has available for representing the sensorimotor data set. This could be done by providing the representation of the source object (for instance, a semantic net representation of the house that is being projected onto the picture of a camel), and constraining the model to use only those concepts that are used in the given representation, or closely related ones.

Thus, the set of concepts that the system would be forced to use would become the source, and the sensorimotor data set that would be conceptualized would become the target. The model would work by producing a conceptualization of the target sensorimotor data set in terms of the source concepts. The resulting representation would be metaphorical, if it would be something that the system would not have produced by itself when the source were not explicitly given.

The architecture of a computational system based on this approach is shown in Figure 10.14. A key difference between the concept networks and sensorimotor data sets, namely the degree of abstraction, must be emphasized here, since it would not do to have the target be presented as a concept network or the source as a sensorimotor data set. You might recall the discussion of the last section about the creation of similarity. If the target sensorimotor data set is already conceptualized in some way, and this representation is provided to the model, instead of the raw data, then only existing similarities between it and the given representation of the source can be gleaned. To create similarities, one must have access to the unrepresented, raw sensory data from the target so that it can be conceptualized anew—that is, represented differently.

Similarly, if the representation of the source is not provided, and only an unrepresented source object is given, then one might not be able to find any similarities at all. For instance, if one is given only the bit-map images of a house and a camel, not much can be gained by a bit by bit comparison of the two images. In fact, if the images were of two very similar houses, even then

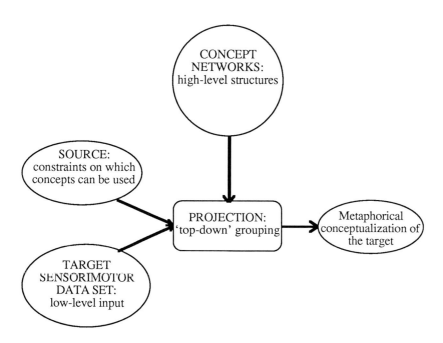

FIGURE 10.14: An architecture for modeling similarity-creating metaphors.

little can be learned from a bit by bit comparison of the images. The reason for this is that it is the concepts that make us see things as similar. It is the concept 'triangle' that makes us see two otherwise very dissimilar figures as alike. It is the concept 'house' that makes us see an igloo and a mansion as similar. Thus, it does not help to do away with the concept networks altogether and always try to find similarities between the sensorimotor data sets corresponding to the source and the target.

Having clarified this point, let us turn back to the architecture of Figure 10.14. One thing to notice is that it is not necessary, or even suggested, that the conventional conceptualization be determined for each sensorimotor data set. Given the source concept network and the target sensorimotor data set, the system would directly project the source onto the target. Computing the conventional representation of the target sensorimotor data set is not needed at all in this process. Only if the system is explicitly asked whether the projection is an instance of creative metaphor, then it would have to figure out the conventional representation of the target sensorimotor data set and compare it with the conceptualization in terms of the source concept network. In this sense, as long as the source is provided, the system does not invoke different processes to compute conventional projection and novel projection. In fact, one might say that in a sense the system is not even aware whether the projection is conventional or novel.

The second thing to notice is that by taking 'conventional' to mean the representation of the sensorimotor data set to which the system naturally settles, I am limiting the sense of 'novel' to include only 'making the familiar strange'; and leaving out those novel projections that result from conceptualizing the sensorimotor data sets that have no natural conceptualizations, corresponding to 'making the strange familiar.' Thus, when a machine vision system that is designed to generate conceptual representation of house scenes, on being presented with a picture of a camel comes up with a representation of it in terms of house-related concepts like 'roof,' 'chimney,' etc., this representation would be termed 'conventional,' and hence non-metaphorical, according to our characterization. While this may seem odd at first, you must remember that as far as the machine vision system is concerned, it is indeed a house that it sees in the camel-picture. It knows of no other conceptualization of that image. It is only we, having the God's-eye view and being fully aware of another more conventional conceptualization of the camel picture, who see the machine vision system's representation of the camel picture as novel, and hence metaphorical.

Indeed, this precise point, made in the context of human cognition, is the theme of Colin Turbayne's excellent *Myth of Metaphor.* Turbayne argued that what we regard as the ontology of reality is only a projection, albeit a conventional one, of our concept networks. However, when we overlook this fact, and take our conventional projections to be the unique immutable ontology of reality, then our view of reality becomes nothing but a myth. The inability of the machine vision system to see beyond its concept network only demonstrates this point more clearly.

For a computational system to be able to regard certain sensorimotor data sets as 'strange' or non-conceptualizable, and yet be able to come up with some reasonable conceptualization when the source is explicitly given, would require a certain degree of self-awareness. Perhaps one way to incorporate this feature would be to have the system generate a confidence factor, along with the conventional conceptualization, when presented with a sensorimotor data set. A low confidence factor, then, would be taken as the sign to mean that the sensorimotor data set is 'strange,' and therefore any conceptualization of it is metaphorical.

With this much background, we can now identify three major research issues in designing and building computational models of creative metaphors. I discuss below how each issue might be addressed within the existing AI technology.

- *Finding a suitable language for the concept networks:* This might seem to be the easiest problem since AI representational languages have evolved quite a bit since semantic nets [Brachman 1978; Brachman *et al.* 1983]. There are also some AI representation schemes especially designed for representing concept networks corresponding to physical systems and processes [Hayes 1979; Forbus 1984; Bobrow 1985], something that would be required to model creative metaphors like 'painting-as-pumping.'

  For now, I would suggest a simple scheme that has 'object,' 'attribute,' and 'action' nodes. Object nodes represent objects and action nodes represent operators that change objects to other objects, or change attributes of an object. Each node would contain a procedure that encapsulates the 'meaning' of the object, action, or attribute represented. For instance, in modeling Schön's painting-as-pumping metaphor that we have already encountered in the earlier chapters, the 'pump' node would contain a procedure to decide when something might be considered a pump. It might include the fact, among others, that a pump needs to be a hollow container with some sort of opening. Exactly how to represent this 'procedural' part of a concept network would depend crucially on how the sensorimotor data sets are described, since it is these 'procedures' that would have to interact with the sensorimotor data sets to determine how the sensorimotor data set might be represented. For instance, in viewing painting as pumping, it is the procedure corresponding to 'pump' that would have to find a suitable chunk in the sensorimotor data set of painting to be identified as 'pump.'

- *Finding a suitable description language for the sensorimotor data sets:* Recall that the sensorimotor data sets are structured objects themselves that resist arbitrary conceptualization. Therefore, one would have to find some way of describing sensorimotor data sets as well. In a model of visual metaphors, for instance, the sensorimotor data set could be described as a set of pixels with attributes, or as a structured set of line segments and regions. In any case, the description of the sensorimotor data set would have to be quite detailed, in terms of minute components and micro-structures; since otherwise, the conceptualization process would not produce anything interesting. Thus, we might not have an object 'brush' in the sensorimotor data set of painting, but, instead, there must be 'fibers,' 'droplets,' etc.; we may not have 'triangle,' 'hexagon' etc. in the sensorimotor data set of the figure of the Star of David, but there must be line segments.

  Also, the description of the sensorimotor data set should be as theory-neutral as possible, since otherwise it would not admit different conceptualizations. For instance, if the sensorimotor data set corresponding to the Star of David is described as two inverted triangles, it can never be reorganized to produce a hexagon in the middle. If the sensorimotor data set of painting is described as a smearing process, then it can no longer be reorganized as pumping. This is because the sensorimotor data sets are at the lowest level of abstraction—they can be grouped together in different ways but cannot be further broken down into smaller units.

- *Modeling the process of projection between the source concept network and the target sensorimotor data set:* This is the heart of the problem. The projection process would result in a conceptual representation of the target sensorimotor data set that is partially isomorphic to the source concept network, and yet does not violate the structure of the target sensorimotor data set. This process can be likened to a somewhat simplified case of speech recognition. In speech recognition, the problem is that of coming up with a grammatical, meaningful sentence, given an acoustic signal. Now the acoustic signal can be considered to be the target sensorimotor data set, and the grammatical, meaningful sentence—the output of the speech recognizer—can be considered to be a concept-level representation of the target. The task is 'somewhat simplified' because, with the source concept network given to us, we are told what the resulting sentence might be, (or that it is 'English' instead of 'French'). That is, instead of trying to find any meaningful pattern in the acoustic signal, we are given a pattern, and are told to find what parts of it, if any, occur in the acoustic signal.

This analogy immediately suggests that the process might be modeled as a 'blackboard system' [Nii 1986]. The blackboard control structure has been successfully used as an underlying architecture for a variety of AI applications including speech recognition [Erman *et al.* 1980], scene analysis [Nagao & Matsuyama 1980], and interpretation of electron density maps of protein crystals [Terry 1983]. In fact, if we consider the example of the Star of David, the process of interaction that generates different conceptual representations of it, such as two overlapping triangles, is essentially a scene analysis problem in disguise.

In modeling the process of interaction underlying generative metaphor as a blackboard system, the procedure attached to each node in the concept network of the source is considered a 'knowledge source.' When the source interacts with the target, all the knowledge sources are activated in parallel, which then compete and cooperate with one another to arrive at a suitable organization, or grouping, of the target sensorimotor data set. These would be the top-down knowledge sources that would be looking for certain specific features in the target sensorimotor data set. One might also include bottom-up knowledge sources that recognize certain features of the target sensorimotor data set and propagate upwards the constraints that the structure of the sensorimotor data set puts on how it might be conceptualized. A suitable interpretation would be found when the top-down expectations of the source agree with the bottom-up constraints of the target. (Notice the absence of quotation marks around the terms top-down and bottom-up here, since I am using both these terms in their traditional sense. As I emphasized earlier using the example of a parser, both the top-down and bottom-up control strategies correspond to the 'top-down' grouping in the sense used in this chapter.)

One might also use a non-deterministic approach similar to that of Hofstadter and Mitchell's Copycat. In fact, in the light of my previous remarks about the relationship of non-determinism to creativity, this approach seems much more promising. A significant difference, though by no means a major architectural one, between the way Copycat is set up and the way I am envisioning the proposed model would be in the initial conditions. Recall that in Copycat, all runs start with a fixed set of bottom-up codelets, with preset urgency levels, in the coderack. In the proposed model, however, the source concept network would cause certain nodes in the slipnet to be activated at the start of a run, thereby creating an initial pressure that would be different for different sources. Thus, the same target sensorimotor data set would be assigned different descriptions when different sources are used; and the same source would be given different interpretations when different target sensorimotor data sets are present. Moreover, the dichotomy of 'novel' *vs.* 'conventional' descriptions can be captured in this initial bias of the slipnet. A description assigned to a given sensorimotor data set would be viewed as 'conventional' if it were arrived at most of the time with no initial bias to the slipnet, and any other description would be considered 'novel.'

10.7   Conclusions

The main points of this chapter can be summarized as follows. First, there is the methodological inadequacy of almost all traditional approaches to metaphor and analogy that focus on finding some existing similarities between the given representations of the source and the target. These approaches are basically flawed—in as far as their potential to model creative analogies or metaphors is concerned—not because they characterize similarity in this way or that way, or whether they use this algorithm or that algorithm in computing the similarities, but because they are always working with some given representations that have been fixed in advance, whereas the creativity of metaphors and analogies, as I have argued in the earlier chapters, comes from changing these a priori representations in novel ways, a process that often generates new cognitive information that was not present in the old representations. Changing representations, however, requires one to interact with the perceptual data directly, since it is the autonomous structure of the perceptual data that constrains the possible ways in which they can be represented.

From this point of view, it is the model of analogy implemented by Hofstadter and Mitchell that seems much more promising. By focusing on the process by which the representations are initially generated, they were able to model many instances of creative analogies that required new ways of looking at the objects. Though this model was confined to an artificial microworld, I argued that once we realize that it is the process of redescription or changing representation that underlies creative metaphors and analogies, we see at once that there are many existing AI systems—in the domains such as scene recognition, handwriting recognition and speech recognition—that can generate instances of creative metaphor or analogy.

Against the backdrop of this discussion, I outlined a system to model creative metaphors and analogies as changes of representation. The idea is that when the source concept network is explicitly given, the system is forced to conceptualize the target sensorimotor data set using only those concepts. This can result in a changed representation of the target sensorimotor data set—changed from what the representation might be when the source is not given—thereby creating similarities between the source and the target.

In this connection, I must note that the process of change of representation plays a key role in many other aspects of cognition. In problem solving, for instance, new approaches and new insights often involve a changed representation. Though this has been recognized as far back as Amarel [1968], it is only recently that change of representation is getting a more serious attention from AI researchers [Korf 1980; Lowry 1990; Subramanian 1990]. The arguments of this chapter serve, I hope, only to highlight this point further.

Finally, I would like to underscore the fact that cognitive modeling of creative metaphors and analogies need not await a complete understanding of syntactic metaphors and analogies, as some might argue. Rather, given that the mechanisms underlying the two classes of metaphors and analogies are very different, the respective research on each class can proceed hand-in-hand. Moreover, as the crucial role played by creative metaphors and analogies in various aspects of cognition cannot be overemphasized, in understanding their underlying cognitive mechanisms lies the key to unraveling the mystery surrounding the creativity of the human mind.

Bibliography

Achinstein P., 1963, "Variety and Analogy in Confirmation Theory," *Philosophy of Science 30,* No. 3, July 1963, pp. 207–227.

Agassi J., 1964, "Analogies as Generalizations," *Philosophy of Science 31,* No. 4, Oct. 1964, pp. 351–356.

Allwood C.M. and Eliasson M., 1987, "Analogy and Other Sources of Difficulty in Novices' Very First Text-Editing," *International Journal of Man-Machine Studies 27,* pp. 1–22.

Amarel S., 1968, "On the Representations of Problems of Reasoning about Actions," in D. Michie (ed.) *Machine Intelligence 3,* American Elsevier, New York, NY.

Anderegg M.A., 1984, *David Lean,* Twayne Publishers, Boston, Mass.

Andersen M., 1967, "An Impression," in S. Rozental (ed.) *Niels Bohr: His life and work as seen by his friends and colleagues,* North-Holland, Amsterdam, The Netherlands, pp. 321–324.

Arbib M.A., 1972, *The Metaphorical Brain,* John Wiley & Sons, Inc., New York, NY.

Arbib M.A. and Hesse M.B., 1986, *The Construction of Reality,* Cambridge Univ. Press, Cambridge, UK.

Barham J., 1990, "A Poincaréan Approach to Evolutionary Epistemology," *Journal of Social and Biological Structures 13,* No. 3, pp. 193–258.

Barker S. and Achinstein P., 1960, "On the New Riddle of Induction," *Philosophical Review 69,* No. 4, pp. 511–522.

Bateson G., 1979, *Mind and Nature: A Necessary Unity,* Dutton, New York, NY.

Berger P.L. and Luckmann T., 1966, *Social Construction of Reality: A Treatise in Sociology of Knowledge,* Double Day & Co. Inc.; Anchor Book Edition 1967.

Berggren D., 1962–63, "The Use and Abuse of Metaphor," *The Review of Metaphysics,* vol. 62, Dec. 1962, pp. 237–258; vol. 63, March 1963, pp. 450–472.

Berlin B. and Kay P., 1969, *Basic Color Terms: Their Universality and Evolution,* Univ. of California Press, Berkley, Calif.

Binkley T., 1974, "On the Truth and Probity of Metaphor," *The Journal of Aesthetics and Art Criticism 33,* no. 2, pp. 171–180; reprinted in M. Johnson (ed.) *Philosophical Perspectives on Metaphor,* Univ. of Minnesota Press (1981), Minneapolis, Minn., pp. 136–153.

Black M., 1962, "Metaphor," in M. Black *Models and Metaphors,* Cornell Univ. Press, Ithaca, NY, pp. 25–47; originally published in *Proceedings of the Aristotelian Society,* N.S. 55 (1954–55), pp. 273–294; reprinted in M. Johnson (ed.) *Philosophical Perspectives on Metaphor,* Univ. of Minnesota Press (1981), Minneapolis, Minn., pp. 63–82.

Black M., 1979, "More about Metaphor," in A. Ortony (ed.) *Metaphor and Thought,* Cambridge Univ. Press, Cambridge, UK, pp. 19–45; originally appeared in a slightly different form in *Dialectica 31,* (1977), pp. 431–457.

Bobrow D. (ed.), 1985, *Qualitative Reasoning About Physical Systems,* MIT Press, Cambridge, MA.

Brachman R.J., 1978, "A Structural Paradigm for Representing Knowledge," Technical Report # 3605, BBN Laboratories, Cambridge, Mass.

Brachman R.J., Fikes R.E., and Levesque H.J., 1983, "Krypton: A Functional Approach to Knowledge Representation," *Computer 16,* no. 10, Oct. 1983, pp. 67–73.

Broad W., 1985, "Subtle Analogies found at the core of Edison's genius," *New York Times,* March 12, pp. C1–C2.

Bunch B.L., 1980, "Rescher on the Goodman Paradox," *Philosophy of Science 47,* pp. 119–123.

Burks A.W., 1977, *Chance, Cause, Reason,* The Univ. of Chicago Press.

Cage J., 1961, *Silence,* Wesleyan University Press, Middletown, Connecticut.

Camac M.K. and Glucksberg S., 1984, "Metaphors do not Use Associations Between Concepts, They are Used to Create Them," *Journal of Psycholinguistic Research 13,* No. 6, pp. 443–455.

Campbell J., 1949, *The Hero with a Thousand Faces,* Pantheon Books, New York, NY.

Campbell J., 1986, *The Inner Reaches of Outer Space: Metaphor as Myth and as Religion,* Harper & Row, New York, NY.

Campbell J., 1988, *The Power of Myth,* with Bill Moyers, Doubleday, New York, NY.

Canguilhem G., 1963, "The Role of Analogies and Models in Biological Discovery," in A.C. Crombie (ed.) *Scientific Change,* Basic Books, New York, NY, pp. 507–520.

Carbonell J.G., 1982, "Metaphor: An Inescapable Phenomenon in Natural Language Comprehension," in W.G. Lehnert & M.H. Ringle (eds.) *Strategies for Natural Language Processing,* Lawrence Erlbaum Associates, Hillsdale, NJ, pp. 415–433.

Carbonell J.G., 1983, "Learning by Analogy: Formulating and Generalizing Plans from Past Experience," in R.S. Michalski *et al.* (eds.) *Machine Learning,* pp. 137–161, Tioga Publishing Co., Palo Alto, Calif.

Carbonell J.G., 1986, "Derivational Analogy: A Theory of Reconstructive Problem Solving and Expertise Acquisition" in R.S. Michalski *et al.* (eds.) *Machine Learning Vol. II,* pp. 371–392, Morgan Kaufmann, Inc., Los Altos, Calif.

Carnap R., 1962, *Logical Foundations of Probability,* The Univ. of Chicago Press, 2nd ed.

Carnap R., 1963, "Variety, Analogy, and Periodicity in Inductive Logic," *Philosophy of Science 30,* No. 3, July 1963, pp. 222–227.

Carroll J.M. and Mack R.L., 1985, "Metaphor, Computing Systems, and Active Learning," *International Journal of Man-Machine Studies 22,* pp. 39–57.

Cassirer E., 1944, *An Essay on Man,* Yale University Press, New Haven, Conn.

Cassirer E., 1946, *Language and Myth,* translated by S.K. Langer, Dover Publications Inc. (1953), New York.

Cassirer E., 1950, *The Problem of Knowledge: Philosophy, Science, and History since Hegel,* translated by W.H. Woglom and C.W. Hendel., Yale Univ. Press, New Haven, Conn.

Cassirer E., 1955, *The Philosophy of Symbolic Forms: Vol. 1–3,* translated by R. Manheim, Yale Univ. Press, New Haven, Conn.

Champa K.S., 1985, *Mondrian Studies,* The University of Chicago Press, Chicago, Ill.

Chase S., 1938, *The Tyranny of Words,* Harcourt Brace Jovanovich, New-York.

Clement C.A. and Gentner D., 1991, "Systematicity as a Selectional Constraint in Analogical Mapping," *Cognitive Science 15,* pp. 89–132.

Cohn P.M., 1981, *Universal Algebra,* revised edition, D. Reidel, Dordrecht, Holland.

Collins A. & Gentner D., 1987, "How People Construct Mental Models," in D.

Holland and N. Quinn (eds.) *Cultural Models in Language and Thought,* Cambridge Univ. Press, Cambridge, U.K.; Chap. 10 (pp. 243–265).

Connor K. and Kogan N., 1980, "Topic-Vehicle Relations in Metaphor: The Issue of Asymmetry," in R.P. Honeck and R.R. Hoffman (eds.) *Cognition and Figurative Language,* Lawrence Erlbaum Associates, Hillsdale, NJ, pp. 283–308.

De Valois R.L., Abramov I., and Jacobs G.H., 1966, "Analysis of Response Patterns of LGN Cells," *Journal of the Optical Society of America 56,* pp. 966–977.

De Valois R.L. and Jacobs G.H., 1968, "Primate Color Vision," *Science 162,* pp. 533–540.

Deregowski J.B., 1980, *Illusions, Patterns and Pictures: A Cross Cultural Perspective,* Academic Press, London, U.K.

Dretske F.I., 1981, *Knowledge and the Flow of Information,* MIT Press, Cambridge, Mass.

Edwards G., 1982, *The Discreet Art of Luis Buñuel,* Marion Boyars, London, U.K.

Emmet D.M., 1945, *The Nature of Metaphysical Thinking,* MacMillan & Co. Ltd., London (1961).

Erman L.D., Hayes-Roth F., Lesser V.R., and Reddy D.R., 1980, "The Hearsay-II Speech-Understanding System: Integrating Knowledge to Resolve Uncertainty," *Computing Surveys 12,* pp. 213–253.

Evans T.G., 1963, *A Heuristic Program to Solve Geometric-Analogy Problems,* Ph.D. Dissertation, Dept. of Mathematics, M.I.T., Cambridge, Mass.

Evans T.G., 1968, "A Program for the Solution of a Class of Geometric-Analogy Intelligence-Test Questions," in M. Minsky (ed.) *Semantic Information Processing,* MIT Press, Cambridge, Mass. (1968), Chap. 5, pp. 271–353.

Falkenhainer B., Forbus K.D. and Gentner D., 1989, "The Structure-Mapping Engine," *Artificial Intelligence 41,* No. 1, pp. 1–63.

Fass D. and Wilks Y., 1983, "Preference Semantics, Ill-Formedness, and Metaphor," *American Journal of Computational Linguistics 9,* Nos. 3–4, July-December 1983, pp. 178–187.

Fass F., 1989, "Met*: A Method for Discriminating Metonymy and Metaphor by Computer," Technical Report CSS/LCCR TR 89–15, Center for Systems Science, Simon Fraser University, Burnaby, BC, Canada.

Fauconnier G., 1985, *Mental Spaces*, MIT Press, Cambridge, Mass.

Favreau O.E. and Corballis M.C., 1976, "Negative Aftereffects in Visual Perception," *Scientific American*, December 1976; reprinted in *The Mind's Eye*, readings from *Scientific American*, W.H. Freeman & Co. (1985), New York, NY; pp. 53–59.

Feynman R., 1986, "Personal Observations on the Reliability of the Shuttle" by Richard Feynman, Appendix F to the *Report to the President by the Presidential Commission on the Space Shuttle Challenger Accident*, Washington D.C. (1986); reprinted in *What do you care what other people think?* by Richard Feynman, W.W. Norton & Co. (1988), New York, pp. 220–237.

Forbus K.D., 1984, "Qualitative Process Theory," *Artificial Intelligence 24*.

Fox H.N., 1982, *Metaphors: New Projects by Contemporary Sculptors*, Smithsonian Institution Press, Wash. D.C.

French R.M. and Hofstadter D.R., 1991, "Tabletop: An Emergent, Stochastic Model of Analogy-Making," Technical Report CRCC-53-1991, Center for Research on Concepts and Cognition, Indiana University, Bloomington, Ind.

Gentner D., 1982, "Are Scientific Analogies Metaphors?," in D.S. Miall (ed.) *Metaphor: Problems and Perspectives*, Harvester Press Ltd., Brighton, U.K., pp. 106–132.

Gentner D., 1983, "Structure-Mapping: A Theoretical Framework for Analogy," *Cognitive Science 7*, pp. 155–170.

Gentner D., 1989, "The Mechanisms of Analogical Learning," in S. Vosniadou and A. Ortony (eds.) *Similarity and Analogical Reasoning*, Cambridge University Press, London, U.K., pp. 199–241.

Gentner D. and Clement C., 1988, "Evidence for Relational Selectivity in the Interpretation of Analogy and Metaphor," in G.H. Bower (ed.) *The Psychology of Learning and Motivation*, Academic Press, New York, NY, pp. 307–358

Gentner D., Falkenhainer B., and Skorstad J., 1987, "Metaphor: The Good, the Bad, and the Ugly," position paper in *Proceedings of TINLAP-3*, Las Cruces, New Mexico, pp. 155–159.

Gentner D. and Gentner D.R., 1983, "Flowing Water or Teeming Crowds: Mental Models of Electricity," in D. Gentner & A.L. Stevens (eds.) *Mental Models*, Lawrence Erlbaum Associates, Hillsdale, NJ, pp. 99–129.

Gentner D. and Jeziorski M., 1989, "Historical Shifts in the Use of Analogy in Science," in B. Gholson *et al.* (eds.) *The Psychology of Science: Contributions to Metascience,* Cambrige University Press, London, U.K,, pp. 296–325.

Gentner D. and Stuart P., 1983, "Metaphor as Structure-Mapping: What Develops," BBN Report No. 5479, Bolt Beranek & Newman, Inc., Cambridge, Mass.

Gerhart M. and Russell A., 1984, *Metaphoric Process: The Creation of Scientific and Religious Understanding,* Texas Christian University Press, Fort Worth, Texas.

Gerrig R.J., "Empirical Constraints on Computational Theories of Metaphor: Comments on Indurkhya," *Cognitive Science 13,* pp. 235–241.

Gick M.L. and Holyoak K.J., 1980, "Analogical Problem Solving," *Cognitive Psychology 12,* pp. 306–355.

Gick M.L. and Holyoak K.J., 1983, "Schema Induction and Analogical Transfer," *Cognitive Psychology 15,* pp. 1–38.

Gillam B., 1980, "Geometrical Illusions," *Scientific American,* January 1980; reprinted in *The Mind's Eye,* readings from *Scientific American,* W.H. Freeman & Co. (1985), New York, NY; pp. 87–94.

Gitter D.L., Gordon W.J.J., and Prince G.M., 1964, *The Operational Mechanisms of Synectics,* Synectics Inc., Cambridge, Mass.

Goodman N., 1955, *Fact, Fiction, and Forecast,* 3rd ed. (1973), Bobbs-Merrill Co., Inc., Indianapolis, Ind.

Goodman N., 1972, *Problems and Projects,* Bobbs-Merrill Co., Inc., Indianapolis, Ind.

Goodman N., 1976, *Languages of Art,* 2nd ed., Hackett Publishing Co., Indianapolis, Ind.

Goodman N., 1978, *Ways of Worldmaking,* Hackett Publishing Co., Indianapolis, Ind.

Gordon W.J.J., 1961, *Synectics: The Development of Creative Capacity,* Harper & Row, New York, NY.

Gordon W.J.J., 1965, "The Metaphorical Way of Knowing," in G. Kepes (ed.) *Education of Vision,* George Braziller, New York, NY, pp. 96–103.

Greiner R., 1985, *Learning by Understanding Analogies,* Ph.D. Dissertation, Computer Science Department, Stanford University, Stanford, Calif.

Gruber H.E., 1978, "Darwin's 'Tree of Nature' and Other Images of Wide Scope," in J. Wechsler (ed.) *On Aesthetics in Science,* MIT Press (1978),

Cambridge, Mass., pp. 121–40.

Halasz F. & Moran T.P., 1982, "Analogies Considered Harmful," *ACM Proc. of Human Factors in Computer Systems,* pp. 383–386.

Halford G.S. and Wilson W.H., 1980, "A Category Theory Approach to Cognitive Development," *Cognitive Psychology 12,* pp.356–411.

Hall R.P., 1989, "Computational Approaches to Analogical Reasoning: A Comparative Analysis," *Artificial Intelligence 39,* pp. 39–120.

Harrod R., 1956, *Foundations of Inductive Logic,* MacMillan, republished 1974.

Hart C., 1985, *The Prehistory of Flight,* University of California Press, Berkeley, Calif.

Hartline H.K., 1967, "Visual Receptors and Retinal Interaction," *Les Prix Nobel en 1967,* Nobel Foundation 1968-1969, pp. 242–259; reprinted in F. Ratliff (ed.) *Studies on Excitation and Inhibition in the Retina,* The Rockefeller University Press (1974), New York, NY, pp. 643–660.

Hausman C.R., 1983, "Metaphors, Referents, and Individuality," *Journal of Aesthetics and Art Criticism 42,* pp. 181–195.

Hausman C.R., 1984, *A Discourse on Novelty and Creation,* SUNY Press, Albany, NY.

Hausman C.R., 1989, *Metaphor and Art: Interactionism and Reference in Verbal and Nonverbal Art,* Cambridge University Press, Cambridge, U.K.

Hayes P.J., 1975, "The Naive Physics Manifesto," in D. Mitchie (ed.) *Expert Systems in the Micro-Electronic Age,* Edinburgh Univ. Press, Edinburgh, Scotland.

Heider E.R. and Olivier D.C., 1972, "The Structure of the Color Space in Naming and Memory for Two Languages," *Cognitive Psychology 3,* pp. 337–353.

Helmreich S., Iverson E. and Laroche F., 1990, "Modular Meta5: Further Research in Collative Semantics," Technical Report MCCS-90-192, Computing Research Labs, New Mexico State University, Las Cruces, NM.

Henle P., 1958, "Metaphor," in P. Henle (ed.) *Language, Thought, and Culture,* Univ. of Michigan Press, pp. 173–195; reprinted in M. Johnson (ed.) *Philosophical Perspectives on Metaphor,* Univ. of Minnesota Press (1981), Minneapolis, Minn., pp. 83–104.

Hesse M.B., 1959a, Analogy-Structure in a Thesaurus, Technical Report ML 101, The Cambridge Language Research Unit, Cambridge, U.K.

Hesse M.B., 1959b, "On Defining Analogy," *Proceedings of the Aristotelian Society LX,* pp. 79–100.

Hesse M.B., 1964, "Analogy and Confirmation Theory," *Philosophy of Science 31,* No. 4, Oct. 1964, pp. 319–327.

Hesse M.B., 1966, *Models and Analogies in Science,* Univ. of Notre Dame Press, Notre Dame, Ind.

Hesse M.B., 1974, *The Structure of Scientific Inferences,* Univ. of California Press, Berkeley, Calif.

Hesse M.B., 1980, *Revolutions and Reconstructions in the Philosophy of Science,* Indiana Univ. Press, Bloomigton, Ind.

Higginbotham V., 1979, *Luis Buñuel,* Twayne Publishers, Boston, Mass.

Hintikka J. and Sandu G., 1990, "Metaphor and the Varieties of Lexical Meaning," *Dialectica 44,* Fasc. 1–2, pp. 55–78.

Hobbs J.R., 1979, "Metaphor, Metaphor Schemata, and Selective Inferencing," Tech. Note 204, SRI International, Menlo Park, Calif.

Hobbs J.R., 1990, *Literature and Cognition,* CSLI Lecture Notes No. 21, Center for the Study of Language and Information, Stanford, CA.

Hoeller S.A., 1982, *The Gnostic Jung and the Seven Sermons to the Dead,* The Theosophical Publishing House, Wheaton, Ill.

Hoffman R.R. and Kemper S., 1987, "What Could Reaction-Time Studies Be Telling Us About Metaphor Comprehension?" *Metaphor and Symbolic Activity 2,* No. 3, pp. 149–186.

Hofstadter D.R., 1981-85, "Metamagical Themas: Roles and Analogies in Human and Machine Thought," *Scientific American,* Vol. 245, No. 3, Sept. 1981; reprinted with much additional material as "Analogies and Role in Human and Machine Thinking," in *Metamagical Themas: Questing for the Essence of Mind and Pattern,* Basic Books, Inc. (1985), New York; Chap. 24 (pp. 547–603).

Hofstadter D.R., 1984, "The Copycat Project: An Experiment in Nondeterminism and Creative Analogies," A.I. Memo 755, Artificial Intelligence Laboratory, MIT, Cambridge, Mass.

Hofstadter D.R., 1985, *Metamagical Themas: Questing for the Essence of Mind and Pattern,* Basic Books, Inc., New York.

Hofstadter D.R. and Mitchell M., 1991, "An Overview of the Copycat Project," Technical Report CRCC-52-1991, Center for Research on Concepts and Cognition, Indiana University, Bloomington, Ind.

Holland D. and Quinn N. (eds.), *Cultural Models in Language & Thought,* Cambridge University Press, Cambridge, UK.

Holland J.H., Holyoak K.J., Nisbett R.E. and Thagard P.R., 1986, *Induction: Processes of Inference, Learning, and Discovery,* MIT Press, Cambridge, Mass.

Holstein B.I., 1970, *Use of Metaphor to Induce Innovative Thinking in Fourth Grade Children,* Ph.D. thesis, School of Education, Boston University, Boston, Mass.

Holyoak K.J. and Thagard P., 1989, "Analogical Mapping by Constraint Satisfaction," *Cognitive Science 13,* No. 3, pp. 295–355.

Hubel D.H. and Wiesel T.N., 1979, "Brain Mechanisms of Vision," in *The Brain,* A Scientific American Book, pp. 84–96, W.H. Freeman & Co., New York, NY.

Hubel D.H., 1988, *Eye, Brain and Vision,* Scientific American Library, W.H. Freeman, New York, NY.

Hume D., 1739, *A Treatise on Human Nature,* Penguin Classics Edition (1987).

Indurkhya B., 1986, "Constrained Semantic Transference: A Formal Theory of Metaphors," *Synthese 68,* no. 3, pp. 515–551.

Indurkhya B., 1987, "Approximate Semantic Transference: A Computational Theory of Metaphors and Analogies," *Cognitive Science 11,* pp. 445–480.

Indurkhya B., 1989, "Modes of Analogy," in K. P. Jantke (ed.) *Analogical and Inductive Inference,* Lecture Notes in Artificial Intelligence 397, Springer-Verlag (1989), Berlin, GDR, pp. 217–230.

Indurkhya B., 1990, "Some Remarks on the Rationality of Induction," *Synthese 85,* (October 1990), pp. 95–114.

Indurkhya B., 1991a, "On the Role of Interpretive Analogy in Learning," *New Generation Computing 8,* pp. 385–402; originally published in *Proceedings of the First International Workshop on Algorithmic Learning Theory,* Japanese Society for Artificial Intelligence, Tokyo, Japan (1990), pp. 174–189.

Indurkhya B., 1991b, "Modes of Metaphor," *Metaphor and Symbolic Activity 6,* No. 1, pp. 1–27.

Indurkhya B., in preparation, "A Cognitive Theory of Reference."

Inhelder B. and Piaget J., 1959, *The Early Growth of Logic in the Child,* translated by E.A. Lunzer and D. Papert (1964), W.W. Norton & Company (1969), New York, NY.

Iwayama M., Tokunaga T. and Tanaka H., 1990, "A Method of Calculating the Measure of Salience in Understanding Metaphor," *Proceedings of the Ninth National Conference on Artificial Intelligence,* Boston, Mass., pp. 298–303.

Johnson M. (ed.), 1981a, *Philosophical Perspectives on Metaphor,* Univ. of Minnesota Press, Minneapolis, Minn.

Johnson M., 1987, *The Body in the Mind,* Univ. of Chicago Press, Chicago, Ill.

Johnson M.G. and Malgady R.G., 1980, "Towards a Perceptual Theory of Metaphoric Comprehension," in R.P. Honeck and R.R. Hoffman (eds.) *Cognition and Figurative Language,* Lawrence Erlbaum Associates, Hillsdale, NJ, pp. 258–282.

Jones R.S., 1962, *Physics as Metaphor,* University of Minnesota Press, Minneapolis, Minn.

Jung C.G., 1963, *Memories, Dreams and Reflection,* edited by Aniela Jaffe, translated by Richard and Clara Winston, Vintage Books, (Random House, Inc.).

Kamp H., 1981, "The Paradox of the Heap," in U. Monnich (ed.) *Aspects of Philosophical Logic,* D. Reidel (1981), Dordrecht, Holland, pp. 225–277.

Kanizsa G., 1976, "Subjective Contours," *Scientific American,* April 1976; reprinted in *The Mind's Eye,* readings from *Scientific American,* W.H. Freeman & Co. (1985), New York, NY; pp. 82–86.

Kant I., 1787, *Critique of Pure Reason,* translated by Norman Kemp Smith, unabridged edition, St. Martin's Press (1965), New York, NY.

Katz A.N., Paivio A. and Marschark M., 1985, "Poetic Comparison: Psychological Dimensions of Metaphoric Processing," *Journal of Psycholinguistic Research 14,* No. 4, pp. 365–383. (See also the Erratum, *Journal of Psycholinguistic Research 15,* No. 1, p. 93.)

Kay P. and McDaniel C.K., 1978, "The Linguistic Significance of the Meanings of Basic Color Terms," *Language 54,* No. 3, pp. 610–646.

Kedar-Cabelli S., 1988, "Analogy: From a Unified Perspective," in D.H. Helman (ed.) *Analogical Reasoning: Perspectives of Artificial Intelligence, Cognitive Science, and Philosophy,* Kluwer Academic Publishers, Dordrecht, The Netherlands, pp. 65–103.

Kelly M.H. and Keil F.C., 1987, "Metaphor Comprehension and Knowledge of Semantic Domains," *Metaphor and Symbolic Activity 2,* No. 1, pp. 33–

51.

Kempton W., 1987, "Two Theories of Home Heat Control," in D. Holland and N. Quinn (eds.) *Cultural Models in Language and Thought,* Cambridge Univ. Press, Cambridge, U.K.; Chap. 9 (pp. 222–242).

Keynes J.M., 1921, *A Treatise on Probability,* MacMillan & Co., London.

Kfoury A.J., Moll R.N., and Arbib M.A., 1982, *A Programming Approach to Computability,* Springer-Verlag, New York, NY.

Kittay E.F., 1982, "The Creation of Similarity: A Discussion of Metaphor in Light of Tversky's Theory of Similarity," *PSA 1982,* (Philosophy of Science Association), Vol. 1, pp. 394–405.

Kittay E.F., 1987, *Metaphor: Its Cognitive Force and Linguistic Structure,* Clarendon Press, Oxford, U.K.

Kling R.E., 1971a, *Reasoning by Analogy with Application to Heuristic Problem-Solving: A Case Study,* Ph.D. Dissertation, Dept. of Computer Science, Stanford University, Palo Alto, Calif.

Kling R.E., 1971b, "A Paradigm for Reasoning by Analogy," *Artificial Intelligence 2,* pp. 147–178.

Koestler A., 1964, *The Act of Creation,* Hutchinsons of London; 2nd Danube ed., 1976.

Köhler W., 1930, "Human Perception," trans. by M. Henle, in M. Henle (ed.) *The Selected Papers of Wolfgang Köhler,* Liveright (1971), New York, NY, pp. 142–167.

Köhler W., 1969, *The Task of Gestalt Psychology,* Princeton Univ. Press, Princeton, NJ.

Kolers P.A., 1972, *Aspects of Motion Perception,* Pergamon Press, Oxford, U.K.

Kolers P.A. and Green M., 1984, "Color Logic of Apparent Motion," *Perception 13,* pp. 249–254.

Korf R. E., 1980, "Toward a Model of Representation Changes," *Artificial Intelligence 14,* pp. 41–78.

Krausser P., 1974, "Kant's Theory of the Structure of Empirical Scientific Inquiry and Two Implied Postulates Regarding Things in Themselves," in L.W. Beck (ed.) *Kant's Theory of Knowledge,* D. Reidel Publishing Co., Dordrecht, Holland, pp. 159–165.

Kuhn T.S., 1957, *The Copernican Revolution,* Harvard University Press, Cambridge, Mass.

Kuhn T.S., 1962, *The Structure of Scientific Revolutions,* Univ. of Chicago Press; 2nd enlarged ed., 1970.

Lakatos I., 1976, *Proofs and Refutations: The Logic of Mathematical Discovery,* edited by J. Worrall and E. Zahar, Cambridge University Press, Cambridge, U.K.

Lakoff G., 1986, "The Meanings of Literal," *Metaphor and Symbolic Activity 1,* No. 4, pp. 291–296.

Lakoff G., 1987, *Women, Fire, and Dangerous Things,* Univ. of Chicago Press, Chicago, Ill.

Lakoff G., 1987a, "The Death of Dead Metaphor," *Metaphor and Symbolic Activity 2,* No. 2, pp. 143–147.

Lakoff G., 1991, "Metaphor and War," paper circulated over computer network.

Lakoff G. and Johnson M., 1980, *Metaphors We Live By,* Univ. of Chicago Press, Chicago.

Lakoff G. and Kövecses Z., 1987, "The Cognitive Model of Anger Inherent in American English," in D. Holland and N. Quinn (eds.) *Cultural Models in Language and Thought,* Cambridge Univ. Press, Cambridge, U.K.; Chap. 8 (pp. 195–221).

Lakoff G. and Turner M., 1989, *More than Cool Reason: A Field Guide to Poetic Metaphor,* University of Chicago Press, Chicago, Ill.

Langer S.K., 1942, *Philosophy in a New Key,* Harvard Univ. Press, Cambridge, Mass., (3rd ed. 1980).

Langer S.K., 1953, *Feeling and Form,* Charles Scribner's Sons, New York.

Lettvin J.Y., Maturana H., McCulloch W.S. and Pitts W.H., 1959, "What the Frog's Eye Tells the Frog's Brain," *Proc. IRE 47,* pp. 1940–1951.

Levin S.R., 1977, *The Semantics of Metaphor,* John Hopkins Press, Baltimore, Maryland.

Levy A., 1979, *Basic Set Theory,* Springer-Verlag, New York, NY.

Libby W., 1922, "Scientific Imagination," *Scientific Monthly XV,* pp. 263–270.

Lippmann R.P., 1987, "An Introduction to Computing with Neural Nets," *IEEE ASSP Magazine,* April 1987, pp. 4–22.

Lowry M., 1990, "STRATA: Problem Reformulation and Abstract Data Types," in D. Paul Benjamin (ed.) *Change of Representation and Inductive Bias,* Kluwer Academic Publishers, Dordrecht, The Netherlands.

Luria A.R., 1976, *Cognitive Development: Its Cultural and Social Foundation,* Harvard University Press, Cambridge, Mass.

Mac Cormac E.R., 1982, "Metaphors and Fuzzy sets," *Fuzzy Sets and systems* 7, pp. 243–256.

Mac Cormac E.R., 1985, *A Cognitive Theory of Metaphor,* MIT Press, Cambridge, Mass.

Mac Lane S., 1986, *Mathematics: Form and Function,* Springer-Verlag, New York, NY.

MacLaury R.E., 1987, "Color-category Evolution and Shuswap Yellow-with-Green," *American Anthropologist 89,* pp. 107–124.

Mal'cev A.I., 1973, *Algebraic Systems,* translated by B.D. Seckler and A.P. Doohovskoy, Springer-Verlag, Berlin, FRG.

Malgady R.G. and Johnson M.G., 1980, "Measurement of Figurative Language: Semantic Feature Models of Comprehension and Appreciation," in R.P. Honeck and R.R. Hoffman (eds.) *Cognition and Figurative Language,* Lawrence Erlbaum Associates, Hillsdale, NJ, pp. 239–258.

Martin J.H., 1988, *A Computational Theory of Metaphor,* Ph.D. Dissertation, Computer Science Department, Univ. of Calif. at Berkeley, Berkeley, Calif.

Maturana H.R. and Varela F., 1987, *The Tree of Knowledge: The Biological Roots of Human Understanding,* translated by R. Paolucci (1988), Shambhala Publications, Boston, Mass.

McCabe A., 1983, "Conceptual Similarity and the Quality of Metaphor in Isolated Sentences Versus Extended Contexts," *Journal of Psycholinguistic Research 12,* No. 1, pp. 41–68.

Miller A.I., 1978, "Visualization Lost and Regained: The Genesis of the Quantum Theory in the Period 1913–27," in J. Wechsler (ed.) *On Aesthetics in Science,* MIT Press (1978), Cambridge, Mass., pp. 73–102.

Miller R.M., 1976, "The Dubious Case for Metaphors in Educational Writing," *Educational Theory 26,* (Spring 1976), pp. 174–181.

Mitchell M. and Hofstadter D.R., 1989a, "The Role of Computational Temperature in a Computer Model of Concepts and Analogy-Making," *Proceedings of the Eleventh Annual Conference of the Cognitive Science Society,* pp. 765–772.

Mitchell M. and Hofstadter D.R., 1989a, "The Emergence of Understanding in a Computer Model of Concepts and Analogy-Making," *Physica D,* 42, pp. 322–334.

Mitchell M. and Hofstadter D.R., 1989a, "The Right Concept at the Right Time: How Concepts Emerge as Relevant in Response to Context-Dependent Pressures," *Proceedings of the Twelfth Annual Conference of the Cognitive Science Society,* pp. 174–181.

Mondrian P., 1934, "The True Value of Oppositions in Life and Art," translated by H. Hotzman and M.S. James, in H. Holtzman and M.S. James (eds.) *The New Art—The New Life: The Collected Writings of Piet Mondrian,* G.K. Hall & Co., Boston, Mass., pp. 283–285.

Moss A.E.St.G., 1989, "Does Russian have a Basic Term for Purple?" *Linguistics 27,* pp. 144–155.

Nagao M. and Matsuyama T., 1980, *A Structural Analysis of Complex Aerial Photographs,* Plenum Press, New York, NY.

Neisser U., 1976, *Cognition and Reality,* W.H. Freeman & Co., San Francisco, Calif.

Nelson T.A., 1982, *Kubrick: Inside a Film Artist's Maze,* Indiana University Press, Bloomington, Ind.

Newman J.R., 1956, *The World of Mathematics,* Volume 2, Simon and Schuster, New York.

Nii H.P., 1986, "Blackboard Systems," Technical Report No. STAN-CS-86-1123 (also numbered KSL-86-18), Dept. of Computer Science, Stanford University, Stanford, Calif.

Nowottny W., 1962, *The Language Poets Use,* The Athlone Press, Univ. of London.

Ortony A., 1979, "Beyond Literal Similarity," *Psychological Review 86,* pp. 161–180.

Ortony A., 1979a, "The Role of Similarity in Similes and Metaphors," in A. Ortony (ed.) *Metaphor and Thought,* Cambridge Univ. Press (1979), Cambridge, UK, pp. 186–201.

Ortony A., 1980, "Some Psycholinguistic Aspects of Metaphor," in R.P. Honeck and R.R. Hoffman (eds.) *Cognition and Figurative Language,* Lawrence Erlbaum Associates, Hillsdale, NJ, pp. 69–83.

Partee B.H., 1979, "Montague Grammar, Mental Representations, and Reality," in P.A. French *at al.* (eds.) *Contemporary Perspectives in the Philosophy of Language,* Univ. of Minnesota Press, Minneapolis, pp. 195–208.

Petrie H.G., 1979, "Metaphor and Learning," A. Ortony (ed.) *Metaphor and Thought,* Cambridge Univ. Press (1979), Cambridge, UK, pp. 438–461.

Piaget J., 1936, *The Origin of Intelligence in the Child,* trans. by Margaret Cook (1953), Penguine (1977), New York, NY.

Piaget J., 1937, *The Construction of Reality in the Child,* trans. by Margaret Cook (1954), Ballantine Books (1971), New York, NY.

Piaget J., 1945, *Play, Dreams and Imitation in Childhood,* trans. by C. Gattegno and F. M. Hodgson (1951), W.W. Norton & Company (1962), New York, NY.

Piaget J., 1946, *The Child's Conception of Time,* trans. by A.J. Pomerans (1969), Ballantine Books (1971), New York, NY.

Piaget J., 1946a, *The Child's Conception of Movement and Speed,* trans. by G.E.T. Holloway and M.J. Mackenzie (1970), Ballantine Books (1971), New York, NY.

Piaget J., 1953, *Logic and Psychology,* Manchester University Press, Manchester, U.K.

Piaget J., 1967, *Biology and Knowledge,* trans. by B. Walsh (1971), The University of Chicago Press, Chicago, Ill.

Piaget J., 1970, *Genetic Epistemology,* trans. by E. Duckworth, Columbia University Press, New York, NY, (W.W.Norton edition, 1971).

Piaget J., 1974, *Adaptation and Intelligence,* translated by S. Eames (1980), Univ. of Chicago Press, Chicago, Ill.

Piaget J., 1975, "Language within Cognition: Schemes of Action and Language Learning," in M. Piatelli-Palmirini (ed.) *Language and Learning: The Debate between Jean Piaget and Noam Chomsky,* Harvard Univ. Press, Cambridge, Mass., Chap. 7.

Piaget J., 1976, *Behavior and Evolution,* translated by D. Nicholson-Smith (1978), Pantheon Books, New York, NY.

Piaget J., 1981, *Possibility and Necessity: Vol. 1, The Role of Possibility in Cognitive Development,* translated by H. Feider (1987), Univ. of Minnesota Press, Minneapolis, Minn.

Piaget J., 1983, *Possibility and Necessity: Vol. 2, The Role of Necessity in Cognitive Development,* translated by H. Feider (1987), Univ. of Minnesota Press, Minneapolis, Minn.

Piaget J. and Inhelder B., 1948, *The Child's Conception of Space,* trans. by F.J. Langdon and J.L. Lunzer (1956), W.W. Norton & Company (1967), New York, NY.

Piaget J. and Inhelder B., 1966, *The Psychology of the Child,* trans. by Helen

Weaver, Basic Books (1969), New York, NY.

Piaget J., Inhelder B., and Szeminska A., 1948a, *The Child's Conception of Geometry,* trans. by E.A. Lunzer (1960), W.W. Norton & Company (1981), New York, NY.

Piaget J. and Szeminska A, 1941, *The Child's Conception of Number,* trans. by C. Gattegno and F.M. Hodgson (1952), W.W. Norton & Company (1965), New York, NY.

Pinker S., 1985, "Visual Cognition: An Introduction," in S. Pinker (ed.) *Visual Cognition,* pp. 1–63, MIT Press, Cambridge, Mass.

Plato, *Theaetetus,* translated by F.M. Cornford, in *Plato's Theory of Knowledge,* Macmillan, New York, NY (1985).

Pollio H.R. and Burns B.C., 1977, "The Anomaly of Anomaly," *Journal of Psycholinguistic Research 6,* No. 3, pp. 247–260.

Pollio H.R. and Smith M.K., 1979, "Sense and Nonsense in Thinking about Anomaly and Metaphor," *Bulletin of Psychonomic Society 13,* pp. 323–326.

Polya G., 1945, *How to Solve it,* Princeton Univ. Press, Princeton, New Jersey, (2nd ed. 1973).

Popper K.R., 1959, *The Logic of Scientific Discovery,* Hutchinson, London.

Popper K.R., 1962, *Conjectures and Refutations: The Growth of Scientific Knowledge,* Basic Books, New York; 2nd ed. 1965; Harper & Row: 1968.

Quinn N., 1986, *American Marriage: A Cultural Analysis,* Draft.

Quinn N., 1987, "Convergent evidence for a cultural model of American marriage," in D. Holland and N. Quinn (eds.) *Cultural Models in Language and Thought,* Cambridge Univ. Press, Cambridge, U.K.; Chap. 7 (pp. 173–192).

Ratliff F., 1976, "On the Psychophysiological Basis of Universal Color Terms," *Proceedings of the American Philosophical Society 120,* no. 5 (October 1976), pp. 311–330.

Reddy M.J., 1979, "The Conduit Metaphor—A Case of Frame Conflict in Our Language about Language," in A. Ortony (ed.) *Metaphor and Thought,* Cambridge Univ. Press (1979), Cambridge, UK, pp. 284–324.

Rescher N., 1976, "Pierce and the Economy of Research," *Philosophy of Science 43,* pp. 71–98.

Reynolds R.E. and Ortony A., 1980, "Some Issues in the Measurement of Children's Comprehension of Metaphorical Language," *Child Develop-*

ment 51, pp. 1110–1119.

Richards I.A., 1936, *The Philosophy of Rhetoric,* Oxford Univ. Press, Oxford, UK; Lecture V (pp. 87–112) of this work is reprinted in M. Johnson (ed.) *Philosophical Perspectives on Metaphor,* Univ. of Minnesota Press (1981), Minneapolis, Minn., pp. 48–62.

Ricoeur P., 1976, *Interpretation Theory: Discourse and the Surplus of Meaning,* The Texas Christian Univ. Press, Fort Worth, Tex.

Ricoeur P., 1977, *The Rule of Metaphor,* translated by R. Czerny *et al.,* Univ. of Toronto Press, Toronto, Can.

Ricoeur P., 1978, "The Metaphorical Process as Cognition, Imagination, and Feeling," *Critical Inquiry 5,* no. 1, pp. 143–159; reprinted in M. Johnson (ed.) *Philosophical Perspectives on Metaphor,* Univ. of Minnesota Press (1981), Minneapolis, Minn., pp. 228–247.

Ricoeur P., 1982, "Imagination et Métaphore," *Psychologie Medicale 14,* No. 12, pp. 1883–1887.

Robbins J., 1991, "Echoes of 1939 on Capitol Hill," *Wall Street Journal,* January 14, 1991, p. A12.

Rifkin N., 1982, *Antonioni's Visual Language,* UMI Research Press, Ann Arbor, Mich.

Rogers H., 1967, *Theory of Recursive Functions and Effective Computability,* McGraw-Hill, New York, NY.

Rosch E., 1978, "Principles of Categorization," in E. Rosch and B.B. Lloyd (eds.) *Cognition and Categorization,* Lawrence Erlbaum Associates, Hillsdale, NJ, pp. 27–48.

Rothbart D., 1984, "The Semantics of Metaphor and the Structure of Science," *Philosophy of Science 51,* pp. 595–615.

Rowell L., 1983, *Thinking About Music,* The University of Massachusetts Press, Amherst, Mass.

Rumelhart D.E., Hinton G.E., and Williams R.J., 1986, "Learning Internal Representation by Error Propagation," in D.E. Rumelhart & J.L. McClelland (eds.) *Parallel Distributed Processing: Explorations in the Microstructure of Cognition, Vol. 1,* MIT Press, Cambridge, Mass.

Russell S.J., 1987, *Analogical and Inductive Reasoning,* Ph.D. Thesis, Computer Science Dept., Stanford University, Palo Alto, Calif.

Russell S.W., 1976, "Computer Understanding of Metaphorically Used Verbs," *American Journal of Computational Linguistics,* Microfiche 44.

Sacks O., 1985, *The Man Who Mistook His Wife for a Hat and Other Clinical Tales,* Harper & Row, New York, NY.

Salmon W.C., 1966, *The Foundations of Scientific Inference,* Univ. of Pittsburgh Press, Pittsburgh, Penn.

Scheffler I., 1979, *Beyond The Letter,* Routledge & Kegan Paul, London, U.K.

Schön D.A., 1963, *Displacement of Concepts,* Humanities Press, New York.

Schön D.A., 1979, "Generative Metaphor: A Perspective on Problem-Setting in Social Policy," in A. Ortony (ed.) *Metaphor and Thought,* Cambridge Univ. Press (1979), Cambridge, UK, pp. 154–283.

Scientific American, 1986, *The Mind's Eye,* readings from *Scientific American,* W.H. Freeman & Co., New York, NY.

Scott W.A., Osgood D.W., and Peterson C., 1979, *Cognitive Structure,* V.H. Winston & Sons, Washington, D.C.

Searle J.R., 1979, "Metaphor," in A. Ortony (ed.) *Metaphor and Thought,* Cambridge University Press (1979), Cambridge, U.K., pp. 92–123.

Segall M.H., Campbell D.T. and Herskovits M.J., 1966, *The Influence of Culture on Visual Perception,* Bobbs-Merrill Co., Indianapolis, Indiana.

Sekuler R. and Levinson E., 1977, "The Perception of Moving Targets," *Scientific American,* January 1977; reprinted in *The Mind's Eye,* readings from *Scientific American,* W.H. Freeman & Co. (1985), New York, NY; pp. 60–68.

Sewell E., 1964, *The Human Metaphor,* Univ. of Notre Dame Press.

Shirley E.S., 1981, "An Unnoticed flaw in Barker and Achinstein's Solution to Goodman's New Riddle of Induction," *Philosophy of Science 48,* pp. 611–617.

Shlain L.M., 1991, *Art & Physics,* William Morrow and Co., New York, NY.

Shurkin J., 1984, *Engines of the Mind: A History of the Computer,* W.W. Norton & Co., New York, NY.

Siegel R.K., 1977, "Hallucinations," *Scientific American,* October 1977; reprinted in *The Mind's Eye,* readings from *Scientific American,* W.H. Freeman & Co. (1985), New York, NY; pp. 109–116.

Simon J., 1978, "Why is the Co-Eatus Always Interruptus?" in J. Mellen (ed.) *The World of Luis Buñuel,* Oxford University Press, New York, pp. 363–368; originally published in *The New York Times,* February 25, 1973.

Solomon S.J., 1973, *The Classic Cinema: Essays in Criticism,* Harcourt Brace Jovanovich, New York, NY.

Sowa J.F., 1984, *Conceptual Structures: Information Processing in Mind and Machine,* Addison-Wesley, Reading, Mass.

Sticht T.G., 1979, "Educational Uses of Metaphor," in A. Ortony (ed.) *Metaphor and Thought,* Cambridge Univ. Press (1979), Cambridge, UK, pp. 474–485.

Stillman J.M., 1924, *The Story of Early Chemistry,* D. Appleton and Company, New York, NY; republished as *The Story of Alchemy and Early Chemistry,* Dover Publications (1960), New York, NY.

Stove D.C., 1986, *The Rationality of Induction,* Clarendon Press, Oxford, U.K.

Stratton G.M., 1897, "Vision without Inversion of Retinal Image," *Psychological Review IV,* No. 5, September 1897.

Subramanian D., 1990, "A Theory of Justified Reformulations," in D. Paul Benjamin (ed.) *Change of Representation and Inductive Bias,* Kluwer Academic Publishers, Dordrecht, The Netherlands.

Sweetser E.E., 1987, "The Definition of 'lie': An Examination of the Folk Models Underlying a Semantic Prototype," in D. Holland and N. Quinn (eds.) *Cultural Models in Language and Thought,* Cambridge Univ. Press, Cambridge, U.K.; Chap. 2 (pp. 43–66).

Terry A., 1983, "The CRYSALIS Project: Hierarchical Control of Production Systems," Technical Report No. HPP-83-19, Heuristic Programming Project, Stanford University, Stanford, Calif.

Tourangeau R. and Sternberg R.J., 1982, "Understanding and Appreciating Metaphors," *Cognition 11,* no. 3, May 1982, pp. 203–244.

Truffaut F., 1984, *Hitchcock,* with the collaboration of H.G. Scott, revised edition, Simon and Schuster, New York, NY.

Turbayne C.M., 1962, *The Myth of Metaphor,* Yale Univ. Press, New-Haven; revised edition with an appendix by R. Eberle "Models, Metaphors, and Formal Interpretations," Univ. of South Carolina Press, Columbia, 1970.

Turner V., 1974, *Dramas, Fields, and Metaphors: Symbolic Action in Human Society,* Cornell University Press, Ithaca, New York.

Ullman S., 1985, "Visual Routines," in S. Pinker (ed.) *Visual Cognition,* pp. 97–159, MIT Press, Cambridge, Mass.

Van Rooten L. d'Antin, 1967, *Mots D'Heures: Gousses, Rames,* Penguin

Edition (1980), New York, NY

Verbrugge R.R., 1980, "Transformations in Knowing: A Realist View of Metaphor," in R.P. Honeck and R.R. Hoffman (eds.) *Cognition and Figurative Language,* Lawrence Erlbaum Associates, Hillsdale, NJ, pp. 87–125.

Von Wright G.H., 1965, *The Logical Problem of Induction,* 2nd revised ed., Oxford Univ. Press.

Vosniadou S., Ortony A., Reynolds R.E., and Wilson P.T., 1984, "Sources of Difficulty in the Young Child's Understanding of Metaphorical Language," *Child Development 55,* pp. 1588–1606.

Waggoner J.E., 1990, "Interaction Theories of Metaphor: Psychological Perspectives," *Metaphor and Symbolic Activity 5,* No. 2, pp. 91–108.

Wallace B. and Srb A.M., 1964, *Adaptation,* 2nd ed., Prentice-Hall, Inc.

Way E.C., 1991, *Knowledge Representation and Metaphor,* Kluwer Academic Publishers, Dordrecht, The Netherlands.

Wegener P., 1885, "The Life of Speech," in D.W. Abse *Speech and Reason,* University of Virginia Press, Charlottesville, Virg., pp. 111–293.

Weiner E.J., 1984, "A Knowledge Representation Approach to Understanding Metaphors," *Computational Linguistics 10,* No. 1, January-March 1984, pp. 1–14.

Weiner E.J., 1985, "Solving the Containment Problem for Figurative Language," *International Journal of Man-Machine Studies 23,* pp. 527–537.

Weitzenfeld J.S., 1984, "Valid Reasoning by Analogy," *Phil. of Science 51,* pp. 137–149.

Wermus H., 1971, "Formalisation de Quelques Structures Initiales de la Psychogenese," *Archives de Psychologie 41,* pp. 271–288.

Wheeler C.J., 1987, "The Magic of Metaphor: A Perspective on Reality Construction," *Metaphor and Symbolic Activity 2,* pp. 223–237.

Wheelwright P.E., 1962, *Metaphor and Reality,* Indiana University Press, Bloomington, Ind.

Whitford F., 1987, *Understanding Abstract Art,* E.P. Dutton, New York, NY.

Whittock T., 1990, *Metaphor and Film,* Cambridge University Press, Cambridge, U.K.

Whorf B.L., 1941, "Languages and Logic," in J.B. Carroll (ed.) *Language, Thought, and Reality: Selected Papers of Benjamin Lee Whorf,* MIT Press (1956), Cambridge, Mass., pp. 233–245.

Whorf B.L., 1950, "An American Indian Model of the Universe," in J.B. Carroll (ed.) *Language, Thought, and Reality: Selected Papers of Benjamin Lee Whorf,* MIT Press (1956), Cambridge, Mass., pp. 57–64.

Wilks Y.A., 1975, "Preference Semantics," in E.L. Keenan (ed.) *Formal Semantics of Natural Language,* Cambridge University Press, Cambridge.

Wilks Y.A., 1978, "Making Preferences more Active," *Artificial Intelligence 11,* pp. 197–223.

Winner E., Engel M., and Gardner H., 1980, "Misunderstanding Metaphor: What's the Problem," *Journal of Experimental Psychology 30,* pp. 22–32.

Winston P.H., 1978, "Learning by Creatifying Transfer Frames," *Artificial Intelligence 10,* pp. 147–172.

Winston P.H., 1981, "Learning New Principles from Precedents and Exercises," AIM 632, Artificial Intelligence Laboratory, MIT, Cambridge, Mass.

Wood R., 1989, *Hitchcock's Films Revisited,* Columbia University Press, New York, NY.

Zadeh L.H., 1965, "Fuzzy Sets," *Information and Control 8,* pp. 338–353.

Name Index

Abbott, Edwin, 135, 180
Abramov, I., 108, 414
Acconci, Vito, 6
Achinstein, P., 325, 349, 411, 428
Agassi, J., 325, 411
Allwood, C.M., 335, 411
Amarel, S., 409, 411
Anderegg, M.A., 23, 24, 411
Andersen, M., 50, 411
Antonioni, Michelangelo, 23–25, 246, 252, 253, 256, 427
Arbib, M.A., 187, 217, 286, 290, 411, 421
Armajani, Siah, 6
Aycock, Alice, 6

Barham, J., 120, 411
Barker, S., 349, 411, 428
Bateson, G., 132, 290, 411
Baum, Frank, 1
Benjamin, Richard, 23
Berger, P.L., 161, 411
Berggren, D., 286, 287, 411
Berlin, B., 107–110, 294, 299, 411
Binkley, T., 306, 307, 411
Black, Max, 3–5, 10, 54, 66, 68–73, 75, 78, 81, 83, 86, 248, 262, 286, 289, 290, 303, 314, 412
Bobrow, D., 405, 412
Bohr, Niels, 50, 55, 60, 411
Boland, Eavan, 41, 48, 246–251, 253–254, 278–279, 292, 307, 310, 311

Brachman, R.J., 405, 412
Broad, W., 56, 63, 412
Buñuel, Luis, 25, 414
Bunch, B.L., 349, 412
Burks, Arthur W., 349, 412
Burns, B.C., 17, 426
Bush, George H.W., 337, 351
Buy, Ugo, 121

Cage, John, 6, 412
Camac, Mary K., 3, 45–46, 412
Campbell, D.T., 104, 428
Campbell, Joseph, 5, 22, 49, 412
Canguilhem, G., 56, 412
Carbonell, J.G., 3, 360, 366, 373, 413
Carnap, R., 33, 324–326, 343, 413
Carnot, Sadi, 57, 333
Carroll, J.M., 371, 413
Carter, Michael, 338
Cassirer, Ernst, 7, 10, 94, 111, 113–115, 132, 144, 186, 286, 287, 290, 292, 298, 413
Champa, K.S., 43, 413
Chaplin, Charlie, 23, 25
Chase, S., 309, 413
Christie, Julie, 23
Clement, C.A., 40, 329–332, 413, 415
Clift, Eleanor, 337
Cohn, P.M., 211, 231, 233, 242, 413
Collins, A., 163, 413
Connor, K., 17, 414

Corballis, M.C., 339, 415

Darwin, Charles, 55, 60, 416
De Kooning, Willem, 6
De Valois, R.L., 108–109, 414
Deregowski, J.B., 104, 414
Descartes, Rene, 106
Desforges, Abbé Pierre, 105
Dretske, Fred I., 250, 414
Dukakis, Michael, 351

Edwards, Gwynne, 25, 414
Ehrenfels, Christian von, 95
Eliasson, M., 335, 411
Eliot, T.S., 48
Emmet, Dorothy M., 286–287, 414
Engel, M., 431
Erman, L.D., 187, 386, 398, 407, 414
Evans, Thomas G., 358, 377–385, 414
Ewing, Lauren, 6

Falkenhainer, B., 3, 39, 366–367, 414, 415
Fass, Dan, 3, 360, 362, 414
Fauconnier, G., 132, 415
Favreau, O.E., 339, 415
Feynman, Richard, 352, 391, 415
Fikes, R.E., 412
Forbus, K.D., 366–367, 405, 414, 415
Fox, H.N., 6, 415
Franklin, Benjamin, 62
French, Robert M., 391, 415

Gacs, Peter, 350
Galileo, Galilei, 336, 350
Gardner, Howard, 431
Gentner, D.R., 258, 307, 308, 415
Gentner, Dedre, 3, 33, 40, 56–58, 163, 258, 307–308, 312, 313,

329–333, 336, 339, 366, 367, 371, 375, 413–416
Gephardt, Richard, 351
Gerhart, Mary, 106, 416
Gerrig, R.J., 87, 416
Gick, Mary L., 33, 40, 56, 263, 267–274, 318, 329–332, 416
Gillam, B., 339, 416
Gineste, Marie-Dominique, 75
Gitter, D.L., 56, 416
Glucksburg, Sam, 3, 45–46, 412
Goodman, Nelson, 7, 9, 10, 35, 94, 111–116, 118, 127, 128, 131, 134, 151, 158, 166, 169, 179, 186, 253, 306, 317, 348, 349, 354, 412, 416, 428
Gordon, William J.J., 56, 58, 60–62, 64, 270, 276, 332, 333, 373, 389, 396, 416
Gray, William, 336
Green, M., 98, 421
Greiner, R., 373, 416
Gruber, H.E., 5, 55–56, 416

Halasz, F., 335, 417
Halford, G.S., 157, 233, 417
Hall, R.P., 365, 417
Harrod, R., 323–326, 343, 417
Hart, C., 104–105, 417
Hartline, H.K., 106, 417
Hausman, Carl R., 3–5, 66, 75–76, 86, 417
Hayes, P.J., 405, 417
Hayes-Roth, F., 414
Hedren, Tippi, 24
Heider, Eleanor, 109, 417
Helmreich, S., 362, 417
Hemingway, Ernest, 1
Henle, P., 2, 417
Herskovits, M.J., 104, 428

Hesse, Mary B., 5, 33, 54, 56, 132, 270, 277, 286, 290, 303, 322, 325, 358, 411, 417–418

Higginbotham, Virginia, 25, 418

Hintikka, Jaakko, 306, 418

Hinton, G.E., 427

Hitchcock, Alfred, 6, 22–24, 44, 64, 115, 116, 252, 429, 431

Hobbs, Jerry R., 360, 362–363, 418

Hoeller, S.A., 158, 418

Hoffman, R.R., 87, 418

Hofstadter, Douglas R., 31, 166, 358–359, 367, 370, 376–378, 384–392, 407, 408, 415, 418, 423–424

Holland, Dorothy, 157, 170, 419

Holland, J.H., 132, 166, 187, 241, 267, 318, 320, 354, 419

Holstein, B.I., 5, 56, 419

Holyoak, Keith J., 33, 40, 56, 263, 267–274, 318, 329–332, 339, 366, 371, 372, 416, 419

Hubel, D.H., 106, 170, 185, 355, 419

Hume, David, 343, 419

Indurkhya, Bipin, 28, 67, 84–86, 236, 256, 258, 274, 304, 344, 396, 416, 419

Inhelder, Bärbel, 116, 419, 425–426

Iverson, E., 362, 417

Iwayama, M., 361, 420

Jacobs, G.H., 108, 414

Jeziorski, M., 56–58, 333, 336, 415

Johnson, Mark, 2, 66, 78, 79, 82, 84, 94, 124–128, 131, 251, 262, 289, 293–297, 306, 307, 360, 420, 422

Johnson, Michael G., 3, 17, 40, 249, 252, 309–311, 420, 423

Jones, Roger S., 106, 420

Jung, Carl G., 158, 160, 418, 420

Köhler, W., 96, 421

Kövecses, Z., 6, 422

Kamp, H., 307, 420

Kanizsa, G., 339, 420

Kant, Immanuel, 7, 94, 111–115, 127, 158, 160, 276, 288, 420, 421

Katz, A.N., 310, 420

Kay, P., 107–110, 294, 299, 411, 420

Kedar-Cabelli, S., 365, 420

Keil, F.C., 46–47, 420

Kekule, 62

Kelly, M.H., 46–47, 420

Kemper, S., 87, 418

Kempton, W., 6, 421

Keynes, J.M., 324, 326–327, 346, 349, 421

Kfoury, A.J., 217, 421

Kittay, Eva F., 4, 5, 48, 65, 67, 86–89, 299, 421

Klee, Paul, 21, 25–26

Kling, R.E., 365, 421

Koestler, A., 56, 62–63, 421

Kogan, N., 17, 414

Kolers, P.A., 98, 102, 118, 354, 421

Korf, R.E., 409, 421

Krausser, P., 112, 158–159, 421

Kubrick, Stanley, 43, 44, 424

Kuhn, Thomas S., 275–276, 421–422

Lakatos, Imre, 169, 422

Lakoff, George, 2, 5, 6, 19–20, 66–67, 78–85, 90, 94, 124–128, 131, 132, 151, 156–157, 262, 263, 286–287, 290, 292–301, 306, 308–309, 360, 422

Langer, Susanne K., 113–114, 413, 422
Laroche, F., 362, 417
Lean, David, 23–25, 411
Leigh, Janet, 6
Lesser, Victor R., 414
Lettvin, J.Y., 106, 422
Levesque, H.J., 412
Levin, S.R., 296, 422
Levine, M.W., 108
Levinson, E., 339, 428
Levy, A., 192, 422
Libby, Walter, 56, 62, 422
Lippmann, R.P., 187, 422
Lowry, M., 409, 422
Luckmann, T., 161, 411
Luria, Alexander R., 100–102, 109, 423

M Cormac, Earl R., 76
Mack, R.L., 371, 413
MacLaury, R.E., 110, 423
Mac Cormac, Earl R., 7, 19, 66, 77–78, 82, 125, 286–287, 290, 292–301, 303, 306, 307, 309, 423
Mac Lane, S., 192, 265, 423
Mal'cev, A.I., 197, 231, 423
Malgady, Robert G., 3, 17, 40, 249, 252, 309–311, 420, 423
Marschark, M., 310, 420
Martin, James H., 3, 360, 423
Matsuyama, T., 407, 424
Maturana, H.R., 120, 422, 423
McCabe, Allyssa, 45, 310, 423
McCulloch, W.S., 422
McDaniel, C.K., 109, 420
Melis, Erica, 335
Melville, Herman, 1, 16, 19
Metzinger, Jean, 49, 55
Miller, A.I., 5, 50, 55–56, 423

Miller, R.M., 263, 341, 423
Mitchell, Melanie, 358, 367, 370, 377–378, 384–392, 399, 407, 408, 418, 423–424
Moll, R.N., 217, 421
Mondrian, Piet, 42–43, 63, 246, 252–254, 278–279, 307, 311, 413, 424
Moran, T.P., 335, 417
Morris, Robert, 6
Moss, A.E.St.G., 110, 424

Nagao, M., 407, 424
Neisser, Ulric, 249, 424
Nelson, Beryl, 197, 347
Nelson, Thomas A., 44, 424
Newman, Barnett, 6
Newman, J.R., 350, 424
Newton, Sir Isaac, 55
Nii, H.P., 407, 424
Nisbett, R.E., 419
Nixon, Richard, 262, 285, 301, 308–309
Nowottny, W., 28, 424

O'Toole, Peter, 24
Oppenheim, Dennis, 6
Ortony, Andrew, 3, 26, 28, 40, 47, 251, 309, 311, 312, 424, 426, 430
Osgood, D.W., 428

Paivio, A., 310, 420
Partee, Barbara H., 155, 424
Peterson, C., 428
Petrie, H.G., 5, 169, 424
Piaget, Jean, 7, 9–10, 94, 116–123, 126, 128, 131–132, 134, 151, 157, 165, 168, 292, 303, 354, 419, 425–426
Pinker, S., 185, 426

Pitts, W.H., 422
Plato, 95, 426
Pollio, H.R., 17, 426
Pollock, Jackson, 6
Polya, G., 56, 426
Popper, Karl R., 164, 242, 426
Prince, G.M., 416

Quinn, Naomi, 6, 157, 170, 286, 309, 419, 426

Ratliff, Floyd, 107–109, 426
Reddy, D.R., 414
Reddy, M.J., 6, 426
Rescher, N., 349, 412, 426
Reynolds, R.E., 28, 426, 430
Richards, I.A., 3, 66, 286, 289, 290, 427
Ricoeur, Paul, 3, 10, 54, 66, 74–75, 81, 86, 251, 286, 290, 396, 427
Rifkin, N., 24, 427
Riguet, J., 197
Robbins, James, 336, 427
Rogers, H., 217, 427
Rosch, Eleanor, 159, 375, 427
Rothbart, D., 5, 55, 427
Rowell, L., 6, 427
Rumelhart, D.E., 187, 427
Russell, Allan, 106, 416
Russell, S.J., 373–374, 427
Russell, Sylvia W., 360, 361, 363, 427
Ryder, Winona, 23

Sacks, Oliver, 110, 428
Salmon, W.C., 343, 428
Sandburg, Carl, 2, 40, 50
Sandu, G., 306, 418
Schön, Donald A., 5, 6, 56, 59–61, 64, 85, 271, 274, 276, 332, 333, 373, 389, 405, 428

Scheffler, I., 307, 428
Scott, W.A., 132, 428
Searle, John R., 296, 428
Segall, M.H., 104, 428
Sekuler, R., 339, 428
Sewell, E., 286–287, 428
Sharif, Omar, 23
Shirley, E.S., 349, 428
Shlain, Leonard M., 50, 428
Shurkin, J., 338, 428
Siegel, R.K., 339, 428
Simon, John, 25, 428
Sizzi, Francesco, 336, 350
Skorstad, J., 3, 39, 415
Smith, M.K., 17, 426
Solomon, Stanley J., 23, 429
Sowa, J.F., 364, 429
Spender, Stephen, 42, 48, 74, 246–247, 249, 251–254, 278, 292, 307
Srb, A.M., 347, 430
Sternberg, R.J., 4, 310–312, 429
Stevens, Wallace, 73
Stewart, James, 22, 23, 44, 64
Sticht, T.G., 5, 429
Stillman, J.M., 336, 429
Stove, David C., 344–348, 429
Stratton, G.M., 167–168, 429
Stuart, P., 3, 416
Subramanian, D., 409, 429
Sweetser, E.E., 304, 429
Szeminska, A., 116, 426

Tanaka, H., 361, 420
Taylor, Rod, 24
Terry, A., 407, 429
Thagard, P.R., 366, 371, 419
Thomas, Dylan, 1
Tokunaga, T., 361, 420
Tourangeau, R., 4, 310–312, 429

Truffaut, Francois, 24, 44, 116, 252, 429
Tubey, Charles, 336
Turbayne, Colin M., 106, 168, 286–289, 405, 429
Turner, Mark, 2, 5, 66, 67, 79, 81, 83, 85, 286, 294, 295, 297, 300, 422
Turner, Victor, 6, 429

Ullman, S., 185, 429

Van Eyck, Jan, 22, 25, 26
Van Rooten, L. d'Antin, 399, 429
Varela, F., 120, 423
Verbrugge, R.R., 4, 5, 17, 28, 30, 249, 430
Vitti, Monica, 23
Von Wright, G.H., 33, 343, 430
Vosniadou, S., 28, 430

Waggoner, J.E., 4, 5, 430
Wallace, B., 347, 430
Way, Eileen C., 360, 363–364, 430
Wegener, P., 290, 430
Weiner, E.J., 3, 360, 361, 430
Weitzenfeld, J.S., 327–329, 341, 366, 373, 430
Wermus, H., 121, 430
Wertheimer, Max, 96
Wheeler, C.J., 286, 430
Wheelwright, P.E., 5, 66, 76–77, 430
Whitford, Frank, 22, 42, 430
Whittock, Trevor, 6, 23–24, 43, 430
Whorf, Benjamin Lee, 80–81, 100, 430–431
Wiesel, T.N., 170, 419
Wilks, Yorick, 360, 362, 414, 431
Williams, R.J., 427
Wilson, P.T., 28, 430

Wilson, W.H., 157, 233, 417
Winner, Ellen, 28, 431
Winston, Patrick, H., 373, 431
Wood, R., 6, 431

Zadeh, L.H., 77, 431

Subject Index

Ω-word algebra, 211

4'33" (Cage), 5

2001: A Space Odyssey (Kubrick), 43

Achilles (Newman), 5

Birds, The (Hitchcock), 24, 26, 252

Cathedral (Pollock), 5

Challenger, space shuttle, 352

Composition with Blue and Yellow (Mondrian), 42, 246, 252

Discreet Charm of the Bourgeoisie, The (Buñuel), 25

Doctor Zhivago (Lean), 23

Excavations (Kooning), 5

Flatland (Abbott), 135–136, 180

Fog (Sandburg), 2, 40

Force that through the green fuse drives the flower, The (Dylan Thomas), 1

Lawrence of Arabia (David Lean), 24

Le Goûter (Metzinger), 49

Love Song of J. Alfred Prufrock (Eliot), 48

Marriage of Giovanni (?), Arnolfini and Giovanna Cenami (?), The (Van Eyck), 22

Mermaids (Richard Benjamin), 23

Moby Dick (Melville), 1, 16, 19, 26

Modern Times (Chaplin), 23, 25

Old Man and the Sea, The (Hemingway), 1

Park near L(ucerne) (Klee), 21

Psycho (Hitchcock), 6, 23

Rear Window (Hitchcock), 22, 44, 64

Red Desert, The (Il Deserto Rosso) (Antonioni), 23

Seascape (Spender), 42, 48, 74, 247

Theaetetus (Plato), 95

Wall Street Journal, 336

White Hawthorn in the West of Ireland (Eavan Boland), 41

Wizard of Oz, The (Baum), 1, 26

Boston Globe, 337, 350

Buffalo News, 1

Abstract symbolism
    in Klee, 21, 25
    in Mondrian, 63

Abstraction, in syntactic metaphor, 263

Accommodation, 164–169
    as 'bottom-up' process, 148, 185, 394
    as restructuring concept networks, 148
    biological, 118
    changes structure of concept network, 133
    examples of
        determining number of days in a year, 166
        imitation, 165
        in mathematical proofs, 169
        mapping a terrain, 133, 166

grouping perspective on, 174
in a parser, 394
in a three-layered cognitive system, 182
in layered cognitive system, 185
Accommodation (Piaget), 118–123, 128
ACME, *see* Analogical Constraint Mapping Engine
Adaptation (Piaget), 119
Admissibility
  of a class of operators, 221
  of an operator, 220
ALG1 (algebra), 209, 216, 224, 227
ALG2 (algebra), 209, 211, 216, 221, 224, 227
Algebra
  definition of, 205
  examples of, 205
  finite, 209
  finitely generated, 216
  infinite, 209
Algebra of classes, definition of, 223
Algebras, product of, 224
Analogical Constraint Mapping Engine, 371–373
Analogical inference, *see* Predictive analogy
Analogical reasoning, *see* Predictive analogy
Analogical symbols, 114
Analogies
  as basis of metaphors, 4
  in political rhetoric, 337
  similarity-based, 50
Analogy
  as a general heuristic, 366
  between biological systems and cognitive systems (Piaget), 120

between fluid-flow and heat-flow, 57
between software and myth, 49
between *Le Gôuter* (Metzinger) and quantum mechanics, 49
creative, *see* Creative analogy
different senses of, 28
predictive, *see* Predictive analogy
proportional, *see* Proportional analogy
simple, *see* Simple analogy
starry-sky-through-the-smoked-glass (Black), 69, 72, 73, 81
Anomaly, 17, 18
Apparent motion
  effect of cultural background, 102
  experiments of Kolers, 96
  experiments of Wertheimer, 96
  experiments with colored figures, 98
Appearances, world of (Kant), 112
Aptness of metaphors, *see* Metaphorical aptness
Argument by analogy, *see* Predictive analogy
Articulating the content domain (Kittay), 88, 89
Assimilation, 118–120
  biological, 118, 134
  cognitive, 134
  formation of memory, 134
  underlies induction, 354
  vs. projection, 134
Associated commonplaces, 68
Astrology, 342
Asymmetry in simple analogy, 30
Asymmetry of metaphor 17, 19, 254
  empirical studies of, 17

in Black's interaction theory, 69–
70
in interaction theories, 4, 5
Augmentation, 85

Baptism, 23
Baseball World Series (1991), 351
Benzene, molecular structure of, 62
Between-domains similarity, crite-
rion of (Tourangeau & Stern-
berg), 312
Bible, 22
Bijection, 201
Bijective function, 203
difunctional relation and, 204
Biological metaphor
underlying Copycat, 386
Biological systems
assimilation and accommodation
in, 118
cognitive systems and, 120
Blackboard system, 407
Bottom-up
knowledge sources, 407
Bottom-up process
in parsing, 394
in visual cognition, 186
vs. 'bottom-up' process, 394
Buddhism, 22, 23
Buddhist metaphysics, 43

Cantor's theorem, 333, 366
Categories (Kant), 112
Chain
of subalgebras, 229
of subclasses, 198
Change of representation
basis of creative analogies, 359
basis of metaphor, 75
in cognition, 409

modeling similarity-creating metaphor
as, 401
Circularity in concept networks, 157
Class, 191
empty, 191
finite, 191
infinite, 191
power of, 194
Classes
disjoint, 192
intersection of, 191
product of, 194
union of, 191
Classes vs. sets, 192
Closed systems (Piaget), 157
Closure
of a class of objects of an algebra, 214
over operators, 216
Clustering effect, in concept networks, 156
Codelets (Copycat), 387, 388, 408
Coderack (Copycat), 387, 408
Codomain, of a relation, 194
Cofunctional
correspondence, 229
relation, 196
Cognition
action-oriented approach to (Piaget), 118
biological basis of, 120
Cognitive domains (Scott *et al.*),
132
Cognitive model, 133
ambiguous, 176
complete, 178, 235, 236
definition of, 233
extension of, 238
full, 178, 235, 236
fully resolved, 235, 236

gives descriptions to objects in environment, 176
groups the environment, 169
in Spinner's world, 141
optimal, 235, 236
refinement of, 178, 238
represents environment by a concept network, 176
restriction of, 238
synonyms in, 178
unambiguous, 235, 236
Cognitive models
'notational systems' and (Goodman), 179
accommodating, 241
concept driven, 240
conceptualized versions of reality, 169
correspond to 'worlds' (Goodman), 169
equivalent, 236
experiential versions of reality, 169
over the same environment, 236
projective, 240
strongly equivalent, 236
Cognitive relation, 161–164
accommodating, 165
concept driven, 165
creates environment, 161
difunctional, 235
environment driven, 165
epimorphic, 235
homomorphic, 240, 241
in Spinner's world, 141
incoherency of, 164, 169
isomorphic, 236
makes concept network meaningful, 161
projective, 165

Cognitive relations, 132
Cognitive system
multi-layered, 182, 247
three layered, 182
Coherency
correctness and, 301
finite representability of, 163, 241
full, 234, 241
is not internal consistency, 146, 303
local, 234, 241
of cognitive models (and relations), 133
of cognitive relations, 163
of projective models, 242
vs. internal consistency, 7
Color blindness, 95
Color perception, 101
Color universals, 109, 110
neurphysiological basis for, 107
Communion ritual, interpretation of, 5, 22
Comparison theory, *see* Theories of metaphor, comparison theory
Complex symbol, 21, 26
Components
of a description, 212
of a symbol, 153
Composition
of correspondences, 226
of functions, 203
of operators, 204
of relations, 194
of transformations, 170
Compositional semantics, 67, 86
Computability of operators, 217
Computable function, 232
Concept network

definition of, 232
finite, 155
generating set of, 153
in a parser, 393
infinite, 156
source, 253
subnetwork of, 153
target, 254
Concept networks, 132, 151–158
as potential representations, 141, 152
at perceptual level, 180
circularity of, 157
closed systems (Piaget) and, 157
clustering effect in, 156
components of, 151
constraints on, 155
derived, 157
examples of
natural number system, 151
street map, 151
finitely generated, 155
inherited, 158
learned, 157
of Spinner, 141
radial structure in, 156
representation langauge for, 405
role of operators in, 152
Concept, wholeness of, 95
Conceptual graph theory (Sowa), 364
Conceptualization, in a parser, 393
Congruences, 231
Constant operator, 204
Constructivism, Piaget's, 121, 128
Constructivist approach to cognition, 111
Content domain (Kittay), 88–89
Context, identifies source and target, 15

Contextual decomposition (in Evans' program), 381
Conventional interpretations
of models, 54
of Spinner's cognitive models, 146
Conventional metaphor, 19, 293
Conventional metaphor schemas, 360
in Hobbs' model, 362
Conventional metaphors, 1, 2, 13, 20, 67, 78, 79, 126, 296–298, 310, 360, 363
computational models of, 360
Conventional-metaphorical dichotomy, 21, 286
in symbols, 21
Copernicus' astronomy, 275
Copycat (Hofstadter & Mitchell), 377, 384–391, 408
major components of, 386
nondeterminism in, 388–390, 407
Correctness
conventional vs. metaphorical, 306
identified with coherency, 301
objectivity of, 307
vs. truth, 303
vs. understanding, 305
Correlation condition (Lakoff), 82
Correspondence
between algebras, 224
difunctional, 229
gives rise to chain of subalgebras, 229
inverse of, 226
preserves closure, 229
between concept network and environment, 148, 161
between concept network and world of Spinner, 141

between sensory states and world
of Spinner, 138
between symbols and objects,
144
Correspondences
between algebras
composition of, 226
examples of, 224
induce groupings, 227
Created World (Jung), 160
Creation of attributes, 84
Creation of similarity
as highlighting and downplaying, 53
between ideas and food, 82
between painting and pumping,
60
between software and mythology, 49
Black's explanantion of, 68
brought about by change in conceptualization, 81
by non-verbal analogies, 49
by projective metaphor, 271
caused by redescription, 54
clues offered by Black, 72
in a machine vision system, 400
in comparison-theoretic framework, 53, 65
in Hausman's approach, 75
in perspectival theory, 4, 86
in pre-theoretic models, 55
in Sandburg's *Fog*, 3
in simile, 48
in *Love Song of J. Alfred Prufrock*
(Eliot), 48
is not arbitrary, 64
Kittay's explanation of, 67
paradox of, 65
problems raised by, 54

psychological studies of, 45
rooted in a cognitive phenomenon,
84
Wheelwright's explanation of,
77
Creative analogies
computational model of, 376
in Copycat, 385–391
Creative analogy, 50
Creative metaphors
in Boland's poem, 41
in computational systems, 395,
399
in Ricoeur's account, 74
Creative problem solving, 56
Creatura (Jung), 160
Cubism, 55, 60

Dani language, color terms in, 109
Dead metaphor, 19, 67, 293
four senses of, 294, 297
Derivation
from 'women' to 'dangerous things',
156
Derivations, 84, 85
circular, 84
Description
as a labeled ordered tree, 153
in a cognitive model, 236
of a symbol, 153
of an object in a cognitive model,
176
Determination rule (Russell), 373
Determining structures (Weitzenfeld),
328
Diaphor (Wheelwright), 66, 76–78
Dichotomy
conventional vs. metaphorical,
21, 286
literal vs. metaphorical, 293
novel vs. conventional, 408

source vs. target, 24, 246, 253
Dictionary meaning, 16, 20, 247
Dictionary meanings, 249
Differences, role of
    in cognition, 290
Differentiation (Piaget), 120, 122
Difunctional
    cognitive relation, 235
    correspondence, 229, 230
    relation, 196, 200, 202
        bijective function and, 204
        equivalence relation and, 201
Digitalization (Dretske), 250
Direct analogy (Gordon), 58, 333
    predictive analogy and, 58
Directed acyclic graph, 211
Directly emergent concepts, 81
Disconnected relation, 198
Discursive symbols, 114
Disjoint (pairwise) groupings, 192
Disjoint classes, 192
Domain of a relation, 194
Domains-interaction theory, *see* The-
      ories of metaphor, domains-
      interaction theory
Dynamic equilibrium (Mondrian),
    43
Dynamic type hierarchy (Eileen Way),
    363
Dynamical objects (Pierce), 76

Effectory vector (Spinner), 136
Einstein's theory of relativity, 275
Electrical circuits, as target realm,
    258
Empty class, 191
Environment, 132, 160
    for Spinner, 144
    grouped in a cognitive model,
      169
    ontology of, 160

structure of, 160
Epimorphism, 230, 235
Epiphor (Wheelwright), 66, 76–78
Epitomization, in Weiner's model
    of metaphor, 361
Equivalence relation, 201
Evaluation function, on structural
    descriptions, 212
Evolution, theory of, 55, 60
Experiential ontology of Spinner's
    world, 144
Experiential view of cognition (Lakoff),
    124
Extension of a cognitive model, 238
Extra-linguistic condition (Hausman),
    4, 76

Finite representability
    of coherency, 163, 241
    of concept networks, 155, 232
Finitely generated algebra, 216, 232
First-Order Logic, 84
Flight, prehistory of, 104, 127
Form (Bateson), 132
Forward grouping, induced by a re-
    lation, 201
Frame of reference, 115, 128
French revolution, 338
Full grouping, 192
Function, definition of, 203
Functional concepts, 141
Functional correspondence, 229
Functional relation, 196, 203
Fuzzy set-theory
    in explaining color 'universals',
      109
    in formalizing metaphors, 77

Generalization (Piaget), 120
Generating class (of an algebra), 215

Generating set (of a concept network), 153
as a set of primitives, 155
minimal, 155
Generation (of symbols), 153
Generation history (of objects in
an algebra), 209
Generative metaphor (Schön), 276,
407
Gestalt psychology, 96, 100
Gestalt structure of preconcepts, 126
Grouping
in gestalt psychology, 96
in Spinner's cognitive models,
144
induced by a relation
backward, 201
forward, 201
involves loss of information, 277
of objects in environment, 169
of transformations in environment, 170–172
over a class
bijective, 201
definition of, 192
examples of, 193
full, 192, 197
induced by relation, 194, 196,
198, 200
pairwise disjoint, 192, 198
partition, 192, 196
over an algebra, 227
Grue paradox (Goodman), 348–349
generalized, 349

Hearsay II (Erman *et al.*), 386, 398,
399
Hering theory (of color vision), 107
Highlighting and downplaying
by syntactic metaphor, 262, 312,
321

creation of similarity and, 53,
65, 68, 70
Hinduism, 23
Homeomorphs (Weitzenfeld), 328
Homomorphism, 240, 241
definition of, 229
Hopi language, 100
Hydraulic systems, theory of
as source concept network, 258

Ichkari women, 101–102, 109
Idealized cognitive models (Lakoff),
132, 151, 156
Identity operator, 204
Identity, concept of, 117
Image
of a homomorphism, 230
of a relation, 194
Imagination
approach to understanding, 250
in understanding metaphor, 251
Imitation
as example of accommodation,
165
Incoherency (of cognitive relation
or cognitive model)
detectable by finite means, 164,
241
Individuality condition (Hausman),
76
Induction
cognitive dimension of, 354
compared with vision, 354
metaphysical dimension of, 355
two dimensions of, 353
Information, loss of
in cognition, 277, 279
reclaimed by projective metaphor,
277
INTEGER (algebra), 206, 209, 215–
221, 224, 226, 236

Interaction between lexical fields and content domains (Kittay), 89

Interpreting Spinner's concept networks, 141

Intersection, of classes, 191

Intrinsic decomposition (in Evans' program), 381

Inverse
of a correspondence, 226
of a function, 203
of a relation, 194

Isomorphism
in Black's theory, 72
in Lakoff's theory, 82
cognitive relation as, 236
definition of, 230

Isomorphism theorem, First, 231

Kernel (of a homomorphism), 230

Kinetoscope, invention of (Edison), 63

Knowledge, biological basis of, 120

Lakoffian approach to cognition, 124

Lateral geniculate nucleus, 108

Latitude and longitude, lines of (as examples of projection), 133, 168

Lavoisier's theory of combustion, 275

Layered cognitive system
accommodation in, 185
multiple 'worlds' (Goodman) and, 187
new insights in, 186
projection in, 182
visual system as, 185

Learning by analogy, 373–375

Learning, two forms of, 374

LENGTH (correspondence between algebras), 226, 227, 236

Lexical decision paradigm, 45

Lexical field (Kittay), 88–89

Lightning conductor, invention of (Franklin), 62

Linguistic metaphors, *see* Metaphors, linguistic

Link preconcept, 125, 126

Literal, 14, 19, 20
four senses of, 294, 297

Literal metaphors, 293

Literal-metaphorical dichotomy, 293

Local coherency, 163, 302
definition of, 234

Logical width (Carnap), 324

Macaque monkey, visual system of, 108

Making the familiar strange (Gordon), 61, 276, 333, 389, 396, 404

Making the strange familiar (Gordon), 60, 270, 396, 404

Map, as a concept network, 151–153, 162

Material models (Hesse), 270

Meaning change, caused by metaphor, 290

Mental models (Holland *et al.*), 132

Mental spaces (Fauconnier), 132

Met* (Fass), 362, 363

Metaphor
'emotional state as blotches of paint', 246, 252, 256
'glass telephone booth as cage of misery', 252
'ideas are food', 82
'life is a journey', 83
'more is up less is down', 81
'ocean as a harp', 246, 278
'paintbrush as a pump', 60, 85, 274, 275, 277, 333

'painting as pumping', 405
'wild flowers as water', 42, 246,
    247, 278, 310
as change of representation, 75,
    401
as projection, 249
asymmetry of, 17, 19, 254
comparative aspect of, 290
emotive force of, 19
in artificial intelligence, 357
in cognition, 5
in creative problem solving, 56
in learning and education, 5
in natural language processing
    systems, 357
in science, 5
induces new structure in the tar-
    get, 85
Lakoff's definition of, 297
Mac Cormac's definition of, 297
natural language processing ap-
    proaches to, 365
open-endedness of, 311
predictive analogy and, 313
reorganizes the target, 85
strong thesis of, 286
subjectivity of, 18
theories of, *see* Theories of metaphor
turns into anomaly, 17
turns into myth, 288
two senses of, 297
Metaphoric content, degree of, 13,
    19, 23
Metaphoric-content continuum, 20,
    31, 34
conventional end of, 20, 22
middle of, 23
novel-metaphorical end of, 20,
    23
Metaphorical aptness, 309–313

open-endedness of metaphor and,
    311
similarities between source and
    target and, 45, 310
Metaphorical interpretation
in Chaplin's *Modern Times*, 23
in contemporary arts, 5
in David Lean's *Lawrence of Ara-
    bia*, 24
of Christ's death and resurrec-
    tion, 22
Metaphorical quality, *see* Metaphor-
    ical aptness
Metaphorical relation, 254
Metaphorical schema (Lakoff), 83
Metaphors
asymmetry of, *see* Asymmetry
    of metaphors
classification of, 1
create associations between words,
    46
in contemporary art, 6
in extended contexts, 45, 310
in films, 6
in music, 6
isolated, 45, 310
linguistic, 13, 24, 25, 67
    computational models of, 360
lose their novelty, 290
non-linguistic, 24, 25
    asymmetric, 25
    optional, 26
open-endedness of, 257
predictive analogy, 56
similarity-based, *see* Similarity-
    based metaphors
similarity-creating, *see* Similarity-
    creating metaphors
subjectivity of, 16
underlying the concept of mar-

riage, 6
Mimetic symbols, 114
Models, 34–35
    conventional interpretations of,
        34, 54
    folk and cultural (Holland & Quinn),
        156
    pre-theoretic, 54
        for quantum mechanics, 55
    unconventional interpretations
        of, 35
MODULO (correspondence between
        algebras), 224, 227, 236
Mythology as computer software,
        49
Myths, metaphorical interpretation
        of, 5

Natural number system (as a con-
        cept network), 151–153, 155,
        156, 162, 313
Necessity, concept of (Piaget), 122
Negative aftereffects of motion, 96
Network models (Hesse), 132
New Testament, 26
Newtonian mechanics, 106, 275
Non-Euclidean geometry, 113
Non-linguistic metaphors, *see* Meta-
        phors, non-linguistic
Nondeterminism, *see* Copycat, non-
        determinism in
Novel projection
    in a machine vision system, 401
    in a speech understanding sys-
        tem, 398
Nursery rhymes (Mother Goose's),
        399

O-subalgebra, 218
    finitely generated, 219
Object permanence,

concept of, 116
construction of, 117
Object-concepts, 141
Objective
    criteria of rightness, 115
    nature of created referent (Haus-
        man), 76
    nature of natural sciences, 112
Objects
    acquire descriptions in cognitive
        model, 176
    counterparts of symbols, 160
    in Spinner's environment, 144
Onto function, 203
Ontology
    does not exist before conceptu-
        alization, 144
    experiential, 132
    of an environment, 160
Ontology and structure
    fixed, 115
    mind-independent, 7, 93, 106,
        111
    objective, 124
    of abstract domains (Lakoff),
        125
    of Spinner's sensorimotor data
        set, 138
    pre-existing, 93, 124
    preconceptual, 111, 125, 131
Operation (Piaget), formal charac-
        teristics of, 121
Operational structures, emergence
        of, 122
Operator, 204
    constant, 204
    identity, 204
    specialization of, 204
Operators
    composition of, 204

computability of, 217
induced, 236
of Spinner's concept networks,
    141
physically realizable, 155
represent actions of hypotheti-
    cal agents, 146
roles of, 152
Optics, influenced by theory of acous-
    tics, 55

Paintbrush as a pump, *see* Metaphor,
    'paintbrush as a pump'
Painting
    as masking a surface, 64
    as pumping, *see* Metaphor, 'paint-
        ing as pumping'
    as smearing, 59, 61
    sensorimotor data set of, 406
Paintings, metaphorical interpreta-
    tions of, 5
Parable of the sower, 29
Paradox
    grue, *see* Grue paradox (Good-
        man)
    in Black's interaction theory, 66,
        73
    in interaction theories of metaphor,
        66
    in interaction view of cognition,
        7, 93, 115, 116, 123, 124,
        127, 128, 131–133, 245
    of creation of similarity, 65, 67,
        72, 75, 79, 81, 89, 90, 93,
        124, 131, 245, 246, 280
    of raven, 344
    Russell's, 192
Parallel terraced scan (Copycat), 390
Paramorphs (Weitzenfeld), 328
Part-whole preconcept, 125
Partition, 192, 201, 203

Perception, goal oriented nature of,
    106
Perspectival theory, *see* Theories of
    metaphor, perspectival the-
    ory
Phenomenal world (Kantian), 160
Phlogiston theory, 275
Phonograph, invention of, 63
Physiological structures, source of
    universals, 110
Platonic concepts, in Copycat, 386
Pleroma (Jung), 158
Polynomial operations, class of, 216,
    232
Positing structure, 85
Possibility, concept of (Piaget), 122
Power, of a class, 194
Pre-image, of a relation, 196
Preconcepts
    as 'universals', 126
    basic logic of, 125
    genesis of, 126
    internal logic of, 125
Predicative metaphors, 28
Predictive analogy, 32–34, 36, 56,
    257
    computational approaches to, 365–
        375
    dark side of, 334
    definition of, 320
    direct analogy and, 58
    first-order generalization, 325,
        374
    general-purpose heuristic, 373
    in alchemy, 336
    in artificial intelligence, 358
    in learning, 373–375
    in sports, 351
    in understanding text-editors,
        335

induction and, 317
logical problem of justification,
  322
making the familiar strange and,
  61
metaphor and, 313
problem-solving heuristic, 33, 316,
  321, 329, 332–334, 365
projective metaphor and, 320
second-order generalization, 327
similarity-based metaphors and,
  57
suggestive metaphor and, 270,
  321
syntactic metaphor and, 321
Predictive disanalogy, 375
Preference semantics (Wilks), 362
Presentational symbols, 114
Primary subject (of a metaphor),
  1, 67
Primary system (of a metaphor),
  254
Primitives, choices of, 84
Principal subject (of a metaphor),
  67, 68
Problem solving
  creation of similarities in, 60
  in real-world situations, 59, 332
Product
  of algebras, 224
  of classes, 194
Projection, 60, 164–168
  as 'top-down' grouping, 392
  as reinterpreting concept net-
    works, 148
  changes experiential ontology of
    environment, 133
  examples of
    in mathematical proofs, 168
    lines of latitude and longitude,

133, 168
  measuring time in hours and
    minutes, 168
  playful activities of children,
    168
  retinal inversion of image, 167
  grouping perspective on, 174
  in a parser, 394
  in computational systems, 394
  in multi-layered cognitive sys-
    tem, 182
  in three-layered cognitive sys-
    tem, 182
  novel vs. conventional, 395
  underlies induction, 354
  vs. assimilation, 134
Projective metaphor
  asset to cognition, 277
  examples of, 271
  reclaims lost information, 277
Projective metaphors, 271–277
  in history of science, 275
Proper subclass, 191
Proportional analogies
  computational models of, 358
  in Hofstadter's microworld, 376,
    384
  of geometric figures, 30, 32, 36,
    51–65, 279, 358, 377, 378
  perceptual, 30, 32, 50, 51
  symmetry of, 31
  verbal, 30
    create similarities, 50
Prototype effect in concept networks,
  156
Prototypicality, in Weiner's model
  of metaphor, 361
Ptolemaic astronomy, 275

Q-morphism (Holland *et al.*), 166,
  241, 320

Quantity, as target domain, 82
Quantum mechanics, 49, 60, 106
    pre-theoretic model for, 55
    product of an analogy, 50

Radial categories (Lakoff), 156
Radial structure, in concept net-
    works, 156
Randomness, of a sample
    over space, 346
    over time, 347
Reality
    constrains possible ontologies,
        133
    construction of, 116
    experiential, 81
    experiential ontology of, 132
    objective, 76, 81, 125
    ontology and structure of, 132
    pre-conceptual structure of, 89
    structures the environment, 144
    three levels of, 158
Realm, 253
    source, 254
    target, 253
Redescription
    creates similarities, 54
    in proportional analogies, 359
    underlies creative metaphors and
        analogies, 359
Reductionist approach to reality, 106
Refinement of a cognitive model,
    238
Refinements of cognitive models, 241
Relation
    codomain of, 194
    definition of, 194
    disconnected, 198
    domain of, 194
    equivalence, 201
    full, 197

    image of, 194
    induces a chain, 198
    induces groupings, 194
    inverse of, 194
    reflexive, 201
    symmetric, 201
    transitive, 201
Relations, composition of, 194
Relativism, 89
Relativity, theory of, 113, 275
Religious symbols, metaphorical na-
    ture of, 5
Representation
    in a cognitive model, 236
    of an object by a concept, 176
Representational languages, 405
Restriction, of a cognitive model,
    238
Retinal inversion of image, as ex-
    ample of projection, 167
Revolution, scientific (Kuhn), 275
Russell's paradox, 192

S-subalgebra, 218
    finitely generated, 218
Salience
    in Weiner's model of metaphor,
        361
    of objects in Copycat, 387
Sampling principle
    in justifying induction, 344–349
    in justifying predictive analogy,
        323
Scale model, of a ship, 291
Schema induction, 263, 373, 375
Schemas (Kant), 112
Schemas (Piaget), 120–123, 126, 132,
    151
Schematas (Goodman), 151
Scope of a proposition (Keynes),
    326

Secondary subject (of a metaphor), 1, 67

Secondary system (of a metaphor), 254

Semantic differential scales, 47

Semantic distance, 28

Semantic field, 87, 88

Semantic net, 400, 401, 405

Semantic proximity, 74

Sensori stimuli, 96

Sensorimotor data set, 132, 159
    description language for, 406
    for Spender's *Seascape*, 248
    for Spinner, 138
    in a parser, 393
    ontology of, 132
    structure of, 132, 159

Sensory vector (Spinner), 136

Sets vs. classes, 192

Shawnee, 80

Shuswap, 'yellow-with-green' category in, 110

Signs vs. Symbols, 114

Similarities
    before and after the metaphor, 56
    creation of, *see* Creation of similarity
    experiential, 79
    mind-independent, 48
    objective, 48, 79
    perception of, 20
    changed by metaphors, 47

Similarity metrics, 80, 81

Similarity-based metaphors, 1–3, 8, 9, 37, 39, 53, 56–60, 63, 245, 246, 254, 256–257, 279–280, 357, 363
    epiphors and, 77
    in artificial intelligence, 358

    in cognition, 40, 56
    predictive analogy and, 57

Similarity-based, account of metaphor, 40, 55, 95, 333

Similarity-creating metaphors, 1–3, 8–9, 35, 37, 40, 49, 56, 271, 278–279, 357
    as change of representation, 401
    empirical studies of, 45
    in cognition, 56, 63
    in films, 43
    in problem solving, 62
    paradox of, 65
    problem of, 6

Similes, 26–28
    as symmetric comparisons, 28
    creation of similarity and, 27
    simple analogies and, 29
    statements of literal similarity and, 27

Simple analogies
    in non-verbal settings, 49
    similes and, 29

Simple analogy, 29–30, 36, 50

Single-instance generalization, 373

Slipnet (Copycat), 386, 408

SME, *see* Structure-Mapping Engine

Source (of a metaphor), 15
    affected by context, 15
    regarded as a system, 68, 73
    supplied by text, 18

Source concept network, 253, 408, 409

Source domain, 1
    'food', 83
    'journey', 83, 85
    'verticality', 81

Source realm, 254

Source semantic field, 89

Soviet Union, 101
Specialization, of an operator, 204
Speech recognition, 407
Speech understanding system, 386
    novel projection in, 398
Spinner, 135–148
    changes bias of sensory organ,
        180
    concept networks of, 141
    effectory organ of, 136
    reinterprets concept networks,
        148
    restructures concept networks,
        148
    sensorimotor data set for, 138
    sensory organ of, 135
    transported to an alien world,
        147
    world of, 138
        dense fog in, 180
        zonal structure of, 158
Split reference (Ricoeur), 74
Star of David, 4, 5, 70–73, 81, 406,
    407
    as sensorimotor data set, 406
STRING (algebra), 206, 209, 214–
    216, 219, 220, 224, 236
Strong thesis of metaphor, 286–293,
    296
    challenges to, 299
    three versions of, 287
Structural correlation, 82
Structural description, 209
    as directed acyclic graph, 211
    components of, 212
    definition of, 212
Structural descriptions
    class of, 211
    evaluation function on, 212
Structure

creation of, 127
in an algebra, 209
objective, of a content domain,
    89
of a description, 212
of a symbol, 153
of an environment, 160
of external world, 7
of Spinner's concept networks,
    141
pre-existing and mind-independent,
    128
represented as axioms, 84
Structure and ontology, *see* Ontol-
    ogy and structure
Structure (Piaget), formal charac-
    teristics of, 121
Structure Mapping Engine, 367–373
Structure-mapping theory (Gentner),
    367
Structure-preserving mapping, 85
Subalgebra, 217
    finitely generated, 218
Subclass, 191
Subnetwork of a concept network,
    153
Subsidiary subject (of a metaphor),
    67, 68
Suggestive metaphor
    example of, 267
Suggestive metaphors, 266–270
    predictive analogy and, 270, 321
Surjective function, 203
Symbolic forms, theory of (Cassirer),
    113
Symbolic system (Cassirer), 114
Symbolic systems, concept networks
    as, 132
Symbolism
    in films, 22

of religion, 22

Symbols
   components of, 153
   creation of, 113
   descriptions of, 153
   non-conventional interpretations
      of, 21
   of Spinner's concept networks,
      141
   structured set of, 21
   structures of, 153
   types of, 114
   vs. signs, 114

Symmetric relation, 201

Symmetry
   in interaction theory of metaphor
      Black, 4, 70
      critique by Lakoff & Turner,
         81
      Hausman, 5, 76
   in proportional analogies, 30,
      31

Syntactic metaphor, 257–267, 280,
      312, 336, 392, 409
   advantages of, 261
   example of, 258
   limits of, 265
   predictive analogy and, 320

Systematicity (Gentner), 331, 332,
      336, 337, 341, 367, 371, 375

Tabletop (French & Hofstadter), 391

Target (of a metaphor), 14
   changed by context, 15
   determined by context, 18
   explicit mention of, 15
   independently structured, 82
   not mentioned or hinted, 16
   not regarded as a system, 73
   referent of, 90
   regarded as a system, 68, 73

Target concept network, 254

Target content domain (Kittay), 88

Target domain, 1
   'life', 83, 85
   'painting', 85
   'quantity', 82

Target realm, 253
   easier cognitive access to, 261

Target sensorimotor data set, 407,
      408
   changed representation of, 409

Tenor (of a metaphor), 1, 254

Theories of metaphor
   comparison theory, 2–4
      discredited, 39
      explanation of creation of simi-
         larity, 65
      failure of, 65
   dead metaphor theory, 294
   domains-interaction theory, 4
   Lakoffian approach, 66
   literal meaning theory, 294, 299
   perspectival theory, 4, 67, 86
   transformation theory, 4

Theory of evolution, 55, 60

Thermodynamics, theory of
   analogy with flow of fluids, 57

Things in themselves, world of (Kan-
      tian), 112, 158, 277, 288,
      289
   cognitive access to, 159
   determines structure of environ-
      ment, 160
   determines structure of senso-
      rimotor data set, 159
   richly connected, 276

Topic (of a metaphor), 1, 67, 88

Topic-less metaphors, 28

Transformation theory, *see* Theo-
      ries of metaphor, transfor-

mation theory
Transformations
    counterparts of operators, 160
    grounded in reality, 144
    in Spinner's environment, 144
Transitive relation, 201
Transsubstantiation doctrine, 5
Tree series, by Mondrian, 63
Truth vs. correctness, 303
Type, of an operator, 161

Unconventional interpretation, 15–
    19, 25, 27, 29, 36
    subjectivity of, 16
Understanding
    as imagining a perceptual ex-
        perience, 249
    as representing internally, 249
    metaphorical description, 251
    non-metaphorical description, 249
    vs. correctness, 305
Union, of classes, 191
Uniqueness condition (Hausman),
    4, 75
Universal Algebra, 9, 190
Universal knowledge structure, 131
Universals, 94, 106
    in color categories, 107
Uzbekistan, 101

Vehicle (of a metaphor), 1, 88, 67,
    254, 311
Verticality, as source domain, 81
Visual cortex, 108
Visual illusions, 100, 101
    effect of cultural background,
        104
Visual system
    as a layered cognitive system,
        185

hallucinations and paradoxes in,
    339
    of macaque monkey, 108
Vividness thesis (Ortony), 251
Vocabulary, 84

Within-domain similarity, criterion
    of (Tourangeau & Sternberg)
    310
Workspace (Copycat), 387
World (Goodman), 115

Young-Helmholtz theory (of color
    vision), 107

ZORBA-I (Kling), 365, 366

STUDIES IN COGNITIVE SYSTEMS

Series Editor: James H. Fetzer, *University of Minnesota, Duluth*

1. J. H. Fetzer (ed.): *Aspects of Artificial Intelligence.* 1988
   ISBN 1-55608-037-9; Pb 1-55608-038-7

2. J. Kulas, J.H. Fetzer and T.L. Rankin (eds.): *Philosophy, Language, and Artificial Intelligence.* Resources for Processing Natural Language. 1988
   ISBN 1-55608-073-5

3. D.J. Cole, J.H. Fetzer and T.L. Rankin (eds.): *Philosophy, Mind and Cognitive Inquiry.* Resources for Understanding Mental Processes. 1990
   ISBN 0-7923-0427-6

4. J.H. Fetzer: *Artificial Intelligence: Its Scope and Limits.* 1990
   ISBN 0-7923-0505-1; Pb 0-7923-0548-5

5. H.E. Kyburg, Jr., R.P. Loui and G.N. Carlson (eds.): *Knowledge Representation and Defeasible Reasoning.* 1990   ISBN 0-7923-0677-5

6. J.H. Fetzer (ed.): *Epistemology and Cognition.* 1991
   ISBN 0-7923-0892-1

7. E.C. Way: *Knowledge Representation and Metaphor.* 1991
   ISBN 0-7923-1005-5

8. J. Dinsmore: *Partitioned Representations.* A Study in Mental Representation, Language Understanding and Linguistic Structure. 1991
   ISBN 0-7923-1348-8

9. T. Horgan and J. Tienson (eds.): *Connectionism and the Philosophy of Mind.* 1991   ISBN 0-7923-1482-4

10. J.A. Michon and A. Akyürek (eds.): *Soar: A Cognitive Architecture in Perspective.* 1992   ISBN 0-7923-1660-6

11. S.C. Coval and P.G. Campbell: *Agency in Action.* The Practical Rational Agency Machine. 1992   ISBN 0-7923-1661-4

12. S. Bringsjord: *What Robots Can and Can't Be.* 1992
    ISBN 0-7923-1662-2

13. B. Indurkhya: *Metaphor and Cognition.* An Interactionist Approach. 1992   ISBN 0-7923-1687-8

KLUWER ACADEMIC PUBLISHERS – DORDRECHT / BOSTON / LONDON

Waynesburg College Library
Waynesburg, Pennsylvania

329.97295   A549p

Anderson, Robert William
AUTHOR

Party Politics in Puerto Rico
TITLE

68051

DATE DUE	BORROWER'S NAME

329.97295   A549p
Anderson, Robert William
Party Politics in Puerto Rico
68051